Taxation Treatment of Interest

Taxation Treatment of Interest

Second edition

E.C.D. Norfolk
LLB, FTII, Solicitor

Butterworths
London, Dublin & Edinburgh
1992

United Kingdom	Butterworth & Co (Publishers) Ltd, 88 Kingsway, LONDON WC2B 6AB and 4 Hill Street, EDINBURGH EH2 3JZ
Australia	Reed International Books Australia Pty Ltd, SYDNEY, MELBOURNE, BRISBANE, ADELAIDE, PERTH, CANBERRA and HOBART
Belgium	Butterworth & Co Publishers, BRUSSELS
Canada	Butterworths Canada Ltd, TORONTO and VANCOUVER
Ireland	Butterworth (Ireland) Ltd, DUBLIN
Malaysia	Malayan Law Journal Sdn Bhd, KUALA LUMPUR
New Zealand	Butterworths of New Zealand Ltd, WELLINGTON and AUCKLAND
Puerto Rico	Equity de Puerto Rico, Inc, HATO REY
Singapore	Malayan Law Journal Pte Ltd, SINGAPORE
USA	Butterworth Legal Publishers, AUSTIN, Texas; BOSTON, Massachusetts; CLEARWATER, Florida (D & S Publishers); ORFORD, New Hampshire (Equity Publishing); ST PAUL, Minnesota; and SEATTLE, Washington

A CIP Catalogue record for this book is available from the British Library
First edition 1984
Second edition 1992

ISBN 0 0406 00285 1

Typeset by Kerrypress Ltd, Luton, Beds
Printed and bound in Great Britain by Mackays of Chatham PLC, Kent

PREFACE

Many changes affecting the taxation treatment of interest have occurred since the publication of the first edition of this book. Apart from the consolidation of the income tax and corporation tax legislation in 1988 (and of the capital gains legislation in 1992), hardly a year has passed without a significant legislative change: quoted Eurobonds and deep discount securities (1984); the accrued income scheme (1985); restrictions on foreign tax credit relief for banks (1987); legislation affecting the £30,000 limit for mortgage interest relief (1988); deep gain securities (1989); TESSAs and qualifying convertible securities (1990); tax deduction at source for bank and building society interest, and the basic rate tax relief restriction for mortgages (1991); and equity notes (1992). In addition, there have been developments in case law and in Inland Revenue practice.

The second edition follows the same form as the first, with the inclusion in Chapter 9 (Special Topics) of a summary of the special rules introduced to deal with discount securities.

In updating the book, I have been greatly helped by my colleagues at Norton Rose who have contributed many suggestions on both technical and practical issues and have given me support and encouragement to prepare this edition. My thanks go to all of them, including Louise Higginbottom and Elizabeth Grist who read and commented on the revised version, and to my secretary, Jill Childs, for undertaking the necessary typing. Notwithstanding their help, I remain responsible for the book in its final form and for the views expressed in it.

The law is stated as at 1 November 1992.

Christopher Norfolk
Kempson House
Camomile Street
London EC3

1 December 1992

PREFACE TO THE FIRST EDITION

'He is happy who, far away from business, like the race of men of old, tills his ancestral fields with his own oxen, unbound by any interest to pay.'

Horace *Epodes*

For about 150 years the law relating to the taxation of interest and relief for interest paid remained largely as it had been established at the beginning of the nineteenth century. Since the introduction of corporation tax in 1965 and the (first) abolition in 1969 of general relief for interest paid, Parliament has continued on almost a yearly basis to change some aspect of the treatment of interest in the UK tax system. These changes have not only involved minor alterations: relief for interest paid was extended in 1972, and again curtailed in 1974; anti-avoidance legislation has been introduced to counter schemes designed to reduce a taxpayer's tax bill by the apparent payment of interest; the way in which relief is given at the basic rate for mortgage interest has been completely altered, effectively reverting to a system which, until 1969, had applied generally since 1803. Further changes, intended to be made in 1983, but deferred by reason of the General Election, are to be introduced in 1984. In recent years also, cases have come before the courts for decision on aspects of the taxation treatment of interest.

Apart from changes in the law, the last ten to fifteen years have seen many developments in financial techniques, not only in the UK but internationally, combined with a very substantial increase in the number of banks established in London – mainly branches or subsidiaries of overseas banks.

Against this background, borrowers, lenders and their professional advisers are regularly faced with a variety of problems concerning the taxation treatment of interest paid and received. The purpose of this book is to provide a complete picture of the law relating to the place of interest in the UK tax system. Principally, this concerns the charge to income tax or corporation tax on interest received, the way in which tax is sometimes collected at source by deduction before the interest reaches the recipient, and the reliefs which may be available to a payer of interest in computing his liability to income tax or corporation tax. However, other taxes can be concerned with the payment (or, in some cases, non-payment) of interest, and Chapter 11 summarises the law relating to interest for the purposes of taxes other than income tax and corporation tax. Much of the relevant law is set out in involved legislation; where appropriate, this legislation is examined closely, but in other cases only a general summary is provided – a book such as this, designed to describe principles of general application and to highlight points which can be important in practice, cannot be a substitute for a detailed consideration of the legislation as it applies to the facts of any given case.

In addition to the legislation and the effect of decided cases, reference is also made to Inland Revenue practices. These are mainly published as Extra-Statutory Concessions or Statements of Practice. However, as with other areas of taxation, there are unpublished practices, sometimes of general application, which are often only discovered by approaching the Inland Revenue for a view on a particular point; inevitably, these do not have the status of published practices, and in appropriate cases should only be relied on after obataining written confirmation from the Inland Revenue.

I have been greatly helped in writing this book by having the opportunity to draw on the experience of colleagues with whom I have been able to discuss practical problems; my thanks also go to David Goldberg, who kindly read a number of the chapters at the final draft stage and provided many useful suggestions, to Louise Higginbottom, who assisted in researching numerous points and in preparing the manuscript and correcting proofs, and to Jill Childs, who devoted many hours to processing and reprocessing the words into a form in which they would be ready for the printer. Notwithstanding their contributions, I remain responsible for the book in its final form and for the views expressed in it.

The law is stated as at 1 March 1984, however, on 13 March 1984 the Inland Revenue published proposals for new legislation to be introduced in connection with the 1984 Budget. Where relevant, reference is made (in the text or in a footnote) to any proposed changes, but two items should be mentioned here. First, the additional rate of income tax on investment income is to be abolished from 1984/85; because of the numerous references in the book to the additional rate (which will continue to be of relevance in settling questions relating to years of assessment up to and including 1983/84) specific reference has not been made in each instance to the abolition of this rate.

Second, the rate of corporation tax is to be reduced to 50 per cent for the financial year 1983 and by 5 per cent per annum to 35 per cent for the financial year 1986. Nevertheless, the examples in Chapter 5 have been left showing a corporation tax rate of 52 per cent; this should avoid any confusion resulting from 50 per cent being both the rate of corporation tax and the rate of the post-tax value of a company's income.

Christopher Norfolk
London EC3

22 March 1984

CONTENTS

TABLE OF STATUTES

TABLE OF CASES

Chapter 1

HISTORICAL BACKGROUND

1-01 The principal provisions now in force concerning the taxation treatment of interest are based on statutory foundations laid at the beginning of the nineteenth century. An understanding of the legislative background to the present legislation is important for two reasons. First, it is helpful to understand how the legislation has arrived in its present state; for example, it explains why there are distinctions between annual interest and other interest in relation to relief for interest and the deduction of income tax at source from interest paid. Second, many of the decided cases, which may be good authority on questions which are relevant in the context of the modern legislation, are concerned with the legislation in an earlier form; in order properly to understand those decisions and the relevance which they now have, it is necessary to understand the statutory framework which applied when those decisions were made by the courts.

1-02 The Duties on Income Act 1799[1] imposed a charge to tax under the heading 'Income from annuities, interest of money, rent charge or other payments of the like nature'[2]. The income taxable was assessed on a preceding year basis. Against both that and other classes of income the taxpayer was permitted to set certain General Deductions, which included 'The amount of annual interest payable for debts owing by the party, or charged upon the property of the party, from which any income shall arise'.

1-03 In 1803 a different basis was introduced in relation to the taxation of interest, a basis which survived in much the same form for over 150 years. By s 208 of the Income Tax Act 1803[3], tax was charged on all 'annuities, yearly interest of money or other annual payments', which tax was to be imposed in the same way as the charge under Schedule D (which did not expressly mention 'interest'). But, where the yearly interest, annuity or other annual payment was paid out of profits or gains brought into charge to tax, the assessment was not levied on the recipient; instead, the payer was to be taxed on the full amount of his income, irrespective of the amount of the payment made by him, but he was also authorised to deduct the tax from the interest or other payment made. By s 209 of the same Act, where a taxpayer had paid interest[4] out of profits or gains which had borne tax, and this was certified by the Commissioners, the payer was entitled to abate the interest paid by an amount calculated by reference to the rate

---

[1] 39 Geo III c 13.
[2] Sixteenth Case of Schedule (A) to the Act.
[3] 43 Geo III c 122.
[4] Not only 'yearly interest'.

1

of tax. In this way, the legislation at the same time provided for the enforcement of the tax liability of the recipient and permitted the payer to obtain effective relief for the payment made; the payer was not obliged to pay the gross amount of the interest out of his net after-tax income, but was required only to pay the net after-tax amount of the interest out of his net after-tax income.

Interest was also mentioned in the provisions of the 1803 Act concerning the taxation of profits of a trade. The Fourth Rule of the First Case of Schedule D prohibited any deduction in computing taxable profits of a trade for, inter alia, any annual interest 'payable out of ... profits or gains'[5]. Here, it was made clear that interest 'payable out of ... profits or gains' was not deductible in computing such profits or gains. Relief would, however, have been available to the trader for such interest under the procedure described above. There was no specific provision disallowing a deduction for other interest paid by the trader. Under the Second Case of Schedule D the 'actual amount' of the profits or gains of a profession or vocation were to be taxed 'without any deduction'.

1-04   In the Income Tax Act 1806[6], Rule 2 of the Third Case of Schedule D imposed duty on 'The profits on all securities bearing interest, payable out of the public revenue (except securities before directed to be charged under the rules of Schedule C) and all discounts, and on all interest of money, not being annual interest.' Sections 114 and 116 incorporated provisions similar to ss 208 and 209 of the Act of 1803. Although the Act referred in Rule 2 of the Third Case of Schedule D to 'annual interest', s 144 followed s 208 of the 1803 Act in using the expression 'yearly interest'. Rule 3 of the First Case of Schedule D, which contained many provisions which can now be found in TA 1988 s 74, included a prohibition against a deduction 'for any sums employed or intended to be employed as capital in such trade, manufacture, adventure, or concern; ... nor on account or under pretence of any interest which might have been made on such sums if laid out at interest'[7]; Rule 4 made the same provision as in the 1803 Act to prevent relief for 'annual interest ... payable out of ... profits or gains'.

1-05   The 1806 procedure for the taxation of interest remained in the Income Tax Act 1842[8]. Under s 105 of that Act, a charity which was entitled to exemption from tax in respect of yearly interest or other annual payments received from which tax was deducted at source was permitted to claim a refund from the Commissioners. The rules for the computation of profits or gains from a trade or profession again included an express prohibition against the deduction of 'any annual Interest, or any Annuity or other annual Payment, payable out of such Profits or Gains'.

1-06   The system for deducting at source an amount equivalent to tax on interest (and other annual payments) was modified by s 40 of the Income Tax Act 1853. This did away with the need for the payer of the interest

---

[5] '... except the interest of debts due to foreigners not resident in Great Britain'.
[6] 46 Geo III c 65.
[7] Cf TA 1988 s 74 (F) and (h).
[8] 5 & 6 Vict c 35; see Second Rule of Third Case of Schedule D and ss 102–103.

to obtain a certificate from the Commissioners that tax had been paid on the profits or gains out of which the payment was made. It was simply provided that a taxpayer paying, inter alia, 'any yearly Interest of Money ... shall be entitled and is hereby authorised, on making such Payment, to deduct and retain thereout the Amount of the Rate of Duty which at the Time when such Payment becomes due shall be payable under this Act'. There was no longer any requirement that the interest be paid out of profits or gains brought into charge to tax. This resulted in the curious position that the payer could deduct tax at source, but was not obliged to account for that deduction (either directly or indirectly) to the Commissioners, although where the interest was paid out of profits or gains brought into charge to tax this provided, as before, effective relief to the payer for the interest paid.

The Income Tax Act 1853 also introduced the requirement that tax should be deducted where 'Interest, Dividends, or annual Payments have been or shall be intrusted to any Person in the United Kingdom for Payment to any Persons, Corporations, Companies or Societies in the United Kingdom'[9]. The system[10] for deducting tax was the same as had been introduced in 1842[10] in relation to 'Annuities, or any Dividends or Share of Annuities, payable out of the Revenue of any Foreign State to any Persons, Corporations, Companies or Societies in Great Britain[11]'.

1-07 The defect in the Income Tax Act 1853 was rectified thirty-five years later by s 24(3) of the Customs and Inland Revenue Act 1888. That subsection provided that, to the extent that 'any interest of money or annuities' taxed under Schedule D were not payable out of profits or gains brought into charge to income tax, the payer was to deduct income tax at the rate in force at the time of payment and account for that tax to the Commissioners of Inland Revenue. This new provision did not apply only to 'annual' or 'yearly' interest, but to interest generally. Thereafter, all interest, whether yearly interest or not and including interest paid to banks (which would treat the interest received as a taxable trading receipt), was subject to deduction of tax at source where not paid out of profits or gains brought into charge to tax[12]. Where the interest was paid out of such profits or gains, the payer remained entitled to deduct and retain the tax for himself.

1-08 Therefore, from 1888 there was an established procedure for:

1   requiring the payer of any interest not paid out of taxed income to collect and account for the tax to the Commissioners of Inland Revenue; and
2   permitting the payer of *yearly* interest paid out of taxed income to recoup for himself an amount equivalent to tax on such interest paid, so giving him effective relief for that interest and at the same time enforcing the tax charge on the recipient. The legislation treated yearly interest in the same way as annuities and other annual payments –

9   16 & 17 Vict c 34 s 10.
10 5 & 6 Vict c 80 s 2 – not the Income Tax Act 1842 (5 & 6 Vict c 35).
11 ITA 1853 s 5 provided that references to 'Great Britain' should be read as references to the United Kingdom.
12 See *Lord Advocate v Edinburgh Corpn* (1903) 40 SLR 632, 4 TC 627; but see also the criticism of this decision by Viscount Radcliffe in *IRC c Frere* [1964] 3 All ER 796, 42 TC 125 at 153, HL.

the taxpayer had effectively transferred part of his income to a third party, so that the recipient rather than the payer should suffer tax on that income. For this reason, yearly interest was later deductible in computing total income for surtax purposes[13].

1-09   Interest paid to banks on ordinary short-term bankers' advances was not treated as 'yearly' interest[14]. This meant that a taxpayer paying such interest out of taxable profits or gains was not able to obtain effective relief for the interest paid, since it would not fall within the procedure under s 40 of the Income Tax Act 1853. This was remedied by FA 1915 s 22 under which a taxpayer paying bank interest was allowed to obtain repayment from the Commissioners of a sum equal to tax on the interest paid, so giving effective tax relief for the interest. This treatment was extended by FA 1917 s 15 to interest (other than yearly interest) paid to a member of a UK stock exchange or a discount house. These two provisions were consolidated in the following year in ITA 1918 s 36. Although these provisions were retained until 1969[15], they were not specifically extended to give relief for surtax purposes, although in practice the Inland Revenue did by concession grant similar relief for surtax[16].

1-10   ITA 1918 was the first consolidation of the legislation, and the basic structure of the taxation treatment of interest was by then established. 'Profits arising from interest' payable in the UK out of any public revenue were taxed under Schedule C which included provisions very similar to those which now apply under Sch C and TA 1988 Sch 3. Other UK source interest was taxable under Case III of Schedule D which was almost identical to the present provisions, although Case III expressly included those instances where interest would be paid without deduction of income tax at source[17]. Interest 'from securities in any place out of the United Kingdom' was taxed under Case IV of Schedule D, subject to a deduction for, inter alia, 'annual interest payable out of the income to a person not resident in the United Kingdom'.

So far as relief for interest paid was concerned, 'yearly interest ... reserved or charged upon any lands' qualified the taxpayer to deduct and retain an amount equal to tax on the interest[18]. There remained the specific prohibition against deducting, in computing the profits or gains of a trade, profession, employment or vocation (taxable under Cases I or II of Schedule D), 'any annual interest ... payable out of the profits or gains[19]. However, relief was available (by way of deduction and retention of tax) for yearly interest of money payable out of taxed profits or gains, under Rule 19 of the General Rules. Rule 21 of the General Rules set out the provisions for deduction

---

[13]   See F(1909-10)A 1910 s 66(2).

[14]   See §**3-06** below.

[15]   See §**1-14** below.

[16]   See *IRC v Frere* [1964] 3 All ER 796, 42 TC 125, HL.

[17]   Eg savings bank interest and interest on certain government securities.

[18]   It is not clear why this specific provision was made, having regard to the provisions of Rule 19 of the Rules applicable to Schedules A to E — see below; in *A-G v LCC* [1907] AC 131, 5 TC 242, HL it was held that tax could be deducted and retained (under ss 102 and 104 of the Income Tax Act 1842) where paid out of income taxable under Schedules other than Schedule D.

[19]   Rule 3(1) of the Special Rules applicable to Cases I and II Schedule D.

of tax to be paid over to the Inland Revenue where interest (whether yearly or not) was paid otherwise than out of profits or gains brought into charge to tax.

1-11 The basic structure remained during the thirty-four years before the next consolidation in 1952, although some modifications were made. These modifications included:

1 Relief, in the same way as for a business loss, for interest paid under deduction of tax under Rule 21 where the interest was paid wholly and exclusively for the purposes of a trade, profession or vocation[20];
2 Annual interest payable out of the profits or gains was permitted as a deduction in computing overseas profits taxable under Case I or Case II of Schedule D where certain conditions were satisfied[1]. This amendment was required because the tax deduction and retention machinery would not apply where non-UK source interest was paid to a non-resident;
3 The Inland Revenue was authorised to make special arrangements relating to interest and building societies[2]. These arrangements provided for special ('composite rate' tax) treatment in respect of interest paid by building societies, and also for interest paid on building society advances to be paid without deduction of tax but for the payer to be granted relief for the interest paid by way of discharge or repayment of tax;
4 Provision was made for information to be given to the Inland Revenue as to interest paid gross by banks and certain other persons carrying on a trade or business[3].

1-12 The next consolidation in ITA 1952 saw the charging provisions in Schedule C and Case III and Case IV of Schedule D only slightly changed since 1918 and in much the same state as they are in TA 1988. The provisions for giving relief for interest paid (which, since 1803 had mainly been the same as the relief for annuities and other 'annual payments' paid by the taxpayer) were firmly established, as was the witholding tax mechanism where interest was paid otherwise than out of taxed income. However, two significant changes were to take place before the next consolidation in 1970.

1-13 First, the system of corporation tax was introduced in 1965. This required a different approach for companies to the way in which relief was to be given for interest paid. Until 1965, companies had paid income tax, and, therefore, the scheme of witholding and retention had been available to provide relief for yearly interest paid out of taxed income; in the case of other interest paid out of taxed profits to banks, stock exchange members and discount houses, relief had been available by means of a repayment equal to income tax at the standard rate[4]. The system would no longer work when companies paid a different tax, and therefore FA 1965 s 52[5]

---

[20] FA 1928 s 19; and see now TA 1988 ss 390 and 393 (9).
[1] FA 1949 s 23; and see now TA 1988 ss 82, 338 (4) and 340.
[2] FA 1951 s 23; and see, until repealed, TA 1970, s 343 (4) and TA 1988 s 476.
[3] FA 1951 s 27; and see now TMA 1970 s 17.
[4] Eg under ITA 1952 s 200.
[5] See now TA 1988 s 338.

specifically provided for relief as a deduction against the 'total profits' of a company for 'charges on income' including:

1   'any yearly interest . . .'; and
2   'any other interest[6] payable in the United Kingdom' on an advance from a UK bank, stock exchange member or discount house[7].

Provision was also made for relief for interest as a charge on income where it was paid to a non-resident[8]. FA 1965 s 53 (5)[9] prevented any deduction in computing 'income' (ie at an earlier stage than the deduction of interest from 'total profits') for any 'yearly interest' or for certain other payments which were mentioned in ITA 1952 s 169, although yearly interest paid on a loan from a UK bank was permitted to qualify as a trading expense[10]. However, unlike s 169, the restriction in FA 1965 s 53(5) did not apply only where the payment was made 'out of profits or gains brought into charge to tax'.

1-14   The other major change was the abolition (after 170 years) by FA 1969 of the general relief for interest paid by taxpayers. This was achieved by deleting references to 'yearly interest' and 'annual interest' in ITA 1952 s 169, leaving the deduction and retention mechanism to continue to apply only to annuities, other 'annual payments' and certain other types of payment. If no further amendment had been made, the s 170 procedure (deduction of tax and accounting to the Inland Revenue) would have applied to interest only where the interest was paid otherwise than out of profits or gains brought into charge to income tax. In order to retain the witholding system for all interest payments, a new witholding system was established by FA 1969 s 26[11], and references to 'interest' were deleted from ITA 1952 s 170. Under this new system, individuals were only required to deduct tax on payments of interest where the recipient did not have his usual place of abode in the UK. It should be noted that s 26 only applied to payments of '*yearly* interest of money', and no tax deduction was required in certain cases of interest paid to, or by, UK banks[12]. To complete the abolition of the general relief for interest paid, ITA 1952 s 200 was repealed, so preventing any repayment of tax in respect of interest not falling within the deduction and retention procedure.

1-15   Although the general relief for interest was abolished in 1969, specific provision was made for relief to continue to be allowed in respect of interest on borrowings for certain purposes (eg to acquire or improve land and buildings, to acquire an interest in a close company, or to contribute capital to a partnership).

1-16   Following the 1970 consolidation, there were many changes to the way in which interest is taxed and relief is given for interest paid; two particular

---

[6] Ie interest which is not 'yearly interest'.
[7] See §8-33 to §8-42 below.
[8] See now TA 1988 ss 338 and 340.
[9] See now TA 1988 s 337(2).
[10] FA 1965 s 54(3), now TA 1988 s 337 (3).
[11] See now TA 1988 s 349(2) and (3).
[12] Cf §§1-09 above.

changes should be noted. In 1983, the wheel came full circle with the introduction of the Mortgage Interest Relief at Source ('MIRAS') system for interest paid to building societies and other qualifying lenders on loans to purchase private residences. Under this system[13], the borrower pays the lender interest net of basic rate income tax, retaining the withheld amount by way of tax relief. The other change first involved the extension, in 1985, of the composite rate tax payment arrangements to interest paid by banks[14], placing them on the same footing as building societies. However, that system no longer survives[15]; from 6 April 1991, interest paid by banks and building societies is now paid to individual depositors (and, in the case of building societies, certain other depositors) net of basic rate income tax deducted at source (except where paid to a non-resident or to a depositor who certifies that his income level qualifies him to receive interest gross)[16].

1-17 The legislation now stands consolidated in 1988 but with amendments made since consolidation which have either been incorporated in the legislation or are contained in subsequent Finance Acts. However, the basic structure remains that interest is taxed under Sch C and Sch D Cases III, IV and V, with interest being available for relief only where it is specifically so provided, the payer of interest being liable to deduct (and account to the Inland Revenue for) income tax on payments of yearly interest (except where paid by an individual to a UK resident, and in relation to certain bank and building society interest).

[13] See §§7-36 to 7-39 and 8-51 below.
[14] TA 1988 s 479.
[15] FA 1990 s 30 and Sch 5.
[16] See §§7-26 to 7-31 below.

Chapter 2

THE NATURE OF INTEREST

1 What is 'interest'?

2-01 Although the word 'interest' is sometimes defined for the purposes of a particular provision in the tax legislation (eg in TA 1988 s 729 (10), where it is to be construed as including a dividend) there is no general definition of the word for the purposes of taxation. TA 1988 s 832 (1) defines the word as meaning 'both annual or yearly interest and interest other than annual or yearly interest', but that does not shed any light on the question of what is 'interest'. This leaves the word to be construed in accordance with its ordinary natural meaning, and, although there have been several cases on the question of what amounts to interest, the decisions have not resulted in there being a special tax meaning of the word[1].

NON-JUDICIAL DEFINITIONS

2-02 Insofar as its meaning can be extracted from a dictionary[2], interest may be regarded as 'money paid for the use of money lent (the principal), or for the forbearance of a debt, according to a fixed ratio (rate per cent)', a meaning which dates back to 1545. It will be seen from a review of the decided cases that this definition includes certain features which have concerned the courts: interest must be for the use of *money*, but this may be either money *lent* or money *outstanding* where the creditor should be compensated for the delay in receiving his money. It will, however, be seen that there is no need for there to be a *fixed* interest rate; money may be lent at a variable or floating rate of interest, or the interest may even be simply a sum of money payable as a premium on redemption.

ECONOMIC FACTORS

2-03 Interest received by a lender can be regarded as made up by the following elements:

1   A payment which reflects the availability of and demand fsor loan finance. This price will vary from time to time, so causing interest rates to

---

[1] Although in *IRC v Barnato* [1936] 2 All ER 1176, 20 TC 455, CA, Lord Wright MR did suggest, at 20 TC 497, that there was a difference between 'money which could be described, in one sense, as interest' and 'interest within the meaning of the Income Tax Acts'.
[2] Shorter Oxford English Dictionary.

change. The prevailing rate when a loan is made and the anticipated trend of changes in rate over the life of the loan will be taken into account by the lender and borrower in negotiating a loan at a fixed rate. On the other hand, the lender may reserve the right to alter the interest rate by reference to a published base rate (eg a bank's own 'base rate'), or the loan agreement may provide for the rate of interest to be kept directly in line with a particular rate such as a London interbank rate for the currency of the loan, typically where the lending bank may be funding itself on the interbank market. It is this element for which a person is compensated where a settlement or award of interest is made in arrears;

2   Payment to compensate the lender for the risk of the loan not being repaid. This factor will cause the interest rate to reflect the borrower's credit standing[3];

3   Payment to the lender for providing the loan and maintaining the loan. A commercial lender will suffer administrative and other costs in connection with making and maintaining the loan, for which he is compensated by the interest payments.

Other factors may contribute to the fixing of the relevant interest rate. For example, where a contract for the sale of property provides for completion on a fixed date, the vendor may stipulate for a higher interest rate than might normally apply to a loan to the purchaser in order to encourage the purchaser not to delay completion of the purchase, as well as to compensate the vendor for anticipated costs resulting from his not receiving payment on the due date.

2-04   Although interest can be analysed in this way, this does not necessarily prevent any part of the payment being 'interest'. In the case of a bank loan, the three elements described above will all be material factors. Where a loan is made at a fixed margin over an interbank rate for deposits of a sum equivalent to the amount of the loan, the floating interbank rate will represent the element described in paragraph 1 in §2-03 above, while the margin (normally a fixed percentage to be added to the interbank rate) will compensate the bank for (and reflect the level of) risk in respect of the particular borrower and will also remunerate the bank for arranging the loan (ie the elements described in paragraphs 2 and 3 of §2-03). However, it will be seen[4] that where a payment in relation to a loan is not calculated in the conventional way but is expressed as a fixed premium on redemption, the payment may not amount to 'interest' where it merely reflects the risk element described in paragraph 2 in §2-03 above.

On the other hand, the terms on which a loan is made might stipulate for a commitment commission to be paid, that is a payment normally calculated at a modest percentage rate by reference to the amount which the lender has agreed to lend but which has not yet been taken up by the borrower. Such a payment compensates the lender for standing ready to make a loan, but cannot be said to be interest since it is a payment in respect of a sum *not lent* rather than in respect of a sum lent. Prior to the enactment of what is now TA 1988 s 77 (under which certain incidental

---

[3] See *Lomax v Peter Dixon & Son Ltd* (1943) 25 TC 353 at 364, CA, and §2-31 below.
[4] See §2-31 below – premium on redemption.

costs of obtaining a loan can be deductible expenditure for tax purposes) it was often attractive to a commercial borrower to seek to arrange the interest rate by reference to a formula which incorporated the commitment commission; having regard to the comments above, it is not certain that such attempts would result in the commitment commission element of the interest being interest properly so called.

2–05 Another factor which might be built into an interest formula is provision for payments by reference to fluctuating exchange rates. For example, a borrower may wish to borrow sterling from a lender having a foreign currency-based business; that lender may be prepared to lend sterling, converted from foreign currency at the 'spot' rate when the loan is made, on terms that the interest paid reflects any loss (or gain) suffered (or enjoyed) by the lender on receiving repayments of the loan in sterling (which he wishes immediately to convert into an amount of foreign currency calculated at the 'spot' rate). If the loan agreement provides for interest to be calculated by reference to this factor (and it might increase or decrease the interest otherwise payable) it would seem that the payment may be treated as interest properly so called; the fluctuating nature of the interest would result from the terms on which the lender is prepared to lend sterling, which in turn depend upon the effective cost to the lender of making and maintaining the loan in sterling having regard to the value to the lender of the asset. The point is not entirely free from doubt in view of the comments of Lord Greene MR in *Lomax v Peter Dixon & Son Ltd*[5] as to the extra cost of repaying a loan by reference to the price of gold. In the light of this it would be preferable not to link the additional payments to the principal repaid, but either to vary the interest (up and down) by reference to fluctuations in the exchange rate as applied to the whole of the outstanding amount of the loan, or for the interest to be increased by the cost to the lender of maintaining forward foreign exchange contracts to provide the required foreign currency on repayments of sterling; in either case it would also be necessary to adjust the amount of the interest payments themselves. It should be noted that a business borrower would not normally be permitted to deduct as a trading expense the increased cost (in sterling terms) of repaying a foreign currency loan employed as part of the fixed capital of his business[6], and by TA 1988 s 77 the relief given for the incidental costs of obtaining loan finance expressly[7] does not extend to permit a deduction for such additional expenditure; however, effective relief might be available where the borrower is entitled to relief for interest which is in part calculated by reference to changes in exchange rates[8].

2–06 There is normally no difficulty in identifying as 'interest' the interest payable under a loan. Interest on an outstanding loan was said to be 'payment

---

[5] (1943) 25 TC 353 at 363.

[6] See *Beauchamp (Inspector of Taxes) v F W Woolworth plc* [1989] STC 510, [1990] 1 AC 478, HL. But relief might be available under legislation to be introduced following consultation on the taxation of foreign exchange gains and losses – see Inland Revenue Press Release, 11 August 1992.

[7] S 77 (7) (a).

[8] See also *Bennett v Underground Electric Rlys Co of London Ltd* [1923] 2 KB 535, 8 TC 475, where the Inland Revenue argued, successfully, that the extra cost, in sterling terms, of paying interest in dollars was part of the interest and was not an expense of management.

by time for the use of money' in *Bennett v Ogston*[9]. In that case, interest received in respect of an outstanding loan in the period after the death of a moneylender was held to be taxable as interest under Case III of Schedule D, notwithstanding that in the period prior to the moneylender's death the return would have been treated as a trading receipt. The interest on a loan will normally be calculated on an annual or more frequent basis, and may be similarly payable. However, the fact that the interest is rolled up and paid on repayment of the loan will not prevent the payment being 'interest'[10].

CONTINGENT INTEREST

2-07 The fact that payment of the interest due on a loan is contingent on other factors, such as the profitability of the borrower, does not necessarily prevent the payment being interest. In *IRC v Pullman Car Co Ltd*[11] interest payable to debenture holders was nonetheless interest where the interest was only payable to the extent that the company had in the year sufficient profits out of which to pay the interest. But the interest was cumulative, in that the obligation to make the payment did not lapse if the profits were insufficient; the deficiency was carried forward to the following year.

2-08 However, a profit share payable to a lender has been held not to be interest. In *A W Walker & Co v IRC*[12], the lender was entitled to be paid £200 per year while the loan was outstanding (which was held to be interest) and also three-twentieths of the profits of the business between £1,000 and £3,000 per year; the latter payment was held to be 'a share of what the business earns, and that is not interest, that is simply a share of the profits'[13]. That decision was considered in *IRC v Mashonaland Rly Co Ltd*[14], where it was held that the consideration for a loan, in the form of a fixed annual amount, or, if lower, the amount of the company's 'net earnings' for the year, was 'a payment for the distribution of profits' for the purposes of corporation profits tax. That was sufficient to determine the question of deductibility for tax purposes, and Rowlatt J expressly declined to decide whether the payment was 'interest'[15]. It would, however, seem arguable that the payment was not one of interest. The difference between the obligations in the *Pullman* and *Mashonaland Rly Co* cases was that in

---

[9] (1930) 15 TC 374 at 379.
[10] See *Re Craven's Mortgage* [1907] 2 Ch 448, 76 LJCh 651, and §3-07 below.
[11] [1954] 2 All ER 491, 35 TC 221.
[12] [1920] 3 KB 648, 12 TC 297.
[13] (1920) 12 TC 297 at 302; see also *Ruskin Investments Ltd v Copeman* [1943] 1 All ER 378, 25 TC 187, CA, where the value received in excess of the original loan on transfer to the lender of valuable property in discharge of the borrower's obligation was held to be of an income nature assessable under Case VI of Schedule D without it being decided that the excess was interest within Case III; and *Bond v Barrow Haematite Steel Co* [1902] 1 Ch 353 at 363: 'interest is compensation for the delay in payment, and is not accurately applied to the share of profits of trading'.
[14] (1926) 12 TC 1159.
[15] See also *Wilson v Mannooch* [1937] 3 All ER 120, 21 TC 178, where a share of profit on resale of a property, subject to a maximum limit, was held to be taxable as annual profits of an income nature, without the court deciding whether that liability fell under Case III (as interest) or Case VI (as a casual profit).

the former any interest unpaid was cumulated and carried forward to be paid in later years when there were sufficient profits; on the other hand, if the *Mashonaland Rly Co* had insufficient profits out of which to pay the agreed amount (5.3125% of the principal) the company was *pro tanto* relieved of the obligation. Although in each case the relationship was one of debtor and creditor, the consideration for the use of the money was not 'fixed' (even in the sense in which a predetermined floating rate formula is 'fixed'); the creditor stipulated for a return on his investment which would not necessarily provide him with any compensation for the use of his money, and the terms of the loan expressly contemplated that possibility[16].

The importance of this question in the case of payments by a company was diminished by a specific legislative provision[17] under which consideration for the use of money lent to a company which is 'to any extent dependent on the results of the company's business' is treated as a dividend distribution rather than as interest. However, this provision does not apply to the extent that the consideration represents a reasonable commercial return, so that such variable payments will not always amount to dividend distributions[18]; therefore, since a company making such a payment is not necessarily prevented from obtaining relief for such payments it may be necessary to determine whether such fluctuating payments are interest. The question may also arise in relation to a loan to an individual or to individuals trading in partnership.

INTEREST ON VOLUNTARY CREDIT

2–09   Where a creditor allows an indebtedness to remain outstanding, the return which he receives is as much interest as would have arisen had he made a loan of an equivalent amount[19]. In *Hudson's Bay Co v Thew*[20] the taxpayer sold land on terms that the purchase money should be paid by instalments which would bear interest. Although the property remained in the legal ownership of the vendor pending payment of all outstanding instalments, the income was held to be interest and not income from land.

2–10   The parties may also contemplate that an indebtedness may at a later date be found to have arisen and provide for compensation to be paid when settlement is made between them. In such a case the payment will be interest properly so called, notwithstanding that it could not be predicted at the outset which party would be in debit. This was the position in *Chevron Petroleum (UK) Ltd v BP Petroleum Development Ltd*[1]. That case concerned the arrangements for developing an oil field which straddled two blocks in the UK sector of the Continental Shelf, which blocks had been licensed

---

[16] Note that s 42 of the Partnership Act 1890 distinguishes between compensation in the form of a share of profit and interest. See also TA 1988 s 209 (2) (d) and reference to 'consideration given by the company for the use of the principal' and not 'interest'; but Cf TA 1988 Sch 18 para 1 (5) (b) – 'interest which depends to any extent on the results of the company's business'.

[17] Now TA 1988 s 209 (2) (d).

[18] See §9–08 below.

[19] A 'debt' remaining outstanding is not the same as a 'loan' – *Potts' Executors v IRC* [1951] 1 All ER 76, 32 TC 211, HL.

[20] [1919] 2 KB 632, 7 TC 206.

[1] [1981] STC 689.

to different groups of oil companies. An agreement had been entered into providing for the joint development of the oil field and for the two groups to bear expenditure and share oil in the same proportions as it would ultimately be agreed that the recoverable oil lay within the two blocks. Pending final determination of those proportions, costs were to be shared in ratios agreed in the light of the most recent geological information, with adjustments to be made from time to time in the light of new information. The agreement provided for an adjustment payment to be made to correct any imbalance in cost sharing, and this adjustment included an 'interest factor'. Even though this element arose from an unusual calculation (the total payment due from the party in debit was the difference between, on the one hand, expenditure which should have been borne by that party plus interest and, on the other hand, expenditure which had actually been borne by that party plus interest) the interest element was held to be interest properly so called. The paying group was merely making good what had transpired to be a previous deficiency in its level of contributions to expenditure, together with compensation to the other group for having originally borne a disproportionately high share of the costs.

INTEREST ON INVOLUNTARY CREDIT

2-11 However, it is not a precondition of a payment being interest that there must have been a prior agreement that interest would be paid. In *Schulze v Bensted (Surveyor of Taxes)*[2] a sum awarded as interest upon the restoration to a trust of money which had been misappropriated was held to be interest 'in reality as well as name'[3]. Judicial approval was given[4] by the Lord President, Lord Strathclyde, in the Court of Session to a dictionary[5] definition of interest:

'Interest of money may be defined as the creditor's share of the profit which the borrower or debtor is presumed to make from the use of the money'[6].

Lord Strathclyde continued:

'Otherwise stated, it is just recompense to the creditor for being deprived of the use of his money.'

So, in that case, the trustees had awarded to them a sum approximating to that which the trust money, had it been in their hands, would have earned[7].

2-12 Similarly, in *IRC v Barnato*[8], where money was wrongfully withheld by trustees who admitted an obligation to pay interest, the compensation was treated as interest notwithstanding that the order made by the Special

---

[2] 1915 SC 188, 7 TC 30.
[3] (1915) 7 TC 30 at 32.
[4] (1915) 7 TC 30 at 33.
[5] *Bell's Dictionary and Digest on the Law of Scotland.*
[6] Note that reference is only made to the 'presumed' profit rather than the actual profit.
[7] See also *Sweet (Inspector of Taxes) v Macdiarmid* (1920) 58 SLR 129, 7 TC 640: interest on *jus relictae* was 'interest of money'.
[8] [1936] 2 All ER 1176, 20 TC 455, CA.

Referee (consequent upon the admission of the principle of liability and subsequent examination of the facts) provided for a payment to be made in a single sum; the payment comprised a clearly identifiable interest element, but the amount was stated in a single sum since it was to be paid in a single sum rather than because it only represented an indivisible liability in respect of a single amount[9].

'DAMAGES' AS INTEREST

2-13   *Barnato* was distinguished from an early decision, *Re National Bank of Wales Ltd*[10], where it had been held that damages for fraudulent misappropriation of money did not include an interest element, notwithstanding that the damages had been increased by reference to a percentage rate per annum. The grounds for that decision were that interest awarded as compensation for delayed payment differed from damages for fraud. However, the decision in *National Bank of Wales* was overruled[11] by the House of Lords in *Riches v Westminster Bank Ltd*[12]. There, it was held that interest on damages awarded from the date when the cause of action arose until judgment was 'interest of money', confirming the earlier decisions in *Schulze v Bensted (Surveyor of Taxes)* and *Barnato*. Lord Simonds[13] adopted the language of Evershed J at first instance[14]:

> 'The proposition that interest is awarded as damages, or by way of damages ..., imports the justification for the award or for the rate awarded, but does not affect the quality of interest as such. ...'

Lord Simonds went on:

> 'Perhaps the position may become even clearer if for "damages" the word "compensation" is substituted. It would be difficult, I suppose, in a case where a man, being deprived of the use of his money, was awarded interest by way of compensation, to say that what he was awarded was not interest but something else. ... The trustee must pay interest to compensate his *cestui que trust* ... for the interest he has lost. It might equally be called damages or interest by way of damages.'

The House of Lords did not overrule *Simpson v Maurice's Executors*[15], where compensation, not in any way referred to as interest, paid for detention of assets in a German bank during the 1914–18 War was found not to be interest. This decision appears to remain distinguished on the grounds that not only did neither the award nor the relevant provisions of the Peace Treaty mention payment by way of interest but also the treaty appears to

---

[9] (1936) 20 TC 455 at 508–509, CA.
[10] [1899] 2 Ch 629, 68 LJCh 634, CA.
[11] As were other cases which had erroneously distinguished compensation by way of damages from compensation by way of interest – see *London, Chatham and Dover Rly Co v South Eastern Rly Co* [1893] AC 429, 63 LJCh 93, HL and *Webster v British Empire Mutual Life Assurance Co* (1880) 15 ChD 169, 49 LJCh 769, CA.
[12] [1947] AC 390, 28 TC 159.
[13] (1947) 28 TC 159 at 195.
[14] (1947) 28 TC 159 at 165.
[15] (1929) 45 TLR 581, 14 TC 580, CA.

proceed on the basis that the payment should be compensation for the owner of the capital having a restricted right of disposition over it during the war rather than for the use of the money by German interests to the exclusion of the English account holder. The relevant German Decree did not seek to confiscate moneys held in German banks, but merely prevented the funds being transferred, directly or indirectly, to the UK; the English customer would have been entitled to draw money from the account to pay a German or other, non-English, creditor[16].

Where a court makes an award it will usually be made clear how the amount is made up, and the interest element will be known. But there may be cases where, although interest forms an element in the calculation, the amount paid is in reality a capital sum of damages and the recipient is not treated as receiving interest income. This was the position in *IRC v Ballantine*[17] (where the award included an amount described as 'interest'), and *Glenboig Union Fireclay Co Ltd v IRC*[18] (where interest was payable in addition to the capital sum payable to a trader for the sterilisation of a capital asset). Neither of these decisions were criticised by the House of Lords in *Riches v Westminster Bank Ltd*[19], and therefore it may remain possible for a plaintiff to be awarded a sum which compensates him for, inter alia, the lost use of the money which he is claiming without the award containing a taxable interest element[20].

2-14 It also remains open for parties to a negotiated settlement to agree a lump sum settlement which may not include any identifiable element of interest[1]. Where it is clear that the amount claimed is paid and that it is paid together with an additional amount it may be reasonable to infer that the additional payment is compensation for delay in restoring the sum in question to the injured party in the absence of any other explanation as to the basis for payment of such additional amount. In *Perrin v Dickson*[2] an annuity paid to the taxpayer was, on a proper construction of the facts, found to amount to a return of capital together with interest, and the principal that the courts may dissect a payment into its true constituent elements has been followed in later cases[3].

On the other hand, the facts may warrant an agreed settlement by way of a lump sum not designated as representing any separately identifiable amounts but merely satisfying claims made against the payer. This might arise where the basis of liability is not clear, the value of the assets withheld or misappropriated is disputed, or the period or percentage to be taken into account in providing compensation by way of interest is not agreed.

---

[16] See also the comments of the Privy Council in *Raja's Commercial College v Gian Singh & Co Ltd* [1976] STC 282 at 287-288.

[17] (1924) 8 TC 595.

[18] 1922 SC(HL) 112, 12 TC 427.

[19] [1947] AC 390, 28 TC 159.

[20] However, even if the compensation is not interest, and therefore not taxable as income, it may be subject to capital gains tax – see TCGA 1992 s 22.

[1] See Lord Denning MR in *Jefford v Gee* [1970] 2 QB 130 at 150, CA. But see also Viscount Simon in *IRC v Wesleyan and General Assurance Society* (1948) 30 TC 11 at 25, HL: 'the name given to a transaction by the parties concerned does not necessarily decide the nature of the transaction'.

[2] [1930] 1 KB 107, 14 TC 608, CA.

[3] See *Lord Howard de Walden v Beck* (1940) 23 TC 384 and *Vestey v IRC* [1961] 3 All ER 978, 40 TC 112; but see also *Sothern-Smith v Clancy* [1941] 1 All ER 111, 24 TC 1, CA.

In such a case, there may be no payment or receipt of interest properly so called.

PAYMENTS DESCRIBED AS 'INTEREST'

2-15   In the same way as the description of interest as 'damages' will not prevent the payment being interest, so the character of a payment which is not interest properly so called cannot be altered by its being described by the parties to a transaction as 'interest'. Moreover, the mere calculation of the payment by reference to a sum of money will not cause the payment to be 'interest'. In *Bond v Barrow Haematite Steel Co*[4] a payment expressed as 'interest' in respect of preference shares of a company was held not to be interest; there was no outstanding indebtedness. In *Pretoria-Pietersburg Rly Co Ltd v Elwood (Surveyor of Taxes)*[5] 'guaranteed interest' paid by the South African government to the railway company at four per cent on the company's share capital was not interest proper. This was merely a subsidy paid by the government to the company, a subsidy which was reduced by any profit earned by the company[6].

2-16   In *Re Euro Hotel (Belgravia) Ltd*[7] the question arose as to whether 'interest' payable under a building agreement was 'yearly interest of money' in respect of which the payer should deduct income tax under what is now TA 1988 s 349 (2). The payer was a development company which had entered into an agreement with another company under which that other company would finance the construction of a building by the developer; on completion of the building the other company would acquire a long lease of the premises and would grant the developer an underlease at a rack rent. Once the construction costs paid by the other company had reached a certain level, the developer was to pay 'interest' on the construction costs until grant of the underlease. Megarry J held that the payment was not a payment of 'interest of money'. It was not sufficient for the 'interest' to be calculated by reference to 'money', but in order for the payment to be interest properly so called the 'money' in question must be sums due to another person in respect of which the interest is paid. The 'money' need not necessarily be owed to the same person as receives the interest; as Megarry J pointed out[8], A might lend money to B on terms that B pays interest to X. On the facts of the case in question, the only 'money' to which the 'interest' related was an out-and-out payment which had been made by the other company (which in effect amounted to the cost to that company of the long lease which it would acquire on completion). Megarry J saw the 'interest' payment as being a spur to the developer to complete the building economically. No doubt it also amounted to a return to the other company on its investment pending the grant of the underlease, when rental income would begin to flow; but, even though that might result in the payments

---

[4] [1902] 1 Ch 353, 71 LJ Ch 246.
[5] (1908) 98 LT 741, 6 TC 508, CA.
[6] See also *Spiller v Turner* [1897] 1 Ch 911, where it was suggested, at 919, that guaranteed interest on preference stock was probably interest rather than dividend, although this was not material to the decision.
[7] [1975] STC 682, [1975] 3 All ER 1075.
[8] [1975] STC 682 at 691*f*.

being income in the hands of the other company, it would not cause the payments to be 'interest', because the payments were in no sense in respect of money which any longer belonged to the other company[9].

2-17   Adjustments to a purchase price are sometimes described as 'interest' when they are no more than part of a formula for calculating that price. For example, negotiations may be undertaken leading to the sale of a business with effect from a previous date – perhaps the date on which broad agreement was reached but before the parties became bound to proceed; a price might be agreed by reference to the value of the business at that date, and, typically, it would be agreed that the purchaser should be entitled to any profits (or should suffer any losses) from that date and that the purchaser should pay interest from that date on the agreed price. In such circumstances, because there would be no indebtedness present until after the parties became bound to buy and sell, there would be no payment of interest properly so called, except insofar as interest is to run after the parties become bound to proceed.

2-18   Payments may even be made in respect of a loan or indebtedness, where the *Euro Hotel* principle would be satisfied, yet not be interest. In *Ridge Securities Ltd v IRC*[10] as part of a tax avoidance scheme a company issued a debenture with 'interest' calculated as 90 per cent of the gross dividends received by the company[11]. Pennycuick J described this interest as being 'grotesquely out of proportion to the principal amount secured'[12], and thought it 'impossible to treat as having the quality of interest a sum greater than the principal advanced and payable a few days after the advance'.
    Ridge Securities was applied by the High Court in *Cairns v MacDiarmid (Inspector of Taxes)*[13]. This case also concerned a tax avoidance scheme under which the taxpayer borrowed a sum from a bank, paid a year's interest in advance and then paid an affiliate of the bank a discounted sum to assume the obligation to repay the loan; another affiliate of the bank then assumed the liability to repay the bank, and, shortly after, the bank accepted early repayment from that affiliate. At first instance, Nourse J[14] noted Lord Strathclyde's approval in *Schulze v Bensted (Surveyor of Taxes)*[15] of the dictionary definition of interest as 'just recompense to the creditor for being deprived of the use of his money' and pointed out that interest must not be excessive or grotesque. He held that, in the circumstances, the 'interest' (calculated for a year) paid by the taxpayer could not be properly described as interest since it was not 'just recompense' for what was only a trivial deprivation of the use of the money lent by the bank. This was because, under the arrangements made by the bank and its affiliates, the bank was not deprived of its money for more than four days. It is not clear what

---

[9] Arguably, although this point was not taken by the paying company, the payments were 'annual payments' in respect of which income tax should bave been deducted under what is now TA 1988 s 349 (1).
[10] [1964] 1 All ER 275, 44 TC 373.
[11] It was not suggested that the payment was not interest, by reference to *A W Walker & Co v IRC* [1920] 3 KB 648, 12 TC 297 – see §2–08 above.
[12] 44 TC 373 at 393*g*.
[13] [1982] STC 226.
[14] [1982] STC 226 at 243*a*.
[15] (1915) 7 TC 30 at 33.

is 'excessive interest'; having regard to several statutory provisions this might be interest which exceeds a reasonable commercial rate or return[16].

The judgment of Nourse J did not proceed on the basis that the taxpayer did not have the use of the money for more than a very few days (nor was intended to) even though the Commissioners found as a fact that the taxpayer confidently expected that a company would be available to take over the loan obligation as in fact happened. It is arguable that the taxpayer should not be affected by arrangements to which he was not a party. If, for some reason, the company which assumed the liability had retained that liability and had discharged it after one year it would seem that the arrangements could not be challenged on the basis of the payment of interest being excessive because, as against the original lender, money would have been borrowed for a year for which reasonable consideration would have been paid. When *Cairns* was upheld in the Court of Appeal[17], the decision did not turn on whether the payment was of 'interest'[18]. However, Sir John Donaldson MR commented that the payment may have been a payment of interest because the amount paid was not excessive having regard to the right to retain the borrowed sum for a year[19]. It would seem that Nourse J's view was influenced by the Commissioners' finding that the loan was never intended to remain outstanding for more than a few days.

2-19 It not infrequently happens that commercial contracts involve a financing element where the transaction is not one involving a loan or credit, but references are sometimes made to 'interest'. Examples include hire purchase or leasing transactions. In the former, there are 'capital' and 'interest' elements in the payments made by the hirer, but, even if the description 'interest' is used, payments made by the hire purchaser which reflect the financing costs charged by the finance company are not payments for the use of money; they are payments for the use of the asset hired, albeit that the hire purchaser is at the same time paying 'capital' instalments of hire from which he derives his right to buy the asset for a nominal price at the termination of the hire period. Similarly, finance leasing contracts often provide for the calculation of the lease rental by reference to a floating interest rate applied to the unamortised element of the original cost of the leased asset. Although the finance lessor may regard this as the commercial return on his investment in the asset, it is not interest properly so called since there is no indebtedness in favour of the lessor. Such contracts may provide for 'interest' to be paid on any delayed payments due to the owner of the asset; this would be interest proper since it would be compensation to the creditor for late payment of sums due to him, but the main payments will not be affected by this. Other commercial contracts which involve calculations by reference to interest rates are interest rate swaps and currency swaps. Normally, interest rate swaps do not involve any direct lending or other indebtedness between the parties to the swap, but merely mutual obligations to make payments according to the spread between two interest rates (floating and fixed), and therefore no 'interest' is paid. This type of arrangement

[16] See, for example, TA 1988 ss 74 (n) and 209 (2) (d) and Sch 18 para 1 (5) (b).
[17] [1983] STC 178.
[18] See §**3-12** below.
[19] [1983] STC 178 at 182*b*.

should be distinguished from payments under an interest subsidy agreement[20] where the payment of the difference between a low rate agreed by the lender with the borrower and a higher rate agreed by the lender with a third party would be 'interest' notwithstanding that the third party has not borrowed any money[1].

Currency swaps developed from parallel loans where, for example, a UK company holding sterling would make a loan in sterling and take a loan (from the sterling borrower, or, more usually, a foreign affiliate of that borrower) in foreign currency. However, currency swaps may or may not (depending upon the particular transaction) involve any exchange of money or of mutual indebtedness obligations in different currencies. Where a currency swap does involve some indebtedness between the parties from the outset then the interest element payable in respect of such indebtedness would be interest properly so called. The essential point (as explained in *Re Euro Hotel (Belgravia) Ltd*[2]) is that in order for there to be interest properly so called not only must there exist a sum of money in respect of which the interest is payable but also that sum of money must not be merely an element in a formula but must be owed to another party (normally, the recipient of the interest).

Although the payments under the transactions described above may not amount to interest properly so called, it should be noted that in some circumstances they may be 'annual payments' and so attract a similar taxation treatment (as to deduction of income tax at source[3], relief for payments made and tax in the hands of the recipient) as if they were 'yearly interest'[4].

ACCRUED INTEREST ON SECURITIES BOUGHT AND SOLD

2-20 A person who sells interest-bearing securities *cum div* does not receive any interest on sale of the securities, but merely receives a price for the asset sold, even though that may include an element calculated by reference to the expectation of the receipt of the interest. This was established in *Wigmore v Thomas Summerson & Sons Ltd*[5] where the vendor of War Stock was held not to be chargeable to income tax in respect of any accrued interest element in stock sold. In that case, Rowlatt J said[6] that the Inland Revenue was

> 'taking up the cudgels, apparently, on behalf of the purchasers, who say that they decline to be assessed to tax in respect of income which has been accruing on the security they have purchased, in a period anterior to the date at which they did purchase'.

---

[20] Eg as made by the Export Credits Guarantee Department.

[1] See *Re Euro Hotel (Belgravia) Ltd* [1975] STC 682 at 691*f*, and §2-16 above; but any countervailing payment by the lender to the third party (if the actual loan rate were to exceed the (floating) subsidy rate) would not be 'interest'.

[2] See note 1 above.

[3] Under TA 1988 ss 348(1) and 349(1).

[4] Although, in practice, the Inland Revenue normally takes the view where payments are made to or by either a bank carrying on a bona fide banking business in the UK or a recognised UK swaps dealer that such payments may be paid gross and still qualify for tax relief (see Extra-Statutory Concession C17).

[5] [1926] 1 KB 131, 9 TC 577.

[6] (1925) 9 TC 577 at 580.

A purchaser took up the cudgels himself in *Schaffer v Cattermole (Inspector of Taxes)*[7], where the *Summerson* case was followed and the taxpayer was held to be taxable on the full amount of the interest received by him on government securities bought *cum div*.

In *IRC v Oakley*[8] it was held that the *Summerson* principle applied notwithstanding that the transfer of the securities was not effected until after the interest payment date; but, the sale had been made *cum div*, and although payment of the interest was made to the vendor he accounted to the purchaser for the interest through his brokers.

Despite the position as a matter of general law, where interest-bearing securities are transferred with accrued interest, the transferor is now normally treated by statute as receiving income equal to the accrued interest, and the transferee is not taxed on that amount when it is subsequently received[9].

INTEREST PAID BY A GUARANTOR

2-21   Where a debtor defaults on a guaranteed loan the guarantor may be called upon to pay any accrued and unpaid interest as well as any principal. Is the interest paid by the guarantor interest proper? This question will not affect the treatment of the interest in the hands of the recipient – it will remain taxable income and, probably, interest from his point of view – but the quality of the payment from the point of view of the guarantor will be relevant in connection with any obligation to deduct (and account to the Inland Revenue for) income tax[10] and any relief which may be allowed in respect of loan interest[11].

2-22   In *Pretoria-Pietersburg Rly Co Ltd v Elwood (Surveyor of Taxes)*[12] the South African government had guaranteed the liability of the company to its debenture holders (as well as guaranteeing to pay 'interest' on the company's share capital[13]). In considering the quality of the payments by the government, Fletcher Moulton LJ (giving the unanimous judgment of the Court of Appeal) said[14]:

> 'So far as it relates to the interest on the debentures which is guaranteed direct to the debenture holders, there is no difficulty. That is clearly payable by the Company as interest on money lent, and so much of the payment under the Government guarantee as goes for that purpose partakes of the same quality and is liable to income tax as interest.'

2-23   That case was not considered by the House of Lords in *IRC v Holder and Holder*[15] which concerned a claim by guarantors for relief for payments under a guarantee in respect of interest due on a bank loan. The claim was made by the taxpayers under ITA 1918, s 36(1). Interest payable on

---

7 [1980] STC 650, CA.
8 [1926] 1 KB 131, 9 TC 582.
9 TA 1988 ss 710 to 728; and see §§9-29 to 9-34 below.
10 See Chapter 7, Part 1.
11 See Chapter 8 below.
12 (1908) 98 LT 741, 6 TC 508, CA.
13 See §2-15 above.
14 (1908) 6 TC 508 at 520.
15 (1932) 16 TC 540.

an advance from a bank was payable gross, and, since relief for interest paid under deduction of income tax was then given by another procedure[16], s 36 (1) made the following provision for interest paid to a bank:

> 'Where interest payable in the United Kingdom on an advance from a bank carrying on a bona fide banking business in the United Kingdom is paid to the bank without deduction of tax out of profits or gains brought into charge to tax, the person by whom the interest is paid shall be entitled, on proof of the facts to the satisfaction of the special commissioners, to repayment of tax on the amount of the interest.'

The House of Lords held that the relief claimed was not available. However, the case does not decide that 'interest' paid by a guarantor is not interest. The case was concerned with relief[17]. Viscount Dunedin (with whom Lord Warrington of Clyffe agreed) said[18] of s 36 (1):

> 'I think that interest payable on an advance from a bank means interest on an advance made to the person paying. The guarantor does not pay on an advance made to him, but pays under his guarantee.'

Lord Macmillian said[19]:

> 'The benefit of the Section, in my opinion, is confined to persons who pay interest to a bank on advances which they themselves have received from the bank.'

Although Lord Thankerton appears to have questioned the possibility that a guarantor could pay interest proper ('I am of the opinion that the guarantor cannot be said to be paying interest to the creditor, though he is making good the loss of interest'[20]), Lord Atkin was tempted to go further and accept that the payments by the guarantors were interest proper. Of the view that the guarantor could not be said to have paid interest 'within the meaning of the section' he said[1]:

> 'I confess to feeling doubts on this point, for there can be no doubt, I think, that as the result of the sum of money paid by the guarantor, the interest due from the principal debtor was in fact paid and that if the principal debtor was sued he could support a plea of payment. Similarly, it might, I think, be said that, if a guarantor of rent pays under the guarantee, he pays the rent, not, it is true, his rent, but the rent of the tenant.'

It would seem that *Holder* is not authority for the view that 'interest' paid by a guarantor is not interest; so that, for example, a guarantor paying interest may be subject to the obligation to deduct income tax at the basic

---

16 See §1–09 above.
17 See also *Hendy (Inspector of Taxes) v Hadley* [1980] STC 292, [1980] 2 All ER 554, where a guarantor of a loan to a close company was held not to be entitled to relief under (what is now) TA 1988 ss 353 and 360 for payments under the guarantee in respect of interest because there had been no loan to the guarantor.
18 (1932) 16 TC 540 at 564.
19 (1932) 16 TC 540 at 569.
20 (1932) 16 TC 540 at 567.
1 (1932) 16 TC 540 at 565.

rate under TA 1988 s 349 (2)[2]. Moreover, it is arguable that a guarantor paying interest to a UK bank would be obliged to deduct tax notwithstanding that s 349 (3) (a) normally prevents s 349 (2) applying to interest 'on an advance from a bank carrying on a bona fide banking business in the United Kingdom', because, as was pointed out in *Holder*, the advance would not have been made to the guarantor. On the other hand, the better view is probably that, because s 349 (3) (a) is a relieving provision vis-à-vis the bank, whereas ITA 1918 s 36 (1) was a relieving provision vis-à-vis the payer of the interest, and the circumstances relating to the interest paid are no different from the bank's point of view (ie the interest is interest paid on an advance by the bank) merely because a person other than the original debtor has paid the interest, the interest would be payable gross.

2–24   The restricted view of *Holder* was taken by Lord Denning MR in *Westminster Bank Executor and Trustee Co (Channel Islands) Ltd v National Bank of Greece SA*[3]. He said[4] that

> '*Holder's* case was a decision on the words in section 36 (1) of the Income Tax Act 1918, "... the person by whom the interest is paid". It is not authority on the words "interest of money" [in other legislation].'

In the House of Lords, the distinction drawn by Lord Denning between *Holder* and the *National Bank of Greece* case was not argued further, although Lord Hailsham LC, delivering the only speech in the House of Lords, referred to it and said[5] that but for *Holder* he would have been attracted by the argument that 'interest' paid by the guarantor was interest within Sch D Case III[6].

In *Re Hawkins*[7] Megarry J reviewed *Holder* and the *National Bank of Greece* case and, while concluding that there was no binding authority either way, preferred the approach of Lord Atkin in *Holder* and of Lord Denning in the *National Bank of Greece* case. He was fortified by the facts of the particular case where the guarantee specifically related to interest payable under a promissory note, but he left open the possibility that payment of interest under a general guarantee of obligations might not amount to a true payment of interest.

2   Discount and premium

2–25   A lender might obtain a return on money lent otherwise than by stipulating for the payment of 'interest'. The borrower might agree to pay a premium to the lender on repayment of the loan; such premium might be the only return to the lender or it may be paid in addition to interest

---

[2] See Chapter 7, Part 1.
[3] [1969] 3 All ER 504, 46 TC 472, CA.
[4] (1969) 46 TC 472 at 485*e*.
[5] (1970) 46 TC 472 at 494*g–h*.
[6] In suggesting that the interest in the *National Bank of Greece* case would fall within Case III it appears that Lord Hailsham overlooked the fact that when considering *Holder* Lord Denning was concerned only with whether the payments were interest proper, and not, at that stage, whether the interest fell within Case III – see (1970) 46 TC 472 at 486*b*.
[7] [1972] 3 All ER 386, [1972] Ch 714.

paid throughout the currency of the loan. Or, the borrower might agree to accept a lower principal sum from the lender in consideration of the loan obligation, as where loan stock is issued at a discount; a financing may be effected by the 'borrower' drawing a bill of exchange for a fixed sum which is then sold to a purchaser (effectively, the lender) at a discount. Cases may also arise where a loan obligation is transferred in consideration of a price greater or less than the face value of the obligation – ie at a premium or a discount. These transactions may involve the 'borrower' or the 'lender' giving or receiving a sum additional to, or instead of, any interest specified, and which flows from the debt obligation and amounts to an additional cost of the financing or an additional return from the investment. Whether or not such amount is interest properly so called might affect the question of whether the borrower is under any obligation to deduct income tax from the payment and whether he is entitled to any tax relief for the payment made, as well as the treatment of the payment in the hands of the recipient.

DISCOUNT

2-26 The tax legislation makes (and has in the past made) special provision for the taxation of a discount but not of a premium. Schedule D Case III is broken into three parts[8]:

> 'Tax in respect of –
> (a) any interest of money, whether yearly or otherwise, or any annuity or other annual payment ..., and
> (b) all discounts, and
> (c) income, except income charged under Schedule C, from securities bearing interest payable out of the public revenue.'

It will be seen that a distinction is made between 'interest of money, whether yearly or otherwise' and 'discounts'.

2-27 In *Brown (Surveyor of Taxes) v National Provident Institution*[9] the taxpayer bought Treasury Bills at a discount. The difference realised on maturity, or earlier sale, between the proceeds received and the cost to the taxpayer was held to be taxable as 'profits ... on all discounts' within Case III of Schedule D as it then stood[10]. The House of Lords rejected the taxpayer's contention that the profit received was merely an accretion to capital. The discount was the taxpayer's return on the money laid out and compensated him for the use of the money and the risk that the money might never be repaid. Lord Sumner said[11]:

> 'It is all one thing, discount, whether the return to the lender is compounded of premiums for risk and interest on money in one ratio or another.'

---

[8] TA 1988 s 18 (3).
[9] [1921] 2 AC 222, 8 TC 57, HL.
[10] Section 100 of the Income Tax Act 1842.
[11] (1921) 8 TC 57 at 96.

A discount is taxable on maturity of the bill or loan or an earlier disposal by the holder[12], which is when the amount of the discount is received by the holder. It is not taxable in the years between acquisition and maturity of the bill or loan; that would involve anticipating a profit which should not be done even where the holder of the bill or loan prepares its commercial accounts on a basis which recognises part of the discount on an accruals basis until maturity[13].

2-28   The House of Lords also held in the *National Provident Institution* case that the profit received by the holder of the bills was taxable whether or not it exceeded the amount of the discount at which the bill was originally sold (or that proportion of it as the time between purchase and sale bore to the life of the bill). In other words, where a bill payable in a year's time and having a face value of £112 is bought at a price of £100, a profit of, say, £7 realised on sale after six months would be chargeable to income tax as a 'profit ... on ... discount', even though it might be said that only £6 of the discount had accrued over the six month period and that the price would have resulted from a change in market interest rates (in this example, a fall in interest rates) or a change in the market appreciation of the level of risk in relation to the obligor under the bill. Viscount Cave said[14]:

> 'The expression "profit on a discount" is unusual, and ... is probably eliptical for "profit on a security bought at (or a transaction involving) a discount"; and if one has embarked on such a transaction, I think the resulting profit, though enhanced by adventitious circumstances, is all profit on the discount. The value of the bill in the market may vary with the rise or fall of the value of money; but there is no real accretion to the capital, for the amount secured by the bill remains the same.'

This latter consequence is unsatisfactory[15], since it results in there being taxed as income the whole of the profit made by a taxpayer who acquires a security at a discount, even though he may be able to sell that security at an advantageous price by reason of a fall in interest rates (or other circumstances) rather than merely by reason of the passage of time. Further, the position is even more unsatisfactory for a subsequent purchaser of a note or bill originally issued at a discount where a rise in interest rates has resulted in a fall in the value of the security; a note issued at a discount of £10 may be traded at a discount of £15, the purchaser being charged to income tax on the whole discount of £15 on maturity or subsequent sale. It might be said that the surplus profit of £5 cannot be a profit from a 'discount' since the original 'discount' was only £10. The Inland Revenue appears not to view discounts in this way, but in principle regards any surplus realised by the holder of an obligation issued at a discount as being a capital

---

12 *Ditchfield (Inspector of Taxes) v Sharp* [1982] STC 124.
13 *Willingale (Inspector of Taxes) v International Commercial Bank Ltd* [1978] STC 75, [1978] 1 All ER 754, HL, although it is understood that the Inland Revenue only accepts this taxation treatment in the case of a financial trader which prepares its commercial accounts on an accruals basis if it can be shown that the accounts could be properly prepared on a basis which does not recognise the discount until maturity.
14 (1921) 8 TC 57 at 87.
15 See Walton J in *Ditchfield (Inspector of Taxes) v Sharp* [1982] STC 124 at 133*j*.

gain where it is realised before maturity of the obligation, whereas the whole of the discount is regarded as taxable income on redemption even though the surplus accruing to a taxpayer who acquired the obligation after it was issued is less (or greater) than the original discount[16]. Having regard to the observations in *Brown (Surveyor of Taxes) v National Provident Institution*[17] and *Ditchfield v Sharp*[18] it seems doubtful whether the Inland Revenue's view is correct. This somewhat unsatisfactory state of affairs has been remedied in relation to certain debt instruments issued at a 'deep discount'; legislation introduced in 1984 permits the 'true' discount element to be treated as income in the hands of a holder, any balance being brought within the capital gains regime, with tax relief available for the corporate issuer[19].

The word 'discount' in this sense does not include every difference between the issue price of an obligation and its face value. Not every 'discount' is potentially taxable under Sch D Case III, but only those discounts where the return for the use of the money is the discount rather than interest. Where the obligation does bear interest but the issue is made 'at a discount' (perhaps because of the risk element in the loan or fluctuations in currency exchange rates between the fixing of the coupon and the date of the issue), the discount element, not being in the nature of interest, will be treated as capital for taxation purposes[20]. However, the fact that interest is payable on a debt does not prevent a discount in respect of the debt being taxable as a discount unless the profit from the discount is of a capital nature[1].

2-29 The *National Provident Institution* case did not decide that a discount was not interest. A case on this point came before two judges of the Northern Ireland High Court in *Torrens v IRC*[2]. There, the taxpayer claimed relief under ITA 1918 s 36[3] in respect of a discount on promissory notes drawn by the taxpayer and purchased by a bank. The Special Commissioners had held that the discount was not interest; the two judges were divided, so that the Commissioners' decision stood. Although the discount was 'the equivalent of the payment of interest in advance'[4], Best LJ found that the relief claimed was not available because the transaction did not involve 'an advance from a bank', and because 'discount' was different from 'interest' and was distinguished from 'interest' in the legislation.

Megaw LJ, on the other hand, saw the discounting of the notes by the bank as involving advances by the bank at 'interest' (being the difference between the amount paid by the bank and the face value of the notes). Megaw LJ was also influenced by the reference, in s 36 (2) to 'interest ... payable ... to a discount house'; he inferred that 'interest' in that sub-

---

[16] Inland Revenue Consultative Document, 'Tax Treatment of Deep Discounted Stock', January 1983, paras 4 to 7.
[17] See §§**2-27** and **2-28** above.
[18] [1983] STC 590 at 594*j*-595*b*, and 596*h*.
[19] See §§**9-69** to **9-73** below, and TA 1988 s 78 and Sch 4.
[20] See *Lomax v Peter Dixon & Son Ltd* (1943) 25 TC 353 at 365-366, CA, and §**2-31** below.
[1] See *Ditchfield (Inspector of Taxes) v Sharp* [1983] STC 590 at 595*f*.
[2] (1933) 18 TC 262.
[3] See §**2-23** above.
[4] Stroud's Judicial Dictionary, 1931 Supplement, referred to by Best LJ, (1933) 18 TC 262 at 266.

section must refer to 'discount'[5], and therefore thought that the word 'interest' 'must have the same broad meaning in sub-section (1)'[6]. He also argued that a contrary view would result in double taxation, since the taxpayer would enjoy no relief for the discount but the bank would include the discount in its profits[7].

A discounting transaction where bills are bought at a discount differs from a transaction where money is lent at interest in that no money is borrowed by the drawer of the bill in a discounting transaction; this is not affected by the fact that the two types of arrangements are ways in which money can be raised, perhaps at the same cost[8]. Nevertheless, this does not prevent a discount being treated as a discount and not as interest where an interest-bearing security is issued at a discount by way of a borrowing.

PREMIUM

2-30   A premium paid by a borrower, normally on the repayment of a loan, may, on the other hand, be treated as interest proper. In *IRC v Thomas Nelson & Sons Ltd*[9] the taxpayer company made a loan on terms that interest was payable at 3 per cent per annum, but a premium, varying in amount according to the date of repayment, was payable on any repayment of the loan. The question before the court was whether the premium paid by the foreign borrower was income chargeable under Case V of Schedule D. It was held that the premium was taxable as income, since it was merely part of 'a reasonable return for the use of ... capital'[10]; the combination of the interest rate and a premium gave the lender a return at the rate of between 5 per cent and 5.5 per cent per annum. It was not suggested that the premium was in fact interest by another name, although Lord Normand said[11] that

> 'the premiums are part of the consideration given by the borrowers for the use of the capital lent to them, and part of the creditor's share of the profit which the borrower ... is presumed to make from the use of the money.'[12]

2-31   The whole question of premiums and discounts and their relationship with interest was reviewed by Lord Greene MR in *Lomax v Peter Dixon & Son Ltd*[13]. In that case, a Finnish company was indebted to the taxpayer; an agreement was reached under which the indebtedness was replaced by the Finnish company issuing, at a discount, notes to the taxpayer, such notes carrying a commercial rate of interest and also being repaid at a premium

---

[5] Quite why he inferred this is not clear. ITA 1918 s 36 (2) (formerly, FA 1917 s 15) was designed to extend to interest paid to discount houses the same relief which had been allowed by s 36 (1) (formerly, FA 1915 s 22) to interest paid to banks – see §1–09 above.

[6] (1933) 18 TC 262 at 270.

[7] This would not seem to have any bearing on the true character of the discount, but only on the question as to whether relief should be available to the drawer of the promissory notes under s 36 (1). This notion was rejected by the House of Lords in *IRC v Frere* [1964] 3 All ER 796, 42 TC 125, HL.

[8] *IRC v Rowntree & Co Ltd* [1948] 1 All ER 482, 27 ATC 28, CA.

[9] 1938 SC 816, 22 TC 175.

[10] (1938) 22 TC 175 at 180.

[11] (1938) 22 TC 175 at 179–180.

[12] See *Schulze v Bensted (Surveyor of Taxes)* (1915) 7 TC 30 at 33, and §2–11 above.

[13] [1943] 2 All ER 255, 25 TC 353, CA.

on maturity if the Finnish company's profits reached a certain level. Neither the discount nor the premium was held to be in the nature of income.

Lord Greene, giving the judgment of the Court of Appeal, considered the treatment of premiums and discounts. Although he said[14] that each case must depend on its own facts (as to which extrinsic evidence could be brought to demonstrate the quality of the sum in question), certain general principles could, in his view, be discerned.

'Where a loan is at or above a reasonable commercial rate of interest applicable to a reasonably sound security, there is no presumption that a "discount" at which the loan is made or a premium at which it is payable is in the nature of interest.'[15]

In such a case, the return for the use of the money would be incorporated in the interest, and the discount or premium would reflect other factors such as

'the security offered ... the taste of the market; the terms of the previous issues by the company; the political or international situation; the expectation of changes in money rates; the instability of the currency etc.'[16]

Although the correct tax treatment will depend upon the terms of the contract and outside factors (such as 'the extent to which, if at all, the parties expressly took or may reasonably be supposed to have taken the capital risk into account in fixing the terms of the contract'[17]), the substance of the arrangement will not necessarily dictate the characterisation of the receipts. Lord Greene considered[18] that a lender who subscribes at a premium and receives a high rate of interest, in part as compensation for the capital risk, would suffer tax on the interest as interest, while a lender who receives a lower rate of interest on a loan issued at par (and whose effective interest rate might be the same as that enjoyed by the first lender having regard to the premium paid by him) would only pay tax on the lower amount received; in the first case, there would be no question of netting off the premium paid (in this case by the lender) against the interest received. A similar position applies in the case of a loan issued at a discount where, if the loan bears a commercial rate of interest, the discount will not normally be taxable as a discount. Nor would a premium payable by the borrower on redemption of an interest-bearing loan normally be taxed as interest. However, where the loan itself bears an uncommeracially low rate of interest, and it can be seen that the premium (or discount) is part of the return for the use of the money lent[19], the premium may be taxed as interest and any discount may be taxed under Case III of Schedule D. As Lord Greene pointed out[20], this will nearly always be the case where the loan is not interest-bearing.

[14] (1943) 25 TC 353 at 363.
[15] (1943) 25 TC 353 at 367.
[16] (1943) 25 TC 353 at 364.
[17] (1943) 25 TC 353 at 367.
[18] (1943) 25 TC 353 at 363-364.
[19] As in *IRC v Thomas Nelson & Sons Ltd* 1938 SC 816, 22 TC 175; and see **§2-30** above.
[20] *Lomax v Peter Dixon & Son Ltd* (1943) 25 TC 353 at 367.

The treatment of a premium on redemption as income or capital can be seen in relation to indexed-linked stocks. Broadly, although each particular case must be examined according to its own circumstances, indexation of the principal amount of the stock to provide compensation to the lender for inflation over the period of the loan is treated as capital; but, if the loan interest is indexed with an additional rolled-up amount payable on redemption, the additional amount would be treated when paid as interest from the point of view of both borrower and lender[1]. The importance of the facts of each case, and the potential effect of some aspects of the terms of an issue of index-linked stock, can be seen from the discussions between certain financial institutions and their advisers and the Inland Revenue which were reviewed in the *MFK Underwriting* case[2] in 1989.

2-32   An example of the premium being treated as interest can be seen in *Davies (Inspector of Taxes) v Premier Investment Co Ltd*[3], where the principles described above were followed. The notes in question bore no interest, but were repayable at a premium of 30 per cent on redemption. Moreover, the terms of the notes were such that in the event of early redemption the premium payable was calculated at a percentage rate for each half year since the issue of the notes. The premium was held, applying *Lomax v Peter Dixon & Son Ltd*[4], to be 'interest of money'.

2-33   The taxation treatment of discounts and premiums outlined above was found to give rise to difficulties in relation to certain types of loan obligations designed for companies to raise finance and becoming increasingly popular (outside the UK) between 1980 and 1982. 'Deep discount stocks' or 'zero coupon stocks' involve the raising of capital by loans which carry little or no interest but which are issued at a substantial discount or repayable at a substantial premium. Applying the principles set out above, on the one hand the recipient would suffer income tax on the surplus or 'profit' received by him, whether on maturity or on sale, and whether he had subscribed on issue or had bought in the market[5]; on the other hand, a discount suffered by a borrowing company would not be 'interest' and so would not qualify for relief as a charge on income[6], or, if a premium paid were interest, it might not be 'yearly interest'[7] – in any event, any relief would only be available for a premium paid on redemption and not year by year for the amount accrued (as may be the proper accountancy treatment)[8].

In practice the Inland Revenue's view of the discount on deep discounted or zero coupon stocks was that it should be treated as rolled-up interest in the hands of the lender[9]. Although this would not seem to be a precise analysis of the position, the lender nevertheless suffers tax on the discount

---

[1] See Inland Revenue Press Release, 'Deep Discounted and Indexed Stock', 25 June 1982.
[2] *R v IRC ex p MFK Underwriting Agencies* [1989] STC 873, [1990] 1 All ER 91.
[3] [1945] 2 All ER 681, 27 TC 27.
[4] [1943] 2 All ER 255, 25 TC 353, CA.
[5] See §2-28 above.
[6] See TA 1988 s 338(3), and §§8-33 to 8-40 below.
[7] See Chapter 3 below.
[8] See TA 1988 s 338(1) and §8-35 below.
[9] Inland Revenue Consultative Document, 'Tax Treatment of Deep Discounted Stock', January 1983.

as income, whether it is treated as a discount or rolled-up interest; if the payment in question is a premium on redemption of a zero coupon stock, the treatment as 'rolled-up interest' is probably correct[10]. However, the Inland Revenue was prepared to go one step further and treat a discount in such circumstances as interest from the borrower's point of view and allowable for corporation tax purposes[11].

2-34 Following discussions on a consultative document published by the Inland Revenue in 1983[12], legislation concerning the taxation treatment of discounts was enacted in the Finance Act 1984. These provisions[13] provide for certain discounts (broadly, those exceeding 0.5 per cent per annum over the life of the stock) to be spread over the life of the stock and relief allowed to the corporate borrower on an annual basis. In the hands of the lender, the discount is taxed as income when the stock is realised on disposal or redemption; the problem, described in **§2-28** above, of confusing the income element of the discount with the capital gain is resolved by treating the accrued amount of the discount as income on disposal or redemption, with any difference between that amount and the surplus or loss on the investment being treated as a gain or loss for capital gains purposes[14]. The legislation only applies to discounts. No mention is made of a premium payable on redemption. However, the discount to which the legislation applies is ascertained by reference to 'the amount payable on redemption' which expressly does not include 'any amount payable by way of interest'[15]; a premium which is part of the income return to the investor would normally be 'interest'[16] and so excluded from the meaning of 'discount'.

---

[10] See §2-32 above.
[11] Inland Revenue Press Release 'Deep Discounted and Indexed Stock', 25 June 1982.
[12] Inland Revenue Press Release, 'Corporate Bonds including Deep Discounted Stock', 15 March 1983.
[13] Now TA 1988 s 57 and Sch 4; see §§9-70 to 9-73 below.
[14] Except for a bank or financial concern, where all the discount would fall to be treated on revenue account as a trading receipt.
[15] See TA 1988 Sch 4 para 1 (1) (e) and (b).
[16] See §2-32 above.

Chapter 3

CATEGORIES OF INTEREST

1 Annual or yearly interest

3-01 For the payer of interest, one of the most important questions to resolve is whether or not the interest is 'annual' or 'yearly' interest. This may affect not only whether income tax must be deducted at source and accounted for to the Inland Revenue but also, in some cases, whether relief is available in computing the payer's own liability to tax (whether income tax or corporation tax).

3-02 Before reviewing the cases in which the meaning of the terms 'annual interest' and 'yearly interest' is considered, the following general propositions can be stated:

1   The tax legislation has historically recognised a distinction between annual or yearly interest on the one hand and interest which is not annual or yearly interest on the other hand, the latter being commonly referred to as 'short interest'. Rule 2 of the Third Case of Schedule D of the Income Tax Act 1806[1] specifically referred to 'all interest of money, not being annual interest';
2   There has been no statutory definition of the terms 'annual interest' or 'yearly interest'. Although TA 1988 s 832(1) includes a definition of 'interest', this is merely said to mean 'both annual or yearly interest and interest other than annual or yearly interest';
3   Even where the word 'interest' alone has been used in a phrase including the words 'annuity, or other annual payment', the word 'interest' is not to be construed as meaning only 'yearly interest'[2];
4   There is no difference between 'annual interest' and 'yearly interest'. The expressions are interchangeable and have been used without any consistency in the legislation[3]. Currently, the expression 'yearly interest' appears to be predominant in the legislation[4]. Regrettably, this untidiness was not dealt with when the legislation was consolidated in 1988. In this chapter the expression 'yearly interest' will be used (except where quoting from the legislation or judicial authorities) to include yearly interest and annual interest;

---

[1] 46 Geo III c 65, and see §1-04 above.
[2] See §7-40 below.
[3] See, for an early example, the Income Tax Act 1806, 46 Geo III c 65, and §1-04 above.
[4] See TA 1988 ss 349(2), 338(3)(a) and 337(2)(b) and (3), but cf the use of 'annual interest' in TA 1988 s 353(1)(a).

5   Yearly interest does not mean simply interest 'of the year', in the same way that 'annual profits or gains' are not required to have any quality of recurrence in order to fall within Schedule D Case VI[5].

3-03   The early cases which came before the courts were concerned with the entitlement, under s 102 of the Income Tax Act 1842, of the payer of the interest to deduct tax on payment of interest into court. In the earliest case, *Holroyd v Wyatt*[6], property had been sold by order of the court and interest was payable on the delayed payment of the purchase price. In that case, the judge based his decision not to permit a deduction on what appeared to be the settled practice of the court, although he observed that he would not have expected tax to have been deducted from the interest any more than it would have been deducted from interest paid on the enforcement of a bill of exchange or a promissory note. The same practice was followed in *Humble v Humble*[7] where no reason was given for the decision. A case concerning a bill of exchange (not bearing interest on the face of the bill) came before the courts in *Dinning v Henderson*[8]. There, Sir J L Knight-Bruce V-C refused to disturb the Chancery Masters' practice, even though that practice was to allow a deduction of tax (ie the reverse of the practice in *Holroyd v Wyatt*), although his own view was that

'according to the true construction of the Act[9], the interest should have been allowed to be paid in full, and the claimant left to pay the income tax himself.'[10]

3-04   *Bebb v Bunny*[11] concerned the payment into court of the price on the purchase of a property together with interest for the delayed payment. Sir W Page Wood V-C held that the interest was yearly interest so that deduction of tax would be allowed under s 40 of the Income Tax Act 1853[12]. In his view, yearly interest was 'at least all interest at a yearly rate, and which may have to be paid *de anno in annum*' even though it may accrue *de die in diem*. In that case, it would have been possible for the interest to run for more than a year if the vendor had been unable to enforce earlier payment by the purchaser. The judge felt unable to distinguish between mortgage interest and interest on delayed purchase money – a mortgage deed normally contained a covenant to repay the principal after, say, six months, even though it anticipated that the loan would remain outstanding for some years with interest payable, normally, half-yearly – and it was clearly accepted that interest on mortgage loans was yearly interest. However, it will be seen[13] that it is not clear that there is no distinction between mortgage interest and interest on delayed purchase money.

---

[5] See *Ryall v Hoare* [1923] 2 KB 447, 8 TC 521 and *Martin v Lowry* [1927] AC 312, 11 TC 297, HL.
[6] (1847) 16 LJ Ch 174.
[7] (1849) 12 Beav 43.
[8] (1850) 19 LJCh 273.
[9] No Act is referred to in the report, but seemingly the relevant provision was s 102 of the Income Tax Act 1842.
[10] (1850) 19 LJ Ch 273 at 274; see also the doubt expressed in *Goslings and Sharpe v Blake* (1889) 2 TC 450, at 454 CA.
[11] (1854) 1 K&J 216.
[12] Although only on payment out of court to the vendor, and not on payment into court; but see note 10 in §**3-15** below on *The Norseman* [1957] 2 All ER 660, [1957] TR 193.
[13] See §3-13 below.

The decision in *Bebb v Bunny* also appears to have been influenced by the judge's belief that 'if this interest be not subject to such deduction, I do not well see how it can be charged with the tax at all'. This may have been based on a consideration of s 102 of the Income Tax Act 1842 which provided that in the case of yearly interest there should be no assessment on the recipient but rather the payer should be assessed without deduction for the interest but with the right for him to withhold an amount equivalent to the tax and retain it for himself. However, that procedure did not apply to interest which was not yearly interest; in such a case, the recipient himself would be taxed under Rule 2 of the Third Case of Schedule D in respect of 'all interest of money not being annual interest'[14].

3-05 Interest on bank loans has been reviewed in the cases, the first being *Mosse v Salt*[15]. There, it was held that, although interest on a banker's short loan was not subject to deduction of tax, tax did fall to be deducted from interest paid on a banker's loan secured by a mortgage, because the loan was of a fixed sum not a fluctuating overdraft. The case did not specifically consider whether the interest was yearly interest or not, but it appears to be the first case to distinguish between interest on a short or fluctuating bank advance and interest on a term loan (only the latter being subject to deduction of tax and therefore, presumably, yearly interest).

Interest on a building society loan was held to be subject to deduction of income tax in *Re Middlesbrough, Redcar, Saltburn-by-the-Sea and Cleveland District Permanent Benefit Building Society*[16], although the judgment did not consider the relevant legislation or specifically state that the interest was yearly interest. Until that decision, the Inland Revenue appears to have believed that the payments made by the borrowers to a building society did not contain an element of interest but that 'the whole of the payments must be regarded as so much money annually set apart to purchase the property'[17]. In a later case, *Leeds Permanent Benefit Building Society v Mallandaine*[18], it was held by one of the two judges in the Divisional Court that building society interest was not yearly interest because of the difficulty that a borrower would have had in calculating the changing (ie reducing) interest element in his instalment payments. The other Divisional Court judge did not express an opinion; nor did the Court of Appeal. The case decided that the society was taxable in respect of the interest received, irrespective of the possibility that the borrowers might have been entitled to deduct tax from the interest paid.

3-06 That interest paid on short-term advances by a bank was not yearly interest was confirmed by the Court of Appeal in *Goslings and Sharpe v Blake*[19]. The case concerned a loan for less than a year, and the court was

---

14 Further, see *Leeds Permanent Benefit Building Society v Mallandaine* [1897] 2 QB 402, 3 TC 577, CA, in relation to the 1853 Act; where interest was received gross it was held to be taxable in the hands of the recipient, even where tax might have been deducted at source; and see §3-05 below.
15 (1863) 32 LJCh 756.
16 (1885) 53 LT 492.
17 (1885) 53 LT 492 at 493 – from 'Instructions to Surveyors' issued by the Board of Inland Revenue (Edn 1855, pp 158, 159).
18 [1897] 2 QB 402, 3 TC 577, CA.
19 (1889) 23 QBD 324, 2 TC 450, CA.

careful to stress that it was only dealing with a bank loan for less than a year. It was held that the interest was not yearly interest; there was no provision in the agreement for the loan that the loan might be outstanding and the interest payable for a year or more, and the position was unaffected by the use of an annual percentage interest rate in calculating the interest. It has since been held, in *Ward (Inspector of Taxes) v Anglo-American Oil Co Ltd*[20], that interest on a loan for exactly one year is yearly interest. In *Goslings and Sharpe*, the court approved the decision in *Bebb v Bunny*[1] and disapproved (without specifically overruling) *Dinning v Henderson*[2].

3-07 *Goslings and Sharpe v Blake*[3] and *Bebb v Bunny*[4] were compared in *Re Craven's Mortgage*[5]. The two earlier decisions were not found to be inconsistent; the *Goslings and Sharpe* case was held to be confined to short loans for periods of less than a year, and *Bebb v Bunny* was said[6] to apply 'where interest is reserved for a period of more or less than a year, but is chargeable by periods of a year'. In *Craven* the question of a short, but extendable, loan did not arise. The arrangements in question were made in 1888 and concerned an indebtedness which had been outstanding since 1887; it was agreed that the indebtedness would remain outstanding, at interest from the earlier date, but secured by mortgage until the death of the debtor or the earlier death of his son. The interest was held to be yearly interest, and this was not affected by the interest not being paid yearly (or more regularly) but being payable only on repayment of the principal. In the light of *Re Craven's Mortgage*, it would seem that where a premium payable on redemption of a loan is interest[7], that interest will be yearly interest unless the loan was made as a short-term advance only.

3-08 It does not seem, however, that the correct test of whether interest is yearly interest is to enquire merely whether the interest *may* become payable for a period of a year or more. In *Re Cooper*[8] a creditor proved in bankruptcy for an amount owing on a judgment debt together with interest on the judgment debt. Although the case could have been decided on the grounds that the bankruptcy notice needed only to show the gross amount of the interest due before any tax was deducted, two members of the Court of Appeal expressly held that the interest was not yearly interest. Cozens-Hardy MR said that there was no contemplation or intention on the part of the debtor and creditor that the indebtedness should remain outstanding as an investment (and, therefore, that the interest should run) for a year or more, and that in those circumstances the interest could not be yearly interest.

3-09 The importance of an element of permanence in the arrangements combined with the quality of investment was taken up in later cases. In

---

[20] (1934) 19 TC 94.
[1] (1854) 1 K&J 216, and see §3-04 above.
[2] (1850) 19 LJCh 273, and see §3-03 above.
[3] (1889) 23 QBD 324, 2 TC 450.
[4] (1854) 1 K&J 216.
[5] [1907] 2 Ch 448.
[6] [1907] 2 Ch 448 at 457.
[7] See §§2-30 to 2-32 above.
[8] [1911] 2 KB 550, 80 LJKB 990, CA.

Gateshead Corpn v Lumsden[9] the corporation collected from the taxpayer his contribution to the cost of making up certain roads (which contribution had been outstanding for some years) together with interest which was prescribed by statute. It was held that this was not yearly interest. The Court of Appeal unanimously followed the principle in *Re Cooper* and held that interest was not yearly interest where there was mere forbearance to enforce payment of the debt. Lord Sumner said[10]:

> 'Whether or not the present case could have been brought into line with the mortgage cases if it had been shewn by the evidence that the corporation followed a regular practice of investing funds by allowing time to the frontagers for payment of the principal moneys due from them with interest it is unnecessary to consider. It is sufficient for the purposes of the case to say that no such facts are shewn here.'

In *Garston Overseers v Carlisle (Surveyor of Taxes)*[11] charitable trustees sought to recover from the Inland Revenue the tax attributable to interest received by them on the fluctuating balance of a bank account. The tax could have been reclaimed under s 105 of the Income Tax Act 1842 only where the interest was yearly interest. Rowlatt J reviewed the earlier cases and concluded[12] that

> 'yearly interest means, substantially, interest irrespective of the precise time in which it is collected, interest on sums which are outstanding by way of investment as opposed to short loans or as opposed to moneys presently payable and held over or anything of that kind'.

That being so, the interest on the bank balance, which was at call and not even a short-term loan, was not yearly interest.

3-10   The authorities were reviewed by the Court of Session in *IRC v Hay*[13] where interest on advances by a solicitor were held to be yearly interest. In the course of his judgment, Lord Anderson listed[14] the following propositions which he derived from the earlier cases:

1   'that interest payable in respect of a short loan is not yearly interest' (*Goslings and Sharpe v Blake*[15]);
2   'that, in order that interest may be held to be yearly interest in the sense of the Income Tax Acts, the loan in respect of which interest is paid must have a measure of permanence';
3   'that the loan must be of the nature – and this is pretty well expressing the second proposition in another form – that the loan must be of the nature of an investment' (*Garston Overseers v Carlisle (Surveyor of Taxes)*[16]);

---

9   [1914] 2 KB 883, 83 LJKB 1121, CA.
10   [1914] 2 KB 8833 at 889.
11   [1915] 3 KB 381, 6 TC 659.
12   (1915) 6 TC 659 at 664.
13   1924 SC 521, 8 TC 636.
14   (1924) 8 TC 636 at 646.
15   (1889) 23 QBD 324, 2 TC 450, CA.
16   [1915] 3 KB 381, 6 TC 659.

4   'that the loan must not be one repayable on demand' (*Gateshead Corpn v Lumsden*[17]);

5   'that the loan must have a "tract of future time"'.

This last proposition is based on the judgment of Lord Johnston in the Court of Session in *Scottish North American Trust Ltd v Farmer (Surveyor of Taxes)*[18], where he said:

> 'the natural inference [from the prohibition against deducting, in computing profits and gains, "any annual interest ... payable out of such profits or gains"] is that a distinction is drawn, with intention, between interest which can be properly described as annual, though it may be paid at shorter terms, and interest which cannot be so described, but is casual or anything from day to day upwards, short of annual. I think that the distinction between the two classes of cases may be somewhat aptly described by the use of a term of the Scots Law. Where the interest is payable in respect of an obligation having "a tract of future time", it may, in the sense of the Statute be understood as annual, and where not, not.'

3-11   The concept of yearly interest being interest on a loan having a degree of permanence can also be seen in Viscount Radcliffe's comments (with which the remainder of the House of Lords agreed) in *IRC v Frere*[19]. In that case, the House of Lords rejected a claim by the taxpayer for surtax relief in respect of interest other than yearly interest and which was not paid to a bank. Considering the apparent anomaly in the different treatment of yearly and other interest, Viscount Radcliffe said:

> 'If you ... set interest on a long term mortgage or the charge of a life annuity against the interest on twenty-four hours' money, seven days' money or a three months' bill, it is possible to see a real difference between their respective impacts on the payer's true taxable income. In the first place there is something like a permanent set-up under which the man's income accrues to him each year subject to a fixed and recurring charge for this outgoing. In the second, the short interest can be regarded as merely part of the cost of getting, using and returning money, and is often accounted for as a discount only, and its relation to the payer's annual income is much less direct. If he is borrowing professionally on short loan to get the return by lending *pro tanto* longer, it is only the difference on the incoming and the outgoing that he would think of as his income. If he is borrowing short to finance a purchase transaction, the interest, as I have said, is part of the cost which has to be set against the final gross return.'

3-12   The view of yearly interest as earned from an investment was followed by the Court of Appeal in *Corinthian Securities Ltd v Cato*[20]. The taxpayer had borrowed £2,800 from bankers (although not, at the time, bankers recognised by the Inland Revenue for the purpose of borrowers obtaining tax relief on interest other than yearly interest[1]). The loan was repayable on demand, but it was agreed that so long as the borrower satisfactorily

[17] [1914] 2 KB 883, 83 LJKB 1121, CA.
[18] (1910) 5 TC 693 at 698.
[19] (1964) 42 TC 125 at 153.
[20] [1969] 3 All ER 1168, 46 TC 93.
[1] Under ITA 1952 s 200.

met his obligations under the loan no demand would be made for six months and the loan would be repaid by two equal instalments, the first after six months and the other when agreed in the light of the performance by the borrower of his obligations. When the borrower did not pay the first instalment the loan was called in and the borrower claimed to deduct income tax under ITA 1952 s 169. The Court of Appeal held that the interest was yearly interest. Lord Denning MR said[2]:

> 'Interest is "yearly interest of money" whenever it is paid on a loan which is in the nature of an investment, no matter whether it is repayable on demand or not. An ordinary loan on mortgage is usually in point of law repayable at six months. But it is still "yearly interest of money". On the other hand, when a banker lends money for a short fixed period, such as three months, and it is not intended to be continued, such a loan is not in the nature of an investment.'

The reference to a short loan by 'a banker' raises a question as to whether the motive or commercial activities of the lender can affect the quality of the interest. Was Lord Denning suggesting that a short loan (of less than a year) by an individual out of his own private resources would be such that the interest on the loan would be yearly interest, whereas in the case of a loan by a bank it would not? In *Mosse v Salt*, although short loans by bankers and merchants were cited as being instances where tax was not deductible from interest which 'would come into the account of profit on a different scale when the profits came to be dealt with'[3], nevertheless the test applied to determine whether the interest was yearly interest (even where no banker or merchant was involved) was whether the transaction giving rise to the interest was one 'in which anybody contemplated or intended anything permanent'[4]. It seems never to have been established (nor argued before the courts) that interest paid by banks on deposit accounts is not yearly interest on the basis that the interest paid is merely a trading expense. In *Garston Overseers v Carlisle (Surveyor of Taxes)*[5] the interest paid by a bank on a fluctuating credit balance was held not to be yearly interest because the monies in the account were not there by way of investment rather than because of the status of the payer. It was only in 1967 that the Inland Revenue stated that, in view of uncertainties over the question, it had reviewed its practice and had decided that it would not thereafter require banks to deduct income tax from deposit interest[6]; this statement did not indicate that the Inland Revenue did not regard such interest as yearly interest. Since 1969 banks have been exempted from the obligations placed on companies to deduct income tax from payments of yearly interest[7].

The better view is probably that interest on a loan is yearly interest where the loan can be seen to be in the nature of an investment for a period of a year or more, or initially for a shorter period but in circumstances that the parties anticipate that the loan will remain outstanding for a year or more. A loan for a fixed period of less than a year is really in the nature of a short-term accommodation and will not have any long-term effect on

[2] (1969) 46 TC 93 at 95.
[3] Cozens-Hardy MR, (1863) 32 Beav 269 at 274.
[4] Cozens-Hardy MR, at 274.
[5] [1915] 3 KB 381, 6 TC 659.
[6] Inland Revenue Press Release, 31 May 1967.
[7] See §1-14 above and §7-25 below.

the income of the lender or the outgoings of the borrower, and the interest payable on such a loan is not of such a nature as would (together with annuities and other annual payments) have been susceptible to the historic taxation treatment as income transferred from one taxpayer to another[8].

The characterisation of interest as yearly interest by reference to its being on a loan by way of an investment was disapproved by Sir John Donaldson MR in *Cairns v MacDiarmid (Inspector of Taxes)*[9], since an investment could be for a very short fixed period (eg an overnight deposit). He thought that the question depended more on the intention of the parties. *Bebb v Bunny*[10] was cited by Sir John Donaldson in support of the view that interest would be yearly interest where the interest on a short-term loan '*may*[11] have to be paid from year to year'. Kerr LJ – also agreeing that the interest in *Cairns* was not yearly interest – thought that interest on a loan for less than a year would be yearly interest where 'the true intention of the parties is that it *should*[12] be a long-term loan, beyond a year and indeed probably over many years'[13]. This approach was followed in *Minsham Properties Ltd v Price*[14], where interest on a demand loan by a parent company, the loan having replaced a bank overdraft, was regarded as yearly interest since the loan had the nature of permanent finance.

It would seem that interest will be yearly interest where it is paid on a loan or indebtedness which is in the nature of an investment which the parties intend or contemplate will or should remain outstanding and accruing, if not produc..ng, interest for a year or more. This wou..u exclude the case where an indebtedness, such as outstanding purchase money, is immediately or imminently due and payable but which in theory could remain outstanding for a year or more.

3-13 This view is consistent with the decided cases, with the possible exception of *Bebb v Bunny*[15]. If delayed completion of the purchase had been agreed on the basis that interest would run on the outstanding balance of the purchase money[16] then the loan may well have had that degree of permanence which would have characterised it as an investment for a year or more so that the interest would have been yearly interest. But, if there was merely a delay on the part of the purchaser in completing the purchase on time (which, since the case arose out of a suit for specific performance may have been the case[17]) there seems to have been no justification for treating the interest as comparable with mortgage interest and therefore as yearly interest; the interest payable in each of *Re Cooper*[18] (interest on a

---

8 See also *Goslings and Sharpe v Blake* (1889) 2 TC 450 at 452, CA, as to 'yearly interest of money, or any annuity or *other* annual payment'. Despite this similar treatment of yearly interest and annual payments, it has not been held that interest paid to a bank is not yearly interest because in the bank's hands the interest is not pure income profit as an annual payment would be.
9 [1983] STC 178 at 181*j*, CA.
10 (1854) 1 K&J 216.
11 Author's italics.
12 Author's italics.
13 [1983] STC at 182*j*.
14 [1990] STC 718.
15 (1854) 1 K&J 216, and see §**3-04** above.
16 Eg as in *Hudson's Bay Co v Thew* [1919] 2 KB 632, 7 TC 206.
17 See also *Re Craven's Mortgage* [1907] 2 Ch 448 at 455.
18 [1911] 2 KB 550.

judgment debt) and *Gateshead Corpn v Lumsden*[19] (interest payable under a statute in respect of an outstanding contribution to street works) – both decisions of the Court of Appeal – was interest which could, and in the second case did, run for well over a year, but was nevertheless not yearly interest since there was no investment at interest but merely an indebtedness where the creditor was compensated for the delay in being paid. The later cases have shown that it is not sufficient to qualify the interest as yearly interest that it 'may be or become payable *de anno in annum*' as Sir W Page Wood V-C put it in *Bebb v Bunny*[20].

When FA 1969 introduced the obligation to deduct tax in certain cases of payment of yearly interest, the view was taken by the Inland Revenue[1] that tax should be deducted from interest paid on delayed completion of a purchase of property, presumably on the basis of the decision in *Bebb v Bunny*, where such interest is paid in the circumstances mentioned in what is now TA 1988 s 349 (2)[2]. An examination of the cases suggests that in the ordinary case of delay beyond the contractual date for completion this view is incorrect. In practice, tax is often deducted from interest on delayed completion monies paid by a company or to a non-resident. However, this is not always done, and in one unreported case in 1987[3], interest was ordered to be paid gross; the judge preferred 'modern authority' – *Cairns v MacDiarmid (Inspector of Taxes)*[4], emphasising the importance of the intention of the parties as to the period of the indebtedness – to the *obiter dicta* about unpaid purchase money in *Bebb v Bunny*[5] and *Goslings and Sharpe v Blake*[6].

3–14   Where a court awards a plaintiff a sum of money by way of damages for personal injury or other compensation for loss it may also award interest to run from the date when the cause of action arose. Such interest is interest properly so called, and will normally be taxable in the hands of the recipient; but, is it yearly interest, from which the defendant may be obliged to deduct tax?

In *Barlow v IRC*[7], the taxpayer claimed relief against surtax for interest paid on the restitution of misappropriated trust funds; such relief was only available if the interest was yearly interest. Finlay J held that the interest was yearly interest; he considered that it fell within the principle of *Bebb v Bunny*[8] without being taken out by *Goslings and Sharpe v Blake*[9]. No reference was made by the judge to *IRC v Hay*[10] or *Gateshead Corpn v*

---

[19] [1914] 2 KB 883, 83 LJKB 1121, CA.
[20] (1854) 1 K&J 216 at 219.
[1] See Law Society's Gazette, February 1970 at p 89; see also Law Society's Gazette, 2 September 1981 at p 928.
[2] Ie mainly, where paid by a company, company partnership or local authority, or where paid to a non-resident.
[3] *Commodities and Services International SA v Bestwood Properties Ltd*, (15 December 1987, unreported).
[4] [1983] STC 178, CA, and see §3–12 above.
[5] (1854) 1 K&J 216, and see §3–04 above.
[6] (1889) 23 QBD 324, 2 TC 450, CA, and see §3–06 above.
[7] (1937) 21 TC 354.
[8] (1854) 1 K&J 216.
[9] (1889) 23 QBD 324, 2 TC 450, CA.
[10] 1924 SC 521, 8 TC 636, and see §3–10 above.

Lumsden[11], although those cases were considered by the Special Commissioners who had held that the interest was not yearly interest. The decision also appears[12] to have relied on the fact that it was not suggested that the interest in an earlier case, *IRC v Barnato*[13], was not yearly interest. However, *Barnato* was merely concerned with whether the payment in question was part of the taxpayer's income for super-tax purposes, and it was held that the payment fell within the words 'all interest of money'; whether the interest was yearly interest was not in issue in that case.

The only case where the court has considered the status of interest on damages as yearly interest appears to be *Regal (Hastings) v Gulliver*[14]. There, the defendants in an action had been ordered, in 1942, to make payments to the plaintiff in respesct of a wrongdoing which took place in 1935, together with interest from that date. The defendants' claim to deduct income tax from the payments of interest was challenged by the plaintiff. Cassels J held that not only were the payments interest but that they were also yearly interest. Brief reference was made to *Re Cooper*[15], which Cassels J thought 'really turned on the validity of a bankruptcy notice in which the interest on the judgment debt was included in full without deduction of tax', and *Gateshead Corpn v Lumsden*[16], neither of which were found very helpful. The learned judge concluded that the circumstances of the case – namely, that the defendants were bound to pay interest since they were to be taken to have invested the money which they obtained in 1935 – distinguished the case from *Goslings and Sharpe v Blake*[17] with the result that the interest was yearly interest. The decision, which has not been reviewed in subsequent cases[18], is unsatisfactory in that there was no discussion of the nature of yearly interest nor consideration of the decision in *IRC v Hay*[19]. In the author's view, the decision is of doubtful authority.

In an Irish case, *Hamilton v Linaker*[20], the judge held interest payable on a legacy after the executor's year to be yearly interest, on the basis that since the loan was not a short loan as in *Goslings and Sharpe v Blake*[1] the interest must be yearly interest. Such an approach does not appear to be supported by other decisions. The distinction is between yearly interest and interest which is not yearly interest, and in any given case the task is to ascertain whether the interest is yearly interest rather than whether it is not interest other than yearly interest. The decision in *Hamilton v Linaker* might be justified on the grounds that a legacy which remains outstanding for a year will thereafter bear interest from year to year until it is paid; it is therefore interest which will only become payable after the indebtedness

---

11 [1914] 2 KB 883, 83 LJKB 1121, CA, and see §3–09 above.
12 (1937) 21 TC 354 at 363.
13 [1936] 2 All ER 1176, 20 TC 455, CA.
14 (1944) 24 ATC 297.
15 [1911] 2 KB 550, 80 LJKB 990, CA, and see §3–08 above.
16 [1914] 2 KB 883, 83 LJKB 1121, CA, and see §3–09 above.
17 (1889) 23 QBD 324, 2 TC 450, CA.
18 Although there was a passing reference to another aspect of the decision – namely, whether the payments were interest or damages – in *Riches v Westminster Bank Ltd* (1947) 28 TC 159 at 177–178, HL.
19 1924 SC 521, 8 TC 636, and see §3–10 above.
20 [1923] 1 IR 104.
1 (1889) 23 QBD 324, 2 TC 450, CA.

has remained outstanding for at least one year, even though the interest only runs from the end of the executor's year[2].

3-15   In *Riches v Westminster Bank Ltd*[3] interest payable on damages under the Law Reform (Miscellaneous Provisions) Act 1934 s 3 was held by the House of Lords to be interest properly so called. The question of whether it was also yearly interest did not arise, because the payment was made otherwise than out of profits or gains brought into charge to tax[4] so that the Rule 21, rather than the Rule 19, procedure applied[5].

Nevertheless, in *Jefford v Gee*[6] Lord Denning MR said[7] that 'When the court awards interest on debt or damages for two, three or four years, the interest is subject to tax because it is "yearly interest of money": see *Riches v Westminster Bank*.' He then went on to mention that there were special statutory provisions about deducting tax, and concluded:

> 'We do not think the courts, when awarding interest, should get involved in such questions. Interest should be computed and awarded as a gross sum payable by the defendant, leaving him to work out whether he should deduct tax or not.'

The suggestion that interest awarded by the court was yearly interest was apparently made without argument on the point before the court and on a mistaken understanding of *Riches v Westminster Bank Ltd.* In argument, both counsel for the appellant and counsel appearing as *amicus curiae* appear to have believed that interest awarded by the court was yearly interest and subject to deduction of tax. This misunderstanding may have resulted from the fact that FA 1969 s 26 had recently changed the provisions as to the deduction of tax from interest. Under the new legislation, tax was only to be deductible from *yearly* interest of money, whereas previously there had only been an *obligation* to deduct tax from all interest under Rule 21 (or ITA 1952 s 170) and a *right* to deduct tax from yearly interest under Rule 19 (or ITA 1952 s 169) – which Rule applied depended in part upon whether or not the payment was made out of profits or gains brought into charge to tax[8]. The 1969 amendments did not cause all interest to be yearly interest, nor direct tax to be deducted from all interest.

In *The Norseman*[9], interest awarded on a claim in an admiralty matter was held to be capable of being subject to deduction of tax, although in that particular case tax was not deductible because of the relieving provisions of the double taxation agreement between the UK and Norway (the country of residence of the plaintiff). The judgment did not focus on the question of whether the interest was yearly interest; indeed, the difference between

---

[2] In *Re Michelham, Michelham v Michelham* [1921] 1 Ch 705, 90 LJCh 432 interest owing at the deceased's death was held to be payable subject to deduction of income tax; however, this was because the payment was only properly made out of capital so that the Rule 21 procedure applied – whether the payment was yearly interest was not in issue.
[3] [1947] 1 All ER 469, 28 TC 159, HL, and see §2-13 above.
[4] See Evershed J (1947) 28 TC 159 at 161, and Lord Simonds, at 197.
[5] See §1-10 above.
[6] [1970] 1 All ER 1202, [1970] 2 QB 130, CA.
[7] [1970] 2 QB 130 at 149*b*.
[8] Generally, see Chapter 1 above.
[9] [1957] 2 All ER 660, [1957] TR 193.

ss 169 and 170 was not recognised[10]. In a more recent case, *Esso Petroleum Co Ltd v Ministry of Defence*[11], the defendant Government department claimed to deduct basic rate income tax from interest on damages. It was initially said that this was on the basis of (what is now) TA 1988 s 349 (2); that would have required the interest to be yearly interest. However, before the court that argument was abandoned in favour of an argument that the deduction was made under the provisions dealing with 'public revenue dividends' chargeable under Sch C[12] – that argument failed. It is not clear whether the s 349 (2) argument was abandoned because the interest was not yearly interest or because, the interest being paid by a Government department to a UK company, it was not paid in circumstances to which the deduction obligation applied. Thus, the question of whether the interest was yearly interest did not arise; however, in the course of his judgment, Harman J said[13] that 'There is ... nothing very surprising in finding that interest payable on damages, which are a one-off payment on behalf of a taxpayer to a wronged victim, is payable gross'. Although entirely *obiter*, this remark is consistent with the view that interest on damages is not yearly interest.

3-16 On the basis that yearly interest arises where the circumstances of the loan or indebtedness indicate a semi-permanent arrangement rather than a temporary accommodation, interest awarded by a court on damages or on property to be restored to its rightful owner should not be treated as yearly interest. In such cases, there is not even a voluntary forebearance to recover the amount due[14], still less a contemplation by the parties that the sum should remain outstanding at interest. There is frequently a dispute as to liability or the amount of that liability, and it is only when that question is resolved that the interest obligation comes into being by order of the court. This approach does not appear to have been considered in *Regal (Hastings) Ltd v Gulliver*[15] where interest awarded by the court was held to be yearly interest.

In conformity with this approach, where a solicitor pays to his client a sum in respect of interest on the client's money held by him otherwise than in a designated deposit account that interest is not normally treated as yearly interest[16]. That interest does not derive from any kind of investment made by the client, but is recompense to him for the use which the solicitor has been able to make of the client's money.

3-17 In *Chevron Petroleum (UK) Ltd v BP Petroleum Development Ltd*[17] a payment of interest which was restrospectively identified and quantified

---

[10] Lord Merriman P said, [1957] P 224 at 234–235, that where tax was deductible the defendant could pay into court a net amount, with an explanation of the point. In *Bebb v Bunny* (1854) 1 K&J 216, Sir W Page Wood V-C had said that payment of interest into court should be gross, but with the defendant having the right to claim that a deduction be made when the interest was released to the plaintiff.

[11] [1989] STC 805, [1990] 1 All ER 163.

[12] See Chapter 6 below.

[13] [1989] STC 805 at 810*f*.

[14] As in *Gateshead Corpn v Lumsden* [1914] 2 KB 883, 83 LJKB 1121, CA.

[15] (1944) 24 ATC 297, and see §3-14 above.

[16] See Note published by the Law Society – Law Society's Gazette, 2 September 1981 at p 928, and see also 4 March 1992 at p 34.

[17] [1981] STC 689, and see §2-10 above.

was treated as yearly interest. In that case, it was not until some years after the original payments had been made that it transpired that one group of companies had overcontributed to certain expenditure and was entitled to be reimbursed with interest. It was not suggested[18] that the interest was not yearly interest. This is consistent with the conclusion set out above, because the original contributions were made on the basis that either the contributions to expenditure would not be excessive, in which case they would be permanent capital expenditure, or the excessive contributions would not fall to be reimbursed until a later date (in most cases falling more than one year after the original payment was made), in which case the overcontributing companies would be compensated with interest. In no sense were the payments temporary advances of less than a year, with the possible exception of contributions made wtihin twelve months before the reimbursement; but it would seem right that all the interest should be characterised in the same way – it was not suggested in *Re Craven's Mortgage*[19] that the element of the interest which accrued prior to the mortgage agreement being entered into was not yearly interest.

3-18   The distinction between yearly interest and other interest is one which applies only for taxation purposes and cannot be resolved by reference to any general legal characteristics inherent in the transaction. It is rooted in the historical approach of the tax legislation to the 'transfer' of annual payments from one taxpayer to another. In view of the difficulties which can arise in practice in determining whether or not any given interest is yearly interest there might be some merit in abolishing the distinction, although it would then be necessary to specify certain transactions (perhaps loans which do not in fact run for one year or more) as qualifying for the payment of interest gross to avoid the 'ridiculous farce' to which commercial transactions would otherwise be reduced (as contemplated by Lord Esher MR in *Goslings and Sharpe v Blake*[20]) if tax were to be deductible from all payments of interest.

2   Schedule D Cases III, IV and V

3-19   It is necessary to distinguish between interest chargeable to tax under Sch D Case III and other interest; this distinction is important in relation to the deduction of tax from yearly interest paid, relief for interest paid and the taxation of interest in the hands of the recipient. Broadly, Cases IV and V relate to foreign source interest, and Case III to UK source interest; interest derived from most UK and foreign government, and other foreign public authority, securities is taxed under Sch C, which is described in Part 3 of this Chapter.

3-20   The basic charging provision under Sch D in relation to interest is in TA 1988 s 18(1)(b), where the income charged is 'all interest of money ... not charged under Schedule ... C ..., and not specially exempted from tax'.

---

[18] See [1981] STC 689 at 692*c*.
[19] [1907] 2 Ch 448, 76 LJCh 651, and see §**3-07** above.
[20] (1889) 2 TC 450 at 455, CA.

The tax under Sch D is charged under separate Cases[1], of which those applicable to interest are:

'Case III – tax in respect of –

(a) any interest of money, whether yearly or otherwise, ... whether such payment is payable within or out of the United Kingdom, either as a charge on any property of the person paying the same or by virtue of any deed or will or otherwise, or as a reservation out of it, or as a personal debt or obligation by virtue of any contract, or whether the same is received and payable half-yearly or at any shorter or more distant periods, ... and
(b) all discounts, and
(c) income, except income charged under Schedule C, from securities bearing interest payable out of the public revenue;

Case IV – tax in respect of income arising from securities out of the United Kingdom, except such as is charged under Schedule C;

Case V – tax in respect of income arising from possessions out of the United Kingdom, not being income consisting of emoluments of any office or employment.'

3–21 It will be observed that the principal difference between Case IV and V lies in the two words 'securities' and 'possessions'. Moreover, the word 'securities' is used in relation to income within Sch C. There is no definition in the tax legislation for these purposes of the word 'securities'. The word is widely defined in TMA 1970 s 21 (7) and in TA 1988 s 709 (2) to include stock and shares generally; in TA 1988 s 254 (1) the word 'security' is defined to include 'securities' which do not create or evidence a charge on assets and debt obligations of a company in respect of which a security is not issued. But neither of these definitions is applied for the purpose of Sch D Case IV.

Although in the case of Sch C it would seem that the word 'securities' bears a meaning as in the expression 'marketable securities' (such as government stock), a more restricted meaning applies for the purposes of Sch D Case IV. In 1919, it had been held by Rowlatt J in *Hudson's Bay Co v Thew*[2] that, even where there was no security over an asset (such as mortgaged land, in that case), interest from a debt obligation was income from a security within Sch D Case IV. By analogy with the case of government securities, Rowlatt J considered that it was sufficient for the indebtedness to be 'secured' by personal covenant to pay. However, in the following year the House of Lords decided, in *Singer v Williams*[3], that the word 'security' did require the loan to be secured in some way. Viscount Cave said[4]:

'The word denotes a debt claim, the payment of which is in some way secured. The security would generally consist of a right to resort to some fund or property for payment; but I am not prepared to say that other forms of security (such as personal guarantee) are excluded. In each case, however, where the word is used in its normal sense, some form of secured liablity is postulated.'

---

[1] See TA 1988 s 18 (3).
[2] [1919] 2 KB 632, 7 TC 206.
[3] [1921] 1 AC 41, 7 TC 419.
[4] (1920) 7 TC 419 at 431.

In *Lord Manton's Trustees v Steele*[5] Rowlatt J decided (and the Court of Appeal agreed) that his earlier decision in *Hudson's Bay* had been incorrect. In *Lord Manton's* case a simple contract debt owed by a company not resident in the UK was held to be a 'possession' the interest from which fell within Case V.

The practical implications of the distinction between interest within Case IV and interest within Case V have now disappeared. Previously, the bases on which the assessable income within those Cases was measured were different, Case IV income being assessed on the basis of the income arising in the year of assessment, but Case V income being assessed by reference to the average of the amount of Case V income remitted to the UK in the three preceding years.

3-22   The source from which interest under Case III is derived is not specified in the legislation. Although it may be necessary to determine whether interest falls within Case III or within Case IV or V, it might be thought that because Case III is not specifically limited to securities or obligations situated within the UK the test to be applied is whether the interest in question falls within Case IV or V - if it does not, it would then fall within Case III. That was the approach adopted by the Court of Appeal in *Westminster Bank Executor and Trustee Co (Channel Islands) Ltd v National Bank of Greece SA*[6]. However, in the House of Lords, Lord Hailsham LC, giving the only full opinion, said that he preferred a simpler approach to that adopted by the Court of Appeal. That approach was to identify 'whether or not the source of the payments [ie the interest] ... was or was not situated within the United Kingdom'; in Lord Hailsham's view, if the source was not in the UK 'it [ie the source] would then be either a foreign security within Case IV or a foreign possession within Case V'. This opinion introduces a concept of source, which concept is not used in the language of the UK tax legislation. Other jurisdictions[7] have used the concept of the source of interest and other income, and have taxed interest where it 'arises' or 'accrues' in, or is 'derived' from, the jurisdiction. This has led the courts of such jurisdictions to identify as the 'originating cause' of the interest paid the provision of the loan or credit, the location of which may have been outside the country where the debtor was resident and from which the interest was paid, so resulting in the interest not being derived from any source in that country[8]. The *National Bank of Greece* case concerned the possible application of ITA 1952 s 170 to payments of interest to be discharged by a guarantor of bonds; that section required the deduction of tax from 'any interest of money, annuity or other annual payment charged with tax under Schedule D', without making any reference to Case III. Lord Hailsham based his approach to the question on the territorial limitation which must apply to cut down the wide language of (what is now) TA 1988 s 18 (1)(b). Unlike the provisions of s 18 (1)(a), there is no limitation in s 18 (1)(b) by reference to 'any person residing in the United Kingdom' or 'any property whatever in the United Kingdom'. Nevertheless, Lord Hailsham pointed out that

---

[5] (1927) 11 TC 549.
[6] [1969] 3 All ER 504, 46 TC 472.
[7] Eg South Africa, Kenya, New Zealand, Hong Kong.
[8] *IRC v Lever Bros and Unilever Ltd* (1946) 14 SATC 1; *Esso Standard Eastern Inc v IT Comrs* [1971] EA 127; *IRC v Phillips Gloeilampenfabrieken* [1955] NZLR 868.

some territorial limitation must apply as explained by Lord Herschell in *Colquhoun v Brooks*[9]:

'The Income Tax Acts, however, themselves impose a territorial limit, either that from which the taxable income is derived must be situate in the United Kingdom or the person whose income is to be taxed must be resident there.'

In the *National Bank of Greece* case Lord Hailsham held that the source of the obligation to pay principal and interest was found in the bonds issued by the original borrower; the bonds were foreign documents, and other aspects of the transaction (namely, the issuer of the bonds, the original guarantor, the successor guarantor, the lands charged as security and the funds out of which payments of principal and interest would be paid) were all foreign. Consequently, the source was situated outside the UK, being securities within Case IV. Lord Hailsham gave no weight to the fact that the original provision of funds to the borrower took place in London in sterling. Although the point does not seem to have been argued in that case, it does not appear that, for UK taxation purposes (unlike the position in other jurisdictions[10]), it is necessary to examine the 'originating cause' of the obligation to pay interest, but rather the characteristics of the obligation itself must be examined.

Further, it appears that the governing factor is not the *situs* of the debt as the same applies for death duty purposes; in the *National Bank of Greece* case the bonds in question were bearer bonds, and it was not suggested that the source of the interest was affected by the location of the bonds. The different approach can be justified, since death duties are concerned with ownership of assets, so that the relevant question may be 'where can the asset be effectively dealt with?'[11]. However, in the case of interest, the more relevant question as to source is 'where can payment of the interest be effectively enforced?' This would tend to lead to an examination of the security for a secured debt obligation, and of the location where the indebtedness can effectively be enforced against the debtor in the case of an unsecured obligation[12]. This should be distinguished from the place where payment of the interest is to be made, which does not appear to affect the question of whether the interest falls within Case III. Paragraph (a) of Case III[13] appears to contemplate that interest, annuities or annual payments may fall within Case III 'whether such payment is payable within or out of the United Kingdom'[14]. Therefore, interest may fall within Case III even though it is payable outside the UK (as is commonly the case with interest on foreign currency borrowings[15]). The fact that the interest is payable outside

---

[9] (1889) 2 TC 490 at 499, HL.

[10] See note 7 above.

[11] See *Brassard v Smith* [1925] AC 371, 94 LJPC 81, PC.

[12] In the case of simple contract debts, the locality for death duty purposes depends on the residence of the debtor against whom the debt could be enforced – see *Stamps Comr v Hope* [1891] AC 476, at 481 to 482, PC; and see in relation to locality for stamp duty purposes, *English, Scottish and Australian Bank Ltd v IRC* [1932] AC 238, 101 LJKB 193, HL.

[13] TA 1988 s 18(2).

[14] It might be argued that 'such payment' only relates to 'any annuity or other annual payment' and not to 'any interest of money, whether yearly or otherwise'; however, there seems to be no reason why such a distinction should be made.

[15] See §7-20 below.

the UK would not prevent payment being enforced in the UK against a UK borrower or where the loan is secured on UK property.

3-23   There appears to have been no decided case[16] concerning what constitutes 'securities out of the United Kingdom'. An example of a secured loan can be found in *IRC v Viscount Broome's Executors*[17]. There, the question at issue was whether General Rule 21[18] required the deduction of tax from interest paid by the executors of an individual who had been resident in both the UK and Kenya and who had borrowed money from a resident of Kenya secured by an equitable mortgage of land in Kenya and shares in an English registered company (albeit one which, carrying on a farming business in Kenya, may not, under the law as it then stood, have been resident in the UK). As with the *National Bank of Greece* case[19] whether the interest fell within Case III or Case IV was not directly in issue; tax would have been deductible if the interest was 'charged with tax under Schedule D'. It was assumed that tax was not deductible during the borrower's lifetime because the *situs* was not in the UK, the borrower having been resident in Kenya where the money was borrowed and the security given. However, the court held that tax was required to be deducted when interest was paid by the deceased borrower's executors (who were resident in the UK) 'out of a source arising in this country'[20]. The Memorandum of Agreement as to the loan was under hand, so that the *situs* of the debt could have been taken to be where the executors were resident, and it does not appear to have been argued that the interest arose out of the UK by reason of the original circumstances surrounding the loan. The reference to the payment of interest 'out of a source arising in this country' appears to have been concerned with the *resources* available to the executors to discharge their obligations in relation to the loan; in the *National Bank of Greece* case, Lord Hailsham noted[1] that the funds out of which the interest would have been paid at the time when the bonds were originally issued were in Greece. This points to the importance of the location where the obligation may *effectively* be enforced in determining the source of interest.

However, it should be noted that in relation to both *Viscount Broome's Executors* and the *National Bank of Greece* case, the determination of the source of the interest arose at a time when the interest was payable by a person other than the original borrower. In the earlier case, it was the executors of the deceased borrower who had become liable to pay the interest, and in the later case the interest was payable by the universal successor to the original guarantor (in circumstances where the interest could not be paid in Greece but could be paid at the successor guarantor's London branch). *Viscount Broome's Executors* was not considered by the House of Lords[2] in the *National Bank of Greece* case, where it was held that subsequent events did not alter the source of the interest on the bonds. It is therefore arguable

[16] Apart from the decision in *Hudson's Bay Co v Thew* [1919] 2 KB 632, 7 TC 206, now overruled – see §3-21 above.
[17] (1935) 19 TC 667.
[18] Subsequently, ITA 1952 s 170 – see §1-10 above.
[19] See §3-22 above.
[20] (1935) 19 TC 667 at 679.
[1] (1970) 46 TC 472 at 494*a*.
[2] It was referred to in argument before the Court of Appeal, but not in any of the judgments.

that *Viscount Broome's Executors* might be decided differently in the light of the *National Bank of Greece* case.

3-24   As to 'possessions out of the United Kingdom', the decided cases have been concerned with property other than loans. In *Pickles v Foulsham*[3] the earnings of an employee working outside the UK were held not to be derived from a possession out of the UK where the employment was with a British company, under an agreement made in the UK, and where the salary was paid into a bank in London. That decision was said by Lord Hailsham, in the *National Bank of Greece* case[4], to be more an authority for the wide meaning of the word 'possession' than a guide to the situation of a source of income in a case where the facts are different.

In *IRC v Anderstrom*[5] alimony payable to a UK resident by virtue of an order of a Swedish court was held to be income from a foreign possession; the source of the payments – the asset which gave the recipient the right to be paid – was the order of a foreign court. Similarly, in *Chamney v Lewis (Inspector of Taxes)*[6] maintenance payments under a separation deed made in India were income from a foreign possession within Case V; the judge commented that the deed provided for remittance of sums from abroad and that in fact sufficient sums to meet the payments were remitted from India in the material years. Other cases concerning maintenance payments have held that payments under a foreign court order[7] or a foreign deed[8] must be paid according to the terms of the foreign obligation irrespective of the residence of the payer, and that payments under an English court order remain payable under deduction of UK income tax notwithstanding that the payer no longer resides in the UK[9]. These decisions do not resolve the question in relation to the source of loan interest, and the first two turned on the rights as between the parties to the arrangement.

3-25   The locality of a simple contract debt is the place where the debtor is to be found[10]. Where the debt in question does not amount to a 'security' within Case IV, how is it determined whether the possession is 'out of the United Kingdom'? In *Bradbury v English Sewing Cotton Co Ltd*[11] dividends paid on shares of an American incorporated company were held not to be income from foreign possessions where the company in question[12] was resident in the UK for taxation purposes. It was decided that the established residence in the UK (as a result of which the company's worldwide income was subject to income tax in the UK) applied for all taxation purposes. Subsequently, when the company transferred its residence from the UK, the dividends paid were, in the hands of the UK shareholders, income from foreign possessions. It is doubtful whether the tax residence of a company is of such importance in determining the source of interest. Dividends are

3   [1925] AC 458, 9 TC 261, HL.
4   (1970) 46 TC 472 at 496*b*.
5   1928 SC 224, 13 TC 482.
6   (1932) 17 TC 318.
7   *Bingham v IRC* [1955] 3 All ER 321, 36 TC 254.
8   *Keiner v Keiner* [1952] 1 All ER 643, 34 TC 346.
9   *Stokes v Bennett (Inspector of Taxes)* [1953] 2 All ER 313, 34 TC 337.
10   *English, Scottish and Australian Bank Ltd v IRC* [1932] AC 238, 101 LJKB 193, HL; and see also *Lord Manton's Trustees v Steele* (1927) 11 TC 549, and §**3-21** above.
11   [1923] AC 744, 8 TC 481, HL.
12   American Thread Company.

paid out of a company's overall profits, not out of gross income, whilst interest can sometimes be identified with a particular element of a company's business (such as a branch) which is not the case with dividends. However, except where interest is clearly identifiable with part only of a company's activities, it would seem that where a non-UK resident company pays interest on an unsecured loan, that interest is income within Case V as being from a possession 'out of the United Kingdom'. This is consistent with the view that regard should also be had to the resources out of which payment of the interest can be enforced, although, as already suggested, this would not be the case where the loan is taken for the purposes of a trade carried on by the non-resident company through a branch in the UK. In relation to such a loan it might be said that the debtor is to be found in the UK; it would have a 'tax presence'[13] in the UK, and should be registered as an overseas company under the Companies Act 1985 Part XXIII, which would facilitate enforcement of the debt in the UK[14].

3-26   The converse of that approach is that an unsecured indebtedness of a UK resident company cannot be a 'possession out of the United Kingdom', except, possibly, where the loan is contracted abroad for the purpose of a branch trade undertaken abroad by that company and where payment of the interest is made out of the resources of that branch.

3-27   It should be noted that in the *National Bank of Greece* case[15] Lord Hailsham expressly left open the possibility that there can 'in certain circumstances be an overlap between Cases III and IV only to be resolved by an election of the Crown'[16]. This possiblity was canvassed in argument before the House of Lords[17], but was not considered further by Lord Hailsham. However, although there might be an overlap between Case I and either Case IV or V where investment income could also form part of the income of a trade[18], there would not appear to be any overlap where the source of the income is purely an investment, where the interest will fall within either Case III (because it has a UK source) or Case IV or V (because it has a foreign source) but not both. It appears from what Lord Hailsham said in the *National Bank of Greece* case that, despite the wide wording of Case III which would be sufficient to cover interest from foreign securities and possessions which are owned by a UK resident taxpayer, interest will only be treated as within Case III where the source is in the UK; if this were not the position, income tax would have been deductible in that case from interest paid to UK resident bondholders.

Although there may be no true overlap between Case III and Case IV or V, circumstances may arise where elements are present which suggest different Cases. This may occur where a UK resident company raises a loan to finance a foreign branch trade, or where such a borrower charges foreign property as security for the loan. In such cases, the circumstances must be

---

[13] See *Clark (Inspector of Taxes) v Oceanic Contractors Inc* [1983] STC 35, [1983] 1 All ER 133, HL.
[14] See also *New York Life Insurance Co v Public Trustee* [1924] 2 Ch 101, 93 LJCh 449, CA.
[15] (1970) 46 TC 472 at 495*f*.
[16] As to the Crown's right of election, see *Liverpool and London and Globe Insurance Co v Bennett* (1913) 6 TC 327 at 376, HL.
[17] See [1971] AC 945 at 951 and 952.
[18] As in *Liverpool and London and Globe Insurance Co v Bennett* [1913] AC 610, 6 TC 327, HL.

examined to determine whether or not the source is in the UK, and also whether the source of the interest can really be said to be a foreign security or foreign posesssion. For example, in the case of a borrowing by a UK resident with dual security, in the UK and abroad, it would seem that the interest would fall within Case III because not only is the borrower resident in the UK and the loan partly secured in the UK, but also by reason of the mixed security it could not be said that the security was 'out of the United Kingdom'.

Cross-border guarantees can give rise to interesting questions. Can either a foreign guarantee cause a UK loan to be a Case IV security, or a UK guarantee cause interest on a loan to a foreign borrower to be within Case III? These questions can arise where a foreign parent company guarantees the indebtedness of a UK subsidiary and vice versa. In the first case, even though the existence of a guarantee might cause the indebtedness to be capable of being regarded as a 'security'[19], it would not be a security 'out of the United Kingdom' so as to fall within Case IV[20]. Thus, the UK borrower would be expected to deduct basic rate income tax from yearly interest payable on such a loan[1]. If the guarantee were called, payments by the foreign guarantor in respect of interest might strictly be UK source interest[2], although in practice the UK Inland Revenue would probably be unable to enforce any withholding obligation.

Where a UK company guarantees a foreign company's borrowing, it seems doubtful whether the existence of a UK guarantee alone is sufficient to turn what would otherwise be foreign source interest into Case III interest. The identity of the guarantor was one of the considerations taken into account by Lord Hailsham in the *National Bank of Greece* case[3], but others – the identity of the issuer, any other security and the funds out of which the payment of interest would be paid – seem to be of no less importance. Even if the interest fell within Case III in such circumstances, the UK Inland Revenue would be unable to enforce any tax withholding obligation, unless and until the guarantor was required to pay interest following a default; if the UK guarantee were insufficient to cause the foreign source interest to fall within Case III initially, then the interest would, in the author's view, retain its Case IV source even when subsequently paid by the guarantor[4].

3–28 In view of the uncertain state of the law, care must be taken in arranging loan obligations, particularly where the borrower is resident in the UK and there is a foreign element in the arrangements, if the interest is not to fall within Case III. This will often be important in relation to the obligation to withhold income tax from interest payments to non-resident lenders[5].

Until 1979, the Inland Revenue was in practice prepared to accept that interest paid by a UK resident borrower did not fall within Case III provided three conditions were satisfied:

[19] See §**3–21** above.
[20] See above.
[1] See §**7–08** below.
[2] See §**2–21** to **2–24** above.
[3] See §**3–22** above.
[4] See §**3–22** above. The interest could have a UK source where the guarantor is substituted as primary obligor following liquidation of (or other default by) the original debtor. However, the Inland Revenue are understood to take the view generally that, where payment can be enforced in the UK against a UK guarantor, interest paid by him has a UK source, irrespective of the residence of the original debtor.
[5] See TA 1988 s 119(2) and Chapter 7 Part 1.

1   the loan documentation was subject to a law other than the law of England and Wales, Scotland or Northern Ireland;
2   the loan obligation was created by a document under seal; and
3   the indebtedness was not secured by a charge over any property in the UK.

It is not entirely clear what was the authority for this approach. Certainly, security on UK property must be avoided if the interest is not to have a UK source, and the loan agreement being subject to foreign law (under which deduction of UK tax would not be permitted) and executed under seal (so constituting it as a speciality debt situated outside the UK) would be indicative of the interest not falling within Case III in the light of the cases on maintenance payments[6]. Corporate borrowers frequently took advantage of this practice when raising loan finance in circumstances where the interest could not otherwise be paid gross to the non-resident creditor by virtue of a double taxation agreement[7]. However, at the end of 1979 the Inland Revenue, concerned that the removal of exchange control restrictions had resulted in a flow of UK investment funds into bearer debt instruments issued by UK companies[8], decided that this practice would no longer be followed. The Inland Revenue reverted to what, apparently, had always been the official view, namely, that interest on borrowings by UK residents fell only within Case III irrespective of other features.

3-29   Such a view, based as it must be on the premise that all interest paid by a UK resident has a UK source, does not withstand close examination. TA 1988 s 338 (4) (c) and (d) clearly contemplate that a resident company might pay interest which is not within Case III. Section 338 (4) requires that, in the case of yearly interest paid by a resident company to a non-resident, the interest may only qualify as a charge on income if either:

1   income tax is deducted at source under TA 1988 s 349 (2) (or the interest is relieved from such deduction by virtue of a double taxation agreement[9]); or
2   the interest is paid on a quoted Eurobond[10]; or
3   the interest falls within TA 1988 s 340; or
4   the interest is paid out of income brought into charge to corporation tax under Case IV or V.

Conditions 3 and 4 must refer to yearly interest which does not fall within Case III, since otherwise s 349 would apply and condition 1 would be satisfied. The Inland Revenue considers that conditions 3 and 4 could still be fulfilled in the case of yearly interest where s 349 (2) does not apply by virtue of a special exemption from tax granted to a foreign lender[11]. However, it seems

---

[6] See §3-24 above.
[7] Typically, in the case of issues of negotiable bonds or subsidised export credit borrowings from Japanese or Korean banks.
[8] So that UK investors might receive gross, and fail to declare for taxation purposes, interest received from UK sources.
[9] See Regulation 6 of the Double Taxation Relief (Taxes on Income) (General) Regulations 1970: SI 1970 No 488; and see §7-19 below.
[10] See §7-13 below.
[11] See, for example, §7-05 below.

unlikely that conditions 3 and 4 were included to cover these few instances of special exemptions.

The origin of TA 1988 s 340 was FA 1949 s 23 which was introduced to permit relief for interest paid out of profits or gains in computing taxable profits of a trade carried on outside the UK. That provision was required because before that time the only way in which a trader could obtain relief for interest paid 'out of profits or gains brought into charge to [income] tax' was by making a deduction authorised under the Rule 19 procedure[12] and retaining the deduction for himself; but a foreign lender would no doubt not permit this, so FA 1949 s 23 was introduced to give relief for that interest so long as it was paid gross[13]. On the introduction of corporation tax in 1965, interest paid by a company was taken out of ITA 1952 s 169 (the old Rule 19 procedure) and transferred to s 170 (formerly, the Rule 21 procedure), imposing an obligation on a company to deduct income tax from interest paid. However, it would seem that Parliament took the view, confirmed by the *National Bank of Greece* case[14] that s 170 would only apply where the interest had a UK source, and therefore introduced what is now TA 1988 s 338 (4) (c) to permit companies to obtain relief for interest paid out of profits or gains brought into charge to corporation tax in circumstances where the interest could be (because it did not fall within s 170), and in practice was required to be (normally, by a foreign lender able to enforce the borrower's obligations otherwise than under English law), paid without deduction of UK income tax. The previous provision under the income tax legislation equivalent of TA 1988 s 338 (4) (c)[15] laid down as one of the conditions for relief for yearly interest paid in relation to a foreign trade that 'payment of the interest is secured mainly upon assets outside the United Kingdom which are employed in the trade and belong to the person by whom the trade is carried on', which reflected the circumstances in which interest paid by a UK resident would fall within Case IV rather than Case III.

TA 1988 s 338 (4) (d) enables interest paid out of Case IV or Case V income to be treated as a charge on income. Again, this implements a similar relief previously available[16] under the income tax legislation for yearly interest payable out of Case IV or Case V income to a person not resident in the UK.

Under the deduction and retention procedure[17], the recipient effectively suffered income tax at the standard rate on yearly interest paid to him, since he was bound to permit the payer to make the deduction. But, as with the modern law concerning Sch D Case III[18], that provision would only have been enforced by the UK courts where the interest had a UK source; where there was no UK source the payer would be bound to make payments gross (unless the contract governing the loan otherwise provided). Having regard, therefore, to the special provision historically made by

---

[12] See Chapter 1 above.
[13] See, however, *Alexandria Water Co Ltd v Musgrave (Surveyor of Taxes)* (1883) 1 TC 521 where Brett MR, at 525 questioned whether a non-resident recipient of interest received from an English (*sic*) company trading abroad should not be liable to income tax.
[14] See §3–22 above.
[15] ITA 1952 s 138.
[16] Eg under ITA 1952 s 132 (1) (c).
[17] See Chapter 1 above.
[18] See §3–22 above.

Parliament in relation to relief for interest paid abroad and out of foreign source income, it cannot be concluded that the mere fact of the UK residence of the payer brands yearly interest with the stamp of Sch D Case III.

3-30　Because of the variety of factors which may be present in relation to any given loan or debt obligation, and the uncertain state of the law, it is not possible to lay down any precise rules as to what interest is within Case III on the one hand or Case IV or V on the other. However, the following illustrations are examples, based on the author's views as set out above, of what may amount to loans in respect of which the interest falls within Case III, Case IV or V.

Case III

1　An unsecured loan to a UK resident (unless the loan is contracted abroad for the purposes of, and is serviced by, the foreign trading branch of the UK resident);

2　A loan to a UK resident, secured wholly or mainly on UK property or by the guarantee of a UK resident;

3　A loan to a non-resident, under English law, secured wholly or mainly on UK property (eg a charge over land in the UK or over shares in a UK resident company);

4　An unsecured loan, under English law, to a non-resident, contracted by and made for the purposes of the UK branch trade carried on by the non-resident;

Case IV

1　A loan to a non-resident, secured on foreign property or by a foreign guarantee (unless UK property rather than the guarantee is the principal security or the loan is taken out for, and serviced by, a UK branch trade);

2　A loan to a UK resident, made under foreign law, secured wholly or mainly on foreign property or (possibly) by a foreign guarantee (particularly where it is taken out for the purposes of a foreign branch trade or for the purchase by the borrower of foreign property)[19];

Case V

1　An unsecured loan under foreign law to a non-resident (except, perhaps, where taken out for the purpose of and serviced by a UK branch trade);

2　An unsecured loan under foreign law to a foreign trading branch of a UK resident;

3　Possibly, an unsecured loan to a UK resident under foreign law where the loan documentation is executed under seal.

---

[19] See, for example, the loan considered in the Case Stated in *Hafton Properties Ltd v McHugh (Inspector of Taxes)* [1987] STC 16 at 19*f* to 21*h*. Although the issue was complicated by other factors, the Special Commissioner found that the interest on the loan did not fall within Sch D Case III, and rejected the Inland Revenue's argument that the debt, and therefore the source of the interest, was in the UK where the ultimate debtor was UK resident; the Inland Revenue did not appeal on this point.

It should be emphasised that the law is not well settled on this subject, and care should be taken in establishing loan arrangements where it is not clear whether or not the interest will fall within Case III but where it is important (in relation to deduction of income tax or relief for interest paid) that the interest should or should not fall within Case III.

3-31 It is unsatisfactory that, in the light of the uncertainty as to the legal position in relation to Cases III, IV and V, the Inland Revenue's stance has effectively prevented UK resident companies from raising foreign loan finance except in circumstances where the interest can be paid gross under a double taxation agreement. A UK resident company is unlikely to risk the possiblity of losing an argument before the courts on the application of Case III, and so be required to gross up the interest to ensure that the lender receives the full amount of interest after deduction of tax under TA 1988 s 349 (2). However, following publication in 1983 of a consultative document concerning the possiblity of companies being allowed to pay interest on Eurobonds without deducting basic rate income tax, legislation was passed in 1984 to permit the payment gross of interest on bearer bonds quoted on a recognised stock exchange, subject to certain conditions[20].

3   Schedule C

3-32 Interest which is chargeable to tax under Sch C is interest which falls within certain classes and which is paid in circumstances specified in the legislation. The description of income[1] within Sch C is set out in TA 1988 s 17.

3-33 The broad class of interest is that which falls within the term 'public revenue dividends' as defined in TA 1988 s 45. In that definition, the word 'dividends' is defined to include 'interest'. 'Public revenue' includes the public revenue of any government, whether of the UK or elsewhere, and the revenue of any public authority or institution in any country *outside* the UK. Consequently, interest on UK or foreign government securities amounts to 'public revenue dividends' as does interest in respect of the borrowings of foreign municipal authorities; but, interest on UK local authority borrowings is not within the expression 'public revenue dividends' and so does not fall within Sch C but within Sch D Case III[2]. In order to amount to public revenue dividends, the interest must be payable in respect of securities. The expression does not apply to interest on damages paid by a government and has been held not to apply to interest on damages paid by a government department[3].

A sub-class of 'public revenue dividends' is 'overseas public revenue dividends', which are public revenue dividends payable outside the UK (even if they are also payable within the UK)[4] except where they are paid out of the public revenue of the UK.

---

[20] See now TA 1988 s 124.
[1] Ie not just interest.
[2] See, for example, TA 1988 s 349(2)(a).
[3] *Esso Petroleum Co Ltd v Ministry of Defence* [1989] STC 805, [1990] 1 All ER 163.
[4] See *Maude v IRC* [1940] 1 All ER 464, 32 TC 63 as to the place where interest is 'payable'.

3-34   The circumstances which give rise to interest falling within Sch C are as follows[5]:

1   Where any public revenue dividends are payable in the UK;
2   Where interest on UK government securities is payable in the Republic of Ireland and the securities are on the register of the Bank of Ireland in Dublin;
3   Where a banker or any other person in the UK obtains payment of any overseas public revenue dividends by means of coupons received from any other person or otherwise obtains such payment on behalf of any other person, where payment was not made through a UK paying agent or (if it was) the securities were held in a recognised clearing system[6]. The reference to a banker or any other person 'in the United Kingdom' clearly extends beyond resident persons, and will include UK branches of non-resident banks;
4   Where a banker[7] in the UK sells or otherwise realises coupons in respect of overseas public revenue dividends and accounts to any person for the proceeds either by payment or by crediting that person's account. This provision prevents the holder of the coupons avoiding the third circumstance described above by selling coupons, so receiving payment in a form which is neither interest nor otherwise within the expression 'public revenue dividends'. Schedule C also applies where a dealer in coupons purchases coupons in respect of public revenue dividends otherwise than from a banker or another dealer in coupons. Consequently, the charge under Sch C would still be imposed where the holder sells coupons to an intermediary and that intermediary is either a dealer in coupons or himself sells the coupons to a dealer in coupons.

It should be noted that, for the purposes of the foregoing, the expression 'banker' includes a person acting as a banker[8]; the expression 'dealer in coupons' is not defined. Further, 'coupons' is widely defined to include 'warrants for or bills of exchange purporting to be drawn or made in payment of any overseas public revenue dividends'[9].

3-35   From the interest falling within the circumstances described in §3-34 above there is excepted[10] half-yearly interest of up to £2.50 payable by the Bank of England, Bank of Ireland or the National Debt Commissioners (except where the interest is obtained by coupon on bearer securities). Such interest is, instead, charged under Sch D Case III.

The Treasury may direct that the interest on certain securities shall be paid without deduction of basic rate income tax[11], although the taxpayer may still claim that Sch C, and the tax deduction procedure relating to it, should apply. Where the interest is paid gross under this provision, the

---

[5] See TA 1988 s 17(1).
[6] Euro-clear, CEDEL or First Chicago Clearing System.
[7] But not 'any other person' – see TA 1988 s 17(1), Sch C para 4(a); but including a person acting as a banker – see TA 1988 s 45.
[8] TA 1988 s 45.
[9] TA 1988 s 45.
[10] By TA 1988 s 17(1), Sch C para 5.
[11] Otherwise deductible in respect of interest falling within Sch C – see Chapter 6 below.

tax is charged under Sch D Case III[12]. The only government security in respect of which the interest is currently paid gross under these provisions is 3.5 per cent War Loan.

3-36 There was a general exemption from tax, under Sch C or otherwise, in respect of interest on tax reserve certificates[13]. These ceased to be issued after 1974, and were replaced by Certificates of Tax Deposit in respect of which interest paid is taxable.

Interest paid on UK Savings Certificates is exempt from tax[14]. The exemption is limited to interest on savings certificates up to the maximum amount which the holder is permitted to purchase[15]. In the case of Ulster Savings Certificates, the exemption only applies where the holder is resident and ordinarily resident in Northern Ireland when the certificates are repaid and was so when they were purchased[16].

Interest received by the Treasury or the National Debt Commissioners is exempt from tax[17]. Partly as a result of this provision, interest paid in respect of securities held on the National Savings Stock Register does not fall within Sch C but within Sch D Case III[18].

3-37 Schedule C imposes a system of deduction of basic rate income tax at source in respect of such interest and other dividends as fall within the Schedule. That system is considered in Chapter 6 below.

---

[12] TA 1988 s 50; a similar power exists under TA 1988 s 51 in respect of Northern Ireland securities.
[13] TA 1988 s 46 (2).
[14] TA 1988 s 46 (1) and TCGA 1992 s 121 including children's bonus bonds.
[15] TA 1988 s 46 (3).
[16] TA 1988 s 46 (4).
[17] TA 1988 s 49.
[18] See §6-04 below.

Chapter 4

TAXATION OF INTEREST WITHIN SCHEDULE D CASE III

4–01 This chapter concerns the taxation of UK source interest, except interest within Sch C[1], in the hands of different classes of taxpayer. It does not deal with the machinery for collecting basic rate income tax at source, which is described in Chapter 7.

1 Resident individual

THE CHARGE TO TAX

4–02 Interest within Sch D Case III and received by an individual resident in the UK is chargeable to income tax by virtue of TA 1988 s 18 (1) (b). Although the taxpayer may own a source producing interest, the interest is only taxable when it is received by the taxpayer or by an agent of the taxpayer or otherwise in circumstances that either the taxpayer can exercise dominion over the interest or it enures for his benefit. Interest which has only accrued but has not been paid will not be taxable as interest, although the special provisions of the accrued income scheme may have the effect of taxing accrued interest when securities are disposed of[2]. However, the general rule that accrued interest is not taxable otherwise remains, even where the taxpayer has not received it as a result of his not claiming payment[3]. In *Dewar v IRC*[4] the taxpayer was held not to be chargeable in respect of interest accruing on a legacy after the executor's year even though sufficient income was available to the estate to discharge the liability and the taxpayer was also an executor and a residuary legatee. The Court of Appeal followed the principle, enunciated by Rowlatt J in *Leigh v IRC*[5], that '"receivability" without receipt is nothing'[6]. Therefore, the taxpayer must actually receive the money. In *Parkside Leasing Ltd v Smith (Inspector of Taxes)*[7] it was held that this meant that, where payment of interest was made by cheque, the interest was not received until the cheque was cleared and the money was placed at the disposal of the taxpayer.

---

[1] See Chapter 6 below.
[2] See TA 1988 ss 710 to 728 and §§9–29 to 9–34 below.
[3] Cf the position in relation to rental income chargeable under Sch A, where rent arising is taxable unless the taxpayer can show that TA 1988 s 41 relieves him from the liability.
[4] [1935] 2 KB 351, 19 TC 561, CA.
[5] (1928) 11 TC 590 at 595.
[6] See also *Whitworth Park Coal Co Ltd v IRC* [1959] 3 All ER 703, 38 TC 531, HL, *Champney's Executors v IRC* (1934) 19 TC 375, CA, and *Lambe v IRC* [1934] 1 KB 178, 18 TC 212.
[7] [1985] STC 63, [1985] 1 WLR 310.

But, this does not mean that, in order to be taxable, the interest must necessarily be freely disposable by the taxpayer. In *Dunmore v McGowan (Inspector of Taxes)*[8] bank interest was credited to the taxpayer's deposit account, but the account had been charged as security for a guarantee given by the taxpayer. The taxpayer failed in his claim that the interest was not taxable when it was credited to the account; even though the interest was not then freely available to him, it did enure for the taxpayer's benefit because it became subject to the charge which he had given in support of the guarantee and would go towards discharging any liability if the guarantee were to be called. But, in a rather similar case, *Macpherson v Bond (Inspector of Taxes)*[9], the interest was held not to be taxable in the hands of an individual who had charged a bank deposit as security for debts owed by a company but without his having given a guarantee. Therefore, the interest credited to the deposit account did not go to reduce the individual's liability, and so did not benefit him; his only right was to receive any balance in the account after the company's liability had been discharged. In effect, his position was much the same as if he had lent money to the company which it had deposited as security for its indebtedness. In such circumstances, the individual would not have been taxed until he received any interest[10], but the company would have received the interest as taxable income[11]; however, there appears to have been no suggestion in this case that the company was regarded as taxable.

Where the amount available to be paid by the debtor to the creditor is insufficient to pay off both principal and interest in full – eg where the debtor is insolvent – the question of how much, if any, of the payment actually made should be treated as interest will depend upon the terms of the indebtedness, any court order concerning it and, in some cases, agreement between the parties[12].

The amount of interest assessable is 'the actual amount... without any deduction'[13]. Therefore, no relief may be claimed for the costs of collecting interest or, normally, for interest paid on a loan raised to make the loan or investment which produces the interest[14].

The fact that the resident individual may not be domiciled in the UK does not affect the liability to tax on UK source interest. The remittance (rather than the arising) basis only applies to foreign source income[15].

---

[8] [1978] STC 217, [1978] 2 All ER 85, CA; applied in *Peracha v Miley* [1990] STC 512, CA.

[9] [1985] STC 678.

[10] See *Dewar v IRC* above.

[11] See *Dunmore v McGowan (Inspector of Taxes)* above.

[12] *Smith v Law Guarantee and Trust Society Ltd* [1904] 2 Ch 569, 73 LJ Ch 733, and *IRC v Oswald* (1945) 26 TC 435 at 455, HL; and note that the position as between debtor company and debenture holders will not necessary apply as between life tenant and remainderman where debentures are held by trustees: See *Re Morris's Will Trusts, Public Trustee v Morris* [1960] 3 All ER 548, [1960] 1 WLR 1210.

[13] This language is used in TA 1988 ss 64 and 66; although the same wording does not appear in s 67 (see §4–07 below) there is no basis for claiming any deductions when s 67 applies which cannot be claimed when s 67 does not apply.

[14] See *Soul v Caillebotte (Inspector of Taxes)* (1964) 43 TC 657.

[15] TA 1988 s 65 and §5–06 and §5–07 below.

Persons chargeable

4-03   Tax may be charged on and, if so, must be paid by 'the person receiving *or* entitled to' the interest, under TA 1988 s 59 (1). In *Aplin v White (Inspector of Taxes)*[16] a claim that an estate agent was not taxable failed where the subject of the assessment was interest received by the taxpayer in respect of clients' money held on a deposit account used for clients' money only (although the taxpayer was not obliged to account to the clients for the interest). Since the taxpayer was the person 'receiving' the interest he was held to be chargeable in respect of the interest. However, where such an assessment is made under s 59 (1) on a person who receives interest otherwise than beneficially he will only be liable to be assessed to basic rate income tax, and the interest which will not form part of *his* total income for the purposes of higher rates of income tax[17].

In practice, where a solicitor earns interest on clients' money held on deposit the Inland Revenue does not assess the solicitor as a person 'receiving' the interest under s 59(1) where the client is resident in the UK, whether the solicitor accounts to the client for interest actually earned on a designated deposit account[18] or for an equivalent sum where the money is not held on a designated account[19].

THE BASIS OF ASSESSMENT GENERALLY

4-04   Generally, interest which is received gross is assessed to income tax on the preceding year basis[20]. In other words, in a year of assessment, the interest assessed is that arising (and received[1]) in the preceding year of assessment. This system does not involve the late assessment of income but is designed to provide a means whereby the Inspector of Taxes may, before the end of the year of assessment, assess the income chargeable for that year. The preceding year basis therefore operates to provide an artificial measure of the income to be assessed in any given year of assessment. For this reason, it is expressly provided that tax continues to be computed on the preceding year basis even though no income arises from the source in a given year[2]. If in the year following a year in which no interest arose, interest starts to flow again the amount chargeable in that year would be nil.

No account is taken of the period over which the interest accrued. So, where interest is paid half-yearly on, say, 1 June and 1 December in a year, the interest paid on those dates will be the interest arising within the year of assessment within which those dates fall, even though part of the interest would have accrued during the previous year of assessment. This can lead

---

[16] [1973] STC 322, [1973] 2 All ER 637.
[17] [1973] STC 322 at 327*e*–328*b*.
[18] Although it will be paid to the solicitor net of basic rate income tax in most cases (see §7-27 below) and he will account to the client for the net amount.
[19] See Solicitors' Accounts Rules 1991; generally, as to interest paid by solicitors on clients' money–see Law Society's Gazette, 2 September 1981 at p928, 2 February 1983 at p260 and 4 March 1992 at p34; see also Inland Revenue Statement of Practice A22.
[20] TA 1988 s 64.
[1] See §4-02 above.
[2] TA 1988 s 71.

to interest which accrues over a number of years being taxable in one year when it is received and so being taxable at higher rates of income tax than would have been the case had it been assessed by reference to the years when it accrued. Particular instances of bunching in this way are interest received on purchase money in respect of compulsory acquisitions[3] and interest on damages[4]. A measure of relief in these circumstances was previously available under TA 1970 s 31, but this was repealed in 1971[5].

Although the preceding year basis and the special rules applicable to opening and closing years are expressed to apply in relation to the computation of income tax under Sch D Case III, these rules only apply to income chargeable under Case III and in respect of which basic rate income tax is not deducted at source[6]. The language of TA 1988 ss 64, 66 and 67 refers to 'income tax', and the previous legislation did so since the time, before 1973/74, when surtax was imposed as a separate tax by reference to an individual's total income. Since 1973/74, the unified tax system has resulted in one tax, income tax, being imposed on an individual's income, albeit calculated at different rates on different slices of income. No assessment is made on the recipient individual in respect of basic rate income tax suffered by deduction at source, and any higher rate liability is assessed by virtue of TA 1988 s 1(2)(b) and the relevant section of the Finance Act for the current year of assessment[7] by reference to an individual's 'total income' for the year of assessment. That 'total income' is the taxpayer's income 'from all sources estimated in accordance with the provisions of the Income Tax Acts'[8], and so, in relation to interest falling within Sch D Case III, would include amounts of interest ascertained normally on the preceding year basis[9]. However, where any income[10] is chargeable with income tax by way of deduction at the basic rate in force for a year, the income is deemed to be income of *that* year for the purposes of ascertaining 'total income'[11].

Consequently, interest which falls within Sch D Case III and which suffers deduction of basic rate income tax at source is not assessed on the preceding year basis, even though the higher rate of tax is a rate of 'income tax'. As explained below[12], any tax at the higher rate in respect of such income is payable following the end of the year of assessment in which the income arises, whereas income tax (at the lower, basic or higher rate) in respect of Case III interest paid gross is generally payable during the year of assessment; the former may only be assessed after the end of the year, whereas the latter may be assessed before the year ends because the measure of the income is generally on the preceding year basis.

The position described above is clear where interest paid under deduction of basic rate income tax is regularly paid year by year. What is less clear is what treatment applies where any such interest fails to be paid in any

---

[3] Eg under Compulsory Purchase Act 1965 s 11(1)
[4] See Chapter 2 Part 1, and also *Regal (Hastings) Ltd v Gulliver* (1944) 24 ATC 297.
[5] FA 1971 s 35 and Sch 14.
[6] See Chapter 7 below.
[7] Eg FA 1992 s 10(1)(c) and (2)(b), in respect of the year of assessment 1992/93.
[8] TA 1988 s 835(1).
[9] Subject to the opening and closing years rules–see §4-06 and §4-07 below.
[10] Such as interest to which TA 1988 s 349(2) applies.
[11] TA 1988 s 835(6)(a), see also TA 1988 s 480C, under which interest in respect of a relevant deposit is taxed on the current year basis even if interest is paid gross.
[12] §4-14.

year of assessment. By virtue of TA 1988 s 71, interest can be assessed by reference to interest arising in the preceding year of assessment even though no interest is received in the current year. In *Postlethwaite v IRC*[13] it was held (obiter) that annual payments normally received under deduction of income tax could be assessed in a year of assessment on the preceding year basis even though no payment was received in that year of assessment; any double taxation which might arise would be prevented by invoking the principle against double taxation. However, it might be argued that no preceding year basis assessment should be made in such a case because assessment on a preceding year basis would presuppose non-deduction of basic rate income tax from the interest, and where interest formerly payable under deduction of tax ceases to be so payable the taxpayer is treated as acquiring a new source of income[14]; consequently, no assessment would be made on the interest in the year when none is received, because, there being a hypothetical new source of income, the preceding year basis would not have taken over from the current year basis[15] which applies on the commencement of a new source.

4-05   In the case of a partnership of individuals, the Case III assessment in respect of interest received by the partnership should, strictly, be made on the partners by reference to the interest received by each of them in the preceding year of assessment. However, in practice, the interest is commonly assessed by dividing the interest received by the partnership in the accounts year ending in the preceding year of assessment between the partners in accordance with their profit-sharing ratios in the year of assessment to which the assessment relates. This keeps the basis of the Case III assessment in line with the Case I or Case II assessment[16] on the partnership's business profits.

Opening years

4-06   Special rules apply in the opening and closing years of a source of interest[17]. In the first year of assessment when interest arises the amount assessed is the interest actually arising in that year[18]. In the second year of assessment, the assessment is generally also on the interest actually arising in that year[19]; however, if the interest first arose on 6 April in the first year, the assessment in the second year is on the basis of the interest arising in the first year, unless the taxpayer elects for the current year basis to apply in the second year also[20]. In the third year of assessment (where interest first arose after 6 April in the first year) the taxpayer may also elect for the current year basis to apply for one further year in place of the preceding year basis which would otherwise then commence.

---

13 (1963) 41 TC 224.
14 see TA 1988 s 66(4), and §4-08 below.
15 see §4-06 below.
16 See TA 1988 s 60(1).
17 See TA 1988 ss 66 and 67.
18 TA 1988 s 66(1)(a).
19 TA 1988 s 66(1)(b).
20 TA 1988 s 66(1)(c).

EXAMPLE

1   Interest first arises on 1 October 1992

Year of assessment	Basis of assessment
1992/93	Actual interest in year
1993/94	Actual interest in year
1994/95	Interest arising within 1993/94, unless taxpayer elects for current year basis
1995/96	Interest arising within 1994/95

2   Interest first arises on 6 April 1992

Year of assessment	Basis of assessment
1992/93	Actual interest in year
1993/94	Interest arising within 1992/93; unless taxpayer elects for current year basis
1994/95	Interest arising within 1993/94.

The application of the preceding year basis of assessment so as to use interest received in one year as the basis of assessment for two years does not involve the double taxation of the same income. The same income is merely used as the measure of the income from the same source in determining the taxable amount in each of the two years[1].

Closing years

4–07 In the year of assessment where the source of interest ceases (but not including a year where the source is retained but no interest is received[2]), the interest assessed is that received in that year (if any) rather than in the preceding year[3]. Further, if the interest received in the penultimate year is greater than the amount in that year assessable on the preceding year basis that actual amount is to be assessed for the penultimate year in place of the preceding year's interest[4]. If in those last two years there is no interest, the taxpayer may claim that the last year when interest did arise and the preceding year shall be treated as the two closing years to which the above special rules should apply, and no preceding year basis assessment is made for the year following that in which interest last arose[5].

EXAMPLE

A source of interest ceases on 30 September 1992. No interest has been paid since before 6 April 1991. In 1991/92 an assessment was made by reference to the interest received in 1990/91.

No assessment will be made on interest from the source in respect of the year 1992/93. The taxpayer may claim to have the assessments for 1989/90 and 1990/91, treated as the last two years of the source. This would result

[1] *Beese v Mackinlay (Inspector of Taxes)* [1980] STC 228; *Moore v Austin (Inspector of Taxes)* [1985] STC 673.
[2] See TA 1988 s 71.
[3] TA 1988 s 67(1)(b).
[4] TA 1988 s 67(1)(b).
[5] TA 1988 s 67(1)(c).

in a revision from the preceding year basis to actual basis for 1990/91, and
any tax paid in 1991/92 (on the preceding year basis) would be repaid. The
assessment for 1989/90 would be increased if the actual interest received in
that year was greater than that received in 1988/89.

4-08 The source of interest, by reference to which the opening and closing
rules apply, will normally be an interest-bearing security or other obligation
or a sum of money placed on deposit. Where the terms on which a deposit
or other indebtedness remains outstanding are changed so that temporarily
interest is not payable, this will not result in the taxpayer ceasing to possess
the original source of interest. In *Cull v Cowcher*[6] it was held that the source
was retained even where it was agreed that thereafter interest would not
be paid on sums deposited, because the source was the deposited sum rather
than the contract which related to the deposit. However, where a sum held
on deposit with a bank is transferred to a current (non-interest-bearing)
account the original source will cease to exist[7]; that is because the interest-
bearing deposit account is no longer in credit and can no longer produce
interest, whereas if there is merely an interruption in the payment of interest,
but otherwise the deposited or lent sum remains in place, the source continues
to exist.

On the other hand, additions to and withdrawals from an interest-bearing
deposit with a bank amount to acquisitions and cessations of separate sources
of interest[8]. In practice, the Inland Revenue does not apply this rule in
relation to alterations in sums held on deposit unless large sums are involved,
although it would be open to the taxpayer to claim the correct treatment[9].

Where interest ceases or begins to be payable under deduction of basic
rate income tax at source, the opening and closing rules apply as if there
had been a cessation and acquisition of the source of income[10]. This provision
is required in order to avoid any confusion between the preceding year basis
and current year basis which apply to interest paid gross and interest paid
under deduction of income tax, respectively[11].

PROCEDURAL REQUIREMENTS – OPENING AND CLOSING YEARS

4-09 TA 1988 ss 66 and 67 lay down various time limits for making claims
relating to the opening and closing rules, and provide for the position in
relation to claims upon the death of the taxpayer.

INVESTMENT INCOME OR EARNED INCOME

4-10 Before the year 1984/85, investment income attracted income tax
at an additional rate as well as at the basic rate and the then higher rates.
Although this no longer applies, a summary of the relevant law on the

---

[6] (1934) 18 TC 449.
[7] (1934) 18 TC 449 at 455.
[8] *Hart (Inspector of Taxes) v Sangster* [1957] 2 All ER 208, 37 TC 231, CA.
[9] So long as it is consistently applied to all his bank deposit transactions.
[10] TA 1988 ss 66(4) and 67(2).
[11] See §**4-04** above.

treatment of interest as earned income or investment income is retained, since a subsequent change in the law might resurrect the distinction. In addition, whether interest should be treated as part of the income of a trade or profession (taxable under Case I or II), rather than under Case III, might affect the incidence of certain reliefs.

Interest received by an individual will normally not be earned income. If it is immediately derived[12] from carrying on a trade (such as a trade of moneylender) the interest would form part of the income of a trade in respect of which the profits would be chargeable under Sch D Case I; but interest received by the trader, or his successors, after the cessation of the trade, albeit from loans made while the trade was carried on, has been held to be interest chargeable under Case III in *Bennett v Ogston*[13].

Some doubt was cast on *Bennett v Ogston* concerning the taxation of income derived from a trade or profession but received after the death of the individual who carried on the trade or profession in *Purchase (Inspector of Taxes) v Stainer's Executors*[14] and *Carson (Inspector of Taxes) v Cheyney's Executor*[15]. In those cases, no reason was given for this doubt, and in the first of the cases approval was given to the statement of the principle in *Bennett v Ogston*, the only concern apparently being as to the application of the principle to the facts[16]. The cases in question concerned royalty income received after the death in respect of acting engagements of, or books written by, the deceased. In *Cheyney*, Lord Reid summarised[17] the ground for the judgment in *Stainer* as being

'that payments which are the fruit of professional activity are only taxable under Case II and cannot be taxed under Case III, even when it is no longer possible when they fall due to tax them under Case II, and when looked at by themselves and without regard to that source they would fall within Case III.'

In the author's view, the interest arising in *Bennett v Ogston* after the moneylender's death was not 'fruit of professional activity' in the same way as royalties which were remuneration for work undertaken during the taxpayer's lifetime; interest was not received in respect of making the loan (which would have been made during the deceased's lifetime) but in respect of the continuing use of the money, so that where a loan remains outstanding after the death the interest is properly taxable, although no longer as a receipt of the trade.

However, the fact that interest is earned by a trader on a deposit account maintained in connection with his trade will not normally result in the interest being earned income, since it will not be immediately derived from the trade[18]. It was previously provided[19] in the context of the additional rate income tax charge on investment income that, in certain circumstances,

---

[12] See TA 1988 s 833(4)(c).
[13] (1930) 15 TC 374.
[14] (1951) 32 TC 367 at 411, HL.
[15] [1958] 3 All ER 573 at 582, 38 TC 240 at 265, HL.
[16] See (1951) 32 TC 367 at 410-411.
[17] (1958) 38 TC 240 at 265.
[18] *College of Preceptors v Jenkins* (1919) 89 LJKB 27, 7 TC 162; *Aplin v White (Inspector of Taxes)* [1973] STC 322, [1973] 2 All ER 637; *Northend (Inspector of Taxes) v White and Leonard and Corbin Greener* [1975] STC 317, [1975] 2 All ER 481.
[19] FA 1971 s 32(4).

interest received by a trader could be treated as earned income. Those circumstances required that his trading income was earned income and that interest was derived from either an investment, the proceeds of sale of which, or a debt which, if proved to be bad, would be taken into account in computing his trading profits. That provision reversed the decision in *Bucks v Bowers (Inspector of Taxes)*[20] where a partner in a bank was held not to be entitled to treat as earned income his share of profits to the extent that it derived from investments made by the partnership.

As in the case of dividends on shares[1] it would be possible for the receipt of interest to be taxed under Sch E where the interest received is part of the remuneration for an employment. However, this would not apply where the taxpayer himself provided the loan (the arrangement to remain outstanding during the employment) since the interest would in reality be payment for the use of the money lent; but the position might be different if a creditor were to agree to hold interest on certain securities on trust for the employee during the employment or where the employer otherwise indirectly provided funds on which interest was earned for the benefit of the employee[2].

INTEREST RECEIVED ON A PARTNERSHIP LOAN

4-11   Where a partner receives interest on capital which he has contributed (otherwise than by way of loan) to the partnership, this will merely amount to an allocation of profit and will not be treated as interest income in his hands. Thus, the partner will effectively have his 'interest' treated as earned income, and the partnership will not obtain a deduction for the interest paid. However, where the partner has lent – rather than contributed – capital to the partnership, so that there is a debtor/creditor relationship subsisting, the interest that he receives should be treated, and taxed, as interest[3]. In such a case, the interest, whilst qualifying for relief so far as the taxation of the partnership profits is concerned, will be taxed as investment income in the hands of the lender. The effect of this is that the lending partner will effectively pay himself part of the interest by reference to his profit share, so converting earned income to unearned income.

INTEREST ON DAMAGES FOR PERSONAL INJURIES OR DEATH

4-12   By TA 1988 s 329, interest on damages awarded under the Law Reform (Miscellaneous Provisions) Act 1934 (or equivalent provisions in Scotland and Northern Ireland), in respect of personal injuries or death, or paid under a settlement or compromise payment in respect of interest on a claim for such damages where the interest would be exempt if judgment were given,

---

[20] [1970] 2 All ER 202, 46 TC 267.
[1] See *Recknell v IRC* [1952] 2 All ER 147, 33 TC 201; *White (Inspector of Taxes) v Franklin* [1965] 1 All ER 692, 42 TC 283, CA.
[2] *O'Leary v McKinlay (Inspector of Taxes)* [1991] STC 42 where the source of the income from a foreign deposit by a foreign trust of which the employee was a beneficiary was held to be within Sch E rather than Sch D Case V.
[3] Note that Partnership Act 1890 s 24 (2) provides for the payment of interest on a loan by a partner in the absence of any contrary agreement.

is not to be regarded as income for any income tax purpose. Such interest is, therefore, disregarded, and does not even operate to affect the payment of a higher rate of income tax on other income. It has been held that this exemption is to benefit the recipient and should not be taken into account in computing the amount payable by the defendant[4].

BANK AND BUILDING SOCIETY INTEREST: TESSAs

4-13 Interest paid by banks and building societies to UK resident individuals is generally paid under deduction of basic rate income tax[5], although individuals who are unlikely to be taxable in respect of the interest are able to have interest paid gross. Where the tax deducted exceeds an individual's liability to tax, the tax will be repaid[6].

4-14 Interest and bonus paid on a tax-exempt special savings account ('TESSA') are not taxable[7]. An individual aged 18 or over may open one TESSA for his own benefit with a bank or building society[8], but the TESSA must be unconnected with any other account[9]. The maximum initial deposit in a TESSA is £3,000, and this may be increased by up to £1,800 a year to a maximum amount deposited of £9,000[10]. The account must remain open for five years from its commencement (or until the earlier death of the depositor[11]), and may not be assigned to a third party (either absolutely or by way of security for a loan)[12]; nor must the account be reduced by withdrawal by more than the post-tax value of any interest credited[13]. If any of these conditions is breached, the account ceases to be a TESSA, and any interest or bonus previously credited to the account is treated as then being credited, so attracting a tax liability on that income[14].

ASSESSMENT AND PAYMENT OF TAX

4-15 Interest is not assessed separately according to each source. Instead, one assessment may be issued in respect of income (including interest) chargeable under Case III generally[15] except to the extent that a new source

---

[4] *Mason v Harman* [1972] RTR 1
[5] See §§**7-26** to **7-31** below.
[6] TMA 1970 s 42 (7).
[7] TA 1988 s 326A; and see TCGA 1992 s 271 (4) in relation to exemption from capital gains tax.
[8] TA 1988 s 326A (4) to (7); joint accounts are not permitted. In England and Wales, a person holding a power of attorney may open an account in the name of the donor of the power who qualifies; by concession, a curator bonis in Scotland, acting in his own name, may open an account for an incapacitated person who qualifies — see Inland Revenue Press Release, 22 October 1992.
[9] TA 1988 s 326A (8).
[10] TA 1988 s 326B (2) (a).
[11] TA 1988 s 326A (2).
[12] TA 1988 s 326B (2) (c).
[13] TA 1988 s 326B (2) (b); the tax element which must remain in the account is tax at the basic rate.
[14] TA 1988 s 326B (3).
[15] TA 1988 s 73.

arises or an existing one ceases so that the preceding year basis does not apply to a particular source[16].

The due date for the payment of income tax in respect of interest which is received gross is 1 January in the year of assessment or, if later, at the end of thirty days from the issue of the assessment[17]. Since such interest is generally assessed on a preceding year basis, the Inspector of Taxes should normally be able to issue the assessment in time for the tax to be paid on 1 January except where the assessment is on the current year basis by reason of the opening or closing year rules.

Where income tax at the basic rate has been deducted from the interest, any income tax assessed in respect of the higher rate is payable on or before 1 December following the end of the year of assessment or, if later, at the end of thirty days after the assessment is issued[18]. The assessment will not be raised until after the end of the year of assessment, by which time the Inspector of Taxes will be able to ascertain how much interest has been received subject to deduction of income tax which falls to be assessed for the purposes of higher rate income tax. Where interest is received under deduction of basic rate income tax and by reason of the availability of personal or other reliefs[19] or because of application of the lower rate of income tax[20] the amount of income tax payable by the taxpayer is less than the amount of tax suffered by deduction of source, any excess tax suffered is repaid to the taxpayer after the end of the year of assessment[1].

RELIEF AGAINST INTEREST

4-16   An individual may be entitled to relief which may reduce or extinguish the amount of interest which would otherwise be liable to income tax. Such relief is not special to interest income, and could arise in respect of the following:

1   a Case I or II[2] trading loss suffered in the same or the preceding year of assessment[3];
2   a Case I or Case II loss incurred in one of the first four years in which the trade, profession or vocation is carried on, the loss being carried back up to three years of assessment[4];
3   an extension of the reliefs mentioned in paragraph 1 or 2 above, where the loss derives from capital allowances made in respect of expenditure on assets used in the trade[5];
4   certain interest paid which qualifies for relief[6];

---

[16] TA 1988 ss 66 (3) and 67 (1) (a).
[17] 1988 s 5 (1).
[18] TA 1988 s 5 (4).
[19] Eg relief for interest paid, see Chapter 8 below.
[20] TA 1988 s 1 (2) (aa).
[1]   TMA 1970 s 42 (7); if the repayment is made more than twelve months after the end of the year of assessment in which the tax was deducted the taxpayer may be entitled to repayment supplement — see TA 1988 s 824.
[2]   But not Case V — TA 1988 s 391 (2).
[3]   TA 1988 s 380 (1) and (2).
[4]   TA 1988 s 381.
[5]   TA 1988 s 383.
[6]   TA 1988 s 353; and see Chapter 8 below.

5   investment under a business expansion scheme[7];
6   personal reliefs[8];
7   capital allowances available by way of discharge or repayment of tax, where the allowances are available in respect of the same or the preceding year of assessment[9].

2   Resident company

THE CHARGE TO TAX

4-17   A company resident in the UK pays corporation tax on its profits, including income, and does not pay income tax[10]. Nevertheless, income tax principles apply for the purposes of computing the amount of income of a company for corporation tax purposes and computations, and assessments are made under the same schedular system (and by reference to the same Cases of the Schedules) as applies for income tax purposes[11]. However, TA 1988 s 59(1), under which a person receiving interest (or other income) may be assessed to income tax even though he is not the beneficial owner of the income[12], does not apply for corporation tax purposes[13].

Interest chargeable under Sch D Case III is taxed, as in the case of an individual, according to the interest which arises to and which is received by or credited to a company[14]. In the computation of the income of a trading company for corporation tax purposes, interest chargeable under Case III is separated from the profit and loss account which will form the starting point for the Case I assessment. Not only will it be necessary in most cases to separate interest from the elements making up the Case I profit, but also the amount of interest shown as a credit in the profit and loss account for an accounting period may be calculated on an accruals basis whereas the Case III assessment is by reference to interest received. In the case of a company carrying on a banking trade, accrued interest due from a borrower will normally be treated as a receipt of the trade assessed under Case I, in which case the amount of interest shown in the profit and loss account would not normally require to be adjusted.

To prevent the exploitation of the different timing treatment of interest paid and received as a result of the decision in *Parkside Leasing Ltd v Smith*[15], certain receipts by a company from an associated company are treated as received on the same day as the payment is treated as made[16]. This rule applies to interest within Sch D Case III which is a charge on income[17]

---

7   TA 1988 s 289.
8   TA 1988 Part VII Chapter I.
9   CAA 1990 s 141 (3).
10   TA 1988 s 6 (1), (2) (a) and (4) (a); a company may be assessable in respect of income tax which it may be obliged to deduct from payments – eg payments of interest, see Chapter 7 below.
11   TA 1988 s 9 (1) and (3).
12   See §4-03 above.
13   TA 1988 s 59 (4).
14   See §§4-02 and 4-03 above.
15   [1985] STC 63, [1985] 1 WLR 310, and see §4-02 above.
16   TA 1988 s 341.
17   See §§8-33 to 8-42 below for relief as a charge on income.

of the company making the payment, where one company controls[18] the other, they are both under common control, one is a 51 per cent subsidiary of the other or they are both 51 per cent subsidiaries of a third company.

THE BASIS OF ASSESSMENT

4-18 The preceding year basis of assessment which applies for income tax purposes does not apply for corporation tax[19]. Instead, corporation tax is assessed under Case III on the 'full amount' of the interest arising within the company's accounting period by reference to which corporation tax is assessed[20]. As in the case of income tax[1], no deduction is permitted from the amount of interest assessable. The Case III assessment is made in one sum[2], there being no different treatment for interest received gross and interest received under deduction of basic rate income tax.

4-19 Normally[3], corporation tax is payable nine months after the end of the accounting period for which the tax is payable. Therefore, after the accounting period has ended the interest arising in the accounting period can be ascertained and, normally, an assessment issued before the due date for payment of the tax, or, following the introduction of the 'pay and file' system, the amount of tax payable can be determined by the company. Where interest received by a company is paid under deduction of basic rate income tax[4], the company is liable to corporation tax on the full amount of the interest received, but is entitled to credit against its corporation tax liability for the income tax suffered by deduction at source[5]. Where, by reason of reliefs available to it, its liability to corporation tax is less than the amount of income tax deducted, the company is entitled to a repayment of the income tax. Until the 'pay and file' system applies, that repayment cannot be obtained until the assessment for the period in question is finally determined and it is clear that a repayment is due[6]. Thereafter, repayment of tax deducted is made following a claim made in the company's corporation tax return[7]. Different rules apply to the receipt of interest received net of basic rate income tax under the MIRAS system[8].

Alternatively, a company receiving interest under deduction of income tax may take credit for the tax deducted by setting it against its obligation to deduct basic rate income tax from interest and other annual payments paid by the company, provided that both the payments received and the payments made occur in the same accounting period[9]. Such set-off accelerates the relief for tax suffered by deduction. Where the amount of interest received

---

[18] 'Control' is defined by TA 1988 s 840 for this purpose.
[19] TA 1988 s 9 (6).
[20] TA 1988 ss 70 (1) and 12 (1).
[1] See §**4-02** above.
[2] TA 1988 s 73.
[3] TA 1988 s 10 (1).
[4] See Chapter 7 below.
[5] TA 1988 s 7 (2).
[6] The company may be entitled to repayment supplement where the repayment is made more than twenty-one months after the end of the accounting period in question – see TA 1988 s 825.
[7] FA 1990 s 98 amending TA 1988 s 7.
[8] TA 1988 s 369 (6); and see §**7-39** below.
[9] TA 1988 s 350 (4) and Sch 16 para 5 and s 341 (4); and see §§**7-11** and **7-12** below.

under deduction of tax in an accounting period exceeds the amount of interest and other charges on income paid in the same accounting period, the amount of basic rate income tax deducted in respect of such excess is credited against the corporation tax liability of the company for the accounting period, or repaid, as described above.

INVESTMENT INCOME AND EARNED INCOME

4-20 The distinction between investment income and earned income is of no direct application to the taxation of interest received by a company except insofar as a company carrying on a banking or financial trade treats interest as a trading receipt in computing its Case I profit.

RELIEF AGAINST INTEREST

4-21 A company may be entitled to relief which may reduce or extinguish the amount of interest which would otherwise be liable to corporation tax. Such relief is not special to interest income, and could arise in respect of the following:

1 a trading loss suffered by the company in the same accounting period[10];
2 a trading loss suffered by the company in the following three years, so long as the trade was being carried on in the first accounting period (and subject to certain timing limitations)[11];
3 charges on income paid in the same accounting period[12];
4 capital allowances made on the company by way of discharge or repayment of tax, where the allowances are made in the same or the succeeding accounting period[13];
5 group relief or consortium relief[14];
6 relief for management expenses of an investment company[15];
7 where a bank or deposit-taker is in compulsory liquidation, relief in respect of trading losses carried forward against interest received after the cessation of trade or the commencement of the winding-up[16].

3 Resident trustees and personal representatives

4-22 There is no special rule concerning the taxation of interest, as compared with other income, in the hands of trustees or personal representatives. The general rules which apply to the assessment of interest received by an individual also apply to interest arising to trustees and personal

[10] TA 1988 s 393 (2).
[11] TA 1988 s 393 (3A).
[12] TA 1988 s 338; see Chapter 8 below.
[13] CAA 1990 s 145 (3).
[14] TA 1988 s 402.
[15] TA 1988 s 75.
[16] F (No 2) A 1992 Sch 12 para 4.

representatives, except that they do not pay higher rate income tax[17]. Consequently, interest will normally suffer basic rate income tax by deduction, or basic rate income tax will be assessed on the preceding year basis (subject to the special rules for opening and closing years). No deduction for expenses is permitted against income otherwise chargeable to income tax, although relief may be available to trustees or personal representatives for certain qualifying interest paid[18] or for trading losses where the trustees or personal representatives carry on a trade. No personal relief is available to trustees or personal representatives. Where interest is mandated direct to a beneficiary, the Inland Revenue normally assesses the beneficiary (in place of the trustees or personal representatives) to lower, basic and higher rates of income tax.

Personal representatives may receive interest which accrued during the deceased's lifetime. This interest will nevertheless be taxed as income of the estate and not as income of the deceased[19]. Where a beneficiary having an absolute interest in residue is treated as receiving income which derives from interest which in part accrued before the date of death, and which so falls to be treated as an asset of the estate for inheritance tax purposes[20], a measure of relief is available in charging the income to higher rate income tax in the beneficiary's hands; this is achieved by reducing the grossed-up income in the beneficiary's hands by the amount of attributable inheritance tax grossed up to allow for basic rate income tax[1].

On a person's death he ceases to possess any source of interest which he may then own[2], so that the closing years rules[3] apply. Similarly, the personal representatives acquire a new source of income, and the opening years rules apply[4].

The trustees of approved pension schemes[5] and retirement annuity trust schemes[6] are generally exempt from income tax in respect of income from investments of the scheme, as are personal pension schemes[7]. Charities are exempt from tax in respect of yearly interest[8]; by concession, this exemption is extended to bank interest generally (whether or not yearly interest) and building society interest and dividends paid gross[9].

4-23   Where trustees or personal representatives suffer basic rate income tax on interest income and distribute the balance, the beneficiaries are treated as receiving income net of basic rate income tax. Those beneficiaries may then suffer higher rate income tax, or be in a position to recover part or all of the basic rate tax related to the distributed income where personal or other reliefs are available or the lower rate of income tax applies.

---

[17] TA 1988 s 1 (2) (b) imposes higher rate income tax on an 'individual's' income.
[18] See, for example, TA 1988 s 364 and §8-62 below.
[19] *IRC v Henderson's Executors* 1931 SC 681, 16 TC 282.
[20] See §11-08 below.
[1] TA 1988 s 699.
[2] TA 1988 s 67 (8).
[3] See §4-07 above.
[4] See §4-06 above.
[5] TA 1988 s 592 (2)
[6] TA 1988 s 620 (6).
[7] TA 1988 s 643 (2).
[8] TA 1988 s 505 (1) (c) (ii).
[9] Extra-statutory Concession B9.

The additional rate may be assessed on trustees of discretionary or accumulation settlements[10]. This does not apply to personal representatives; where personal representatives make payments of income to trustees where the additional rate would have applied to the income had the personal representatives been trustees, the payments are treated as made subject to deduction of basic rate income tax[11].

EMPLOYEE SHARE SCHEMES

4-24 TA 1988 s 688 provides special treatment in relation to certain schemes for employees to acquire shares in their employing company (or a related company)[12]. This provision is designed to avoid a charge to income tax where trustees of a scheme both receive and pay out interest in circumstances where, but for the exemption, the interest received would be taxable but the interest paid out would not qualify for relief[13]. For example, under the scheme the company might lend funds to the trustees of the scheme, who would then onlend the funds to employees to acquire shares in the company. Under s 688, the interest received by the trustees is exempt from tax under Sch D Case III[14] to the extent that an equivalent amount is paid out by the trustees to the company, so effectively giving relief for the interest paid which would not otherwise be available. However, it should be noted that where the interest paid to the company exceeds the interest received by the trustees it is not possible for any excess relief to be carried forward to later years.

4 Non-resident individual

GENERAL PRINCIPLES

4-25 Interest within Sch D Case III and received by an individual not resident in the UK is chargeable to income tax by virtue of TA 1988 s 18 (1) (b).

4-26 The circumstances in which interest arises to a non-resident so as to be taxable in his hands are the same as those which apply to a resident individual[15]. The rules concerning the chargeability of a non-resident individual to income tax in respect of UK source interest are generally no different from those which apply to an individual resident in the UK[16]. A non-resident will not normally have available any personal reliefs to reduce or extinguish the income liable to interest. However, Commonwealth citizens and certain other categories of person are entitled to personal reliefs[17]; a

---

10 TA 1988 s 686.
11 TA 1988 s 686.
12 Where the scheme is set up to comply with Companies Act 1985 s 153 (4) (b), or Companies (Northern Ireland) Order 1986 art 163 (4) (b).
13 See Chapter 8 as to relief for interest paid.
14 The interest would not be taxable under any other Case unless, exceptionally, the borrowing employees were resident outside the UK.
15 See §4-02 above.
16 See §§4-03 to 4-15 above.
17 TA 1988 s 278.

non-resident might also be entitled to personal reliefs under the non-discrimination clause in a double taxation agreement between the UK and his country of residence.

COLLECTION OF INCOME TAX

4-27 As a general rule, the courts of one country will not enforce the taxation laws of another country[18]. Therefore, where a non-resident receives interest from the UK it will not normally be possible for the Inland Revenue to recover from him any income tax chargeable by enforcing an assessment against the non-resident and his assets abroad. If the non-resident has assets in the UK it may be possible for the tax to be recovered against such assets.

Income tax at the basic rate may be recovered by deduction at source where the interest is paid to a non-resident[19]. But, this will not enable the recovery of income tax assessable at the higher rate which tax remains assessable notwithstanding that the recipient individual is a non-resident[20]. Moreover, even where interest is paid to a non-resident, it is not required to be paid under deduction of basic rate income tax where it is paid by a bank in the ordinary course of carrying on a bona fide banking business in the UK[1]. Although such bank interest remains within the charge to income tax under the legislation, the Inland Revenue has stated[2] that where interest is paid by such a bank to a non-resident it will not normally take steps to recover income tax in respect of the interest paid gross where the non-resident has neither a trustee or other person[3] in the UK, nor a branch or agent in the UK having the management or control of the interest, whom the Inland Revenue may assess under TMA 1970 s 78. Therefore, where this concession applies, the non-resident will not suffer income tax in respect of UK source bank interest even where he has assets in the UK against which the tax could be recovered, although the Inland Revenue would set off any tax assessable against any tax in respect of which a repayment claim might be made; such a set-off could arise where a non-resident entitled to personal allowances under TA 1988 s 278 makes a claim to have repaid income tax deducted at source in respect of UK source income[4].

4-28 Where the non-resident has an agent in the UK, tax in respect of Case III interest arising to the non-resident may be assessed on and collected from the agent under TMA 1970 s 78. This procedure applies irrespective of whether the agent has himself received the interest. However, it appears that, in order to be assessed on behalf of the non-resident, the agent must have been concerned with the arrangements under which the interest arose;

---

[18] See *Government of India, Ministry of Finance (Revenue Division) v Taylor* [1955] 1 All ER 292, [1955] AC 491, HL.
[19] Strictly, where it is paid to 'a person whose usual place of abode is outside the United Kingdom' – see TA 1988 s 349 (2) (c), and §7-16 below.
[20] TA 1988 s 1 (2) (b) refers to income of an 'individual', irrespective of his residence.
[1] TA 1988 s 349 (3) (b) and §7-25 below.
[2] Extra-statutory concession B13.
[3] See TMA 1970 s 72.
[4] Eg tax on UK company dividends or interest paid by a UK company other than bank interest.

in *Nielsen, Andersen & Co v Collins*[5] Rowlatt J said that 'nobody would dream of charging an agent in respect of profits or gains that did not arise from sales or transactions carried out by him'. Thus, where an agent of a non-resident holding funds of the non-resident places them on deposit with a bank in his own name but on behalf of the non-resident the agent may be asesssable under s 78 even if he arranges for the interest on the account to be credited direct to an account in the name of the non-resident. But, where the agent has no involvement in the deposit, or merely pays money due to the non-resident into a deposit account in the non-resident's name (and over which the agent has no control), the agent would appear not to be assessable in respect of interest arising on the account. A solicitor who places money belonging to a non-resident client in a designated deposit account[6] will not normally be treated as assessable under s 78 in respect of the interest arising on the account and paid to or applied for the benefit of the client, unless the solicitor/client relationship goes beyond the solicitor's usual representative capacity[7]; no question arises of assessment on the solicitor where the money is not placed in a designated deposit account but the solicitor accounts to the client for an amount equivalent to the interest which would have been earned on a designated account[8].

Income tax is not chargeable under TMA 1970 s 78 in the name of an agent who carries out 'investment transactions' – including the placing of money at interest[9] – where, broadly, the agent provides investment management services to the non-resident as one of a number of clients and is remunerated at the customary rate for providing those services[10]. This let-out does not apply where the non-resident and the UK agent are connected[11].

Even where the agent does arrange the transaction which produces the interest, he might avoid being assessed by the proviso to TMA 1970 s 82 (1) where he is acting as a bona fide broker or general commission agent in the ordinary course of business who is remunerated at the customary rate for his services. The Inland Revenue considers that an assessment under s 78 on an agent who receives the interest cannot be avoided by the main part of s 82 (1) which normally prevents a s 78 assessment where the agent does not carry on the regular agency of the non-resident. This view is based on the decision in *Scales v Atalanta SS Co of Copenhagen*[12] which held that the original version of s 82 (1)[13] only applied where the agent did not receive the profits which were assessed. But the proviso to s 82 (1)[14] did not apply in relation to the *Atalanta SS Co* case; it is therefore arguable that where a broker or general commission agent receives interest on behalf of his

---

[5] (1927) 13 TC 91 at 110, HL; see also *Scales v Atalanta SS Co of Copenhagen* (1925) 9 TC 586 at 593.
[6] Under Solicitors' Accounts Rules 1991; the interest will have been paid gross to the solicitor if he has certified the beneficial owner as non-ordinarily resident – see §§7-27 and 7-28 below.
[7] See Law Society's Gazette, 4 March 1992 at p 34.
[8] See §4-03 above.
[9] TMA 1970 s 78 (3) (c).
[10] TMA 1970 s 78 (2).
[11] TMA 1970 s 78 (5).
[12] (1925) 9 TC 586.
[13] F (No 2) A 1915 s 31 (6).
[14] Originally FA 1925 s 17.

principal in the course of providing ordinary 'broker-like'[15] services for which he receives customary remuneration he may not be assessed in respect of that interest under TMA 1970 s 78. Further, the 'double foreigner' relief in TMA 1970 s 82 (2) might apply where the source of the interest is a deposit with a UK branch of a non-resident bank, but in this case it is also important that the agent does not handle the interest itself[16].

A person who is assessed under s 78 on behalf of a non-resident may recover the amount of tax paid by him out of moneys which he receives on behalf of the non-resident[17].

Irrespective of the application of TMA 1970 s 78, basic rate income tax may be assessed on an agent or other person *receiving the interest* on behalf of a non-resident person[18], although in practice the Inland Revenue does not assess such an agent or other person who is excluded from the application of s 78 by the special provisions described above which apply in relation to investment transactions.

DOUBLE TAXATION AGREEMENTS

4-29   The position described above applies in the absence of any special relief accorded to a non-resident under a double taxation agreement between the UK and the individual's country of residence. Commonly, the rate of tax which may be imposed by the UK in respect of UK source interest is reduced by such an agreement below the basic rate (currently, 25 per cent); the reduced rates which commonly apply are 15 per cent[19], 12 per cent[20] and 10 per cent[1]. In some cases, the agreement provides that interest shall be exempt from taxation in the country where it arises; examples of agreements where interest arising in the UK is exempt from income tax in the hands of a resident of the other country are the agreements with the United States, Switzerland, the Netherlands, Luxembourg[2], Norway, Sweden, Denmark, France and Germany.

4-30   It is beyond the scope of this book to review the relevant provisions of all the double taxation agreements entered into by the UK, but the following is a summary of the principal considerations which arise in relation to any relief or exemption from income tax in respect of UK source interest under the terms of a double taxation agreement:

1   The relief will normally be accorded to a person who is resident in the other country for the purposes of the agreement. The agreement will usually include an Article concerned with the determination of the residence of individuals for the purposes of the agreement;

2   The Article providing for the taxation of interest will normally specify what interest is to be treated as arising in one of the states which is

---

[15] See *Fleming (Inspector of Taxes) v London Produce Co Ltd* (1968) 44 TC 582 at 596h.
[16] See Viscount Cave LC in *Maclaine & Co v Eccott (Inspector of Taxes)* (1926) 10 TC 481 at 576, HL.
[17] TMA 1970 s 83 (2).
[18] TA 1988 s 59 (1); see §4-03 above.
[19] Eg India, Malaysia, Singapore.
[20] Eg Spain.
[1] Eg Australia and Canada.
[2] But see §4-36 below.

a party to the agreement. In the case of the UK, this will usually coincide with interest within Sch D Case III in that it will apply to interest paid by a resident of the UK and also to interest paid by a non-resident where the interest is borne by a permanent establishment or fixed base of that non-resident in the UK[3];

3   The special treament of interest in the UK will not affect the taxation of the interest in the hands of the recipient in the country where he is resident (although he may be entitled to credit or other relief in respect of any UK income tax suffered);

4   The special treatment of the interest may only be available where the resident of the other country is the beneficial owner of the interest or where the recipient bears tax on the interest in the country of which he is a resident. Consequently, relief will not be available by reason of the securities or loan being held in the name of a nominee, although the beneficial owner himself may be able to claim relief under a double taxation agreement applicable to him irrespective of the country of residence of his nominee. Where trustees receive the income on trust for a beneficiary who is entitled as of right to the income, the beneficiary may be able to claim relief under an agreement applicable to him[4]; where trustees do not hold income on trust for a beneficiary entitled as of right, the trustees themselves may be entitled to relief from income tax under the double taxation agreement. Care should be taken in relation to any arrangements which involve routeing loan interest through a country having a double taxation agreement with the UK solely for the purpose of enabling interest to be paid from the UK without the deduction of basic rate income tax; the circumstances may be such that the recipient is so bound as to how he deals with the interest received that he cannot be said to be the beneficial owner;

5   The interest may be exempt from tax in the UK or subject to a reduced rate of tax. This will enable the recipient to claim that income tax should not be deducted at the full basic rate. If tax is deducted at a higher rate than is authorised by the agreement, the recipient will be entitled to reclaim the over-deducted tax from the Inland Revenue. The existence of a double taxation agreement providing for reduced UK tax on interest – or for a complete exemption – does not of itself permit the payer to pay the interest subject to a modified, if any, tax deduction. The procedure to be followed where interest is eligible to be paid to a non-resident otherwise than subject to a full deduction of basic rate income tax is described in Chapter 7 below[5];

6   The recipient will not be entitled to relief where the interest is received in connection with a trade or business carried on by him through a permanent establishment or fixed base maintained by him in the UK. In such a case the interest will fall into the computation of business profits to be taxed in the ordinary way or may be subject to tax under Case III. An example of this would be where an overseas bank receives interest on a loan made by the bank to a UK borrower through the bank's London branch;

---

[3] See §3-30 above; it will also include UK government interest taxable under Sch C.
[4] See, as to the taxation of income beneficiaries under trusts, *Baker v Archer-Shee* [1927] AC 844, 11 TC 749, HL and *Archer-Shee v Garland* [1931] AC 212, 15 TC 693, HL.
[5] See §7-19 below.

7   The relieving provisions will not be available to the extent that an excessive amount of interest is paid, perhaps by reason of a special relationship between the payer and recipient directly or indirectly through any other person. The non-excessive element may still qualify for the special treatment under the agreement. The circumstances in which interest may be treated as excessive most frequently arise in relation to the financing of UK subsidiaries by foreign parent companies, where the position is complicated by special provisions concerning the payment of interest by companies to certain non-resident affiliates; this is considered in more detail below, together with the factors to be taken into account generally in relation to whether the interest is excessive[6]. Those special provisions depend upon, broadly, a 75 per cent or greater level of common control, but a 'special relationship' may nevertheless exist where there is a lesser degree of common shareholding; further, a 'special relationship' may exist between individuals, or between an individual and a company or trust, in circumstances which prevent the relief from UK taxation applying. It is understood that the Inland Revenue considers that a 'special relationship' can exist where a loan from an unconnected party is guaranteed by an affiliate of the borrower. Generally, the onus is on the non-resident recipient of the interest to show that there is no special relationship or to show that the interest paid is not excessive[7].

8   The relieving provisions may be stated not to apply where the loan has been made mainly for the purpose of taking advantage of the relieving provisions. It is not entirely clear in what circumstances this restriction would apply, although the Inland Revenue considers that this provision can be invoked where a lender resident in a country having a suitable double taxation agreement with the UK has been inserted in a financing chain in order to avoid UK tax on interest within Case III. However, if a loan is made there is usually a commercial use to which the proceeds of the loan are put. That may be sufficient to dispose of an argument that the restriction should apply, even where the borrower and lender are under common control and the borrower could have been funded by some other means[8], because the use of the proceeds of the loan would indicate that the loan was not made mainly for the purpose of taking advantage of the double taxation agreement. Probably, the relief would not be available in the circumstances which occurred in *Cairns v MacDiarmid (Inspector of Taxes)*[9].

4-31   In the absence of a relieving provision under a double taxation agreement it would be unusual for a non-resident individual to be able to recover from the Inland Revenue any part of any income tax deducted at source from interest paid. This is because of the limited extent to which personal reliefs are available to non-residents[10], although it would be possible for a non-resident individual to be able to claim relief in respect of certain losses or capital allowances as summarised in §**4-16** above.

---

[6] See §**9-12** below.
[7] TA 1988 s 808A (3).
[8] Eg by share capital or a capital contribution.
[9] [1983] STC 178, CA; see §**2-18** above.
[10] See TA 1988 s 278.

5 Non-resident company

GENERAL PRINCIPLES

4-32 In the case of a non-resident company, a distinction must be made between a company which carries on a trade in the UK through a branch or agency and one which does not. In the case of the former, it is liable to corporation tax in respect of both trading income arising directly or indirectly through or from the branch or agency trade, and also in respect of any other income from property used by or held by or for the branch or agency[11]. Therefore, a non-resident company carrying on a banking trade in the UK would treat interest income as part of its trading income in computing its Case I profits; a non-resident company carrying on some other (non-finance) trade in the UK but receiving UK source interest (eg bank deposit interest) in relation to its UK trading activities would be assessed to corporation tax under Case III in respect of such interest. In that regard, the non-resident company is treated effectively in the same way as a UK resident company; credit may be taken for tax deducted at source from interest received against the company's corporation tax liability – any excess of income tax suffered by deduction may be reclaimed from the Inland Revenue[12]. However, a non-resident company may not credit income tax deducted at source from interest and other charges on income received against income tax deductible by the company from similar payments made by the company under the procedure which applies to resident companies[13]. This is because the provisions of TA 1988 Sch 16 which set out that procedure only apply to resident companies[14].

Where interest is paid to a non-resident company, albeit one which will suffer corporation tax in respect of its interest income, it may remain necessary for basic rate income tax to be deducted at source from yearly interest paid by reason of the company's usual place of abode being outside the UK[15], unless the company carries on a branch banking business in the UK and is eligible to receive interest gross[16].

4-33 A non-resident company carrying on a trade in the UK through a branch or agency would not normally be entitled to relief under a double taxation agreement in respect of UK source interest, unless the interest is unrelated to that trade[17].

4-34 Where the non-resident company does not have a branch or agency trade in the UK – or where the interest received is unrelated to the non-resident company's trade in the UK – the interest is chargeable to income tax under TA 1988 s 18 (1) (b) (and not to corporation tax). TA 1988 s 59 (1) expresses income tax to be chargeable on any 'persons', not 'individuals', and companies are liable to corporation tax rather than income tax only

---

[11] TA 1988 s 11 (2) (a).
[12] TA 1988 s 11 (3), as amended, in relation to the application of 'pay and file' by FA 1990 s 98 (3) and (4). There are special rules in s 417 for overseas life insurance companies.
[13] See §§7-11 and 7-12 below.
[14] TA 1988 s 350 (4).
[15] TA 1988 s 349 (2) (c). and see §7-16 below.
[16] See TA 1988 s 349 (3) (a), and §§7-20 to 7-23 below.
[17] See §4-30(1) above.

where they are resident in the UK or the income in question relates to a trade carried on in the UK through a branch or agency[18]. To that extent, a non-resident company in receipt of Case III interest is in the same position as a non-resident individual[19]. However, a non-resident company is not liable to the higher rate of income tax, nor taxable at the lower rate, because that only applies to an 'individual'[20].

DOUBLE TAXATION AGREEMENTS

4-35   A non-resident company may be able to claim relief from income tax in respect of interest within Sch D Case III, and in this connection will be in the same position as a non-resident individual who receives interest otherwise than in connection with a business establishment in the UK[1]. A non-resident company would be unlikely to be able to claim relief from corporation tax under a double taxation agreement in respect of Case III interest, because the circumstances which give rise to a corporation tax charge would probably cause the interest in question to be so related to the non-resident's UK trading presence that the double taxation agreement would not operate to relieve the interest from corporation tax[2]. However, if any such exemption does remain available, the interest is not to be excluded from trading income or profits so as to give rise to tax losses to be relieved against other income[3].

4-36   Under certain double taxation agreements the status of the non-resident recipient company may be such as to disqualify it from taking advantage of the provision of the agreement relieving interest from taxation in the UK. An example of this is an investment holding company in Luxembourg[4].

EUROPEAN COMMUNITY PROPOSALS

4-37   The European Commission has proposed a Directive under which interest (and royalties) paid by a company established in one member state of the European Community should be exempt from tax in that member state where it is paid to a company established in another member state which owns at least 25 per cent of the capital of the paying company. The draft Directive[5] is still under discussion, although the Commission had originally hoped that the Directive would have effect from 1 January 1993.

---

[18] TA 1988 s 6 (2).
[19] See §§**4-25** to **4-28** above.
[20] See TA 1988 s 1 (2)(aa) and (b).
[1] See §§**4-29** and **4-30** above.
[2] See §**4-30 (6)** above.
[3] Under TA 1988 ss 393 or 436; see TA 1988 s 808.
[4] See Article XXX of the UK/Luxembourg Double Taxation Agreement dated 24 May 1967, SI 1968 No 1100.
[5] COM (90) 571 Final – OJ C53 28.2.91 p 26.

6 Non-resident trustees and personal representatives

4-38 UK source interest is taxable in the hands of non-resident trustees and personal representatives by virtue of TA 1988 s 18 (1) (b). As in the case of resident trustees and personal representatives, no special rule applies to the taxation of interest in the hands of non-resident trustees or personal representatives[6]. Interest within Sch D Case III is subject to income tax in their hands, but not at the lower or higher rate[7]. Consequently, the same position obtains as in the case of resident trustees or personal representatives. Interest to which a trust beneficiary is entitled as of right will be assessed as his income.

4-39 Where Case III interest is received by the non-resident trustees of a discretionary or accumulation settlement, the question of the charge to the additional rate would arise because the income has a UK source[8].

DOUBLE TAXATION AGREEMENTS

4-40 Subject to any special provisions relating to trustees or personal representatives, non-resident trustees or personal representatives (or beneficiaries entitled to trust income as of right) may be entitled to relief from income tax under the provisions of a double taxation agreement. In that connection, the same general considerations as are summarised in §**4-30** above will be relevant.

---

[6] See §§**4-22** to **4-23** above.
[7] Trustees and personal representatives are not 'individuals', as mentioned in TA 1988 s 1 (2) (aa) and (b).
[8] See, for example, the assessment of non-resident trustees in respect of dividend income derived from UK companies in *IRC v Regent Trust Co Ltd* [1980] STC 140, [1980] 1 WLR 688.

Chapter 5

TAXATION OF FOREIGN SOURCE INTEREST (SCHEDULE D CASE IV OR CASE V)

5-01   Part 2 of Chapter 3 explains the circumstances in which interest may fall within Sch D Case IV or V – that is foreign source interest other than interest which falls within Sch C. This chapter concerns the taxation of such foreign source interest, principally where it is received by UK resident taxpayers.

As is explained in Chapter 3[1], the practical significance of the distinction between Cases IV and V has now disappeared. For the purpose of this chapter, interest falling within either of those Cases is referred to as 'foreign source interest'. It should be noted that there are two ways in which the charge to tax can be collected in respect of foreign source interest. Either it can be assessed directly on the owner of the interest in the ordinary way, or basic rate income tax may be collected under the paying agent or collecting agent procedure[2] in which case a further assessment to higher rate income tax or corporation tax may be made on the owner, or a repayment claim may be available if an excessive amount of tax has been suffered by deduction. This chapter is principally concerned with foreign source interest which is not subject to the paying agent or collecting agent withholding procedure, although certain provisions (eg those relating to the availability of foreign tax credit relief) apply to all foreign source interest; any special treatment which follows from the operation of the withholding procedure is explained in Chapter 7.

1   Resident individual

THE CHARGE TO TAX

5-02   Foreign source interest is chargeable to income tax under Sch D by virtue of TA 1988 s 18(1)(b) in the hands of a taxpayer resident in the UK. Although the charge to income tax in respect of 'interest of money' is not qualified in the legislation by reference to the residence of the recipient where the interest has a foreign source – as is the case with other foreign source income chargeable to income tax under Sch D[3] – it is clear that the principle of the territorial limitation on the charge to tax prevents a

---

[1] See §3-21.
[2] See Chapter 7 Part 3.
[3] See TA 1988 s 18(1)(a)(i).

non-resident being charged to income tax in respect of foreign source interest unless the legislation specifically provides otherwise[4].

Although there is no authority on the point, it would seem that the charge to tax depends – as in the case of interest within Sch D Case III[5] – on the interest being received by or on behalf of the taxpayer, and that foreign source interest is not taxable when it is only due but is not paid. However, in connection with the receipt of foreign source interest there is a material distinction between the treatment of individuals domiciled within the UK[6] and the treatment of individuals not so domiciled[7].

ARISING BASIS

5–03 Generally, an individual domiciled within the UK[8] suffers income tax in respect of foreign source interest by reference to interest which arises and is paid to him or otherwise comes under his control. He is taxed on 'the full amount' of the interest 'whether the income has been or will be received in the United Kingdom or not'[9]. This is not affected by the individual being a national of another country.

5–04 An exception from the arising basis of assessment can operate where the taxpayer is prevented by the exchange control or other regulations of the country where the interest arises from remitting the interest to the UK. In those circumstances, TA 1988 s 584 provides relief to the taxpayer by deferring the charge to tax until the income can be remitted to the UK.

The relief applies where the foreign source interest cannot be remitted to the UK by reason of the local laws or 'executive action' of the foreign government or by reason of the impossibility of obtaining foreign currency in the foreign country where the interest arose[10]; the fact that foreign currency can only be obtained at what might be regarded as an excessive exchange rate would not satisfy the condition. The taxpayer must also satisfy the Board of Inland Revenue that either of these conditions would continue to apply notwithstanding any reasonable endeavours on his part to remit the income. A further condition must also be satisfied if the relief is to be available, namely, that the taxpayer has not realised the income by selling it outside the foreign country in question for sterling or for some other currency which he is not prevented from remitting to the UK[11].

In order that the relief should apply, the taxpayer must notify the Board of Inland Revenue before the assessment in respect of the interest has become final and conclusive. When the conditions for relief cease to be satisfied, an assessment may be made on the interest irrespective of whether it is in fact then remitted to the UK. The legislation provides that the assessment

---

[4] See *National Bank of Greece SA v Westminster Bank Executor and Trustee Co (Channel Islands) Ltd* [1971] 1 All ER 233, 46 TC 472, HL – see §3–22 above.
[5] See §4–02 above.
[6] Ie in England and Wales, Scotland or Northern Ireland.
[7] See §§5–06 to 5–08 below.
[8] But see §5–04 below, and §5–06 below in the case of certain other individuals including a Commonwealth citizen not ordinarily resident in the UK.
[9] TA 1988 s 65(1).
[10] TA 1988 s 584(1)(a).
[11] TA 1988 s 584(1)(b).

shall be made by reference to the value of the interest at the date when the conditions for deferral of tax cease to be satisfied[12]. This requires reference to the exchange rate ruling on that date (if necessary, the official rate of exchange in the foreign country in question)[13] and also seems to require the assessment to be made as if the income arose on that date, rather than on the date when it actually did arise; the time limit for making the assessment is six years from the date when the Board of Inland Revenue considers that the conditions for relief are no longer satisfied. Any appeal against the Board's decision as to the application of the section lies to the Special Commissioners[14].

The conditions for relief under s 584 will not be treated as satisfied where the taxpayer has received a payment in respect of unremittable interest from the Export Credits Guarantee Department. No further charge to tax is then suffered when the unremittable interest subsequently ceases to be subject to the conditions for relief[15].

5-05   A similar relief applies, by concession[16], where a bank or other financial concern which is entitled to loan interest taxable on the accruals basis cannot remit that interest to the UK because of overseas exchange control restrictions.

REMITTANCE BASIS

5-06   In the case of either

1   an individual who is not domiciled within the UK, or
2   a Commonwealth citizen or a citizen of the Republic of Ireland who is not ordinarily resident in the UK,

the remittance basis is substituted for the arising basis. Here, foreign source interest is assessed to income tax by reference to the 'full amount... of the sums received in the United Kingdom'[17]. Category 2 above does not arise in practice as frequently as category 1; since the charge to income tax under Sch D Case IV or V on foreign source interest only applies where the taxpayer is resident in the UK, for category 2 to apply the Commonwealth citizen or citizen of the Republic of Ireland must be domiciled within the UK yet be on a temporary visit to the UK when he is resident but not ordinarily resident. The remittance basis does not apply to interest having its source in the Republic of Ireland; in that case the arising basis applies irrespective of the domicile of the taxpayer[18].

5-07   It is beyond the scope of this book to examine in detail the law concerning what constitutes, or is treated as, a remittance of interest to the UK. The law which applies to interest is no different from that which

---

[12] TA 1988 s 584 (2).
[13] TA 1988 s 584 (8).
[14] TA 1988 s 584(9).
[15] TA 1988 s 584 (5).
[16] Extra-statutory Concession B38, para 9.
[17] TA 1988 s 65 (4) and (5)(a) and (b); curiously, in relation to Case V income, s 65 (5) (b) uses the expression '*actual* sums', but there appears to be no material distinction between sums which are 'actual' and sums which are not.
[18] TA 1988 s 68 (1).

applies to other foreign source income[19]. The following is a summary of the principal points which arise in relation to remittances:

1   The language of the legislation as to remittances in respect of Case IV income and Case V income, respectively, is slightly different[20], but it appears that little, if anything, turns on this, so that the rules as to remittances of foreign source interest should be treated as being the same whether the interest is derived from 'securities' or other indebtedness[1].

2   There is no requirement that money is brought into the UK, still less that the foreign income itself should be paid direct to the UK[2]. Income can be remitted to the UK where, for example, the taxpayer draws a cheque on a foreign bank account which cheque is then sold to or collected by a bank in the UK without money actually being transferred to the UK.

3   The mere entry of the income in books of account maintained in the UK does not amount to remittance to the UK[3].

4   A series of indirectly related transactions may be taken together to result in a receipt of foreign income in the UK where the amount in question can be traced from the foreign source through what is in effect a conduit to the UK[4].

5   A remittance from an overseas bank account to which has been credited both capital and income will probably be treated as a remittance of income, on the basis that prudence normally dictates the application of income before capital[5]. Nor is income converted into capital by being reinvested. For this reason, it is wise for a non-domiciled individual maintaining bank accounts outside the UK to keep separate accounts for income and capital so that remittances of (non-taxable) capital can be clearly identified. Nevertheless, it may be arguable that where an individual remits a sum from a mixed bank account for a capital purpose (eg the purchase of a house) the remittance could be treated as a remittance of capital where the sum remitted is no greater than the capital element in the account.

6   Where the taxpayer is ordinarily resident in the UK, additional wide-ranging anti-avoidance provisions can apply to treat foreign income as remitted to the UK. Even though there may not be a remittance of foreign income under the general rules, income may be treated as remitted to the UK where it is applied outside the UK in or towards satisfaction of certain loans made to the taxpayer. This rule applies whether the loan was made in the UK or was made outside the UK and brought to the UK, and can apply where the loan in question was used to satisfy

---

[19] Eg dividends from foreign companies, and profits from foreign partnerships.
[20] See TA 1988 s 65 (5) (a) and (b).
[1] See *Thomson (Inspector of Taxes) v Moyse* (1960) 39 TC 291 at 335, HL; and see Chapter 3 Part 2.
[2] See *Thomson (Inspector of Taxes) v Moyse* (1960) 39 TC 291 at 329–330, HL.
[3] *Gresham Life Assurance Society v Bishop* [1902] AC 287, 4 TC 464; but see *Scottish Mortgage Co of New Mexico v McKelvie* (1886) 2 TC 165, HL, where the taxpayer was treated as effectively acting as its own banker through book entries exchanging capital raised in the UK for interest on overseas securities.
[4] *Harmel v Wright (Inspector of Taxes)* [1974] STC 88, [1974] 1 All ER 945.
[5] *Scottish Provident Institution v Allan* (1901) 4 TC 409.

such a loan and even if the loan was satisfied before the proceeds were brought to the UK[6].

7   Where the taxpayer outside the UK makes an outright and irrevocable payment out of income to a third party and that third party remits the amount to the UK, that will not involve a remittance of the income unless any of the foregoing provisions operate (eg by virtue of there being an arrangement whereby the taxpayer can in the UK enjoy the income or other amounts representing it[7]).

TAXABLE AMOUNT OF FOREIGN SOURCE INCOME

5-08   Relief is available against Case IV or V interest taxable on the arising basis for an annuity or other annual payment (but not interest) payable out of the income to a non-resident[8]. This relief results from the way in which relief is given for annual payments under the deduction and retention procedure; that procedure only applies to certain payments falling within Sch D Case III[9], and therefore specific provision is made to relieve annual payments which are not within Case III (such as maintenance payments under a foreign obligation[10]). Where foreign source interest is charged to basic rate income tax under the paying agent or collecting agent procedure[11], relief in respect of such annuities or annual payments is given by way of repayment of the excess tax suffered. However, such payments might not qualify for relief in respect of interest taxable at rates in excess of the basic rate[12]. Until April 1982, interest paid out of foreign source interest to a non-resident could qualify for relief[13], but now interest paid does not qualify for relief against foreign source interest[14] except insofar as interest paid by the taxpayer is available for relief against his income generally[15].

In the case of foreign source interest chargeable on the remittance basis, it is expressly provided that the income is chargeable 'without any deduction or abatement'[16]. Therefore, no relief is available in respect of annuities or other annual payments paid out of the interest after it has been remitted to the UK.

THE BASIS OF ASSESSMENT GENERALLY

5-09   As with interest chargeable under Sch D Case III[17], and subject to one exception, foreign source interest is generally assessed to income tax on the preceding year basis, whether it is chargeable on the arising basis

---

6 TA 1988 s 65(6) to (9).
7 *Carter v Sharon* [1936] 1 All ER 720, 20 TC 229.
8 TA 1988 s 65(1)(b).
9 See TA 1988 s 348(1).
10 *Keiner v Keiner* [1952] 1 All ER 643, 34 TC 346.
11 See §§**7-40** to **7-52** below.
12 TA 1988 s 683.
13 TA 1970 s 122(1)(c).
14 See, in relation to interest claimed against foreign source rental income, *Ockenden (Inspector of Taxes) v Mackley* [1982] STC 513, [1982] 1 WLR 787.
15 See Chapter 8 below.
16 TA 1988 s65(5)(a) and (b).
17 §**4-04** above.

or the remittance basis[18]. In this respect the basis of assessment is identical to that which applies in relation to interest within Case III, and the same special rules apply as to opening and closing years[19]. Similarly, the rules as to the basis of assessment only apply where the interest is not subject to the deduction of basic rate income tax under the paying agent or collecting agent procedure[20]; where interest from a foreign source ceases or begins to be subject to the collection of basic rate income tax before the interest is received by the taxpayer, there is treated as being a commencement or cessation of the source for the purposes of the opening or closing years rules for the same reason as applies for Case III purposes[1].

The exception referred to above is that interest having its source in the Republic of Ireland is assessed on the current year basis[2].

5–10 Interest which is chargeable on the remittance basis is charged by reference to the interest received in the UK in the relevant (normally, preceding) year of assessment[3]. The operation of the opening years rules[4] in relation to foreign source interest chargeable on the remittance basis is illustrated by the following example where interest first arises on 1 October 1992.

Year of assessment	Interest arising	Remittance to UK	Assessed
1992/93	50	30	30
1993/94	100	100	100
1994/95	100	120	100[5]
1995/96	100	90	120

Where an individual is assesssed on the remittance basis he may, subject to any practical constraints, remit interest in such a way that his income tax liability is kept to the minimum; taking into account his other taxable income, any reliefs and allowances and his expectation of the level of income tax rates, he may make remittances so that the lowest rates of tax apply. One practical constraint may be his inability to remit income from the foreign country; this may work to his disadvantage. The taxpayer might incur expenditure in the UK, perhaps financed by a loan[6] to be repaid out of subsequent remittances; on making a remittance of several years' income he could suffer tax at higher marginal rates than would have applied had the income been remitted on a regular basis. TA 1988 s 585 provides relief when the taxpayer remits income in a year where that income arose in earlier years and he was unable, despite reasonable endeavours on his part, to remit

---

[18] TA 1988 s 65 (1) and (5)(a) and (b).
[19] TA 1988 s 66 and 67; and see §§**4–06** to **4–08** above.
[20] See Chapter 7 Part 3.
[1] See §**4–08** above, TA 1988 ss 66 (5) and 67(3).
[2] TA 1988 s 68 (1).
[3] TA 1988 s 65 (5)(a) and (b).
[4] TA 1988 s 66.
[5] No election made for current year basis under TA 1988 s 66 (1)(c); see §**4–06** above.
[6] Consideration would need to be given to the deemed remittance rules in TA 1988 s 65 (6) to (9); see §**5–07(6)** above.

the income in the earlier years by reason of local laws or executive government action in the source country or the impossibility of obtaining foreign currency in that country[7]. The relief permits the taxpayer to have the income assessed by reference to the years in which the income arose. It should be noted that special provision is made for the position where the income in question is the basis for assessment of tax in more than one year of assessment, as can happen where the opening and closing rules apply[8].

5-11   Where an individual formerly living abroad establishes residence in the UK, he is not treated as acquiring a new source of interest where he continues to hold a foreign source of interest which belonged to him before he came to the UK[9]. Therefore, in such circumstances foreign source interest will immediately be assessed on the preceding year basis unless (a) the individual arrives in the UK within the first two years (or three years, if he can make an election under TA 1988 s 66(1)(c) for the current year basis to apply) of receiving interest from the source, or (b) upon his arriving in the UK the interest becomes subject to the paying agent or collecting agent procedure[10]. In practice, where an individual becomes resident in the course of a year of assessment, the assessment in the first year is only made on the proportion of the preceding year's income which the period of residence in the first year bears to a full year[11]. However, where the individual has a foreign domicile (or is a Commonwealth citizen or citizen of the Republic of Ireland, and not ordinarily resident in the UK) his liability to income tax would depend upon the amount of interest remitted to the UK in the preceding year of assessment, which may prevent any liability to income tax in the first year. If the source ceases in the year of arrival or in the following year, special rules are applied in practice[12].

5-12   Where a source of income has ceased to belong to the taxpayer, no subsequent liability to income tax can arise in relation to income from that source. Consequently, where an individual is chargeable on the remittance basis, interest remitted to the UK in a year of assessment when the taxpayer no longer owns the source will not be taxable, and interest accumulated before the year of assessment in which the source ceased can be remitted to the UK free of income tax in later years of assessment. However, where an individual chargeable to tax on the arising basis obtains relief under TA 1988 s 584 in respect of income which he is unable to remit[13], it would seem that he remains liable to be assessed in respect of the income upon the conditions for relief ceasing to be satisfied notwithstanding that by that time he no longer owns the source from which the interest originally arose. This point is not specifically addressed in s 584, but, since the section provides

---

[7] Cf the similar relief under TA 1988 s 584 where income is assessed on the arising basis: §**5-04** above.

[8] TA 1988 s 585(5) and (6), and see §§**4-06** to **4-08** and **5-09** above.

[9] *Back v Whitlock* [1932] 1 KB 747, 16 TC 723.

[10] See Chapter 7 Part 3 and §**5-09** above.

[11] Inland Revenue Booklet IR20 (1992): 'Residents and Non-residents, Liability to tax in the United Kingdom' para 7.15; see also para 7.16 where the remittance basis applies.

[12] See Inland Revenue Booklet IR20: para 7.15; and para 7.16 for the remittance basis.

[13] See §**5-04** above.

for relief from assessment to tax in respect of income so long as certain conditions are satisfied and provides that when the income ceases to be subject to the conditions for relief 'such assessments... shall be made as may be necessary to take account of it', it would seem that the income then becomes assessable notwithstanding that the source of the interest no longer belongs to the taxpayer.

INVESTMENT INCOME OR EARNED INCOME

5–13 Normally, foreign source interest belonging to an individual will be investment income, as in the case of UK source interest. Exceptionally, the interest might be immediately derived from a trade carried on by the individual, in which case the income would fall within either Sch D Case V, where the income is wholly carried on outside the UK (as in the case of a foreign partnership)[14], or Sch D Case I where the trade is carried on wholly or partly in the UK[15]. As to whether the foreign source interest can be earned income, the same considerations arise as in the case of UK source interest[16].

INTEREST ON DAMAGES FOR PERSONAL INJURIES OR DEATH

5–14 The exemption which applies under TA 1988 s 329 in respect of interest awarded by a court on certain damages for personal injuries or death[17] has been extended by Inland Revenue concession to interest awarded in corresponding circumstances by a foreign court provided that the interest is exempt from tax in the country in which the award was made[18]. This latter condition may not be satisfied, and this may result in full income tax being suffered in the UK (subject to the availability of credit for foreign tax). However, it appears that it is not necessary for any exemption from foreign tax to apply by reason of the circumstances in which the interest is paid, so that even if an exemption is available under a double taxation agreement with the UK the concession should apply. This concessionary treatment does not exactly mirror the exemption in s 329, because it does not take account of the exemption applying to interest not awarded by the court but paid in respect of a compromise or settlement payment[19]. However, should interest be received in respect of a compromised or settled claim in a foreign jurisdiction to damages for personal injuries or death, the Inland Revenue might be expected to give sympathetic consideration to an extension of the concession.

---

[14] *Colquhoun v Brooks* (1889) 14 App Cas 493, 2 TC 490, HL.
[15] *Ogilvie v Kitton (Surveyor of Taxes)* 1908 SC 1003, 5 TC 338.
[16] See §4–10 above.
[17] See §4–12 above.
[18] Extra-statutory Concession A30.
[19] See TA 1988 s 329 (3).

DOUBLE TAXATION RELIEF

5-15   Foreign source interest may be subject to taxation in the country where the interest arises; this may be the country where the payer of the interest is resident or perhaps the country where the payer has a business establishment or other asset (eg land) for which the loan or credit was raised. Because of the difficulty in enforcing payment of taxes in other countries, the source country might impose tax in respect of the interest by deduction at source.

The withholding tax suffered may be reduced from the rate which normally applies in the source country, either by reason of a special relief or exemption designed to encourage foreign investment and to reduce the cost of economic development in the source country[20] or by the operation of the provisions of a double taxation agreement between the source country and the UK.

5-16   Where an individual resident taxpayer suffers foreign tax in respect of the foreign source interest, relief in respect of the foreign tax can be given in one of two ways:

(1) Credit Method

The recipient is entitled to credit for the foreign tax against the income tax calculated by reference to the source income. This credit is available whether there is a double taxation agreement in force which provides for the credit[1] or not[2]. Where credit is claimed, income tax is first computed by reference to the whole of the foreign income disregarding the foreign tax suffered[3]. For example, where interest of 100 is paid subject to foreign tax at the rate of 10 per cent, the taxpayer only receives cash of 90 but income tax is first computed as if his income included interest of 100, and the foreign tax of 10 is then credited against his income tax liability. Where the taxpayer is chargeable to tax on the remittance basis in respect of the foreign source interest[4], the amount remitted to the UK is first grossed up by the foreign tax attributable to that income[5].

The amount of credit which can be set against the income tax otherwise payable is subject to a limitation. The credit may not exceed the income tax which would otherwise be payable in respect of the foreign interest, treating that interest as the top slice of the taxpayer's income[6]; if the taxpayer has more than one source of foreign income, this limitation is applied successively down through the various sources of income[7], the taxpayer being entitled to choose the order in which they are taken so as to maximise the relief. The foreign tax suffered at the highest rate would normally be set against the top slice of income and so on.

---

[20] In the absence of an exemption, the lender would normally require the interest to be grossed up so that the net after-tax receipt is the same as it would have been in the absence of any tax deduction.
[1] TA 1988 s 788.
[2] TA 1988 s 790.
[3] TA 1988 s 795 (2).
[4] See §5-06 above.
[5] TA 1988 s 795 (6).
[6] TA 1988 s 796 (1).
[7] TA 1988 s 796 (2).

The total amount of credit may not exceed the total income tax liability of the taxpayer for the year, after deducting the amount of income tax which he is entitled to charge against any other person. This latter deduction is in respect of that income tax which the taxpayer suffers at the basic rate in respect of an amount of his income equal to annual payments paid out of profits or gains brought into charge to income tax and in respect of which he is entitled to recoup himself when making payment to the recipient of the annual payment[8]. If this were not taken into account, it would be possible for a taxpayer fully to extinguish his income tax liability by foreign tax credits and also to withhold amounts equal to basic rate income tax from annual payments paid by him without effectively accounting to the Inland Revenue for such basic rate income tax; this would represent a net loss to the Inland Revenue because the deduction from the annual payments represents the basic rate income tax suffered by the recipient of those payments.

Where income tax is assessed on a preceding year basis, the preceding year's income is merely the artificial measure of the current year's income which is being taxed. Nevertheless, for the purposes of foreign tax credit, the relevant foreign tax is the tax paid by reference to the foreign income used as the basis of the computation of the income tax liability. Both TA 1988 s 790 (4), in relation to unilateral relief, and the typical language of a double taxation agreement provide for credit given for foreign tax in respect of foreign income to be allowed against any UK tax 'computed by reference to' that foreign income. This leads to a difficulty in the opening years of a source of income, where the same item of foreign income may be used as the basis for the income tax assessment for more than one year[9]. This difficulty is dealt with by TA 1988 s 804, which permits the foreign tax to be credited more than once, subject to certain adjustments where the foreign period of assessment does not coincide with the UK year of assessment[10]. A further adjustment may later be made where, by reason of the closing years rules[11], the income in one year of assessment is not taken as a basis for assessment[12].

Further limitations apply in relation to foreign tax credit on loan interest[13]. However, these limitations are rarely likely to be relevant in the case of individuals. For this reason, they are considered below in relation to companies[14]. Similarly, because it is mainly relevant to banks and other financial institutions, 'spared tax' credit relief is also considered below[15], although it could apply in the case of individuals.

(2) Deduction method

The taxpayer may elect not to take relief by way of credit[16]. In that case, the foreign tax is treated as a deduction from the foreign source interest

---

[8] See TA 1988 s 348.
[9] See §5-09 above.
[10] TA 1988 s 804 (3) and (4).
[11] See §§4-07 and 5-09 above.
[12] TA 1988 s 804 (5).
[13] TA 1988 s 798.
[14] See §5-28 below.
[15] See §5-29 below.
[16] TA 1988 s 805.

chargeable to income tax[17]. Where an election is made against credit relief in respect of foreign source interest which is chargeable to income tax on the remittance basis, no further deduction is made; the taxpayer is simply taxable in respect of the amount remitted to the UK.

It will not normally be advantageous to elect against credit relief, since the net after-tax position is better where credit is taken. This is illustrated by the following example:

EXAMPLE

Interest of 100 is taxable on the arising basis, subject to foreign tax of 20; the taxpayer's marginal rate of UK income tax (which applies to the foreign source interest) is 40 per cent.

(a) Credit method:

Interest actually received	80	80
Add, foreign tax	20	
Taxable in UK	100	
UK tax = 100 × 40%	40	
Less, foreign tax credit	20	
Net UK tax payable		20
Net after-tax amount		60

(b) Deduction method:

Interest actually received	80
UK tax = 80 × 40%	32
Net after-tax amount	48

PAYMENT OF TAX

5-17   Income tax assessed in respect of foreign source interest chargeable on the preceding year basis is payable on 1 January of the year of assessment to which the assessment relates or, if later, thirty days after the assessment is issued[18]. Where income tax is only assessable at the higher rate, because basic rate income tax has been collected under the paying agent or collecting agent procedure[19], the interest is assessed on the current year basis and tax is payable on or before 1 December following the year of assessment to which the assessment relates or, if later, thirty days after the assessment is issued[20]. The dates for payment of tax are therefore the same for foreign source interest as they are for interest within Sch D Case III[1].

RELIEF AGAINST INTEREST

5-18   An individual may be entitled to relief which may reduce or extinguish the amount of foreign source interest which would otherwise be liable to

---

[17] TA 1988 s 511.
[18] TA 1988 s 5 (1).
[19] See Chapter 7 Part 3.
[20] TA 1988 ss 5 (4) and 835(6)(a).
[1] See §4-15 above.

income tax in the same way as relief may be available against interest within Sch D Case III[2]. Foreign source interest may not be relieved by Case V trading and other business losses, in the same way as such losses may not shelter interest within Sch D Case III[3].

Where foreign source interest carring a foreign tax credit is relieved by allowances or other reliefs the foreign tax credit lapses, because it cannot be carried forward against income in later years of assessment. In these circumstances, the taxpayer might be better advised to elect against credit and allow the deduction method to apply if otherwise allowances or reliefs which could be carried forward were to be exhausted.

2 Resident company

THE CHARGE TO TAX

5-19 A company resident in the UK pays corporation tax in respect of foreign source interest and does not suffer income tax; in this respect, it is in the same position as in relation to the taxation of interest within Sch D Case III[4]. Income tax principles apply for the purposes of computing the foreign source interest subject to corporation tax which is charged under Case IV or V in one sum, together with other foreign income taxable under the relevant Case[5]. The preceding year basis does not apply[6], and foreign source interest is taxed according to income arising during the accounting period for which the liability is computed.

5-20 The remittance basis, which is available to non–domiciled (and certain other) individuals in respect of foreign source interest[7] is not available to companies, even though it is possible for a company to be domiciled outside the UK[8]. This is because it is expressly provided that for corporation tax purposes income is computed under Cases I to VI 'on the full amount of the profits or gains or income arising in the [accounting] period (whether or not received in or transmitted to the United Kingdom)'[9].

A company may, however, claim relief under TA 1988 s 584 where foreign source interest is not capable of being remitted to the UK. The relief operates for a company in the same way as it does for an individual[10], although provision is now made for the liability to corporation tax to arise in respect of income becoming remittable without an assessment being made when the 'pay and file' system of accounting for corporation tax applies[11].

5-21 As with interest within Case III, foreign source interest income of a company must normally be separated from the elements in the profit and

---

[2] See §**4-16** above.
[3] TA 1988 s 391 (2).
[4] See §**4-17** above.
[5] TA 1988 ss 9 (1), 70(1) and 73.
[6] TA 1988 s 9 (6).
[7] See §§**5-06** and **5-07** above.
[8] *Gasque v IRC* [1940] 2 KB 80, 23 TC 210.
[9] TA 1988 s 70 (1).
[10] See §§**5-04** and **5-05** above.
[11] See TA 1988 s 584 (3), (4) and (10).

loss account of the company which make up the company's trading receipts, and interest received (by or on behalf of the company[12]) substituted for interest included in the profit and loss account on an accruals basis. This will not apply in the case of a company carrying on a banking trade, when the foreign source interest will normally comprise part of its income for the purposes of the Case I computation.

DOUBLE TAXATION RELIEF

5-22   Like an individual, a resident company may be entitled to a reduction in or exemption from any foreign tax suffered in respect of foreign source interest where a double taxation agreement exists between the UK and the country where the interest arises[13].

5-23   A resident company will also be entitled to relief from UK tax for foreign tax suffered in respect of foreign source interest. The deduction method is available to resident companies, by making an election against the credit method[14], but, as for individuals[15], the credit method will normally be preferred unless the company would have a lower liability to corporation tax in one or more accounting periods by reason of losses or other reliefs if relief by deduction were taken.

CREDIT FOR FOREIGN TAX SUFFERED

5-24   Relief by way of credit is available to a resident company, whether there is a double taxation agreement in force which provides for relief in the specific instance[16] or not[17]. The full amount of the foreign source interest, including any amount which may have been deducted by way of foreign tax, is then brought into account for the purposes of corporation tax[18].

5-25   The amount of the foreign tax which may be credited is limited to the corporation tax 'attributable' to the income carrying the credit[19]. The basic rule is that the limit is found by applying the rate of corporation tax payable by the company to the foreign source interest in question[20].

5-26   However, the company may have available relief in respect of interest and annual payments, management expenses or other reliefs which may be set against the company's taxable profits generally. In such a case, the company may choose the order in which these are to be set off[1], and will normally choose to set them first against such income and chargeable gains as do

---

12   See §§**4-02, 4-03** and **4-17**.
13   See §**5-15** above.
14   TA 1988 s 805 and 811.
15   §**5-16 (2)** above.
16   TA 1988 s 788.
17   TA 1988 s 790.
18   TA 1988 s 795 (2).
19   See TA 1988 s 797.
20   TA 1988 s 797 (2).
 1   TA 1988 s 797 (3).

not carry a foreign tax credit, and thereafter against income (and chargeable gains) which carry foreign tax credit, starting with the income (or gains) which carries credit at the lowest percentage rate and so on until the highest rate of foreign tax credit is reached. In this way, the company will preserve the greatest amount of foreign tax credit and so limit the overall amount of tax suffered. In some cases, it will be in the company's interest to arrange matters so that foreign source interest is received into a separate group company to which losses and other amounts can be surrendered by way of group relief as required on a selected basis in order so far as possible to prevent losses and other amounts extinguishing the foreign source income and the related foreign tax credit.

5-27 Foreign tax credits are offset before any advance corporation tax (ACT). ACT is offset against any corporation tax remaining after relief by way of foreign tax credit has been allocated against any item of income (as described above), with the ACT offset limit being the normal limit under TA 1988 s 239(2) or, if lower, the corporation tax liability remaining in respect of that item of income after the foreign tax credit relief[2].

5-28 Before April 1982, a bank was treated as being entitled to full credit for the foreign tax suffered in respect of foreign source interest even though the interest received was not fully taxed as income within Case IV or V but formed part of the income which was taken into account in computing the bank's Case I trading profit. A bank's profit in respect of a given loan – if it were to be notionally isolated from the bank's Case I profit generally but were to take into account the bank's related funding costs – is likely to be such that the foreign tax credit in respect of the interest received exceeds the corporation tax notionally attributable to that isolated profit. Thus, the availability of full relief for foreign tax suffered effectively resulted in tax on UK source profits being relieved by foreign tax credits. Because the effect of this was to divert tax from the UK Exchequer to the borrower's country, the rules as to foreign tax credit relief for banks were amended in 1982[3] and again in 1987[4]. The special provisions in effect only apply to banks and similar financial institutions[5], because it is a condition of the restriction applying that in computing the profits brought into charge to tax which include the foreign source interest there is deductible 'expenditure related to the earning of the foreign loan interest'. Therefore, where an investment company receives foreign loan interest which is effectively relieved by interest paid as a charge on income the restriction appears not to apply, because such interest is paid out of the company's profits brought into charge to corporation tax and is not deductible in computing these profits.

Two restrictions on foreign tax credit are imposed. First, any foreign tax in excess of 15 per cent of the interest is disregarded for the purposes both of computing the taxable profits[6] and of giving credit against UK tax[7]. Second,

---

[2] TA 1988 s 797(4) and (5).
[3] FA 1982 s 65(7).
[4] F (No 2) A 1987 s 67.
[5] The provisions also apply to individuals. TA 1988 s 798(1)(a) applies to 'persons' and in relation to both income tax and corporation tax, although normally the 'persons' affected will be banks.
[6] TA 1988 s 798(5)(b)(ii).
[7] TA 1988 s 798(6)(b).

the foreign tax credit is further limited by treating the foreign loan interest, by reference to which the foreign tax credit is limited by TA 1988 s 797, as reduced by the 'lender's financial expenditure in relation to the loan'[8]. The lender's financial expenditure is, broadly, the lender's funding costs[9], but includes sums paid to the borrower[10] (such as a rebate of a gross-up payment where the lender has obtained credit for foreign tax against UK tax). Where the lender's actual funding costs are not readily ascertainable, perhaps because there is no deposit with or borrowing by the lender which is identifiable as supporting the loan, the costs are to be attributed on a just and reasonable basis having regard to market rates of interest and in the light of regulations[11] made by the Board of Inland Revenue.

SPARED TAX CREDIT

5-29   In some countries legislation provides for an exemption or reduction from the tax imposed on interest on a loan made to a local borrower, particularly where the borrowing is to finance local industrial, commercial or other development. The effect of such a provision is that the foreign borrower may pay interest to a bank resident in the UK without being obliged to deduct local tax from the interest paid and so without suffering an obligation (imposed by the lender) to gross up the interest paid to compensate the lender for the deduction of tax. If this were taken no further, the benefit conferred on the borrower would be entirely at the expense of the local revenue and would benefit the UK Exchequer.

5-30   Because the object of the relief granted in the source country is not to benefit the exchequer of the lender country, several double taxation agreements entered into by the UK incorporate a provision which is designed to preclude the UK Exchequer from enjoying the benefit of the relief from foreign tax. The countries with which these arrangements are made are normally developing countries and are often members of the Commonwealth. The special treatment is not necessarily limited to tax credit in respect of loan interest, but may also extend to tax on business profits earned in the overseas country by a UK resident trader and to tax on dividends derived by a UK resident shareholder from an overseas company.

In the case of interest, the special provisions apply in the operation of the Article of the double taxation agreement which provides for credit to be given against UK tax in respect of tax payable in the other country. Typically, the Article contains a paragraph which defines foreign 'tax payable' as including tax which would have been payable but for an exemption or reduction pursuant to certain legislation in the overseas country concerned. It is beyond the scope of this book to examine the detailed conditions which must be satisfied for the credit to be available, but it should be noted that it is normally necessary not only for the double taxation agreement to contain the appropriate provisions but also for the relevant legislation of the overseas

---

[8]   TA 1988 s 798 (6) (a).
[9]   TA 1988 s 798 (7).
[10]   TA 1988 s 798 (7) (d).
[11]   TA 1988 s 798 (8) and (9) and see the Double Taxation Relief (Taxes on Income) (Foreign Loan Interest) Regulations 1988: SI 1988 No 88.

country to apply to the particular loan or type of loan; the fact that a double taxation agreement includes a 'spared tax' provision, or that it can apply to loan interest, will not mean that spared tax credit will necessarily be available in respect of loans made to borrowers in that country. Changes in the local overseas legislation since the double taxation agreement was entered into might result in the particular exemption or reduction now being available under legislation other than that specified in the agreement. The relevant Article of the agreement might assist in such a case where it provides that spared tax credit is also available where the exemption or reduction falls under other legislation which is agreed by the taxation authorities of both countries to be 'of a substantially similar character'.

The availability of credit provided for under the provisions of a double taxation agreement is always made subject to the requirements of the UK legislation as to foreign tax credit. That 'spared tax' – that is tax not payable – as well as tax actually payable overseas may be credited against UK tax is contemplated by TA 1988 s 788 (5), which permits credit where a double taxation agreement so provides and, broadly, the relief for tax in the overseas country is with a view to promoting industrial, commercial, scientific, educational or other development outside the UK. Spared tax credit is not available in the absence of a double taxation agreement between the UK and the country from which the interest is derived.

5–31 Before 1982, the impact of the availability of spared tax credit was to improve significantly the net after-tax position of a lender, particularly a bank lender where, as has been seen[12], a bank enjoyed the whole of the credit calculated by reference to the gross income although it paid UK tax by reference to its profits after deducting expenditure such as loan interest and deposit interest paid. In the case of spared tax credit, the net after-tax profit of the bank was increased because, unlike the position where overseas tax was actually suffered on the loan interest, the 'surplus' credit which was used against tax notionally attributable to other profits was not required to compensate the bank for any cash loss since no foreign tax was suffered. The way in which spared tax credit relief operated for banks was such that a lender bank which was confident that it would, over the period of the loan, have sufficient taxable profits to absorb the credit not 'used' against the profit notionally attributable to the loan in question would be able to offer to the borrower a reduced interest rate, whilst at the same time achieving a net after-tax profit no lower than would have been realised under a conventional loan.

5–32 The development of spared tax lending before 1982 – particularly having regard to the substantially reduced interest rates offered to certain overseas borrowers – led to a change in the law in 1982 concerning foreign tax credit in relation to spared tax. This only applies in relation to lenders who are entitled to deduct expenditure related to earning the foreign loan interest in computing the profits which are brought into charge to income tax or corporation tax, and so in practice normally only applies to banks[13]. Where such a lender is entitled to credit for spared tax, the foreign loan interest is treated as increased by the amount of the spared tax credit up

[12] §5–28 above.
[13] See also §5–28 above.

to a limit of 15 per cent[14], and the credit available is in any event limited to 15 per cent[15]. The notional increase in the borrower's income effectively neutralises the effect of the spared tax credit.

UNDERLYING TAX CREDIT: RESTRICTIONS

5-33 The restrictions which apply in relation to tax credit in respect of foreign source interest were accompanied by restriction on the availability of relief for underlying tax where a company carrying on a banking or similar[16] business, or a company 'connected' with such a company[17], receives dividends from an overseas company carrying on a business of lending money where if that overseas company had been resident in the UK it would have been entitled to relief for expenditure incurred in making or maintaining a loan. This further restriction was necessary in order to avoid greater relief being available against corporation tax by virtue of the underlying tax credit provisions than would have been available had the resident company received the foreign loan interest direct. Because underlying tax credit relief is available only to companies, this restriction, unlike the 15 per cent limitation on foreign tax credit and provisions in relation to spared tax credit, applies only to companies.

The underlying credit provisions permit a resident company holding 10 per cent or more of the voting power of an overseas company to claim credit for, broadly, the tax suffered on the profits out of which dividends are paid to that company. This might be authorised by a double taxation agreement or, in the case of unilateral relief, by TA 1988 s 790 (6)[18]. That tax might include overseas tax deducted at source from interest paid and, further, might included spared tax. To prevent a company obtaining relief for more credit by the underlying credit system, TA 1988 s 803 provides that where a bank or company carrying on[19] a similar lending business receives dividends from an overseas company:

1   the amount of the underlying tax attributable to tax (whether actual or spared) on loan interest is limited to 15 per cent of the amount of the interest or, if lower, of an amount equal to the excess of the foreign loan interest over what would have been the lender's 'financial expenditure in relation to the loan'[20];
2   the taxable amount of the dividend is reduced by the excess over 15 per cent of any tax actually suffered in respect of foreign loan interest comprised in the profits out of which the dividend is paid; and
3   the taxable amount of the dividend is increased by any spared tax (up to 15 per cent of the foreign loan interest) included in the underlying tax.

---

[14] TA 1988 s 798 (3).
[15] See §**5-28** above.
[16] TA 1988 s 803(10) (b).
[17] TA 1988 s 803(10) (a).
[18] See also TA 1988 ss 799 to 801.
[19] Whether in the UK or elsewhere – TA 1988 s 803(10).
[20] See §**5-28** above.

INTEREST AS 'DIVIDEND' — UNDERLYING TAX

5-34 The provisions under which a company holding 10 per cent or more of the voting power of an overseas company is entitled to credit against corporation tax on dividends received for tax on profits underlying the dividends do not include a definition of 'dividends'. This is the case whether the relief is claimed under the unilateral relief legislation[1] or, normally, under a double taxation agreement; double taxation agreements normally contain a definition of 'dividends', but usually only for the purposes of the Article concerning the tax which may be imposed on dividends in the source country[2], the Article relating to credit for foreign tax being a separate Article.

However, circumstances may arise where, under the law of the source country, interest paid to a UK resident company is treated for taxation purposes as a dividend distribution rather than as interest. Typically, this would be the case where the payer and recipient are associated in some way or where the payer company is so capitalised that it is considered that the taxation treatment of the payer would more properly reflect the payer's economic position if the payment were treated as a distribution out of profits[3]. In such a case a double taxation agreement may permit the interest paid to be treated as an interest payment, although usually the agreement will require the payment to be treated as interest only to the extent that it does not exceed a commercial amount[4].

5-35 Whether or not the interest received is affected by a double taxation agreement, the resident company may nevertheless receive interest which has been treated in the source country as a dividend. This will normally mean that the payment is not allowable as a deduction to reduce taxable profits of the payer company and that a different amount of tax is deducted from the payment by way of withholding than would have been deducted had the payment been interest. In such a case, the recipient company will be subject to corporation tax on the income as interest within either Case IV or Case V and would not strictly be entitled to any credit for underlying tax notwithstanding that the payment is treated as a dividend for the purposes of taxation in the source country. However, it is thought that the Inland Revenue might be prepared to give sympathetic consideration to a claim for relief in respect of the underlying tax as if the payment were in fact a dividend.

RELIEF AGAINST INTEREST

5-36 A company may be entitled to relief against foreign loan interest in the same way as against interest falling within Sch D Case III[5]. Where relief in respect of interest paid as a charge on income is claimed against

---

[1] TA 1988 s 788.
[2] Eg see Article 10.3 of the OECD Model Convention with respect to taxes on income and capital – 'The term "dividends" as used in this Article...'.
[3] Eg see section 385 of the Internal Revenue Code of the USA.
[4] See Chapter 9 Part 1 below as to the position where interest is paid *by* a UK resident company in circumstances where it is treated as a dividend distribution under TA 1988 s 209.
[5] See §4-21 above.

foreign source interest and the interest paid is payable to a non-resident out of the foreign source interest, it is not necessary for the company to have deducted basic rate income tax from the interest paid[6], although an obligation to deduct tax may nevertheless apply[7].

3   Resident trustees and personal representatives

5-37   There is no special rule concerning the taxation of foreign source interest in the hands of personal representatives or trustees. Reference should be made to §§4-22 and 4-23 above as to the taxation of interest in the hands of personal representatives or trustees. Relief by way of credit may be claimed in respect of any foreign tax suffered, whether the interest in question is ultimately taxed in the hands of beneficiaries entitled to the income or in the hands of the trustees. The statutory exemption from tax on yearly interest received by a charity[8] is by concession extended to apply to foreign source bank interest[9].

4   Non-residents

5-38   Persons not resident in the UK are not normally liable to taxation in the UK in respect of foreign source interest, liability to UK taxation being based on the UK residence of the taxpayer or on the income having a UK source. However, a non-resident may be liable to UK taxation in respect of the profits of a trade, profession or vocation carried on in the UK as an individual alone[10], as a company alone[11], or as an individual or company in partnership with others[12]. In these circumstances foreign source interest may be received as part of the income of the business carried on in the UK (eg by a banking business), and so would fall to be included in ascertaining the taxable profits. In the case of a company, the corporation tax net extends more widely, since the definition of 'chargeable profits' of a non-resident company trading in the UK through a branch or agency includes not only 'trading income arising directly or indirectly through or from a branch or agency', but also 'any income from property or rights used by, or held by, or for, the branch or agency....'[13]. Consequently, interest on surplus funds of the UK business held on a deposit account maintained outside the UK could fall within the definition of 'chargeable profits'.

5-39   A non-resident and non-domiciled individual liable to income tax in respect of profits of a trade, profession or vocation carried on in the UK is not taxed on the remittance basis in respect of foreign source interest received as part of the income of that business. This is because the profits

---

[6] See TA 1988 s 338 (4) (d) and TA 1988 s 65 (1) (b).
[7] See Chapter 7 Part I below.
[8] TA 1988 s 505 (1) (c)(ii).
[9] Extra-statutory Concession B9.
[10] TA 1988 s 18 (1) (a)(iii).
[11] TA 1988 s 11 (1).
[12] TA 1988 ss 112 (2) and 115(4).
[13] TA 1988 s 11 (2) (a).

are taxed under Sch D Case I or II and the remittance basis only applies to income taxed under Case IV or V[14].

A company is domiciled outside the UK where its place of incorporation is outside the UK[15]. As explained above[16], a non-resident company may be liable to corporation tax in respect of foreign source interest related to, but not forming part of the income of, a trade carried on in the UK. That interest would be assessed under Case IV or V as appropriate[17], although the applicable Case will not affect the amount of tax payable. However, even where the company is not domiciled in the UK the remittance basis will not be available to it. Although for corporation tax purposes the income is computed under Case IV or V[18], the amount taxable is the full amount of income arising in the accounting period whether or not received in or transmitted to the UK[19].

RELIEF FOR FOREIGN TAX SUFFERED

5–40 Generally, relief by way of credit for overseas tax is only available against UK income tax or corporation tax where the taxpayer is resident in the UK[20], whether the credit is available under the provisions of a double taxation agreement or by way of unilateral relief. This does not normally give rise to any hardship since non-residents trading in the UK will normally be able to arrange that any foreign source income arises otherwise than through the UK trading establishment. However, UK branches of overseas banks are in a different position from other non-residents trading in the UK because they will regularly make loans internationally; London is a major financial centre, and in many cases it will be more convenient for overseas banks to lend through their London branches (rather than through their separate UK resident subsidiaries) having regard to the assets base of, and banking ratios as they apply to, those branches.

5–41 Consequently, there is an exception to the general rule laid down by TA 1988 s 794(1) that a taxpayer must be resident to obtain relief by way of credit for overseas tax. The relief only applies to tax *paid* – and so does not include spared tax – under the law of an overseas country in respect of interest on a loan made through the UK taxable branch or agency through which the non-resident carries on a *banking* business. The relief only applies to banks; there is no definition of 'banking business', although in practice it is likely to be regarded as applying to those non-residents which are regarded as carrying on a bona fide banking business in the UK[1]. Moreover, the tax must be suffered in a country other than one where the bank is liable to tax by reason of domicile, residence or place of management; this condition is applied not by reference to the *tax* imposed on the bank but by reference to the *country* where the tax is imposed, so that a withholding

---

[14] TA 1988 s 65, and §5–06 above.
[15] *Gasque v IRC* [1940] 2 KB 80, 23 TC 210.
[16] §5–38.
[17] See §3–21 as to the distinction between the Cases.
[18] See TA 1988 s 70(1).
[19] See TA 1988 ss 70(1), 12(1) and 9(6).
[20] TA 1988 s 794(1).
[1] For the purposes of eg TA 1988 s 349(3)(a).

tax suffered on loan interest paid from the country of the bank's residence will not be creditable even though the tax suffered does not depend on the bank being resident in that country.

5–42   The credit to which a non-resident branch bank is entitled is also limited to the tax which would have been suffered if the bank had been resident in the UK. This means that if the tax suffered in respect of loan interest payable from the overseas country in question to a UK resident bank would be limited to, say, 10 per cent under the double taxation agreement between the UK and the overseas country, the branch of a non-resident bank will be limited to credit at the rate of 10 per cent even though a higher rate of tax may in fact be suffered because of the absence of, or by reason of the terms of, a double taxation agreement between the overseas country and the country of residence of the bank. On the other hand, credit will only be available for tax actually suffered, so that if the branch bank only suffers tax at the rate of 10 per cent but a UK resident bank would have suffered tax at a higher rate, credit will only be available at the rate of 10 per cent.

The special limitations on foreign tax credit relief apply to branches of non-resident banks as they apply to resident banks[2]. Any tax suffered which may not be relieved by credit by reason of either of the limitations described above may be relieved by deduction[3].

DOUBLE TAXATION AGREEMENTS

5–43   A double taxation agreement, but normally only an agreement between the UK and the country of residence of the recipient, might provide some relief from UK taxation. However, in *IRC v. Commerzbank AG*[4], a German bank carrying on business through a UK branch was held to be entitled to exemption from UK tax on United States source interest, by reason of the terms of the UK/United States Double Taxation Agreement then in force. This arose from the wording of that Agreement, which is no longer applicable but which previously prevented the UK from taxing United States source interest except in the hands of a UK resident.

Although credit relief for foreign tax is normally only available to UK residents, the non-discrimination clause of a double taxation agreement might be available to permit the non-resident (taxable in respect of a UK permanent establishment business, other than a UK branch bank) to obtain credit for foreign tax on loan interest in the same way as a UK resident enterprise would be entitled.

RELIEF AGAINST INTEREST

5–44   A non-resident company or individual may be entitled to relief against foreign loan interest in the same way as relief is available against other income

---

[2] See §§**5–28** and **5–32** above.
[3] TA 1988 s 811; see §**5–16** above.
[4] [1990] STC 285.

including interest falling within Sch D Case III[5]. For example, a non-resident company carrying on a branch or agency trade in the UK and also being taxable in respect of foreign loan interest as part of the company's 'chargeable profits'[6] may have trading losses available for relief against that interest under TA 1988 s 393 (2).

NON-RESIDENT DISCRETIONARY TRUSTS

5-45 Although non–resident trustees of a discretionary or accumulation trust may be subject to the additional rate of income tax in respect of UK source income[7], this does not apply in relation to foreign source income.

---

[5] See §§**4–16** and **4–21** above.
[6] See TA 1988 s 11.
[7] See §**4–39** above.

Chapter 6

TAXATION OF INTEREST WITHIN SCHEDULE C

6-01   This chapter is concerned with the system under which interest is taxed under Sch C. Part 3 of Chapter 3 describes the interest which falls within Sch C, and it will be apparent from that description that Sch C does not so much establish a code for the taxation of certain types or classes of interest, but is more concerned with providing a system for the collection of basic rate income tax by deduction in particular circumstances where certain classes of interest and other 'public revenue dividends' are paid or collected; these circumstances are, principally[1], concerned with the payments of interest made in the UK and the collection of interest through an agent in the UK.

THE SYSTEM IN OUTLINE

6-02   TA 1988 s 17(1) sets out the income to which, and the circumstances in which, the Sch C provisions apply, and Sch 3 to that Act provides the machinery for collection and assessment of income tax at the basic rate[2].

6-03   Where an individual receives interest within Sch C net of basic rate income tax, the interest is treated as part of the individual's total income and may be liable to higher rate income tax on the current year basis[3]. As with interest within Sch D (either Case III[4] or Case IV or V[5]) where it is received under deduction of basic rate income tax, interest within Sch C is always assessed on the current year basis rather than the preceding year basis. Any income tax in excess of the basic rate tax deducted from the interest paid to the taxpayer is payable on or before 1 December following the year of assessment for which the interest is assessed or, if later, thirty days after the issue of the notice of assessment[6]. Where, by reason of personal reliefs or otherwise, the income tax suffered by deduction exceeds the tax for which the recipient is liable, a repayment claim may be made after the end of the year of assessment.

Where interest on any UK government securities is not paid under deduction of income tax but is taxed under Sch D Case III[7] that interest

---

[1] The provisions of TA 1988 s 17(1) Sch C para 2, relating to payments in the Republic of Ireland, are an exception.
[2] See TA 1988 Sch 3 paras 1(c) and 6A(2).
[3] See TA 1988 s 835(6)(a).
[4] See §4-04 above.
[5] See §5-09 above.
[6] TA 1988 s 5(4).
[7] See §3-35 above.

will be charged to tax on the preceding year basis[8]. If such securities are exchanged for securities on which interest is paid under deduction of income tax the closing years rules would apply[9]; moreover, if in the year in which the exchange takes place the aggregate amount of interest taxable exceeds one full year's interest on the first holding of securities, the taxpayer may claim to have the excess taxed to higher rate income tax and his marginal rate of income tax calculated excluding the amount of the excess, and otherwise to have the excess disregarded in computing his total income for the year[10]. Such a claim may also be made where a taxpayer applies for interest on certain government securities, formerly paid gross, to be paid under deduction of income tax[11], although such a change should not result in an increased amount of interest being chargeable in the year of the change because the closing years rules would apply[12].

Where interest within Sch C is received by a company and is chargeable to corporation tax, the interest is taxable in respect of the accounting period in which it is received, the company being entitled to credit for the income tax deducted at source which may be set against the company's corporation tax liability for the period or recovered[13] or, in the case of a resident company, set against any income tax for which the company is liable in respect of interest and other payments made[14].

6-04   Although it might otherwise fall within Sch C, there is a general exemption[15] from the application of Sch C in respect of half-yearly interest and other dividends payable by the Bank of England, the Bank of Ireland or National Debt Commissioners which does not exceed £2.50. Such interest then falls within Sch D Case III[16] and, being paid gross, is generally assessed on the preceding year basis. This exemption does not apply to interest and other public revenue dividends payable by overseas governments or public authorities.

Government stock held on the National Savings Stock Register is held in the name of the National Debt Commissioners, and interest on such stock paid to them is exempt from tax under Sch C[17]. Interest paid to investors in respect of such stock on the Register is not subject to tax under Sch C because such interest is paid by the Director of Savings[18] rather than by the National Debt Commissioners in whose name the stock is held, and the obligation to deduct tax in TA 1988 Sch 3 para 2 (2) does not apply to the Director of Savings. Such interest is therefore paid gross, and is subject to tax under Sch D Case III[19].

---

[8] See §4-04 above.
[9] TA 1988 s 67, and see §4-07 above.
[10] TA 1988 s 52 (1).
[11] See TA 1988 ss 50 (2) and 52(2); and §3-35 above.
[12] TA 1988 s 67 (2), and §4-07 above.
[13] TA 1988 ss 7 (2) and 11(3).
[14] TA 1988 Sch 16 para 5, and see §§7-11 and 7-12 below.
[15] TA 1988 s 17 (1) Sch C para 5.
[16] See TA 1988 s 18 (1) (b) Sch D, Case III(c).
[17] TA 1988 s 49 (1).
[18] Regulations 21 and 22, the National Savings Stock Register Regulations 1976: SI 1976 No 2012.
[19] See TA 1988 s 18((1) (b) Sch D Case III(c).

INTEREST PAYABLE IN THE UK

6-05   Where interest which amounts to 'public revenue dividends' is payable in the UK, the Sch C charge normally applies[20]. Such interest could be interest on UK or foreign government securities or interest paid by overseas public or municipal authorities, but not interest paid by local and other non-governmental authorities in the UK[1]. Where a foreign government or public authority raises funds through an issue of bonds, notes or other securities – particularly where the funds are raised in sterling or are listed on the London Stock Exchange – the issuer will normally appoint a paying agent in the UK to be responsible for making payments of interest; in those circumstances the Sch C charge will apply to the interest paid through that paying agent.

6-06   The deduction of tax does not apply to interest which is exempt from tax by reason of its being paid on securities held by non-residents and being either

1   UK government securities issued subject to a condition that they should be exempt from tax while held by persons not ordinarily resident in the UK[2], or
2   securities of any 'state or territory' outside the UK where the person owning the security is not resident in the UK[3].

As to the former, the government has not for some years issued securities subject to that condition[4], but interest on certain securities issued before March 1977 subject to that condition continues to be exempt from UK tax when held by non-ordinarily resident persons. Before such interest may be paid gross, the holder of the securities must apply to the Inland Revenue (Claims Division) and show that the condition is satisfied[5]. Where securities are held by a trust and the beneficiary entitled as of right to the income is not ordinarily resident in the UK the exemption may be available[6]. By concession, the exemption is also available where the interest forms part of the residuary income of the estate of a deceased person where the residuary legatee is neither resident nor ordinarily resident in the UK[7]. Where the interest is paid out of a discretionary trust to a non-resident beneficiary, he may be able to reclaim the tax from the Inland Revenue[8]. The exemption is not available where the beneficial owner of the security is a non-ordinarily resident person but where the income is deemed to be the income of a resident person (eg under TA 1988 s 739)[9].

---

[20]   TA 1988 s 17(1) Sch C para 1.
[1]   See §3-33 above.
[2]   TA 1988 s 47(1).
[3]   TA 1988 s 48(1); note that, for this purpose, foreign consular offices and employees in the UK are treated as not being resident in the UK – TA 1988 s 322(1).
[4]   House of Commons Written Answer, 18 March 1977, Vol 928, col 351.
[5]   See §6-18 below.
[6]   See *Baker v Archer-Shee* [1927] AC 844, 11 TC 749, HL and *Archer-Shee v Garland* [1931] AC 212, 15 TC 693, HL.
[7]   Extra-statutory Concession A14.
[8]   Extra-statutory Concession B18.
[9]   TA 1988 s 47(3).

So far as the second type of security is concerned, it is specifically provided[10] that a beneficiary under a trust who is able to require the trustee to transfer the securities to him free from the trust is deemed to be a person owning the securities for the purpose of claiming the exemption. Yet, this special provision does not prevent the application of the general rule that the exemption can be claimed where the non-resident beneficiary is entitled to the income as of right, even though he may not be able to require the securities themselves to be transferred to him[11]. A non-resident residuary legatee may also claim the exemption in respect of interest forming part of the residuary income of an estate[12]; a non-resident beneficiary receiving a distribution from a discretionary trust may be able to reclaim any tax deducted[13].

The expression 'state or territory', although seemingly narrower than the expression 'government... public authority or institution' in the definition of 'public revenue' as it applies for the purpose of the definition of 'overseas public revenue dividends'[14], is in practice treated as including public authorities or institutions, so that interest within the expression 'overseas public revenue dividends' can generally qualify for the exemption in the hands of non-residents.

Interest on securities of foreign states is excluded from Sch C, and therefore not subject to deduction of UK tax when paid in the UK, if the securities are held in a recognised clearing system[15].

6-07 Interest within Sch C may also be exempt from tax by virtue of a double taxation agreement between the UK and the country of residence of the recipient of the interest. This may arise where UK source interest is specifically exempt from UK tax in the hands of the recipient[16], or where the interest arises on non-UK government securities and falls within the category of income not specifically mentioned in the double taxation agreement and is so exempt from UK tax in the hands of a resident of the other territory[17]. In the case of interest on UK government securities issued after 1977, a non-resident will need to rely on a double taxation agreement if the interest is to be exempt from UK taxation[18]; in practice, a recipient is unlikely to need to rely on a double taxation agreement in the case of interest on securities of foreign states[19] unless the recipient is technically resident in both the UK and another country but is a resident of the other country (and not of the UK) for the purpose of the relevant double taxation agreement.

---

10 TA 1988 s 48 (2).
11 See note 6 above.
12 Extra statutory Concession A14.
13 Extra-statutory Concession B18.
14 TA 1988 s 45.
15 Euro-clear, CEDEL or First Chicago Clearing System; see TA 1988 s 48 (4).
16 Eg see Article 11 of the UK/USA Double Taxation Agreement: SI 1980 No 568; in some cases, the interest may only be subject to a reduced rate of tax – see §4-29 above.
17 Eg see Article 22 of the UK/USA Double Taxation Agreement.
18 See §6-06 above.
19 See §6-06(2) above.

MACHINERY OF DEDUCTION

6-08 The machinery for the deduction of tax under Sch C is set out in TA 1988 Sch 3. The person in the UK responsible for paying the interest – being the Bank of England, the Bank of Ireland at its office in Belfast or the National Debt Commissioners[20], or any other person acting as paying agent in the UK in respect of the payment of interest out of the public revenue of Northern Ireland or of any overseas government or other public authority[1] – must deduct basic rate income tax and pay it over to the Inland Revenue[2] unless payment is made on foreign securities shown to be held in a recognised clearing system[3] or the non-resident holder of the securities has qualified to receive interest gross[4].

Where interest is paid on securities issued by an overseas government or public authority through a paying agent in the UK, the securities may be held by a non-resident who has not made, or is not able to make, a claim for exemption[5] or by a resident person at an address outside the UK. A paying agent, other than the Bank of England[6], may not be required to deduct tax in those circumstances because, notwithstanding the wide language of Sch C para 1, Sch 3 para 6(1)(a), which establishes who is a 'chargeable person' for the purpose of the machinery of collection of income tax, refers to the payment of interest and other 'dividends' out of any public revenue other than that of the UK or Northern Ireland 'to any persons *in the United Kingdom*'. Consequently, the payment by a UK paying agent of foreign source interest within Sch C to a person who is not present[7] in the UK does not require the deduction of tax. This language in para 6(1)(a) is similar to language in TA 1988 s 123 (2) which relates to the payment by a UK paying agent of interest and other 'foreign dividends' to 'any persons in the United Kingdom'. It is not clear what is a 'person in the United Kingdom'. In practice, the Inland Revenue does not require tax to be deducted in the case of interest within Sch C where

1   payment is made direct to an address abroad (including a foreign branch of a UK bank), and
2   the paying agent does not recognise that the payment is being made to or for the account of a person in the UK[8], and
3   in the case of registered issues, the registered address of the holder of the security is outside the UK and the paying agent does not recognise the registered holder as a person in the UK.

---

[20] TA 1988 Sch 3 para 2.
[1] TA 1988 Sch 3 para 6(1)(a).
[2] TA 1988 Sch 3 paras 3 and 6A.
[3] TA 1988 s 48 (4).
[4] See §§**6-18** to **6-20** below.
[5] Under TA 1988 s 48, see §**6-06 (2)** above.
[6] The Bank of England is required to deduct income tax by TA 1988 Sch 3 para 2 (2)(c), irrespective of whether the recipient is a person 'in the United Kingdom'. In practice, the Bank of England pays interest gross to persons not 'in the United Kingdom' in the limited circumstances of certain securities where it has taken over as paying agent from another person.
[7] There is no mention of *residence*.
[8] The Inland Revenue guidelines do not indicate what is regarded as 'a person in the United Kingdom'.

6-09 The Inland Revenue operates two concessionary practices in the case of payments by a UK paying agent of interest which falls within Sch C. First, a payment of interest may be made gross to a bank in the UK where it is recognised by the Inland Revenue as carrying on a bona fide banking business, provided that the bank certifies in each case that it owns the security in question and that it is beneficially entitled to the interest. Second[9], funds for the payment of interest may be transferred by a principal paying agent in the UK to sub-paying agents without deduction of tax and without evidence of non-residence where the sub-paying agents are appointed by the issuer of the securities and not merely by the principal paying agent; a sub-paying agent in the UK remains subject to the Sch C procedures when making payments to holders of securities. Where the principal paying agent appoints sub-paying agents, funds may be transferred gross by the principal paying agent to a sub-paying agent in the UK so long as the principal paying agent ensures that the sub-paying agent is aware of its obligations under Sch C and makes returns to the Inland Revenue.

These practices do not apply in relation to the collection of income tax in relation to coupons for interest[10].

6-10 No income tax is deducted from payments of interest made by the Bank of England, the Bank of Ireland or the National Debt Commissioners on any securities in the name of the official custodian for charities or where the Bank of England receives a certificate from the Charity Commissioners that the interest is subject only to charitable trusts and is exempt from tax[11].

6-11 The obligations of paying agents in relation to returns and accounting for income tax are summarised in §**10-06** below.

INTEREST PAYABLE IN THE REPUBLIC OF IRELAND

6-12 Where interest is paid in the Republic of Ireland in respect of UK government securities entered on the register of the Bank of Ireland in Dublin, tax must normally be deducted under Sch C[12]. The procedure for collection of the tax is that the interest due to be paid is first transferred to the Bank of England which deducts tax at the basic rate and then pays the balance to the Bank of Ireland for payment to the holders of the securities[13]. In this case, it is the Bank of England which is responsible for collecting the tax.

COLLECTION OF INTEREST THROUGH COUPONS

6-13 Interest on securities issued by overseas governments and public authorities will, if the securities are in bearer form, be paid by means of

---

[9] This treatment applies to Sch C income whether or not it is interest.
[10] Described in §§**6-13** to **6-16** below.
[11] TA 1988 Sch 3 para 4.
[12] TA 1988 s 17(1) Sch C para 2.
[13] TA 1988 Sch 3 para 2(3).

coupons. The coupons attached to the securities when the securities are issued will be detached and presented for payment by a paying agent on the due date for the payment of the interest. However, the paying agent may be outside the UK, in which case a coupon holder may obtain payment by handing the coupon to a banker or other person in the UK and requesting him to obtain payment of the interest from the paying agent abroad. In other cases, a person receiving payment of foreign source interest within Sch C may receive a warrant or bill of exchange for payment in foreign currency of the interest, and may deliver it to a UK bank to obtain payment of the instrument overseas. The Sch C charge applies in these circumstances[14], and, indeed, applies irrespective of the residence or presence in the UK of the holder of the 'coupon' (subject to any special exemption which may be claimed by reason of the coupon holder not being resident in the UK) where the person collecting payment of the interest is 'a person in the United Kingdom'[15]. The Sch C charge also applies where the securities in respect of which the interest is collected are held in a 'recognised clearing system', because, the recognised clearing systems being outside the UK, interest will have been paid gross to the clearing system even if paid by a UK paying agent[16].

The Inland Revenue considers that a person 'obtains payment'

1   where he receives payment of the interest, or
2   where he either presents coupons in respect of bearer securities to a foreign paying agent or the coupons are passed, directly or indirectly, to a person abroad who acts as his agent for the purpose of presentation to a foreign paying agent whether or not he receives payment.

It seems doubtful whether the mere passive receipt by a bank or other person of interest on behalf of a third party amounts to the bank or other person 'obtaining payment'. Certainly, this may be the case where a bank receives a dividend warrant which it then presents for payment, but not where an amount in respect of interest is paid to a bank on behalf of the owner of the security when the bank has not played an active role in obtaining payment.

In practice, a bank which obtains payment of interest and other dividends on behalf of an authorised unit trust – whether or not the bank itself is the trustee of the trust – is normally permitted not to deduct income tax. This results in part from an interpretation of the position where the bank is the trustee and in part from an extension of that practice to other cases where the bank is not the trustee[17]. It was at one time proposed that this practice should be discontinued so that tax would be deducted by a bank obtaining payment of interest and other dividends on behalf of a unit trust, whether or not it was the trustee, but the government abandoned its intention

---

14   The expression coupon includes warrants for or bills of exchange purporting to be drawn or made in payment of any 'overseas public revenue dividends' TA 1988 s 45.
15   See TA 1988 s 17(1) Sch C para 3(a).
16   TA 1988 s 17(1) Sch C para 3(b).
17   See paragraphs 9 and 10 of Inland Revenue Consultative Document, 'The Paying and Collecting Agent Rules etc', September 1982, [1982] STI 434 at p 436.

to legislate on this point[18]. It is understood that this practice is also applied to managers and trustees of authorised unit trusts which are not banks.

By concession, a collecting agent may be specifically authorised by the Inland Revenue to pay interest gross to an approved pension fund or a charity.

6-14 In the case of the collection of interest through coupons, the person chargeable with income tax at the basic rate and required to deduct it from the payment made to the coupon holder is the banker or other person obtaining payment. That person must make returns to the Inland Revenue and account for the tax deducted in the same way as a paying agent who deducts tax from interest payable to persons in the UK on securities issued by overseas governments or public authorities[19].

DEALINGS IN COUPONS

6-15 The arrangements described in §§**6-13** and **6-14** above would not enable tax to be collected where the coupon holder, instead of using a bank to collect payment of the interest on his behalf, either asks the bank to sell the coupons for him and account to him for the proceeds of sale, or simply sells the coupons to the bank or another dealer in coupons[20]. It is therefore provided that tax must be collected in either of these cases where the bank or dealer in coupons is 'in the United Kingdom' (irrespective of the location of the coupon holder), so that tax is collected either before the bank (acting as agent for the coupon holder) accounts for the proceeds of sale of the coupon or when a dealer in coupons pays the price for the coupons purchased[1]. The latter deduction does not apply where the dealer buys the coupon from a banker or another dealer in coupons; this does not provide a loophole in the system, since the banker or dealer – bankers probably being dealers in coupons for this purpose – would deduct tax on paying the purchase price on the initial purchase from the coupon holder. However, there could be a double deduction of tax (eg where a dealer who has purchased coupons (and deducted tax) obtains payment of interest through a bank in circumstances that the bank must deduct tax[2]), and in that case the tax deducted on the subsequent occasion may be repaid on a claim being made to the Inland Revenue[3].

The machinery of collection of tax in those circumstances operates in the same way as it does for paying agents[4], the bank or dealer in coupons being charged with the tax and obliged to make returns[5].

[18] See Written Answer on behalf of Chancellor of the Exchequer, HC Deb, 5 May 1983, Vol 42, col 113 – [1983] STI 219-220.
[19] TA 1988 Sch 3 paras 6A to 6F and 11 to 14; see §**10-06** below.
[20] Coupons on bearer securities can themselves normally be traded as bearer securities, and bills of exchange may similarly be sold.
[1] TA 1988 s 17(1) Sch C para 4.
[2] §**6-13** above.
[3] TA 1988 Sch 3 para 12.
[4] See §**6-11** above.
[5] TA 1988 Sch 3 para 6(1)(d); see §**10-06** below.

NON-RESIDENTS: COUPONS

6-16   A person entitled to an exemption in respect of foreign source interest prima facie within Sch C by reason of his non-residence[6] will be entitled to exemption whether the interest is paid by a UK paying agent or is collected in respect of or by means of sales of coupons[7].

NON-RESIDENTS: PROCEDURE FOR CLAIMS FOR EXEMPTION

6-17   Where the securities in question are in registered form, and where, in the case of UK government securities, the interest is payable gross where the recipient is not ordinarily resident in the UK[8], the non-resident may claim payment of interest without deduction of income tax by applying to the Inspector of Foreign Dividends[9]. Where the Inspector is satisfied as to the applicant's non-residence, authority will be given to the paying agent to make payment without deducting tax under Sch C. The Inspector of Foreign Dividends will require completion of an application for continuation of the exemption from time to time, failing which the authority to pay gross may be cancelled. The authority may similarly be cancelled where there is any alteration in the registration of the security unless the authority is renewed.

6-18   It is also possible for a banker or stockbroker in the UK to obtain payment gross of interest on registered securities (both exempt UK government securities and overseas securities) under the 'E' Arrangement without applying for authority to be issued by the Inspector of Foreign Dividends, where the securities in question are held in a block account as nominee on behalf of customers of the banker or stockbroker who are neither resident nor ordinarily resident in the UK. An authorised signatory of the banker or stockbroker must complete and lodge with the Inspector of Foreign Dividends a form[10] in respect of each payment of interest received gross; that form sets out information designed to satisfy the Inspector of Foreign Dividends that payment gross is justified, and requires the banker or stockbroker in the UK to undertake to refund to the Inland Revenue any income tax not deducted which results from any inaccurate statement on the form.

6-19   In the case of bearer securities, a non-resident owner of the securities may complete a form[11] claiming payment of interest gross; the form must be presented to the person in the UK from whom payment gross is sought by a banker or merchant in the UK who must also present a completed

---

[6] See §§**6-06(2)** and **6-07** above.
[7] See §§**6-13** to **6-15** above.
[8] See §**6-06(1)** above.
[9] On Form A3 (or Form A2 where interest is payable by means of coupons).
[10] Form C9 in the case of UK government securities, and Form C4 in the case of other securities.
[11] Form A in the case of foreign source interest payable gross to a non-resident person or Form A2 in the case of interest on UK government securities payable gross to a non-ordinarily resident person.

Form B undertaking to refund the Inland Revenue any income tax erroneously not deducted from that payment.

Claims for payment gross may be made on behalf of the non-resident by a banker outside the UK where the banker is authorised to do so by the Inland Revenue. Such claims may be made in respect of coupons on UK government securities[12] or coupons on securities issued by overseas governments or public authorities[13], and must be lodged with the person making payment by a banker or merchant in the UK who must also lodge a Form B undertaking to refund any income tax erroneously not deducted.

Claims may also be made on behalf of non-residents by bankers or merchants in the UK where payment of interest is being made on presentation of coupons on bearer securities[14] or where coupons are purchased or interest on coupons is collected abroad[15]. Similarly, claims may be made by a banker, merchant, solicitor, law agent or trust company in the UK on behalf of a non-ordinarily resident person entitled to payment of interest on UK government securities without deduction of income tax under TA 1988 s 47 where the securities are in bearer form or where the interest on registered bonds is payable by means of coupons[16]. In these cases, the claim must be signed by an authorised officer who has sufficient information available to complete the details of the form as to the non-resident's circumstances, and the claimant must undertake to refund to the Inland Revenue any income tax not deducted by reason of any inaccuracy in the completion of the claim form.

Although some of the forms for claiming payment gross refer to payment of interest (and other 'dividends') by means of 'coupons', those forms are also used where payment of interest does not require presentation of a coupon but merely requires presentation of evidence of ownership of the bearer security.

6-20 In cases where these procedures are not applicable but where the non-resident claims payment gross (eg by reason of a double taxation agreement[17]) the non-resident should make application to the Inspector of Foreign Dividends on the appropriate claim form[18].

INTERACTION OF SCH C WITH SCH D

6-21 Interest which is taxable under Sch C cannot fall within Sch D also, and since income taxed under Sch C is taxed by deduction before it is received by the taxpayer it is excluded from Sch D even where it is income of a trade carried on by the taxpayer[19]. This should be contrasted with the position where income falls within more than one Case of Sch D, in which

[12] Form D1.
[13] Form D.
[14] Form C.
[15] Form C3. Under the 'F' arrangement, coupon dealers may make payments gross to UK banks which may then make payment gross to foreign customers provided that Form C3 has been completed.
[16] Form C6.
[17] See §**6-07** above.
[18] See §**7-19** below.
[19] *Thompson v Trust and Loan Co of Canada* [1932] 1 KB 517, 16 TC 394, CA.

circumstances the Crown has the option as to the Case under which the income should be assessed[20]. In this way, the treatment of interest within Sch C differs from the treatment of interest chargeable under Sch D Case III, IV or V which can also be treated as income of a banking trade chargeable under Case I. However, it is specifically provided that where interest falls within Sch C relief may be available against it in respect of carried forward trading losses where the interest would have been treated as a receipt of the trade had it not been taxed under Sch C[1].

6-22   Where the interest in question, although prima facie falling within Sch C, is not subject to tax by reason of the exemption available to non-residents, does that interest fall to be taxed under Sch D Case I where the interest is income of a trade carried on in the UK through a branch or agency? Before the law changed, that question was answered in the negative by the House of Lords in *Hughes v Bank of New Zealand Ltd*[2]; it was held that the exemption applied generally and not only to the charge to tax under Sch C.

As a result of that decision, the Treasury's power to issue securities subject to the condition that interest thereon should be free from tax in the hands of non-ordinarily resident persons[3] was amended[4] to enable a qualification to be imposed to prevent the exemption applying so as to exclude the interest from the computation of profits of a trade or business carried on by the non-resident in the UK; further, it is provided[5] that, in computing the profits of a banking business, an insurance business or a business of dealing in securities carried on in the UK by a non-resident, interest on securities issued by overseas states or territories should be included notwithstanding the exemption in TA 1988 s 48[6]. It therefore remains necessary, in the appropriate cases, to consider whether such interest income would, apart from the exemption, fall to be included in computing the profits of the business carried on in the UK. An example of this can be seen in *Owen (Inspector of Taxes) v Sassoon* [7] where a non-resident Lloyd's underwriter claimed that interest on certain UK and overseas government securities – in respect of which exemption from tax under Sch C had been granted – should not be treated as part of the income of his underwriting business where the securities were deposited as security against his default as an underwriter; it was held that the interest did form part of that income, since the capital from which the income was derived was employed and risked in the business.

In order to reverse another aspect of the decision in the *Bank of New Zealand* case, it is also provided[8] that where in computing the profits of a banking, insurance or security-dealing business carried on by a non-resident in the UK there is excluded from the computation any interest received

[20] See *Liverpool and London and Globe Insurance Co v Bennett* [1913] AC 610, TC 327, HL and §**3-27** above.
[1] TA 1988 ss 385(4) and 393(8).
[2] [1938] 1 All ER 778, 21 TC 472, HL.
[3] See §**6-06(1)** above.
[4] FA 1940 s 60(1).
[5] FA 1940 s 21(1), now TA 1988 ss 474(1) and 445(8)(a).
[6] See §**6-06(2)** above.
[7] [1951] 1 Lloyd's Rep 266, (1951) 32 TC 101.
[8] TA 1988 ss 474(2) and 475 – originally FA 1940 s 21(2).

on UK government securities, there shall also be excluded any expenses (including interest) and profits or losses attributable to the acquisition, holding or any transactions in the securities. This provision is necessary because it was considered that the basis on which exempt government securities had been issued before 1940 could not be changed, but if income were to be excluded from the charge to tax then any related expenditure should also be excluded to prevent the taxpayer obtaining a deduction for expenditure related to non-taxable income. A similar provision applies in relation to the computation of profits of overseas life assurance companies carrying on business in the UK[9].

INTEREST DERIVED FROM THE REPUBLIC OF IRELAND

6-23 Where interest payable out of the public revenue of the Republic of Ireland is payable to persons in the UK it is taken out of Sch C and the collection machinery which would otherwise apply, and it is charged under Sch D Case IV or V. This special treatment only applies so long as the paying agent delivers to the Inland Revenue details of the interest, the names and addresses of recipients and the amounts received by each recipient[10].

CREDIT FOR OVERSEAS TAX

6-24 Where there is a requirement that UK tax is deducted by a paying agent or otherwise in relation to the collection of foreign source interest taxable under Sch C, a deduction may already have been made in respect of tax imposed by the country where the interest had its source. The Inland Revenue publishes a list of countries from which interest etc may be received subject to deduction of local tax for which credit may be given by the paying or collecting agent and the maximum amount of credit which may be given against the basic rate income tax to be accounted for by the UK paying or collecting agent[11]. In the event that the permitted amount for which credit may be given by the agent is exceeded by the overseas tax in fact suffered at source, an adjustment is made when the income is assessed.

---

9 TA 1988 s 445 (8) (b).
10 TA 1988 Sch 3 para 13.
11 Inland Revenue Circular to Paying Agents and Collecting Agents, 1 July 1991.

Chapter 7

INTEREST CHARGEABLE UNDER SCHEDULE D: DEDUCTION OF INCOME TAX AT SOURCE

7-01 Historically[1] it has been the policy of the income tax legislation to collect income tax in respect of recurring payments by deduction, normally at the source of the payment by requiring the person making the payment to make a deduction on account of income tax. The procedures insofar as they apply to interest falling within Sch C are explained in Chapter 6. This chapter is concerned with the collection of basic rate income tax from certain payments of interest falling within Sch D, namely yearly interest chargeable under Case III, most payments of mortgage interest and foreign source interest chargeable under Case IV or V.

1 Yearly interest chargeable under Case III: TA 1988 s 349 (2)

7-02 Before considering the present law, it should be noted that the present system of deducting income tax at source has only existed since 1969[2]. Before then, interest fell to be treated in the same way as annual payments and annuities and was subject to deduction of income tax under the predecessors of TA 1988 ss 348 and 349 (1). There was a material difference between the circumstances where the payer was merely entitled to deduct an amount equivalent to income tax from a payment of yearly interest under the deduction and retention procedure, and those where the payer was bound to deduct and account for income tax because the interest (whether or not yearly interest) was not wholly payable out of profits brought into charge to income tax[3]. In this connection, interest paid by companies had, since 1965, been subject to an obligation to deduct income tax because from that year the profits of companies were brought into charge to corporation tax rather than income tax[4]. There have only been two decided cases concerned with deduction of income tax under the post-1969 legislation[5] and those have been limited to considering whether the payments in question were interest[6]. Care should be taken in relation to the present application of decisions in the earlier cases where the issues concerned not only whether the payment in question

---

[1] See Chapter 1.
[2] FA 1969 s 26.
[3] See, generally, Chapter 1 above; in particular, §1-10.
[4] See §1-13 above.
[5] *Re Euro Hotel (Belgravia) Ltd* [1975] STC 682, [1975] 3 All ER 1075 and *Chevron Petroleum (UK) Ltd v BP Petroleum Development Ltd* [1981] STC 689.
[6] See §§2-10 and 2-16 above.

was interest or yearly interest but also whether there was a right or an obligation to deduct tax.

7–03 The obligation to deduct tax from certain payments of interest is now principally set out in TA 1988 s 349 (2). There is also a right for certain borrowers to deduct income tax from payments of interest on mortgage advances to finance house purchases, but this is considered separately[7].

INTEREST SUBJECT TO DEDUCTION

7–04 The deduction obligation under s 349 (2) applies only to 'yearly interest of money chargeable to tax under Case III of Schedule D'. Chapter 2 considers what amounts to 'interest' and Part I of Chapter 3 deals with the expression 'yearly interest'. From there it will be seen that not all payments described as 'interest' will be subject to deduction of income tax; the payment may not be interest properly so called, and, even if it is, it may be interest on a short-term loan of less than a year which does not amount to 'yearly interest'. On the other hand, payments not described as interest may in fact be yearly interest and may be subject to the deduction obligation.

7–05 In order for the interest to be subject to the deduction procedure, it must be chargeable to tax under Sch D Case III. 'Tax' means either income tax or corporation tax[8], and therefore, for this purpose, the status of the recipient is not relevant. Nor does it matter that the recipient may not be assessed under Sch D Case III in respect of the interest so long as the interest is capable of being charged under Case III. For example, in the case of a bank receiving interest, the interest would normally fall to be taken into account as a receipt in computing the profits of the banking trade chargeable under Sch D Case I. But the interest may nevertheless also fall within Sch D Case III, and the obligation to deduct tax is not affected by the choice ultimately exercised by the Inland Revenue between the Cases of Sch D under which the interest may be charged[9].

But where the interest is subject to an exemption from tax in the hands of the recipient, the interest may not be 'chargeable' to tax at all and therefore not subject to s 349 (2). This does not mean that interest may necessarily be paid free of any deduction where the recipient claims an exemption under a double taxation agreement, because the payer must first be notified by the Inland Revenue not to deduct tax[10]. On the other hand, certain persons (eg the European Investment Bank[11]) are exempt from tax on interest on loans made to borrowers in the UK and interest payable to them is not 'chargeable' to tax.

7–06 If the interest is only chargeable under another Case (eg Case IV or V), the deduction obligation under s 349 (2) will not apply. This was

---

[7] See Chapter 7 Part 2 below.
[8] TA 1988 s 832 (3).
[9] See *Liverpool and London and Globe Insurance Co v Bennett* [1913] AC 610, 6 TC 327, HL.
[10] See §7-19 below.
[11] See Treaty Establishing the European Economic Community, Protocol on the Privileges and Immunities of the European Communities, Articles 3 and 22.

the position in *National Bank of Greece SA v Westminster Bank Executor and Trustee Co (Channel Islands) Ltd*[12], where it was held that, because the source of the interest was not in the UK and the interest on the bonds fell within Sch D Case IV, there was no requirement for tax to be deducted[13]. But, where there is an overlap between Case III and Case IV or V, the interest may fall within the deduction procedure[14].

7-07   The obligation to deduct tax only applies where the yearly interest is 'paid'. Therefore, there is no obligation to deduct tax where interest only accrues but is not paid[15], although crediting interest to a bank account of a depositor would constitute payment; this would be the case even if the recipient were unable to use the money transferred or credited so long as it enures for his benefit, as might be the case where the taxpayer has pledged an account together with accruing interest as security for an obligation[16].

On the other hand, where interest is debited by a bank to the customer's account[17] – and even where both lender and borrower make corresponding book entries which record the payment of interest by an increase in the loan account[18] – or outstanding interest on a loan is capitalised[19], this does not amount to payment of interest. Consequently, the interest is only 'paid', and a s 349(2) deduction obligation only arises, when the capitalised interest is repaid[20]. However, in certain circumstances where interest on a debt is satisfied by the issue of further securities there may be an obligation to account for income tax to the Inland Revenue[1].

CIRCUMSTANCES WHEN DEDUCTION IS NORMALLY REQUIRED

7-08   Income tax must be deducted from yearly interest paid by a company[2] or local authority[3], otherwise than where the payment is made in a fiduciary or representative capacity[4], and from yearly interest paid by any person to a recipient whose usual place of abode is outside the UK. Both these general rules are subject to a number of exceptions.

---

[12] [1971] 1 All ER 233, 46 TC 472, HL.
[13] Note that that case concerned the application of ITA 1952, s 170, which did not require the payments to be within Case III, but nevertheless it was held that there had to be a UK source for the deduction obligation to apply – see §3–22 above.
[14] See §§3–27 and 7–05 above.
[15] See §4–02 above.
[16] See *Dunmore v McGowan (Inspector of Taxes)* [1978] STC 217, [1978] 2 All ER 85, CA, but also *Macpherson v Bond (Inspector of Taxes)* [1985] STC 678, [1985] 1 WLR 1157; and see §4–02 above, in particular where the amount paid is less than the aggregate of the outstanding principal and interest.
[17] *Paton v IRC* [1938] 1 All ER 786, 21 TC 626, HL.
[18] *Minsham Properties v Price (Inspector of Taxes)* [1990] STC 718; but cf where a bank or building society credits interest – §§7–27 and 7–28 below.
[19] *IRC v Oswald* [1945] 1 All ER 641, 26 TC 435, HL.
[20] As to which the parties may appropriate any repayment of less than the whole of the balance outstanding between principal and interest, as in *IRC v Oswald*.
[1] See §7–09 below.
[2] Defined in TA 1988 s 832(1).
[3] Defined in TA 1988 s 842A.
[4] TA 1988 s 349(2).

Tax does not have to be deducted only because payment is made by a company in its capacity as trustee for another person, although the circumstances of the payment might be such that tax must be deducted in any event (eg the true payer may itself be a company or local authority, or the trustee may be paying on behalf of an individual to a person living outside the UK[5]). Tax must also be deducted from payments of yearly interest made on behalf of a partnership of which a company is a member[6].

That companies and local authorities should be required to deduct tax from yearly interest payments followed from the pre-1969 system under which tax was required to be deducted from interest payments and annual payments where they were not paid wholly out of profits or gains brought into charge to income tax; companies have paid corporation tax, not income tax, since 1965, and local authorities were and are exempt from income tax[7].

The obligation of a company to deduct basic rate income tax from yearly interest extends to a European Economic Interest Grouping ('EEIG'), at least where its official address is in the UK. This is because such an EEIG is treated as a body corporate[8] and hence is a 'company' for UK taxation purposes[9]. An EEIG whose official address is outside the UK is not stated to be a body corporate under any UK legislation, but arguably it would be, particularly if it has legal personality[10]. However, since the obligation to deduct basic rate income tax only applies in relation to UK source interest[11], it will be relatively unusual for an EEIG which has its official address outside the UK to pay UK source interest, as its seat, and perhaps also its operations, will be outside the UK[12].

Tax is not required to be deducted where interest is paid by an international organisation designated by the Treasury under TA 1988 s 582A[13], or by a partnership of which such an organisation is a member.

FUNDING BONDS

7-09 Although not dealt with by s 349 (2), it is convenient here to mention circumstances where a deduction obligation may be imposed on a company or local authority which satisfies an obligation to pay interest by issuing 'funding bonds' in place of making a payment of the interest. As already explained[14], interest which is capitalised is not 'paid'. In *Cross (Inspector*

---

[5] See §**7-16** below.
[6] TA 1988 s 349 (2) (b).
[7] FA 1965, s 66 (1), now TA 1988 s 519.
[8] Regulations 3 and 9 of the European Economic Interest Grouping Regulations 1989: SI 1989 No 639; as to Northern Ireland, see Regulations 3 and 9 of the European Economic Interest Grouping Regulations (Northern Ireland): SI 1989 No 216.
[9] TA 1988 s 832 (1); see also Inland Revenue Press Release, 19 April 1990: 'Taxation of European Economic Interest Groupings'.
[10] See Article 1.3 of Council Regulation on the European Economic Interest Grouping, No 2137 of 25 July 1985.
[11] See §§**7-05** and **7-06** above.
[12] See §§**3-19** to **3-31** above.
[13] See the International Organisations (Miscellaneous Exemptions) Order 1991: SI 1991 No 1694, designating the European Bank for Reconstruction and Development.
[14] §**7-07** above.

of Taxes) v London and Provincial Trust Ltd[15] it was held that, where a
company issued bonds promising to make payment at a later date in
satisfaction of its earlier obligation to pay interest, that did not amount to
a payment of interest, notwithstanding that the bonds were marketable and
indeed were sold from time to time by the creditor; such an arrangement
merely involved deferral of payment of the interest. However, that decision
meant that the creditor could realise the value of the funding bonds and
thereby receive the interest in non-taxable form. The law was therefore
changed[16] to provide for the issue of funding bonds to be treated as payment
of the interest.

The provisions only apply in relation to interest on a debt incurred by
any government, public authority, public institution or body corporate[17],
and therefore do not apply to discharge of interest by individuals, trustees
or personal representatives. Where bonds, stocks, shares[18], securities or
certificates of indebtedness (called 'funding bonds' for the purposes of the
legislation) are issued to a creditor in respect of any liability to interest
on such a debt, the issue is treated for taxation purposes as the payment
of interest of an amount equal to the value of the funding bonds at that
time, and the subsequent redemption of the bonds is not treated as the
payment of interest[19]. In those circumstances, the person by or through
whom the issue is made is required to retain bonds to a value equal to
income tax calculated at the basic rate on the value of the bonds issued
and to account to the Inland Revenue for such an amount of tax, although
he may tender bonds in satisfaction. If the Board of Inland Revenue is
satisfied that it is impracticable to retain the bonds in this way it may relieve
the person otherwise responsible for retaining the bonds from that obligation
so long as he provides the Inland Revenue with details of the persons to
whom the bonds are issued, and those persons are then to be charged to
tax under Sch D Case VI on the interest which is treated as having been
received.

COMPANIES – SPECIAL RULES

7-10   A company is not obliged to deduct tax from interest paid to another
where a valid group income election is in force[20]. Such an election may
be made where the two companies are resident in the UK and

1   one is a 51 per cent subsidiary of the other[1];
2   the two companies are 51 per cent subsidiaries of another resident
company; or

[15] [1938] 1 All ER 428, 21 TC 705, CA.
[16] FA 1938 s 25(1), now TA 1988 s 582.
[17] TA 1988 s 582(3).
[18] It is doubtful whether shares, amounting to an interest in the capital of a company rather
than a promise to pay at a later date, would be within the principle established in the
London and Provincial Trust case.
[19] TA 1988 s 582(1).
[20] TA 1988 s 247.
[1] The payment can be made from parent to subsidiary as well as by subsidiary to parent
– TA 1988 s 247(4)(b).

3   the company paying the interest is a trading company or a holding company of trading companies[2] and is owned by a consortium of which the recipient is a member.

Interest cannot be paid gross where it is paid in respect of an investment held as trading stock of the recipient[3]. The term '51 per cent subsidiary' is defined in TA 1988 s 838 (1) (a), and, broadly, requires the parent to own beneficially, directly or indirectly, not less than 51 per cent of the ordinary share capital[4] of the subsidiary; however, holdings in or through non-resident companies are disregarded for this purpose, as are certain shareholdings which are held as trading stock and not as investments[5]. A company is not treated as a 51 per cent subsidiary of another company unless the parent company would be beneficially entitled to more than 50 per cent of the profits available for distribution to equity holders and to more than 50 per cent of the assets of the subsidiary available to equity holders on a winding up[6]. For the purpose of these additional tests, TA 1988 Sch 18 applies as it does for group relief purposes[7]. A consortium is constituted where five or fewer companies resident in the UK beneficially own between them not less than 75 per cent of the ordinary share capital of the company in question and none of which owns less than 5 per cent or has less than a 5 per cent or greater interest in profit distributions and assets on a winding up to which equity holders are entitled[8]. A company owned by a consortium may not participate in a group income election if it is a 75 per cent subsidiary of another company or if arrangements exist under which it could become such a subsidiary[9]. Beneficial ownership of shares may be lost where a company enters into a contract, whether conditional or unconditional, for the sale of the shares in the other company[10]; therefore, if any interest is to be paid between group companies prior to the sale of a subsidiary it is important to ensure that such interest is paid and received before any contractual relationship is brought into being which has the effect of severing the beneficial ownership if the interest is to be paid without deduction of basic rate income tax.

An election to pay interest gross must be made jointly by the payer and recipient[11] in writing to the Inspector of Taxes[12], and once an election is in force TA 1988 s 349 (2) does not apply. The election must provide the Inspector with the necessary details in its support, and is not valid until either the Inspector has accepted the election or three months have elapsed

---

[2] TA 1988 s 247 (9) (a).
[3] TA 1988 s 247 (5).
[4] As defined in TA 1988 s 832 (1).
[5] TA 1988 s 247 (8).
[6] TA 1988 s 247(8A).
[7] TA 1988 s 247(9A).
[8] TA 1988 s 247 (9) (c) and (9A). The rules as to when interest can be paid gross to and from a company owned by a consortium are not quite the same as those which permit group relief between a company owned by a consortium and another company – see TA 1988 ss 402 (3) and 413 (6).
[9] TA 1988 s 247 (1) (b) and (1A).
[10] *Wood Preservation Ltd v Prior (Inspector of Taxes)* [1969] 1 All ER 364, 45 TC 112, CA; see also *J Sainsbury plc v O'Connor* [1991] STC 318, [1991] 1 WLR 763, CA.
[11] TA 1988 s 247 (4).
[12] TA 1988 s 248 (1); see guidance note as to form of elections, published by CCAB after consultation with the Inland Revenue – CCAB TR 340, 16 May 1979, [1979] STI 199.

without the Inspector notifying both companies that he is not satisfied with the election; an appeal may be made against the Inspector's refusal to accept the election[13]. Once the election is in force it will remain in force until either the conditions of the election cease to apply (eg one company ceases to have beneficial ownership of the shares in the other)[14], or either company gives notice to the Inspector revoking the election[15].

7-11   Where the company making the payment of interest is resident in the UK[16], the procedure for making returns and accounting for any tax deducted is set out in TA 1988 Sch 16[17]. This requires the company to make a return to the Collector of Taxes on a quarterly basis[18] showing, inter alia, yearly interest payments made and the tax for which the company is accountable[19]. The returns must be delivered, and tax paid, within fourteen days of the date to which any return is made, so that tax deducted by a resident company from interest payments must normally be paid to the Inland Revenue within between two and fifteen weeks of the payment of the interest.

Moreover, a resident company may set off against any income tax deductible from any payments of interest made in an accounting period any income tax suffered by deduction in respect of any interest or other payments received in the same accounting period under deduction of income tax[20]. If tax deducted from payments made is paid to the Inland Revenue before the claim is made (which would happen where the payment of interest is made earlier in the accounting period than when the receipt is received) any overpaid tax is repayable when the claim to set off tax suffered is allowed.

7-12   Any net amount of income tax deducted by a company from yearly interest and other payments made by it and accounted for to the Inland Revenue does not affect the company's liability to corporation tax in respect of its profits. It is only the net amount of income tax suffered by the company on payments received by it, after deducting any amount of tax set off against tax on payments made, which is available for set-off against the company's liability to corporation tax or eligible for repayment if the net amount suffered by deduction exceeds the company's liability to corporation tax[1].

QUOTED EUROBONDS

7-13   An exception to the obligation on a company to deduct tax in respect of yearly interest applies in relation to interest on quoted Eurobonds[2] – namely, bearer securities quoted on a recognised stock exchange[3]. In this

13 TA 1988 s 248 (2).
14 TA 1988 s 248 (4).
15 TA 1988 s 248 (5).
16 But not where it is non-resident– TA 1988 s 350 (4).
17 TA 1988 s 350 (1), (3) and (4).
18 With additional returns where the end of the accounting period does not coincide with the calendar quarter date – TA 1988 Sch 16 para 2 (2).
19 TA 1988 Sch 16 para 3.
20 TA 1988 Sch 16 para 5.
1 See TA 1988 Sch 16 para 7 and TA 1988 s 7 (2) (as amended in relation to the application of 'pay and file' by FA 1990 s 98).
2 TA 1988 s 124.
3 TA 1988 s 124 (6).

case, tax is not deductible where the company or agent[4] through which interest is paid is not in the UK[5], or the payment is made by or through a person in the UK but either it is paid to a non-resident[6] or the quoted Eurobond is held in a recognised clearing system[7]. However, in order to ensure that interest paid gross but collected on behalf of a person in the UK from a non-UK paying agent or through a recognised clearing system is subject to deduction of tax before the interest is accounted for to the UK person, the collecting agent rules in TA 1988 s 123 (3) to (6)[8] are applied (as modified) in relation to interest paid on quoted Eurobonds[9].

INDUSTRIAL AND PROVIDENT SOCIETIES

7-14   Share interest and loan interest paid by a registered industrial and provident society is paid without deduction of tax, unless the usual place of abode of the recipient is not within the UK[10]. Where such interest is paid to a person having his usual place of abode outside the UK, tax is deductible by the society under the s 349 (2) procedure in the same way 'as it applies to a payment of yearly interest'. This language indicates that tax is deductible in those circumstances even where the interest is not yearly interest[11].

LOCAL AUTHORITIES AND STATUTORY CORPORATIONS – EXEMPT INTEREST ON CERTAIN BORROWINGS

7-15   The Treasury may direct that special treatment shall apply to foreign currency securities issued by a local authority[12]. If such a direction is made, the interest on such securities is paid without deduction of income tax (irrespective of the identity of the recipient), and so long as the beneficial owner of the securities is not resident in the UK the interest is exempt from income tax[13]. The exemption from tax on the interest does not extend to corporation tax, so the exemption is not available to a non-resident bank holding such securities as assets of a banking business carried on in the UK through a branch or agency. Because the interest is automatically paid gross there is no need for a claim to be made for exemption by a non-resident; but, if the interest is received gross by a person not entitled to

---

[4] Including a sub-paying agent who receives the funds through a principal paying agent: Inland Revenue Statement of Practice SP 8/84.
[5] TA 1988 s 124 (1) (a).
[6] When the interest is for tax purposes deemed to be the income of any other person, the condition of non-residence applies in relation to that person; and note that any person claiming payment of interest gross as a non-resident must use the appropriate claim form (Form A6, C10 or D2).
[7] TA 1988 s 124 (1) (b) and (2); recognised clearing systems are Euro-clear, CEDEL and First Chicago Clearing System.
[8] See §§7-46 to 7-48.
[9] TA 1988 s 124 (5); Form C11 is used to claim payment gross on behalf of non-residents.
[10] TA 1988 s 486 (2) and (3) – see §7-16 below as to 'usual place of abode'.
[11] Almost certainly, any such interest paid by an industrial or provident society as defined in TA 1988 s 486 (12) would be chargeable to tax within Sch D Case III.
[12] Defined in TA 1988 s 842A.
[13] TA 1988 s 581 (1).

exemption from tax the interest will be charged to tax under Sch D Case III on the preceding year basis in the case of an individual[14] and for the relevant accounting period in which the interest is received in the case of a company.

If the securities can be repaid in one of several currencies (whether or not one of those currencies is sterling) but the option as to which currency can be used for repayment is exercisable only by the holder, the exemption may apply, but not otherwise where there is an option as to the currency of repayment[15]. The exemption is not available where the income is treated by another provision[16] as the income of a person resident in the UK[17].

This special treatment may also apply, if the Treasury so directs, to the interest on loans raised by statutory corporations[18].

YEARLY INTEREST PAID ABROAD

7-16 Tax must be deducted where any person (including an individual, a partnership of individuals, trustees or personal representatives) pays yearly interest within Sch D Case III to another person whose 'usual place of abode' is outside the UK[19]. This obligation is not determined according to the tax residence of the recipient, but uses the same language as is used in relation to payment of copyright royalties to a person abroad[20] and in relation to payment to persons abroad of rent chargeable to tax under Sch A[1]. The expression is not defined in the legislation and has not been considered judicially in relation to tax legislation. Consideration of this expression in other contexts is not of direct authority, particularly because although the words are not terms of art, they take their meaning from the context in which they are used[2]. The expression does appear to refer to a geographical location – 'place' – and one which has some degree of permanence – 'usual ... abode'. In *Levene v IRC*[3], the Oxford English Dictionary definition of 'reside' as 'to dwell permanently or for a considerable time, to have one's settled or usual abode, to live in or at a particular place' was cited with approval. Thus, it should probably be taken as referring to the address at which the person in question will normally be found: in the case of an individual, his principal or permanent home; in the case of a company or partnership, its principal place of business; more difficulty would be found in the case of trustees or personal representatives, depending on their individual places of abode and whether there is an address at which they could be regarded as being found[4]. What does seem to be clear is that a

---

[14] Except in the opening or closing years – see §§**4-06** and **4-07** above.

[15] TA 1988 s 581 (2).

[16] Eg TA 1988 s 739.

[17] TA 1988 s 581 (3).

[18] TA 1988 s 581(4).

[19] TA 1988 s 349 (2) (c). There is a special exemption for interest paid to Netherlands Antilles subsidiaries of UK companies in connection with pre- 26 July 1984 issues of quoted Eurobonds – FA 1989 s 116.

[20] TA 1988 s 536.

[1] TA 1988 s 43.

[2] See *Price v West London Investment Building Society* [1964] 2 All ER 318 at 321c, CA.

[3] (1928) 13 TC 486, HL – see Viscount Cave, LC, at 505.

[4] Eg the address of a solicitor or other agent.

person's 'usual place of abode' is not necessarily the same as his residence for taxation purposes, so that a person who is technically resident in the UK[5] could have a usual place of abode outside the UK, whereas a person on a year-long world tour, and not resident in the UK in that year, could continue to have his usual place of abode in the UK[6]. Further, an individual (and, perhaps, even a company) could have no 'usual place of abode', in which case he would not suffer the deduction of income tax under s 349 (2).

Clearly, a person paying yearly interest should take care if there is a foreign element in the circumstances, and this would particularly be the case if the payee were to be a company incorporated outside the UK or where the interest is to be transmitted to an overseas address or to a bank account outside the UK. The Inland Revenue has stated that it will not seek to make a solicitor accountable for tax which should have been deducted under s 349 (2) where payment is made gross on the basis of an assurance by the recipient's solicitor that to the best of his knowledge the recipient's usual place of abode is in the UK[7]. In relation to similar wording concerning development land tax[8] the Inland Revenue was empowered to direct that the withholding obligation should not apply to a person making a payment who believed, and who took reasonable steps to establish, that the person receiving the payment was not a person whose usual place of abode was outside the UK; in practice, it may be unlikely that the Inland Revenue would seek to assess a person paying interest without deducting tax in circumstances where reasonable care has been taken.

7-17 Proposals made by the European Commission are expected to lead to a Directive requiring EC member states not to impose tax on interest (or royalties) paid between companies resident in different Member States where one holds 25 per cent or more of the capital of the other. Such a Directive would require UK domestic legislation to be amended. The draft Directive[9] is still under discussion, although the Commission had originally hoped that the Directive would have effect from 1 January 1993.

DOUBLE TAXATION AGREEMENTS

7-18 The recipient of yearly interest may be entitled to claim the benefit of a double taxation agreement between the UK and the country of which he is a resident under which he may be exempt from taxation in the UK on interest falling within Sch D Case III or under which he should only be taxed at a rate lower than the basic rate[10] of income tax[11]. This relief

---

[5] Eg by reason of occasional visits to the UK averaging more than three months in any tax year.
[6] In this case the individual would probably remain 'ordinarily resident' in the UK.
[7] Law Society's Gazette, October 1971, p 458; strictly, this assurance is too narrow, since the payer's solicitor should only need to be told that the recipient does not have his usual place of abode outside the UK.
[8] See Regulation 5 (1) of the Development Land Tax (Disposals by Non-residents) Regulations 1976: SI 1976 No 1190.
[9] COM (90) 571 Final – OJ C53 28.2.91 p 26.
[10] See §7-33 below.
[11] Generally, see §§4-29 to 4-31 as to double taxation agreements.

may protect the recipient in a case where his usual place of abode is outside the UK[12].

7-19   The availability of relief under a double taxation agreement does not entitle the recipient to payment of yearly interest gross or subject to a reduced rate of deduction of tax without any further steps being taken. The Inland Revenue must first notify the payer of the interest that an exemption or reduction applies[13]. In order to obtain such a notification the recipient of the interest must first complete a form provided by the Inspector of Foreign Dividends giving details of the relief claimed and information in support of the claim. That form is then sent to the claimant's own local tax office to be certified that the claimant is tax resident in the other country. The form is then sent to the Inspector of Foreign Dividends in the UK and, provided that the claim is approved, the payer's own Inspector of Taxes is authorised to notify the payer to pay the interest gross or subject to a reduced rate of deduction. This procedure is only available where the non-resident recipient of the interest is beneficially entitled to the income[14]. It should be noted that not all double taxation agreements make beneficial ownership of the interest a precondition of relief, although another condition which often applies – that the recipient is taxable on the interest in his country of residence – may have the same effect in practice.

If the claim has not been made and accepted before the due date for payment of interest, the interest must be paid subject to deduction of tax at the full basic rate. The non-resident recipient may then claim repayment of the tax which has been deducted in excess of the correct amount[15]. If a claim for relief is refused, an appeal against such refusal may be made within thirty days of receipt of written notice of the refusal being received by the claimant[16].

INTEREST PAID TO UK BANKS AND BUILDING SOCIETIES

7-20   The deduction obligation under s 349 (2) does not apply to interest payable in the UK on an advance[17] from a bank carrying on a bona fide banking business in the UK[18]. It will be observed that this only applies to interest 'payable in the UK'. Strictly, interest is only payable in the UK where the borrower is entitled to tender the interest in payment at a branch of the bank in the UK, although interest would also remain payable in the UK where the borrower is also entitled to pay the interest abroad[19]. This could give rise to difficulties in the case of banks making foreign currency loans where the interest would ordinarily be payable only to an account

---

[12] See §**7-16** above.

[13] Regulation 2 of the Double Taxation Relief (Taxes on Income) (General) Regulations 1970: SI 1970 No 488.

[14] Regulation 2(1) of the Double Taxation Relief (Taxes on Income) (General) Regulations 1970: SI 1970 No 488.

[15] The claim form can be used either to claim payment gross (or subject to a reduced rate of deduction) or to reclaim any tax already deducted.

[16] TMA 1970 s 42(3) – see TA 1988 s 788(6) as to claims for relief.

[17] 'Advance' appears to extend to the proceeds of bills or notes discounted by the bank and placed to the credit of its customer – *Grahame v Grahame* (1887) 19 LRIr 249.

[18] TA 1988 s 349(3)(a).

[19] *Maude v IRC* [1940] 1 All ER 464, 23 TC 63.

outside the UK at a location where the foreign currency is normally dealt in (eg dollars in New York). Although it might be argued that interest remains payable in the UK where it is paid to a bank overseas for the credit of a bank in the UK, the Inland Revenue has published a practice of treating yearly interest as 'payable in the United Kingdom' for this purpose[20] where the loan is made in foreign currency by a bank carrying on a bona fide banking business in the UK, on terms that

1   the interest falls to be brought into account as a trading receipt of the business carried on in the UK, and
2   the interest is so brought into account, notwithstanding any provision in the loan agreement for the payment of interest abroad[1].

Where a borrower takes a loan in such circumstances, he should ensure that the bank provides satisfactory assurances that the above two conditions of the Inland Revenue practice will be satisfied if the loan agreement requires the borrower to gross up the interest on account of any tax deducted if tax does become deductible.

7-21   The exemption prevents a deduction of tax being required where the borrower is a company, a partnership including a company, or a local authority[2]. It also applies to interest paid by individuals and others where the lender bank is a non-resident company, whose usual place of abode is probably outside the UK[3], lending through a branch in the UK; such a foreign bank would not be entitled to any exemption from the deduction of tax by reason of a provision in a double taxation agreement[4].

7-22   There is no definition of what is a banking business, although in *United Dominions Trust Ltd v Kirkwood*[5] Lord Denning MR reviewed the matter and concluded[6] that the essentials of the business lay in accepting money from, and collecting cheques for, customers, honouring cheques or orders drawn on the bank and keeping current accounts to enter the credits and debits relating to customers' transactions. Having regard to the provisions of TA 1988 s 349 (3) (b)[7], the taking of interest-bearing deposits should probably also be included[8].

In order to be recognised by the Inland Revenue that it is carrying on a bona fide banking business in the UK the bank must satisfy the Inland Revenue that it does provide conventional banking services (ie broadly, it operates current accounts and takes deposits). The fact that a company is authorised to carry on deposit-taking business under the Banking Act 1987 will not be conclusive evidence of this. Nor does it appear to be conclusive

---

[20]   And also for TA 1988 s 337 (3) – see §**8-29** below – and (although this is not published) for TA 1988 ss 338 (2) (b) and 353 (1) (b).
[1]   Inland Revenue Statement of Practice C5. In practice, this treatment also applies where the loan is taken from an overseas banking branch of a bank which is a company resident in the UK.
[2]   See §**7-08** above.
[3]   See §**7-16** above.
[4]   See §**4-30(6)** above.
[5]   [1966] 1 All ER 968, [1966] 2 QB 431, CA.
[6]   [1966] 1 All ER 968 at 975*h*.
[7]   See §**7-25** below.
[8]   Regarded by Lord Denning MR as a characteristic of banking 'in the old days' – [1966] 1 All ER 968 at 975*b*; see also Harman LJ at 981*i*–982*e*, and Diplock LJ at 986*f*–*g*.

that a company which is not an authorised institution under that Act is not a bank, although it might be open to question whether a company which is not so authorised can be carrying on a *bona fide* banking business in the UK. In *Hafton Properties Ltd v McHugh (Inspector of Taxes)*[9], an Isle of Man bank was held not to have been carrying on a bona fide banking business in the UK, notwithstanding that it had made several loans secured on UK property and that these had been arranged through UK agents. It was held that lending alone was not enough; a banking business involved taking deposits and the other matters referred to in the *United Dominions Trust* case.

7-23   The exemption also requires the interest to be paid on an advance *from* a bank carrying on a bona fide banking business in the UK. This appears to mean that where a borrower takes a loan from such a bank the interest may be paid gross even if the loan is subsequently assigned to a third party which does not qualify as such a bank, and would mean that a guarantor of a loan from such a bank could pay gross to the bank any sum which amounts to yearly interest paid by him[10]. On the other hand, interest paid to such a bank would not strictly appear to qualify for the exemption where the bank has acquired the loan by assignment from the original lender which was not a bank carrying on a bona fide banking business in the UK. In practice, the Inland Revenue accepts that interest may be paid gross to a UK bank where the loan was originally made by a UK bank and the bank receiving the interest has acquired the loan by assignment directly, or indirectly through a chain of UK banks, from the original lender.

7-24   TA 1988 s 349 (2) does not apply to require income tax to be deducted from yearly interest payable by a company or local authority on an advance from a building society to which regulations apply requiring basic rate income tax to be deducted from interest and dividends paid by the society[11].

BANK INTEREST - GENERAL RULE

7-25   Subject to what is said in §§7-26 and 7-27 below, yearly interest paid by a bank carrying on a bona fide banking business in the UK[12] is not subject to the deduction of income tax under s 349 (2) where the interest is paid 'in the ordinary course of that business'[13]. As will be seen from §7-22 above, it is not clear what is the ordinary course of business of banking. In *Royal Bank of Canada v IRC*[14], Megarry J considered the expression 'ordinary banking transactions between the bank and the customer in the ordinary course of banking business' where this was relevant to determine whether the bank was required to provide to the Inland Revenue information about certain transactions under what is now TA 1988 s 745 (5)[15]. That case

9 [1987] STC 16.
10 See §§2-21 to 2-24 above, as to interest paid by a guarantor.
11 See TA 1988 s 477A (7) and the Income Tax (Building Societies) (Dividends and Interest) Regulations 1990: SI 1990 No 2231; and see §7-28 below.
12 See §7-22 above as to this.
13 TA 1988 s 349 (3) (b).
14 [1972] 1 All ER 225, 47 TC 565.
15 Then, ITA 1952 s 414 (5).

was more concerned with whether particular transactions were 'ordinary banking transactions' rather than with the nature of the business generally; there was no doubt that the company was a 'bank', but it did not follow that all business transacted by the bank was ordinary banking business. Megarry J thought that a statement of the essentials of banking, such as was given in *United Dominions Trust Ltd v Kirkwood*[16] was not exhaustive of all that is ordinary in that business. It was said in *United Dominions Trust Ltd v Kirkwood* that deposit accounts kept by bankers are ordinarily subject to withdrawal at notice by the depositor[17]. Banks do, however, issue deposit receipts for sums deposited for a fixed period[18], and certificates of deposit[19]. It seems that these transactions are now sufficiently commonplace as to fall within the ordinary course of banking business.

For many years, the Inland Revenue took the view that interest paid by a bank on money raised as part of the bank's capital was not paid in the ordinary course of banking business. Moreover, the Inland Revenue considered that borrowings for over seven years were 'capital' in nature and so prevented interest on such loans being paid 'in the ordinary course of that business'. However, placing reliance on the *Royal Bank of Canada* case, the Inland Revenue now considers[20] that regard should be had to banking business generally to determine whether interest is paid in the ordinary course of that business; in practice, borrowings which are on terms comparable to those offered by other banks will normally be regarded as meeting the test. In cases of doubt, the Inland Revenue will usually regard interest as paid in the ordinary course of banking business, unless a tax avoidance motive is present or the borrowing is tier 1 or tier 2 capital for the bank[1] (in which case the interest will always fail the ordinary course of banking business test).

What may not satisfy the test of interest paid in the ordinary course of banking business is interest paid on a deposit which is made on terms that interest will be paid and repayment of principal made only to the extent that interest and repayment is received on a loan made by the bank to a third party at the depositor's request[2]. In such circumstances, other arrangements should be considered[3] if the bank is to be satisfied that interest paid to the depositor falls within the exemption from the obligation to deduct tax. However, back-to-back deposits are commonly arranged by banks by way of sub-participation of other banks in commercial loans[4], and interest on such deposits can amount to interest paid by a bank in the ordinary course of banking business.

---

[16] [1966] 1 All ER 968, [1966] 2 QB 431, CA.

[17] See Harman LJ at 982c and Diplock LJ at 986g.

[18] If the fixed period is less than a year the interest would not be 'yearly interest' – see §3–06 above – and so would not fall within s 349 (2) – see §7–04 above.

[19] Normally, for periods of up to five years.

[20] See Inland Revenue Statement of Practice SP12/91.

[1] As defined by the Bank for International Settlements, irrespective of whether the borrowing counts towards tier 1 or tier 2 for regulatory purposes.

[2] Typically, a loan to a UK resident affiliate of a non-resident depositor where tax would be deductible under s 349 (2) were the non-resident to make the loan direct.

[3] Eg a guarantee secured by a charge over a conventional deposit.

[4] Payment of interest and repayment of principal on the deposit being contingent upon receipt of interest and principal on the loan – the depositor in effect taking the risk in place of the original lender bank.

BANK AND BUILDING SOCIETY INTEREST – SPECIAL RULES

7-26   Prior to 6 April 1991, payments of interest by banks and building societies to individuals were governed by the composite rate tax scheme, under which the bank or building society accounted to the Inland Revenue for tax at a special rate in respect of all deposits by individuals and the interest was treated as paid net of basic rate income tax. However, depositors who did not pay tax at that rate on all their income could not recover any of the basic rate income tax treated as paid. Under the present provisions, introduced with effect from 6 April 1991, income tax at the basic rate is required to be deducted from interest paid or credited to individuals by banks and certain deposit-takers and by building societies to individuals and certain others, but this rule is subject to a number of exceptions. In the case of banks and other deposit-takers, the requirements are set out in TA 1988 ss 480A to 482A and regulations made thereunder[5]. In relation to the (similar but not identical) provisions which apply to building societies, the provisions are contained in regulations[6] made under TA 1988 s 477A.

7-27   In addition to banks authorised under the Banking Act 1987, the following are deposit-takers for the purposes of the provisions relating to deduction of income tax from interest[7]:

1   the Bank of England;
2   the Post Office;
3   any local authority; and
4   any body which receives deposits in the course of its business or activities and is so prescribed by order made by the Treasury[8].

When a bank or other deposit-taker makes a payment of interest in respect of a relevant deposit, including where interest is credited to an account of the depositor[9], it must deduct out of it income tax at the basic rate for the year of assessment in which the payment is made[10].

A deposit is only a relevant deposit if it is beneficially owned by an individual or individuals, or (in Scotland) a partnership of individuals, or the personal representatives of a deceased person[11]. However, the following are specifically excluded from the meaning of the expression 'relevant deposit'[12]:

1   a qualifying time deposit – that is, a deposit of not less than £50,000 or, if in foreign currency, not less than the equivalent of £50,000 at the time when the deposit is made, and on terms which require repayment at the end of a specified period of not more than five years, do not

---

[5] The Income Tax (Deposit-takers) (Interest Payments) Regulations 1990: SI 1990 No 2232; the Income Tax (Deposit-takers) (Audit Powers) Regulations 1992: SI 1992 No 12.
[6] The Income Tax (Building Societies) (Dividends and Interest) Regulations 1990: SI 1990 No 2231; the Income Tax (Building Societies) (Audit Powers) Regulations 1992: SI 1992 No 10.
[7] TA 1988 s 481 (2).
[8] See SI 1984 No 1801 and SI 1985 No 1696.
[9] TA 1988 s 480A (5).
[10] TA 1988 ss 480A (1) and (4).
[11] TA 1988 s 481 (3) and (4).
[12] TA 1988 s 481 (5).

make provision for the transfer of the right to repayment and prevent
partial withdrawals of or additions to the deposit[13];

2   a qualifying certificate of deposit – that is, a certificate of deposit issued
     by a deposit-taker and under which the amount payable by the deposit-
     taker exclusive of interest is not less than £50,000 (or the foreign currency
     equivalent of £50,000 at the time when the deposit was made), and
     which requires repayment within five years of the date on which the
     deposit was made[14];

3   a debenture issued by the deposit-taker, or a debt on a security which
     is listed on a recognised stock exchange;

4   a loan made by another deposit-taker in the ordinary course of its
     business;

5   a general client account deposit maintained by a person (eg a solicitor)
     who is under an obligation to operate such an account, except where
     the account is identified by the deposit-taker as being held for the benefit
     of one or more particular clients (eg a designated account)[15];

6   a deposit which forms part of a premiums trust fund of an underwriting
     member of Lloyd's;

7   a deposit made by a London Stock Exchange money broker (recognised
     by the Bank of England) who is acting in the course of his business
     as such a broker;

8   a deposit held at a non-UK branch of the deposit-taker;

9   a deposit where a written declaration has been made to the deposit-
     taker that the person who is beneficially entitled to the interest, or
     all the persons who are so entitled, are not ordinarily resident in the
     UK. Such a declaration can also be made by a personal representative
     of an individual who, immediately before his death, was not ordinarily
     resident in the UK. Where a declaration of non-ordinary residence does
     not include the address of the person making it, interest is subject to
     deduction of tax unless the deposit-taker completes a certificate
     supporting the declaration[16];

10   a deposit pending investment under a Personal Equity Plan[17].

A deposit-taker must treat a deposit as a relevant deposit unless he is
satisfied that it is not a relevant deposit[18].

The requirement to deduct tax from interest on a relevant deposit does
not apply if the deposit-taker has been supplied with a certificate that the
person beneficially entitled to the payment of interest is unlikely to be liable
to pay any amount by way of income tax in the year in which the payment
is made. If the depositor is aged 16 or over, the certificate must be given
by the person who is beneficially entitled to the payment. Special provisions
apply where the beneficiary is either under the age of 16 throughout the
year of assessment or reaches the age during that year. A certificate can
also be given by any one of the following:

---

[13] TA 1988 s 482 (6).
[14] *Ibid*; where no certificate has been issued but the circumstances fall within TA 1988 s 56A,
    the deposit is not a relevant deposit.
[15] TA 1988 s 482 (6).
[16] The Income Tax (Deposit-takers) (Non-residents) Regulations 1992: SI 1992 No 14; the
    Inland Revenue does not regard an overseas PO Box number as an adequate address.
[17] Regulation 17 (2)(a) of the Personal Equity Plan Regulations 1989: SI 1989 No 469.
[18] TA 1988 s 482 (5).

1   a donee of a power of attorney which authorises the donee to administer the financial affairs of the person who is beneficially entitled to the interest; or

2   a parent, guardian, spouse or son or daughter of a person suffering from mental disorder; or

3   a court-appointed receiver of a person incapable of managing his affairs.

Persons completing the certificate must certify that, to the best of their knowledge, they do not expect to be liable to pay income tax and that the information given on the form is correct. The certificate must contain an undertaking by the person giving it that if either he or the beneficiary (if different) becomes liable to pay any amount by way of income tax for the year in which the payment is made, he will notify the deposit-taker. The detailed provisions relating to interest being paid gross in these circumstances are set out in regulations made under TA 1988 ss 480B and 482 (11)[19].

7–28   Subject to certain exceptions, when paying or crediting[20] dividends or interest to an individual or any person other than a company[20a], a building society must deduct an amount representing basic rate income tax[1]; this requirement does not apply in relation to certain securities listed on a recognised stock exchange[2]. The exceptions to this requirement are similar (but not identical) to the provisions outlined above for deposit-takers. A building society may pay interest gross if the payment is within one of the following categories:

1   to an individual beneficially entitled to the interest, or to individuals who are jointly so entitled (including the partners of a Scottish partnership of individuals), and who is or all of whom are not ordinarily resident in the UK[3];

2   to the trustees of a trust where the income of the trust is only enjoyed by individuals who are not ordinarily resident in the UK[4];

3   to personal representatives in respect of an investment forming part of a deceased person's estate, where that person was not ordinarily resident in the UK at the time of his death (or in respect of replacement investments for such investments or dividends or interest thereon)[5];

4   to a charity which is eligible for exemption from tax on interest;

5   to an exempt friendly society;

6   to an exempt pension fund;

7   to a company resident in the UK which is a 51 per cent subsidiary of the building society making the payment, provided that the building society and the company have jointly elected that the payment should be made gross;

---

[19] The Income Tax (Deposit-takers) (Interest Payments) Regulations 1990: SI 1990 No 2232.

[20] Regulation 2 of the Income Tax (Building Societies) (Dividends and Interest) Regulations 1990: SI 1990 No 2231.

[20a] See Inland Revenue Press Release, 24 November 1992, and the Income Tax (Building Societies) (Dividends and Interest) (Amendment No 2) Regulations 1992.

[1] TA 1988 s 477A and Regulation 3 of the Income Tax (Building Societies) (Dividends and Interest) Regulations 1990: SI 1990 No 2231.

[2] Regulation 3(2)(b) of the Income Tax (Building Societies) (Dividends and Interest) Regulations 1990: SI 1990 No 2231.

[3] *Ibid*, Regulation 11.

[4] *Ibid.*

[5] *Ibid.*

8 on a loan from a bank or building society;
9 in respect of a qualifying certificate of deposit or qualifying time deposit[6];
10 in respect of a general client account deposit;
11 for the purposes of approved personal pension arrangements within TA 1988 s 630;
12 in respect of an investment forming part of a premiums trust fund of an underwriting member at Lloyd's;
13 to a local authority;
14 on a deposit pending investment under a Personal Equity Plan[7].
15 to a health service body[7a]; and
16 to the trustees of a unit trust scheme[7a].

In addition, a building society may pay interest gross where a certificate is supplied to it to the effect that the investor is unlikely to be liable to pay income tax in the year in which the payment is made, in the same circumstances as apply in relation to interest paid by banks and other deposit-takers[8]. Where a building society converts to company status under the Building Societies Act 1986, certificates will, by concession, be treated as given to the successor company[9].

7-29 In other cases, where a building society pays a dividend or interest on certain securities (other than deposits) which are quoted, or are capable of being quoted, on a recognised stock exchange, basic rate income tax must be deducted unless the security is a quoted Eurobond[10]. Dividends paid by building societies are not treated as distributions for corporation tax purposes[11]; therefore, no ACT is payable in respect of building society dividends.

7-30 The provisions outlined above in relation to interest paid by banks, other deposit-takers and building societies only relate to the machinery of collection. Where the tax deducted exceeds the depositor's liability to income tax for the year of assessment, then the excess tax deducted can be reclaimed from the Inland Revenue[12]; in practice, where £50 or more tax is reclaimed, this can be done before the end of the year of assessment in which the interest is received[13]. Any liability to income tax at the higher rate or at the additional rate will be payable in addition to the tax deducted at source. Where interest is permitted to be paid gross, the income may nevertheless remain subject to income tax or corporation tax assessed on the recipient of the interest. However, where for any year of assessment during the whole of which he is treated as not being resident in the UK, a person receives interest from a bank, other deposit-taker or building society without deduction of income tax, no action will be taken by the Inland Revenue to pursue his liability to income tax on the interest unless the interest is assessable

---

[6] Defined in TA 1988 s 482 (6); see §7-27 above; where no certificate has been issued but the circumstances fall within TA 1988 s 56A, tax is not deductible from interest on the deposit – TA 1988 s 477 (1A) and (10); see also, Inland Revenue Press Release, 24 November 1992.
[7] Regulation 17 (2) (b) of the Personal Equity Plan Regulations 1989: SI 1989 No 469.
[7a] See Inland Revenue Press Release, 24 November 1992.
[8] Regulations 5 to 8 of the Income Tax (Building Societies) (Dividends and Interest) Regulations 1990: SI 1990 No 2231; and see §7-27 above.
[9] Extra-statutory Concession A69.
[10] TA 1988 s 349 (3A) and (3B).
[11] TA 1988 s 477A (3) (b).
[12] TMA 1970 s 42 (7).
[13] Inland Revenue Press Release: 'Bank and Building Society Interest', 20 January 1992.

on a UK branch or agent or other person within the terms of TMA 1970 s 78 or can be recovered by set-off in a claim to relief in respect of taxed income from UK sources[14]; a non-resident company or other person trading in the UK through a branch or agency is taxable in the ordinary way where the deposit is held in connection with that UK trade.

7-31   Banks, other deposit-takers[15] and building societies[16] account for income tax deducted under these provisions under the same procedure under which companies account for income tax deducted from yearly interest and annual payments[17].

DEDUCTION OF INCOME TAX - PROCEDURE

7-32   Income tax is required to be deducted under TA 1988 s 349 (2) by the person by whom the payment is made or by the person through whom the payment is made. Consequently, an agent (eg a solicitor or trustee) who makes a payment of yearly interest on behalf of a third party can be liable to deduct the tax[18]. Where a mortgagee has taken possession of the mortgaged property he may retain out of the assets held by him funds sufficient to discharge the gross amount of the interest payable to him without accounting to the Inland Revenue for basic rate income tax deducted from the interest[19]. A receiver who is the agent of the mortgagor rather than of the mortgagee, or an administrative receiver (who is deemed to be the agent of the company), is bound to deduct tax from interest paid (where so required) as the person 'by or through whom the payment is made'[20].

The person responsible for making the deduction must 'forthwith'[1] deliver to the Inspector of Taxes an account of the payment made and is assessable and chargeable to income tax on the interest. An assessment may be made on that person[2], and interest will run on any unpaid tax under such assessment in the ordinary way[3]. In the bankruptcy or winding-up of a person who has made a deduction of tax, the Inland Revenue is not able to claim that any trust is imposed on the withheld amount so as to give the Inland Revenue any advantage over other creditors[4]. The existence of a power to assess the payer in respect of tax which should have been deducted from interest does not prevent the Inland Revenue assessing the recipient where the tax has

---

[14] Extra-statutory Concession B13.

[15] TA 1988 s 480A (2).

[16] Regulation 10 of the Income Tax (Building Societies) (Dividends and Interest) Regulations 1990: SI 1990 No 2231.

[17] TA 1988 Sch 16, as modified by TA 1988 s 480A (3) and (4) and by Regulation 10 of SI 1990 No 2231.

[18] See *Rye and Eyre v IRC* [1935] AC 274, 19 TC 164, HL, where solicitors who were directed by a client to pay money on his behalf were held to be persons 'through whom' payment was made.

[19] *Hollis v Wingfield* [1940] 1 All ER 531, [1940] Ch 336, CA is not directly in point, but concerned a case where a mortgagee was entitled to retain the gross amount of the interest; prior to 1969 this could raise an important point for the mortgagor, because it was by deducting income tax from yearly interest paid that the mortgagor obtained effective relief for the interest.

[20] See Law of Property Act 1925 s 109 (2) and Insolvency Act 1986 s 44(1)(a).

[1] TA 1988 s 350 (1).

[2] TA 1988 ss 350 (1) and (3).

[3] TMA 1970 s 86.

[4] In *Re Lang Propeller Ltd* [1927] 1 Ch 120, 11 TC 46, CA.

not been deducted[5]. However, although not expressly stated in the legislation, the Inland Revenue would not be permitted to recover tax from both the payer and the recipient of the interest, as this would be contrary to the general principle against double taxation[6]; thus, if a person paying interest fails to deduct tax and the recipient pays tax in respect of the gross amount of the interest, the Inland Revenue cannot subsequently assess the payer[7]. Moreover, if interest which is required to be paid under deduction of tax is paid net of basic rate income tax but the payer fails to account to the Inland Revenue for the tax, the recipient cannot be assessed to basic rate income tax on the payments made[8].

The procedure under which a UK resident company accounts for income tax deducted from yearly interest is explained in §7-11 above.

7-33 The tax to be deducted is that equal to the basic rate in force for the year of assessment in which the interest is paid[9]. Where it is proposed that the basic rate of income tax should be altered and a resolution of the House of Commons to that effect is passed, any deduction of tax under s 349 (2) is thereafter made at the proposed new rate[10]. If a proposed increase in the basic rate does not in fact take place, any excess tax deducted and paid to the Inland Revenue is repaid so that the payer can account to the recipient for the amount overdeducted[11]. Where an underdeduction has been made by virtue of an increase in the basic rate implemented by the Finance Act after a payment of interest has already been made in the year of assessment, the payer must recover the underdeduction out of the next payment after the passing of the Act; if there is no further payment due he may recover it as a debt due from the recipient of the interest[12]. Where an overdeduction of tax has been made, as a result of a reduction in the basic rate after the payment has been made the overdeduction must be made good by the payer of the interest[13]; in the case of a payment of interest by a company, the adjustment is made to the next interest payment, even though the person who is then entitled to the interest may be different from the person who suffered the overdeduction[14].

7-34 If a person paying yearly interest fails to deduct income tax from a payment, this cannot be made good by a deduction from interest subsequently paid on the same loan[15]; although it appears that, if an amount of interest due has not been paid in full, tax in respect of the whole of the interest in question can be deducted from the balance when it is paid.[16] An agreement for payment of interest without allowing any deduction of income tax is void[17], and if a person refuses to allow a deduction he is

---

[5] See *Grosvenor Place Estates Ltd v Roberts* [1961] Ch 148, CA.
[6] *Ibid*, at 163 and 176.
[7] Thereby preventing the Inland Revenue from recovering interest under TMA s 86 or s 88.
[8] *Stokes v Bennett (Inspector of Taxes)* [1953] 2 All ER 313, 34 TC 337.
[9] TA 1988 ss 4 (1) and (2) (b) and 350 (1).
[10] Provisional Collection of Taxes Act 1968 s 1 (2).
[11] Provisional Collection of Taxes Act 1968 ss 1 (6) and (7) and 2 and TA 1988 s 822.
[12] TA 1988 s 821 (2).
[13] Provisional Collection of Taxes Act 1968 ss 1 (7) and 2.
[14] TA 1988 s 822 (2).
[15] *Currie v Goold* (1817) 2 Madd 163; *Taylor v Taylor* [1937] 3 All ER 571, [1938] 1 KB 320, CA; *Johnson v Johnson* [1946] P 205 [1946] 1 All ER 573, CA.
[16] *Tenbry Investments Ltd v Peugeot Talbot Motor Co Ltd* [1992] STC 791.
[17] TMA 1970 s 106 (2).

subject to a penalty of £50[18]. Refusal to allow a deduction should not normally arise, since if the payer tenders the interest due less basic rate income tax that would discharge his obligation to pay the interest and the creditor would not be able to recover any additional amount by an action before the courts in the UK. If, however, a creditor were to be able to enforce repayment of a loan and yearly interest falling within Case III before a court outside the UK it is probable that that court would not recognise the payer's obligation to deduct UK tax from the interest paid[19].

If an agreement is made for the payment of interest 'less tax', that is treated as an agreement for the payment of the full amount of the interest for the purpose of calculating the tax to be deducted[20]. Similarly, if interest is agreed to be paid at such a rate as shall, after deduction of income tax, amount to a stated rate, the interest is treated as being interest payable at the gross rate[1].

Where a lender wishes to receive the full amount of interest without any reduction on account of UK tax[2], the loan agreement should provide that, in the event of the borrower being required by law to make any deduction or withholding for or on account of UK tax, then the interest payable should be increased to such an amount as after making the deduction or withholding shall leave an amount received by the lender equal to the contractual amount of interest originally due. If the lender is established in a jurisdiction where tax is likely to be suffered in respect of income or profits including the interest received from the borrower with credit being given for any foreign tax suffered, the borrower should consider seeking an undertaking from the lender to repay to the borrower so much of the additional interest paid by the borrower under the grossing-up arrangement as is equal to the amount of any credit against the lender's own liability to tax which may be enjoyed by the lender in respect of the UK tax deducted.

7-35 The obligation to deduct tax must be performed by the person by or through whom the payment is made 'on making the payment'[3], and the account must be delivered to the Inspector of Taxes 'forthwith'[4], unless the special rules applying to interest paid by UK resident companies operate[5]. Where a cheque or warrant for payment of interest is posted to the recipient those obligations arise at the time when the posting is effected, and not the time when the cheque or warrant is encashed[6]. A person paying interest may be required to provide the recipient with written details of the interest paid and tax deducted, as explained in §§**10-02** and **10-03** below.

Where the interest is paid in foreign currency, the amount of tax to be accounted for is the sterling equivalent at the rate of exchange prevailing at the date of payment of the percentage of the foreign currency calculated

---

[18] TMA 1970 s 106(1).
[19] See Chapter 3 Part 2 as to the source of interest where there is a foreign element.
[20] TA 1988 s 818.
[1] TA 1988 s 818(2); such an arrangement could give rise to a fluctuating interest rate affected by changes in the basic rate of income tax.
[2] As may be the case where an overseas lender makes a loan to a UK borrower.
[3] TA 1988 s 349(2).
[4] TA 1988 s 350(1).
[5] See §**7-11** above.
[6] *Rhokana Corpn Ltd v IRC* [1938] 2 All ER 51, 21 TC 552, HL.

at the basic rate of income tax at the same date. In *Rhokana Corpn Ltd v IRC*[7] the House of Lords held that tax should be deducted from the sterling amounts of interest paid by warrant even though the recipients of the interest were entitled to encash the warrants in foreign currencies at fixed rates of exchange which amounted in sterling terms to greater value than the original sterling warrants. This decision was based upon the view that payment of the interest in the special circumstances of that case was made when the warrants were posted and that it cannot have been intended by the legislation that the company should account to the Inspector of Taxes 'forthwith' after every warrant was encashed over a period of time; nor was it clear how the company would in those circumstances have fulfilled its obligation to provide the recipient with a written statement of the tax deducted[8].

2 Mortgage interest relief at source (MIRAS)

7-36 In most cases, relief for mortgage interest on loans to acquire living accommodation is given at source, by permitting borrowers to deduct a sum equivalent to basic rate income tax on 'relevant loan interest' paid on a mortgage advance[9]. This system is similar to the system for giving income tax relief on yearly interest which applied before 1969[10].

The borrower is to be charged with tax at the basic rate[11] on an amount of his income equal to the amount of loan interest which is deductible in computing his total income[12], except that if his income is of such a level that he cannot benefit in full from personal reliefs[13] the amount of income on which he is so chargeable to income tax at the basic rate is reduced accordingly[14].

7-37 The system only applies to[15]

1   interest on a loan to purchase or improve land, or to purchase a caravan or house-boat, in the UK[16] used, wholly or to a substantial extent, as a residence of the borrower[17], in circumstances that the interest would otherwise qualify in full for relief from tax, or to pay off a previously qualifying loan of that kind;

---

[7] [1938] 2 All ER 51, 21 TC 552.
[8] Under FA 1924 s 33, now (effectively) TA 1988 s 234A.
[9] TA 1988 s 369.
[10] See §1-10 above.
[11] Or, as to part of the amount chargeable, at the lower rate where this is applicable – see TA 1988 ss 369 (5A) and (5B) and 1 (2) (aa).
[12] See §8-51 below.
[13] Disregarding certain reliefs in respect of life assurance and deferred annuity premiums – TA 1988 s 369 (5).
[14] TA 1988 s 369 (4).
[15] TA 1988 s 370.
[16] TA 1988 ss 370 (2) and (5) and 354 (1).
[17] TA 1988 ss 370 (2) (c), (6) and (7) and 355. The Inland Revenue considers that the property is not used by the borrower 'to a substantial extent' if more than one-third of the property is let – see Inland Revenue Booklet IR87, p 4.

2   interest on a loan to purchase a life annuity where the interest would otherwise qualify for relief from income tax[18]; and

3   interest on a loan under the Option Mortgage Scheme and outstanding on 1 April 1983[19].

The circumstances where interest would otherwise qualify for relief from income tax are explained in Chapter 8 Part 4 below.

Where the loan is to improve, rather than purchase, land or buildings, the interest is only 'relevant loan interest' where the lender is a building society or local authority, or the lender has notified the Inland Revenue that the interest on the loan is to be brought within the scheme[20] or the loan was made under the Option Mortgage Scheme[1].

The interest is only 'relevant loan interest' where it is payable *and* paid in the UK[2], and is paid by a 'qualifying borrower' to a 'qualifying lender'. A 'qualifying borrower' is an individual, unless he or his spouse[3] is specially exempt from tax under Sch E Case I, II or III (eg certain employees of foreign governments working in the UK)[4]; this limitation applies even where one of the husband and wife is fully taxable under Sch E. Normally, because MIRAS only applies to interest on a loan to purchase or improve the borrower's residence, only resident individuals can be 'qualifying borrowers'. However, where a temporary absence is by concession ignored[5] an individual living and working abroad may qualify to pay interest under the MIRAS scheme even though the property is let at a rent and he is not at the time resident in the UK for taxation purposes. Interest paid by personal representatives or trustees of a will may, in certain cases, be treated as 'relevant loan interest'[6].

'Qualifying lenders' include building societies, local authorities, certain insurance companies, registered friendly societies and other institutions specified in TA 1988 s 376 (4), together with other lenders prescribed by Treasury Order[7].

Where there is one loan to a borrower, only part of which qualifies as 'relevant loan interest' – because, for example, the loan was made both to finance the purchase of a residence and to finance other expenditure – none of the interest under the loan will be 'relevant loan interest'[8]. In such a case, in order to bring the loan on which interest is relievable within MIRAS, it is necessary to arrange for the loan to be split into two loans, the interest on one being 'relevant loan interest', the interest on the other not being so. This situation is to be contrasted with the position where the interest

---

[18] TA 1988 s 365; except where the loan is secured on land in the Republic of Ireland – TA 1988 s 370 (5); see also §8–61 below.

[19] TA 1988 s 370 (3).

[20] TA 1988 s 372; see §8–44(2) below as to loans to improve land.

[1] TA 1988 ss 372 and 870 (3).

[2] TA 1988 s 370 (1).

[3] Except in the case of a separated spouse – TA 1988 s 376 (3).

[4] TA 1988 s 376 (1) and (2); this provision is not prevented from operating in relation to an official of the European Communities by Articles 5 and 7 of the Protocol on the Privileges and Immunities of the European Communities – see *Tither v IRC*: C-333/88 [1990] STC 416, [1990] 2 CMLR 779, ECJ.

[5] See Extra-statutory Concession A27, and §8–55 below.

[6] Regulation 7A of the Income Tax (Interest Relief) Regulations 1982: SI 1982 No 1236.

[7] TA 1988 s 376 (4) and (5).

[8] *R v Inspector of Taxes, ex p Kelly* [1991] STC 566n, CA.

on a loan would be 'relevant loan interest' but the loan in question exceeds the amount on which tax relief is available[9]. In such a case, only so much of the interest is 'relevant loan interest' as would, apart from the scheme, be eligible for relief; this applies where the loan was made after 5 April 1987 or where the lender notifies the Inland Revenue that it is prepared to have loans which are subject to limited interest relief brought within the scheme[10]. Where two or more loans are taken into account for the purpose of determining the limit of relief, these provisions can only apply if both or all the loans were made by the same lender[11].

Where there are joint borrowers, not being husband and wife (unless they are separated[12]), the provisions of the deduction scheme do not apply unless each of the borrowers is a 'qualifying borrower' and the interest is 'relevant loan interest' in relation to each of them[13].

7-38 The legislation and regulations made under it[14] provide for notices to be given in relation to the implementation of the scheme and the cessation of the application of the scheme where the interest ceases to be 'relevant loan interest'[15]. Provision is also made for arrangements for making payments by the Inland Revenue to qualifying lenders of tax deducted at source to make up the sums received by lenders to the full amount to which they are entitled.

7-39 So far as the qualifying lenders are concerned, they receive interest payments net of basic rate income tax, but are permitted to make an immediate claim to recover that tax from the Inland Revenue. The limitations[16] which normally prevent a company reclaiming any tax deducted at source until the corporation tax assessment for the relevant accounting period is finally determined do not apply in the case of tax deducted under the MIRAS scheme[17]. The total of the net amount of interest paid and the tax recovered is treated as the lender's income for taxation purposes.

3   Interest paid by non-resident bodies: TA 1988 s 123

7-40 Where foreign source loan interest is paid by a paying agent in the UK or is collected through a UK banker or other person (whether by the sale of coupons or the collection of interest due on coupons) an obligation to deduct basic rate income tax may arise. This obligation is imposed by TA 1988 s 123 which applies in relation to 'foreign dividends' in the same way as the provisions of Sch C operate in relation to 'overseas public revenue

---

[9] See §**8-56** below.
[10] TA 1988 s 373 (2).
[11] TA 1988 s 373 (4) and (5).
[12] TA 1988 s 373 (7).
[13] TA 1988 s 373 (6).
[14] See FA 1982 s 29.
[15] See FA 1982 Sch 7 paras 7 to 11.
[16] TA 1988 ss 7 (2) and 11 (3).
[17] TA 1988 s 369 (6). See as to claims by lenders for repayment of tax deducted – Regulations 9 to 17 of the Income Tax (Interest Relief) Regulations 1982: SI 1982 No 1236, as amended.

dividends'[18]. Interest chargeable to tax under Case IV or V will often, but not always, fall within these deduction procedures. The definition[19] of 'foreign dividends' includes 'interest, dividends or other annual payments payable out of or in respect of the stocks, funds, shares or securities of any body of persons not resident in the United Kingdom'; discounts are not included. Deduction of tax under s 123 does not apply to foreign source interest payable by individuals, trustees or partnerships nor to foreign source interest payable by UK resident companies[20]. Interest paid by a non-resident company but which falls within Sch D Case III (for example, because it is paid in respect of a liability of a UK branch business) would nevertheless fall within the definition of 'foreign dividends'[1]. However, the Inland Revenue do not regard interest paid on an account outside the UK with a non-UK resident bank as falling within the definition.

It will be seen that 'foreign dividends' includes 'interest', not *'yearly interest'*. However, does the use of the expression 'or other annual payments' require 'interest' to be construed as 'yearly interest'? There is no clear case law on the point. In *IRC v Frere*[2] it was held that the expression 'interest, annuities or other annual payments' referred to 'yearly interest', but that expression was used in a provision relating to forms and declarations in the context of relief from surtax where the substantive liability was charged on total income which was only reduced by yearly interest, annuities or other annual payments[3]. In *Lord Advocate v Edinburgh Corpn*[4], an obligation to deduct income tax from 'any interest of money or annuities' was held to apply to all interest, whether or not yearly interest. The original language from which the definition of 'foreign dividends' is drawn[5] similarly referred to 'Interest, Dividends, or other annual Payments'. Not only did the same Act make it clear that UK residents were chargeable in respect of income from foreign possessions or securities without any exclusion for interest which was not yearly interest[6], but also the same Act referred to 'any yearly Interest of Money, or any Annuity or other annual Payment'[7] in relation to the deduction and retention procedure, so indicating that the draftsman could have limited the paying agency provisions to yearly interest if he had wished. Therefore, it would seem that the better view is that the provisions of TA 1988 s 123 should also apply to all interest and not merely to yearly interest.

'Foreign dividends' do not include interest etc which is a liability of an international organisation designated by the Treasury under TA 1988 s 586A[8].

7-41   Although s 123 refers only to 'income tax', the tax to be collected under this procedure is income tax at the basic rate[9].

---

18 See Chapter 6 above.
19 In TA 1988 s 123 (1) (a).
20 See §§**3-28** to **3-31** above.
1 But see §**7-44** below.
2 (1964) 42 TC 125, at 153, HL.
3 See Viscount Radcliffe at 147 to 150; and ITA 1842 s 164 and Sch G Rule XVII.
4 (1903) 40 SLR 632, 4 TC 627.
5 ITA 1853 s 10; see §**1-06** above.
6 ITA 1853 s 6.
7 ITA 1853 s 40.
8 See the International Organisations (Miscellaneous Exemptions) Order 1991: SI 1991 No 1694, designating the European Bank for Reconstruction and Development.
9 TA 1988 Sch 3 para 6A (1).

7-42   The deduction of tax under s 123 does not apply to a recipient who shows that he is not resident in the UK[10]. Unless the circumstances are such that in practice the paying agent may make payments gross without authority, evidence of non-residence must be produced as under Sch C[11].

A non-resident beneficiary under a trust who is able to call for the securities in question to be transferred to him absolutely is treated as the owner of the securities and so entitled to claim payment of interest gross[12], and in practice where the non-resident beneficiary is entitled to the income of the trust as of right he may be entitled to claim payment of interest gross notwithstanding that he is only entitled to the income of the trust and cannot call for the trust assets to be transferred to him[13]. By concession, a residuary legatee who is neither resident nor ordinarily resident in the UK is treated as being entitled to receive interest gross[14], and a non-resident discretionary beneficiary who receives payments net under TA 1988 s 687(2) is able to make a repayment claim in respect of tax suffered where the underlying income would have been exempt from tax under s 123 had it been received by him directly[15]. However, the ownership of the securities by a non-resident does not permit payment of interest gross where some other provision of the tax legislation (eg TA 1988 s 739) requires the interest to be treated as the income of a resident person[16].

The exemption from tax does not apply where the non-resident carries on a banking, insurance or security-dealing business in the UK and the interest in question forms part of the income of that business[17].

UK PAYING AGENTS

7-43   Section 123(2) imposes a charge to tax on any paying agent who is entrusted with the payment of interest and other foreign dividends to 'persons in the United Kingdom', except where securities on which the interest is paid are held in a recognised clearing system[18]; in the latter case, UK tax would be withheld on collection on behalf of a UK person to whose order the securities are held in the clearing system[19]. The machinery which applies under TA 1988 Sch 3 Parts III and IV to Sch C deductions also applies for the purposes of s 123(2), and the reader is referred to §§6-08 to 6-11 above, insofar as they are not concerned with interest on UK or Republic of Ireland government securities, for an outline of the procedure which is the same as that which applies in relation to Sch C.

The practices in relation to payments, described in §§6-09 and 6-10 above, also apply to the deduction obligation under s 123.

---

[10]   TA 1988 s 123(4).
[11]   See §§6-18 to 6-20 above.
[12]   TA 1988 s 123(5).
[13]   See *Baker v Archer-Shee* [1927] AC 844, 11 TC 749, HL and *Archer-Shee v Garland* [1931] AC 212, 15 TC 693, HL.
[14]   Extra-statutory Concession A14.
[15]   Extra-statutory Concession B18.
[16]   TA 1988 s 123(6).
[17]   TA 1988 ss 474(1) and 445(8)(a); and see §6-22 above in relation to Sch C.
[18]   See TA 1988 s 123(2) and (1)(b); 'recognised clearing systems' are Euro-clear, CEDEL and First Chicago Clearing System.
[19]   See TA 1988 s 123(3)(a)(ii); and §7-41 above.

7-44   As already mentioned, s 123 applies to interest paid by non-resident companies, not merely to foreign source interest within Sch D Case IV or V. Thus, interest paid through a UK paying agent on behalf of a UK branch of a non-resident company would be within these provisions. In practice, where a UK branch of a non-resident bank pays interest through a UK paying agent on securities issued in the UK (as it might where, for example, it pays interest on the issue of tradeable certificates of deposit or deposit notes), the Inland Revenue by concession considers that interest paid in the ordinary course of banking business (so as to be exempted from the withholding obligation in respect of Sch D Case III interest[20]) need not be subject to the deduction of tax under s 123 (2)[1].

7-45   If the circumstances referred to above do not apply, payment in respect of interest on registered securities may only be made gross to a non-resident after the Inspector of Foreign Dividends has authorised payment gross following receipt of a claim on Form A3 or, where payment gross is claimed by a banker or merchant, on Form C4 under the 'E' Arrangement[2]. Interest on bearer securities may be paid without deduction of tax where Forms A or D are submitted as described in §6-19 above.

COLLECTION OF INTEREST ON COUPONS ETC

7-46   The procedure for deduction of basic rate income tax from foreign source interest represented by coupons is the same as that which applies for Sch C purposes[3]. The circumstances are as follows:

1   Where a banker[4] obtains payment of 'foreign dividends' outside the UK[5], and either the interest was not paid through a UK paying agent or the securities in respect of which the interest was paid were held in a recognised clearing system. This applies whether or not the interest is collected by means of coupons, and would arise where a bank in the UK is instructed by its customer to obtain payment of foreign source interest from a paying agent outside the UK. It would also apply where a customer hands to his bank in the UK a cheque or warrant which either on its face or by reason of a counterfoil attached was clearly in payment of a foreign source interest. But if the bank merely obtains payment of foreign currency cheque which happens to be in payment of foreign source interest this would not, in the author's view, amount to obtaining payment of 'any foreign dividends'. The reader is referred to §6-13 above for further comment on the expression 'obtains payment'.

2   Where a banker[6] in the UK sells or otherwise realises coupons for interest amounting to 'foreign dividends' and accounts to his customer for the

---

[20] TA 1988 s 349 (3)(b).
[1] This practice does not apply in relation to the deduction obligation which applies to collecting agents under TA 1988 s 123 (3): see §§7-46 to 7-49 below.
[2] See §6-18 above.
[3] See §§6-13 to 6-16 above.
[4] Which includes 'any person acting as a banker' – TA 1988 s 123 (1)(c).
[5] TA 1988 s 123 (3)(a).
[6] Which includes 'any person acting as a banker' – TA 1988 s 123 (1)(c).

proceeds (whether or not that customer is a 'person in the United Kingdom')[7].

3   Where any dealer in coupons in the UK buys coupons otherwise than from a banker or another dealer[8].

7–47   The procedure under TA 1988 Sch 3 for the collection of the tax is the same as that which applies for the purposes of Sch C. Reference should therefore be made to §§**6–13** to **6–17** above for a summary of the procedure. Similarly, reference should be made to §§**6–19** and **6–20** above for a summary of the procedure for a non-resident to claim payment of interest gross on coupons.

7–48   It should be noted that the question of presence of the *recipient* of the interest 'in the United Kingdom' is not relevant in connection with the circumstances described in §**7–46** above, and therefore the practice described in §**6–08** above is of no application in those cases. However, a non-resident obtaining payment of foreign source interest on coupons in this way is entitled to claim payment of the interest gross[9].

Moreover, the Inland Revenue does not apply its concessionary practice where interest is paid to UK banks recognised by the Inland Revenue[10] to cases other than those involving payments by paying agents in the UK. Therefore, where a UK bank 'obtains payment' outside the UK of foreign source interest payable by a foreign company (eg by presentation of bills of exchange drawn in payment of interest) it will then be obliged to deduct tax[11] on making payment to other banks (eg in a syndicate of UK banks) unless the necessary procedure has been satisfied to enable payment gross in the case of non-resident recipients.

7–49   Under the practice known as the Company Arrangement, a collecting agent who collects interest on behalf of a company which controls, directly or indirectly, not less than 10 per cent of the voting power of the non-resident paying company is not required to deduct income tax.

CREDIT FOR FOREIGN TAX DEDUCTED

7–50   Foreign source interest to which the deduction procedure under s 123 applies may also be subject to the deduction of foreign tax. The Inland Revenue has published a practice under which paying agents may, in certain cases, take into account the foreign tax already deducted before deducting the balance of UK tax at the basic rate[12]. So long as the foreign tax does not exceed the basic rate of income tax to be deducted under s 123, credit may be given, in applying s 123, for the foreign tax deducted against the basic rate income tax to be deducted. If the foreign tax is deducted at a rate greater than the basic rate of income tax, then no UK tax would be

[7] TA 1988 s 123(3)(b) – see §**6–15** above.
[8] TA 1988 s 123(3)(c) – see §**6–15** above.
[9] See §**7–42** above.
[10] See §**6–09** above.
[11] For which it will be liable to account to the Inland Revenue.
[12] Inland Revenue Circular to Paying and Collecting Agents, July 1991.

deducted under s 123. Credit may only be given in the cases of interest deriving from certain countries in respect of which the Inland Revenue has published the rates of foreign tax which may be allowed by way of credit against tax deductible under s 123. If any credit is due for foreign tax which has been deducted but not taken into account in deducting tax under s 123, this will be taken into account when the income is assessed.

TREATMENT OF TAX DEDUCTED UNDER S 123

7-51   Where tax is deducted under s 123, the foreign source interest is assessed on the current year basis and the net interest received in a year of assessment is grossed up to include the tax deducted and included in the recipient's total income for that year[13]. Where an individual's income and allowances are such that he does not bear income tax on all his income, part of the tax suffered by way of deduction may be reclaimed from the Inland Revenue.

The application of the s 123 procedure does not affect the assessment to corporation tax in respect of foreign source interest. Any tax suffered by the company under s 123 may be either set against tax deductible in respect of certain payments made by a resident company[14], or set against the corporation tax payable by the company in respect of its profits for the relevant accounting period or reclaimed by the company if it has insufficient profits[15].

The application of s 123 does not depend upon the income being chargeable to tax under Sch D Case IV or V. It may therefore apply where the interest forms part of the income of a company chargeable to tax under Case I or Case III. The tax deducted would, again, be credited against the taxpayer's income tax or corporation tax liability for the period in question, or reclaimed if it exceeds that tax liability.

7-52   The obligations of paying and collecting agents in relation to returns and accounting for tax deducted are summarised in §§**10-06** and **10-07** below.

---

[13] TA 1988 s 835 (6) (a).
[14] TA 1988 Sch 16 para 5 and see §**7-11** above.
[15] TA 1988 ss 7 (2) and 11 (3).

Chapter 8

RELIEF FOR INTEREST

8-01 From 1803 until 1969, relief for interest was normally available to the taxpayer under the deduction and retention procedure[1], although that only applied to yearly interest, and in 1965 special rules were introduced for companies upon the introduction of corporation tax. Since 1969, many changes have been made; principally, the restriction of general relief for interest in 1969, the reintroduction in 1972 of a wider measure of relief for interest and the imposition of further limitations in 1974. This chapter describes the circumstances where a taxpayer paying interest may now obtain relief for interest against income or other gains which are liable to taxation in his hands.

1 Interest as a business expense – income tax

THE PREVIOUS SYSTEM OF RELIEF

8-02 There is limited judicial authority on the availability of relief for interest as a business expense, and most of the decided cases concern earlier legislation which has now been altered. However, it is helpful to understand how the law has developed, particularly in relation to the different treatment which now applies to a company paying interest as a trading expense and interest as a charge on income[2].

8-03 As explained in Chapter 1, the system which applied for income tax purposes from 1803 to 1969 provided a taxpayer with relief for yearly interest paid under the deduction and retention procedure. Whether the interest was incurred as an expense in a business or a private capacity, a taxpayer paying yearly interest was permitted to retain out of the interest paid a sum representing income tax on that interest. No provision was made for a taxpayer to deduct the interest from his income in computing his liability to income tax (except, from 1949, where the interest related to an overseas trade[3]), and, therefore, although he paid income tax on the full amount of his income, he obtained relief for yearly interest paid by retaining for himself the income tax relating to that interest. In view of this, the legislation specifically provided that in computing profits or gains of a trade or profession no deduction could be made in respect of any yearly interest payable out of such gains. An early case which illustrates the operation of this prohibition

[1] Described in Chapter 1.
[2] See Chapter 8 Part 3 below.
[3] See §1-11 (2).

is *Alexandria Water Co v Musgrave*[4]. In that case, a company carried on its trade outside the UK and paid interest to non-residents on debentures issued to raise money to finance its business. However, as against the recipients of the interest the taxpayer company could not, and did not, deduct an amount in respect of income tax, and so the company claimed a deduction in computing its taxable profits. This was refused, the court holding that there was no reason to override the ordinary meaning of the prohibition against deduction for yearly interest.

8-04   The prohibition on deduction only applied when the payment was made out of the profits or gains of the trade. In *Gresham Life Assurance Society v Styles (Surveyor of Taxes)*[5] it was held that an insurance company which paid annuities was not prevented from obtaining a deduction in respect of annuities paid in the course of its trade despite the prohibition against deduction which applied to annuities or other annual payments as well as to yearly interest. This was because where the payment was made in the course of a trade the profits or gains of the trade could not be ascertained without first deducting the annuities[6]. Accordingly, a bank paying interest on deposits would have been entitled to deduct the interest in computing profits or gains[7].

8-05   Not content with preventing a deduction in respect of yearly interest, the Crown also successfully resisted claims for deduction of interest not being yearly interest on the basis that what was to be assessed was the profits of gains of the *trade* and that was not affected by the way in which the taxpayer, the owner of the trade, chose to finance it. In *Anglo-Continental Guano Works v Bell*[8] the London branch of an overseas company which had taken a short-term loan from its bank was compared with a case where two partners financed their business, in one case from their own resources and in the other with borrowed money; the profits of the *trade*, it was held, were unaffected by the financing arrangements[9].

Anglo-Continental Guano Works was seriously questioned by the House of Lords in *Farmer v Scottish North American Trust Ltd*[10]. The taxpayer was an investment company which paid non-yearly interest on six-month loans from its bankers. The deduction of the interest was challenged on the basis that the interest was expenditure 'for sums employed ... as capital' in the trade[11]. The House of Lords held unanimously that temporary fluctuating borrowings did not amount to 'capital' for the purposes of this prohibition, and that the taxpayer was entitled to a deduction for the interest paid as 'any similar outgoing should be deducted from the receipts, to ascertain the taxable profits and gains which the Company earns'[12]. The *Anglo-*

---

[4]   (1883) 11 QBD 174, 1 TC 521, CA.
[5]   [1892] AC 309, 3 TC 185, HL.
[6]   The dispute with the Inland Revenue, relating to a year before 1888, arose because until 1888 the payer was not obliged to deduct income tax from interest or annuities *not* paid out of profits or gains – see §**1-06** above.
[7]   See Lord Herschell in *Gresham* (1892) 3 TC 185 at 197, disapproving the decision in *Mersey Loan and Discount Co v Wootton* (1887) 4 TLR 164, 2 TC 316.
[8]   (1894) 70 LT 670, 3 TC 239.
[9]   See also *Portobello Town Council v Sulley* (1890) 2 TC 647.
[10]   [1912] AC 118, 5 TC 693.
[11]   Under the then equivalent of TA 1988 s 74 (f) without the proviso added.
[12]   Lord Atkinson, (1911) 5 TC 693 at 707.

Continental Guano Works decision was not expressly overruled. In the only full opinion, Lord Atkinson did not think that the view that interest on borrowed money should not be deductible could apply to a bank whose business was borrowing and lending money, or even to an investment company such as the *Scottish North American Trust.*

8-06 The picture was confused in 1932 by the decision in *European Investment Trust Co Ltd v Jackson*[13]. There, the Court of Appeal refused to disturb a finding by the appellate Commissioners that interest paid on fluctuating advances from a bank was not deductible as being in respect of capital in the trade; the Court of Appeal held that there was sufficient evidence for the Commissioners to come to that conclusion. It was pointed out that each case depended on its own facts and that no general rule could be laid down. Lord Hanworth MR considered[14] that the question to be decided was whether the money was used as fixed or circulating capital, although Romer LJ[15] thought that *Farmer v Scottish North American Trust*[16] neither laid down any general rule that circulating capital was not 'capital' for the purposes of the exemption nor overruled *Anglo-Continental Guano Works v Bell*[17]. It is doubtful whether the distinction between fixed and circulating capital was relevant, because if the borrowing was on capital account, interest paid in respect of it would fall within the prohibition even if the borrowed capital were applied in the circulation of that trader's trade (eg the purchase and sale of goods) so as to be treated as *circulating* capital. The relevant distinction appears to be between a capital liability and a current liability, as discussed in *Pattison (Inspector of Taxes) v Marine Midland Ltd*[18].

   European Investment Trust Co Ltd v Jackson was followed in *Ward v Anglo-American Oil Co Ltd*[19] where interest on Notes issued by the taxpayer was disallowed on the grounds that it was yearly interest[20] and also because it was in respect of capital employed in the trade in that the Notes issued by the taxpayer were not in the category of short loans or temporary trading facilities. *European Investment Trust* was further followed in *Ascot Gas Water Heaters Ltd v Duff*[1] where a guarantee payment was allowed where the purchase price in respect of raw materials was left outstanding on credit, whereas a similar payment was not allowed where a fifteen-year debenture stock was guaranteed. In *Bridgwater and Bridgwater v King (Inspector of Taxes)*[2] a premium or bonus payable on repayment of a loan was not allowable where the loan was more than a mere temporary accommodation[3]. More recently, the view that interest was previously disallowed on the grounds that it was expenditure 'in respect of capital' has been seriously questioned by the Court of Appeal in *Beauchamp (Inspector of Taxes) v F W Woolworth*

[13] (1932) 18 TC 1.
[14] (1932) 18 TC 1 at 13.
[15] (1932) 18 TC 1 at 16–17.
[16] [1912] AC 118, 5 TC 693, HL – see §8-05 above.
[17] (1894) 70 LT 670, 3 TC 239.
[18] [1981] STC 540 at 553g–560h, but not pursued in the Court of Appeal or House of Lords.
[19] (1934) 19 TC 94.
[20] See §8-03 above, which alone would have been sufficient to dispose of the case; see §3-06 above as to yearly interest.
[1] (1942) 24 TC 171.
[2] (1943) 25 TC 385.
[3] See also *Arizona Copper Co v Smiles (Surveyor of Taxes)* (1891) 19 R 150, 3 TC 149 as to premium on repayment of a loan; but it was not argued that the premium was interest.

plc[4]. The words 'in respect of' were considered to be no more than the equivalent of 'on account of' or 'for', which were the words originally used in the Income Tax Act 1842[5]. This point is no longer of any significance in relation to interest, as explained in §8–07 below, but is relevant in relation to foreign currency losses[6] and relief for certain discounts.

THE PRESENT SYSTEM OF RELIEF

8–07   Most of the foregoing difficulties were swept away in 1969 by two changes in the law. In that year, the deduction and retention provisions were abandoned upon the introduction of general limitations on the relief for interest paid. But in order that relief was allowable as a deductible expense of a trade, yearly interest was removed from the prohibition against deduction[7]. Further, the prohibition against any deduction 'in respect of ... any sum employed or intended to be employed as capital in [the] trade, profession or vocation'[8] was not to be treated as disallowing the deduction of any interest[9].

Consequently, subject to a qualification in the case of interest paid abroad[10], both yearly and non-yearly interest may qualify as a trading expense provided of course that it is incurred on revenue account and is wholly and exclusively incurred for the purposes of the trade, profession or vocation [11]. This means that relief is available for interest on both bank overdrafts and other temporary facilities and also on long-term loans to provide capital assets for the trade (eg to finance the purchase of a farm by a farmer). Even interest paid on a loan to purchase a business is regarded as being incurred for the purpose of a trade[12], presumably on the basis that it is incurred 'for the purpose of enabling a person to carry on and earn profits in the trade'[13]. However, where the trader borrows to draw out of the business more than his accumulated realised profits (current and capital), the Inland Revenue may regard the borrowing as not being for the purposes of the trade[14]. Thus, if the trader anticipates that he might want to withdraw his invested capital at a later stage, he should consider financing part of his initial investment in the business through borrowings, rather than raise borrowings at a later date to replace his own capital. However, it does not necessarily follow that, where the trader's capital account is reduced or overdrawn, interest on an equivalent amount of the trade borrowings should be disallowed; what is

---

[4] [1988] STC 714 at 716*c*–718*b*.
[5] Section 100 – Third Rule of Sch D Case I.
[6] The issue in the *F W Woolworth* case.
[7] See FA 1969 s 18 (4) and Sch 13 para 22, amending ITA 1952 s 137 (1) (now TA 1988 s 74 (m)).
[8] See ITA 1952 s 137 (f) (now TA 1988 s 74 (f)).
[9] FA 1969 Sch 13 para 4 (1), effective from 1968.
[10] See §§8–09 to 8–12 below.
[11] See *Marine Management Ltd v Deputy Comr of Inland Revenue* [1986] STC 251, PC, where interest on a loan to acquire a controlling shareholding in a company did not qualify as a trade expense even though the purpose of acquiring control was to obtain a management agreement with the company.
[12] See Inland Revenue Booklet: IR11 (1985) para 38 (although this booklet is no longer current).
[13] Lord Davey in *Strong & Co of Romsey Ltd v Woodifield (Surveyor of Taxes)* (1906) 5 TC 215 at 220, HL.
[14] Inland Revenue, 'Tax Bulletin', November 1991, p 4; see also Inland Revenue Booklet IR11 (1985) para 45 (although this booklet is no longer current).

required is an examination of the accounts and of the application of the borrowing to ascertain the purpose of the borrowing.

Where a loan is obtained partly for the purpose of the business and partly for some other purpose, an apportionment of the interest may be possible in order that relief is available for part of the interest paid. This will depend upon the general rules and the 'wholly and exclusively' test[15]. Examples of such an apportionment might be where a loan relates to the purchase of both business premises and private residential accommodation, or where a loan is used to acquire a motor car used for both business and private travel[16].

It will be noted that the relaxation of the rules in 1969 applied only to 'interest'. Thus, other forms of expenditure related to loans or credit, such as guarantee payments, are subject to the previous rules. In the case of a premium payable on repayment of a loan, this may amount to interest properly so called and thereby qualify for relief under the law as amended in 1969[17].

8–08 Where expenditure is to qualify for relief as a business expense it must be incurred on revenue rather than capital account. From this it would appear that if interest is charged to capital, or is otherwise not charged to profit and loss account, it will not be allowed as a revenue expense of the trade[18]. It was decided[19], in relation to claims for relief from income tax under the pre-1969 deduction and retention procedure as it applied to companies before 1965, that where a company capitalised interest it could not also claim that the interest had been paid out of profits or gains brought into charge to income tax. Similarly, it would seem that interest which is capitalised cannot at the same time be regarded as a deductible expense of earning the profits of a trade. Although the 1969 amendment to the prohibition against any deduction 'in respect of ... any sum employed or intended to be employed as capital in the trade' prevents that prohibition disallowing a deduction of interest[20], in the author's view that amendment reversed the decision that interest on a capital borrowing was expenditure 'in respect of ... capital' but did not extend to permit capitalised interest to be deducted as a trading expense.

Capitalised interest paid on a loan raised to purchase machinery or plant will not qualify for capital allowances as expenditure on the provision of the machinery or plant[1]. Such capitalised interest is only incurred in putting the trader in a position to incur the expenditure on the machinery or plant, and is not sufficiently closely related to the provision of the equipment to qualify for capital allowances.

---

[15] See, for example, *Mallalieu v Drummond (Inspector of Taxes)* [1983] STC 665, [1983] 2 All ER 1095, HL.

[16] See Inland Revenue Booklet: IR11 (1985), paras 38 and 39 (although this booklet is no longer current).

[17] See §§**2–30** to **2–32** and **2–34** above.

[18] See *Odeon Associated Theatres Ltd v Jones (Inspector of Taxes)* [1972] 1 All ER 681, 48 TC 257 CA; and *Symons (Inspector of Taxes) v Weeks* [1983] STC 195 at 233d–234e.

[19] *Central London Rly Co v IRC* [1936] 2 All ER 375, 20 TC 102, HL; *Chancery Lane Safe Deposit and Offices Co Ltd v IRC* [1966] 1 All ER 1, 43 TC 83, HL and *Fitzleet Estates Ltd v Cherry (Inspector of Taxes)* [1977] STC 397, [1977] 3 All ER 996, HL.

[20] See now TA 1988 s 74 (f), and see §**8–07** above.

[1] *Ben-Odeco v Powlson (Inspector of Taxes)* [1978] STC 460, [1978] 2 All ER 1111, HL.

A company which capitalises interest paid may, however, be able to obtain relief for such interest as a charge on income (but not as an expense of the trade)[2].

INTEREST PAID ABROAD

8-09   Where interest is paid to a person not resident within the UK[3], further conditions must be satisfied before the interest can qualify for relief as trade expenditure. First, no relief is available 'if and so far as it is interest at more than a commercial rate'[4]. What is a commercial rate of interest must depend upon all the circumstances of the case (including the currency of the loan, its term, the credit risk and the security, if any, given). If the interest does exceed a commercial rate then, by reason of the words 'so far as', relief will only be denied for the excess element of the interest. If the creditor and debtor are related or connected by any special relationship, the circumstances of an excessive interest rate may also prejudice any relief from UK income tax on the interest to which the creditor may be entitled under a double taxation agreement[5].

8-10   Yearly interest paid to a non-resident must also satisfy one of the conditions of TA 1988 s 82. The first condition is that the person paying the interest must have deducted income tax from the interest under TA 1988 s 349 (2)[6] and have paid over the tax to the Inland Revenue. This condition will be satisfied where the recipient is relieved from the deduction of income tax, or is entitled to a deduction at a reduced rate only, by reason of the provisions of a double taxation agreement and the Inland Revenue has previously authorised a reduced withholding of income tax or payment gross[7]. Further, where the interest paid falls within an exemption from the deduction obligation under s 349 (2) – ie it is paid to the UK branch of a non-resident bank carrying on a bona fide banking business in the UK[8] – the payment of interest will be 'in accordance with s 349 (2), so as to satisfy the condition. But, where the interest is not chargeable under Sch D Case III, so that s 349 (2) does not apply at all, the payment of interest gross will not satisfy this condition.

Where this condition is satisfied, the amount of interest which qualifies as a deductible expense is the gross amount – not the net amount after deduction of income tax[9] – subject always to the limitation which applies to interest in excess of the commercial rate[10].

---

[2] TA 1988 s 338 (5) (a); and see §8–38 below.
[3] Cf TA 1988 s 349 (2) (c), which applies to a person whose usual place of abode is outside the UK – see §7–16 above.
[4] TA 1988 s 74 (n).
[5] See §4–30 above.
[6] TA 1988 s 82 (1) (a); and see Chapter 7 Part I above.
[7] Although Regulation 6 of the Double Taxation Relief (Taxes on Income) (General) Regulations 1970: SI 1970 No 488 is stated to apply only in relation to TA 1970 s 248 (4) (now TA 1988 s 338 (4)), the Inland Revenue in practice treats Regulation 6 as applying for the purpose of TA 1988 s 82 (1) (a).
[8] TA 1988 s 349 (3) (a); and see §§7–20 to 7–23 above.
[9] TA 1988 s 82 (5).
[10] TA 1988 s 74 (n), and §8–09 above.

8-11   Where the taxpayer cannot satisfy the condition as to the deduction of income tax under s 349 (2), the interest may still qualify as a deductible trading expense if other conditions are satisfied[11]. These circumstances could arise where s 349 (2) does not apply by reason of

1   the interest not falling within Sch D Case III because the source is not within the UK; this is discussed in §§**3-28** to **3-31** above, and might be said by the Inland Revenue not to be capable of applying having regard to the further condition that the trade, profession or vocation is carried on by a UK resident;
2   the interest not falling within Sch D Case III by reason of a special exemption from tax enjoyed by the recipient of the interest[12]; or
3   the non-resident not having his usual place of abode outside the UK[13].

In these circumstances, the following conditions must be satisfied in order for interest paid to the non-resident to qualify for relief as a trading expense:

1   The trade, profession or vocation must be carried on by a person residing in the UK. Because this condition will not be satisfied by a non-resident trading in the UK through a branch or agency, such a person may only obtain relief for interest as a trading expense where a loan is taken up in the UK such that the interest falls within Sch D Case III and the alternative condition (described in §**8-10** above) can be satisfied. Similarly, where a resident individual is a partner in a partnership managed abroad his taxable share of partnership profits will be computed under the Case I or Case II rules[14], yet the trade will be deemed to be carried on by persons resident outside the UK[15] so that this condition cannot be satisfied to obtain relief for interest as a trading expense; and
2   The liability to pay the interest must have been incurred wholly and exclusively for the purposes of the trade, profession or vocation. This condition must be satisfied in respect of all deductible trading expenditure[16]; its inclusion in these conditions appears to be a relic from the time when special provision was made to grant relief for interest paid in an overseas trade and yearly interest was otherwise not a deductible trading expense[17]; and
3   Either the interest was incurred wholly or mainly for the purposes of activities of the trade, profession or vocation carried on outside the UK or the interest is payable in foreign currency. In the first part of this condition, the words 'carried on outside the United Kingdom' qualify the 'activities' rather than the 'trade, profession or vocation'; the word 'activities' is not preceded by the definite article, and a trade, profession or vocation chargeable to tax under Case I or II will normally

---

[11]   TA 1988 s 82 (1) (b).
[12]   See §**7-05** above.
[13]   As to this unlikely event, see §**7-16** above.
[14]   TA 1988 s 65 (3).
[15]   TA 1988 s 112 (1).
[16]   TA 1988 s 74 (a).
[17]   FA 1949 s 23 (1) (a).

be one carried on, in part at least, in the UK[18]. It is therefore necessary to be able to show that the proceeds of the loan or other credit are applied in the overseas activities of the business where the borrowing is in sterling; and

4   Not only must the interest be required to be paid outside the UK under or pursuant to the loan agreement or other contract under which the interest is payable, but also the interest must in fact be paid outside the UK.

8-12   However, there are certain cases where the conditions described in §8-11 above cannot be used to qualify interest paid to a non-resident as a trading expense. First, no relief is available where the business in question is carried on by a partnership and the interest is paid to any of the partners, whether on a loan to the partnership or in respect of a share in the partnership capital[19]. Neither can interest be relieved as a trading expense on this basis where the business is carried on by a body of persons controlled by the person entitled to the interest, where the person entitled to the interest is a body of persons over whom the person carrying on the business has control, or where both parties are bodies of persons and some other person has control over both of them[20]. For this purpose, 'control' is defined in TA 1988 s 840 as, broadly, existing where a party can secure that the affairs of a body corporate are conducted in accordance with that party's wishes or, where a partnership is the subject of the control, where the first party has the right to a share of more than one-half of the partnership's assets or income[1]. 'Bodies of persons' includes companies but probably not partnerships[2]; the provisions are of no application where the body of persons carrying on the business (rather than receiving the interest) is a company, since a company would be liable to corporation tax rather than income tax and these rules as to relief for interest as a trading expense do not apply for corporation tax purposes[3]. The fact that s 82 does not apply for corporation tax purposes can give rise to difficulty where the trade is carried on by a partnership of which a company is a member. In such a case, the corporate partner's share of taxable profits is computed as if the partnership were a company[4] and the individual partner's income tax liability is calculated 'by reference to the computations made for corporation tax'[5]. It would seem that, if the interest in question can be treated as a charge on income rather than as a trade expense[6], then relief may be available, for both corporate and individual partners, by reference to, and subject to the conditions of, the provisions of TA 1988 s 338[7].

---

[18] *San Paulo (Brazilian) Rly Co v Carter* [1896] AC 31, 3 TC 407, HL, and *Ogilvie v Kitton (Surveyor of Taxes)* 1908 SC 1003, 5 TC 338.
[19] TA 1988 s 82 (3); see §4-11 above as to interest paid by a partnership to a partner.
[20] TA 1988 s 82 (4).
[1] Curiously, not 'profit', although in the context it probably means profits and other income (such as interest income).
[2] See TA 1988 s 832 (1) and *Padmore v IRC* [1989] STC 493; see also TA 1988 s 773 (2).
[3] TA 1988 s 82 (6).
[4] TA 1988 s 114 (1).
[5] TA 1988 s 114 (3) (a).
[6] As to whether the taxpayer has any choice in this, see §8-34 below.
[7] See §§8-33 to 8-41 below.

2 Other income tax reliefs for business-related interest

8-13 Ever since the 1969 restrictions were introduced to limit the general relief for interest paid, certain interest on loans related to investment in an individual's business activities have qualified for relief even though the interest may not qualify as a trade or other business expense. These reliefs have been adapted in the course of the changes made in 1972 and 1974, and have been subject to other amendments and extensions, and the circumstances in which these reliefs are available are described below. Relief cannot be given for interest both as a business expense and under the special provisions, nor can the basis for relief be changed from year to year[8]. In practice, the Inspector of Taxes may be prepared to agree that the basis on which relief is claimed may be changed, but this can give rise to a loss of relief for interest in the year of assessment when the change is made where the basis is changed from a special claim to a business expense claim. This is because, relief having already been given in the past under the special provisions, the Inspector of Taxes may refuse to allow the same interest to be treated as an expense in the computation of the trading profits of the basis period ending within the preceding year of assessment.

8-14 These special reliefs are provided under TA 1988 ss 353 and 359 to 363. Relief is only available where the interest either is yearly interest chargeable under Sch D Case III[9], or is interest payable in the UK on an advance from a bank carrying on a bona fide banking business in the UK or from a UK Stock Exchange member or discount house; interest paid in the Republic of Ireland to Republic of Ireland banks, Stock Exchange members and discount houses is also eligible for relief[10]. The practice relating to interest on foreign currency bank loans paid outside the UK (described in §7-20 above), although not expressed to apply for the purpose of s 353, is in practice so applied. Relief will not normally be available where a taxpayer raises a loan from an overseas bank (except through its UK branch) even though it might be for a qualifying purpose. Neither overdraft interest nor credit card interest can any longer qualify for relief under these provisions[11]. However, where an overdraft is used exclusively for a qualifying purpose and is replaced within 12 months by a loan, the Inland Revenue will, in practice, give relief for interest on the loan provided that the other conditions are met[12].

8-15 In order to obtain relief, the taxpayer must make a claim[13], and the interest is then deducted from his income for the year in which he pays

---

8 TA 1988 s 368 (3) and (4).
9 TA 1988 s 353 (1) (a); and see Chapter 3 Part 3 above.
10 TA 1988 s 353 (1) (b).
11 TA 1988 s 353 (3) (a); see also *Walcot-Bather v Golding (Inspector of Taxes)* [1979] STC 707 and *Lawson (Inspector of Taxes) v Brooks* [1992] STC 76.
12 See Inland Revenue Booklet IR11 (1985) para 33; although this booklet is no longer current, it is understood that the practice still applies and that it extends to qualifying loans other than loans to purchase land and buildings – see ICAEW 'Taxline', May 1992, p 4. See also *Lawson (Inspector of Taxes) v Brooks* [1992] STC 76 as to whether this is a concession or a correct interpretation of TA 1988 s 367 (2).
13 TA 1988 s 353 (1).

the interest; normally, there is no provision for the carry forward of unused relief. If the taxpayer has suffered income tax by deduction on any income, any tax found to be overpaid is repayable to the taxpayer when the claim for relief in respect of interest is allowed[14].

Relief is not available in respect of so much of any interest paid as exceeds a commercial rate of interest[15]. This is determined by reference to both general market conditions and the circumstances of the particular loan.

8-16   All the circumstances described below which qualify interest paid for relief where it is related to a business require that the loan in question is made 'to defray money applied' by the borrower. This language differs from that used in connection with other provisions[16] which permit relief for interest paid in specific circumstances and which require that 'the proceeds of a loan' are 'applied' in a particular way. The word 'defray' means 'to provide money to pay', which is consistent with the legislation providing relief for interest paid which in most cases[17] requires the loan to be made on the occasion of the application of the money for the qualifying purpose 'or within what in the circumstances is a reasonable time from its application'[18]. Normally, the loan will be made at or before the time of its application, but where there is sufficient identification between the loan and its purpose (eg where it replaces a temporary overdraft drawn down to finance the acquisition), relief may still be available where the loan is made after the qualifying expenditure is incurred[19]. What is a reasonable time between the making of the loan and the application for the specified purpose will depend upon the circumstances of each case, but the Inland Revenue considers that a period of up to six months is reasonable in all cases[20]. Relief will not be available where the proceeds of the loan are first used for some extraneous purpose[1].

References to 'loan' include credit given for unpaid purchase money[2].

In relation to loans to acquire an interest in a close company or a partnership (but it is unclear whether or not also in relation to other loans), if the loan is made to a husband and wife jointly, the Inland Revenue will allow tax relief for interest to whichever spouse satisfies the qualifying conditions. This will apply even if the interest is paid out of a joint account[3].

INVESTMENT IN A CLOSE COMPANY

8-17   TA 1988 s 360 provides that interest is eligible for relief for income tax purposes where it is paid on a loan applied[4] in acquiring ordinary share

---

[14] TMA 1970 s 42 (7).
[15] TA 1988 s 353 (3) (b).
[16] TA 1988 ss 364 (1) and 365 (1) (a).
[17] But not in relation to loans to buy machinery or plant.
[18] TA 1988 s 367 (2).
[19] See §8-14 above.
[20] Inland Revenue Booklet IR11 (1985) para 7 (although this booklet is no longer current).
[1] TA1988 s 367 (2).
[2] TA 1988 s 367(3). Unpaid purchase money is not normally a 'loan' - *IRC v City of Buenos Ayres Tramways Co (1904) Ltd* (1926) 12 TC 1125 at 1146.
[3] Inland Revenue, 'Tax Bulletin', February 1992, p 14.
[4] The statutory language is 'on a loan ... to defray money applied'; this expression is considered in §8-16 above.

capital (whether by purchase or subscription) in a close company which is not a close investment holding company[5]; ordinary share capital does not include fixed rate preference shares[6]. Relief is also available where the loan is applied in making a loan – which need not be interest-bearing – to such a close company where the loan is used wholly and exclusively for the purposes of the business of the company or of a similar close company which is associated[7] with the borrowing company[8]. These provisions do not permit a shareholder in a close company to obtain relief for interest paid by him under a guarantee of a loan from a third party to the company; such an arrangement does not involve either a loan to the individual shareholder or a loan by him to the company[9].

To prevent a close company being a close investment-holding company, it must exist for one or more of the following purposes:

1   carrying on a trade on a commercial basis[10];
2   making investments in land to be let to persons other than any person 'connected' with a company or any spouse or relative of his[11]; or
3   certain purposes concerned with the organisation and administration of a group of companies which exists for one or both of the above purposes[12].

The legislation requires that the company in which the investment is made is not a close investment-holding company at the time when the investment is made. However, arguably this will not be the case where an investment is made in a newly-established close company which thereafter establishes a trade or otherwise satisfies the conditions; the Inland Revenue takes the view, which is arguable, that a company which is established to acquire and carry on a trade but which has not yet acquired a trade does not 'exist wholly or mainly for ... the purpose of carrying on a trade or trades on a commercial basis'[13]. Previously, the Inland Revenue used, in practice, to regard the requirement as met where the company satisfied one of the conditions within a reasonable time after the money was invested in the company by the individual; the time up to the end of the accounting period in which the investment is made was regarded as reasonable for this purpose. However, it appears that the Inland Revenue is no longer applying this practice, but requires the company to have commenced trading (or to have made appropriate investments in land) no later than the time when the investment in the close company is made.

---

5   TA 1988 s 360 (1) (a).
6   TA 1988 s 832 (1).
7   The expression 'associated company' is defined for these purposes in TA 1988 s 416 (1) – see TA 1988 s 360 (4).
8   TA 1988 s 360 (1) (b).
9   *Hendy (Inspector of Taxes) v Hadley* [1980] STC 292, [1980] 2 All ER 554 – and see §§2-22 to 2-24 above as to payment of interest under a guarantee.
10 TA 1988 s 13A (2) (a).
11 TA 1988 s 13A (2) (b).
12 TA 1988 s 13A (2) (c) to (f).
13 TA 1988 s 13A (2) (a).

8-18   Not all investments in close companies are sufficient to qualify the loan interest for relief. The taxpayer must also be able to show either:

1   That when the interest was paid the company exists for one of the purposes summarised in §8-17 above, and the taxpayer has a 'material interest' in the company[14]. Although the condition of the company is determined by reference to TA 1988 s 13A (2) – which relates only to close companies – the legislation only requires the company to be a close company at the time when the taxpayer makes the investment in the company. TA 1988 s 13A (2) only applies to close companies, but the description of companies in s 13A (2) is not expressed to relate to close companies only, so that it is possible for a company to satisfy the conditions in that subsection – and so qualify the interest paid for relief – even though the company is no longer a close company[15]. As to the requirement that the taxpayer must also have a 'material interest' in the company when the interest is paid, this means, broadly, that, together with relatives, partners and other 'associates'[16], the taxpayer has or controls more than a 5 per cent interest in the company[17]. Further, if the company mainly holds land or investments, no property must be used as a residence by the taxpayer unless he has worked for the greater part of his time in the 'actual management or conduct'[18] of the business of the company or of an associated company of that company; or

2   That, the company continuing to exist for one of the purposes set out in TA 1988 s 13A (2) and the taxpayer holding *any* part (ie including a holding of 5 per cent or less) of the ordinary share capital in the company, the taxpayer has worked for the greater part of his time in the 'actual management or conduct' of the company[19] or of an associated company of that company[20].

Where under condition 1 above the individual must have a 'material interest' in the close company, the condition does not require that the loan be raised to acquire that interest or the whole of it, but once all the conditions are satisfied the relief will thereafter be available. For example, the individual might have made a loan to the company out of borrowed money and later acquire a material interest; the relief will thereupon apply to the interest on the original loan. Similarly, if an individual having borrowed money to finance the purchase of, say, 3 per cent of the ordinary share capital subsequently acquires more than a further 2 per cent (eg by inheritance) he would thereafter qualify for relief on the original loan interest. On the other hand, the loss of the material interest, whether by disposal of part of the holding or by a further issue of shares to other shareholders, and, where the loss is by disposal, whether or not this involves disposal of the shares whose acquisition was financed by the loan, will result in the taxpayer no longer being eligible for relief.

---

[14]   TA 1988 s 360 (2) (a).
[15]   See Inland Revenue Statement of Practice SP 3/78.
[16]   TA 1988 s 360A (2).
[17]   See TA 1988 s 360A as to the definiton of 'material interest'.
[18]   See §8-19 below.
[19]   Not the *business* of the company.
[20]   TA 1988 s 360 (3) (a) and (b).

8-19 Where the individual does not have a material interest in the company, he must have spent the greater part of his time from the raising of the loan until the payment of the interest in the management or conduct of the company or an associate. The individual's 'time' is regarded by the Inland Revenue as being normal working time[1]; his period of work need not be constant, so long as on a cumulative basis he has spent more than half his normal working time on the company's affairs. It will be seen that the reference to the taxpayer's 'time' in the exception to the restriction in §8-18(1) above (ie where the taxpayer resides in accommodation owned by the company) is not qualified by reference to the period between taking up the loan and paying the interest; nor is it clear at what point that restriction operates where the property is used as the taxpayer's residence. It is likely that, in practice, the period from taking up the loan to paying the interest would be regarded as the relevant period for both purposes.

It will be seen that, where the taxpayer seeks to qualify for relief under the conditions outlined in §8-18(2) above, he must work in 'the actual management or conduct of the company' or an associate. This language is to be contrasted with both the language of the exception to the restriction relating to residence in company property mentioned in §8-18(1) above and the original language of the relief as introduced in 1974. In each of those cases reference was made to 'management or conduct of the business of the company'. Nevertheless, the Inland Revenue construes the present language strictly and considers that relief is only available to directors and senior managers on the basis that the aim of the legislation was (so it is said) to limit relief to those who have a significant stake in the ownership and management of the company[2]. Some support for the view that this was the Government's intention can be drawn from the Committee Stage debate on the Finance Bill in 1982[3], but it is far from clear what amounts to 'the conduct of the company'. Having regard to the scope of the relief in the case of co-operatives and employee-controlled companies[4], this language perhaps deserves further attention in the form of the insertion of the words 'the business of' so as to make available the relief to all shareholder/employees in close companies who work for the greater part of their time in the business of the company.

CO-OPERATIVES

8-20 Relief is available for interest on loans to finance investment in a common ownership enterprise or a co-operative enterprise[5] (commonly referred to as a 'co-operative'). Here, relief may be available where the taxpayer uses the borrowed money to invest in a share or shares[6] or to make a loan to the co-operative which is used for its business or for the business of

---

[1] See Inland Revenue Booklet IR11 (1985) para 61 (although this booklet is no longer current).
[2] CCAB Notes on Taxation Anomalies and Practical Difficulties, 9 June 1983 – [1983] STI 256 at p 258.
[3] HC Official Report, Standing Committee A, 25 May 1982, cols 430–432.
[4] See below.
[5] As defined in Industrial Common Ownership Act 1976, s 2 – see TA 1988 s 363 (5).
[6] There is no condition as to 'ordinary share capital' – a company qualifying under the Industrial Common Ownership Act 1976 s 2 (1) (a) (i) is required to have no share capital.

a subsidiary[7]. For this relief to be available, the body in which the investment is made must continue to be a co-operative when the interest is paid[8] and the individual must work for the greater part of his time[9] as an employee of the co-operative or of a subsidiary[10]. In this case, there is no requirement that the taxpayer must be concerned at a senior management level.

EMPLOYEE-CONTROLLED COMPANIES

8-21   Relief is also given for interest on loans to invest in 'employee-controlled companies'. Here, relief is available for loan interest where the loan is applied in acquiring ordinary share capital[11] of – not, as in the two cases described above, extended to include the taxpayer making a loan to – an 'employee-controlled company'[12]. Broadly, a company qualifies as such a company when more than 50 per cent of the issued ordinary share capital *and* of the voting power in the company is beneficially owned by full-time employees[13] of the company (or of a 51 per cent subsidiary of the company)[14], but for this purpose there is disregarded the excess over 10 per cent of any such employee holding[15]. A full-time employee is a person who works for the greater part of his time as an employee or director[16].

8-22   Several conditions must all be satisfied if the relief is to be available[17]. Generally,

1   the company must be an unquoted UK resident trading company;
2   the shares must be acquired not later than twelve months after the company became employee-controlled;
3   the company must normally be employee-controlled for at least nine months in each year of assessment; and
4   normally, the taxpayer must be a full-time employee of the company from when the loan is taken up until when the interest is paid.

LOANS FOR PARTNERSHIP INTERESTS

8-23   Loan interest is also eligible for relief where the loan is applied in purchasing a share in a partnership – as where a payment is made to an outgoing partner in consideration of acquiring his share in the assets (including any goodwill) of the partnership – or in contributing capital to the partnership or making a loan to the partnership where the money contributed or lent

---

[7]   TA 1988 s 361 (1) (a) or (b).
[8]   TA 1988 s 361 (2) (b).
[9]   See §**8-19** above.
[10]   TA 1988 s 361 (2) (c).
[11]   Defined in TA 1988 s 832 (1).
[12]   TA 1988 s 361 (3) (a).
[13]   In relation to qualifying loans applied before 6 April 1990, the employment of a spouse may also be taken into account for this purpose – FA 1988 Sch 3 para 15 (1) and (2) and Sch 14 Part VIII.
[14]   TA 1988 s 361 (5).
[15]   TA 1988 s 361 (6).
[16]   TA 1988 s 361 (8) – see §**8-19** above.
[17]   TA 1988 s 361 (4).

is used wholly for the purposes of the partnership trade, profession or vocation[18]. It is a condition of obtaining relief that the taxpayer is a member of the partnership, other than a limited partner, from the raising of the loan until the payment of the interest[19]. Although a limited partner may not take part in the management of the partnership without prejudicing his limited liability[20], it is not necessary in order for a general partner to obtain relief that he acts in the conduct of the partnership business[1]. In practice, the Inland Revenue treats a salaried partner in a professional partnership – who is not for taxation purposes a partner but a salaried employee taxable under Sch E – as eligible for relief under this provision, provided that he is allowed independence of action in handling affairs of the partnership and generally acts in such a way as to be indistinguishable from general partners in relations with clients of the partnership[2].

REPLACEMENT OF LOANS

8-24 The special reliefs described above all apply whether the loan is the original loan applied for the qualifying purpose or the loan is applied in paying off another loan on which interest was eligible for relief under TA 1988 s 353 or would have been so eligible had it not been interest-free[3].

RECOVERY OF CAPITAL

8-25 All the reliefs described above are subject to loss or restriction where the taxpayer receives a capital payment from or in respect of his interest in the company, co-operative or partnership which payment is assumed to be applied in repayment of a pro rata share of the loan on which interest relief is claimed[4]. Such a capital payment is treated as being received where[5] the taxpayer receives consideration for the disposal of the shares or of his partnership interest or receives a repayment of any of the share or partnership capital, or he receives a repayment of a loan made to the company or partnership or receives consideration for assigning any debt due to him from the company or partnership. Where the sale is not by way of a bargain made at arm's length, the relevant consideration is adjusted to the market value of what is disposed of. It should be noted that for these provisions to apply it is not necessary for the taxpayer to dispose of (or, in the case of a loan, receive repayment of) the shares or loan the acquisition of which is financed by the loan on which the interest relief is claimed. For example, the taxpayer would lose relief in respect of a loan to finance the acquisition

---

[18] TA 1988 s 361 (2) (a) and (b).
[19] TA 1988 s 362 (2) (a).
[20] Limited Partnerships Act 1907 s 6 (1).
[1] The law was changed in 1981 – FA 1981 s 25 (2).
[2] See Inland Revenue Statement of Practice A33.
[3] TA 1988 ss 360 (1) (c), 361 (1) (c) and (3) (b) and 362 (1) (c).
[4] TA 1988 ss 360 (2) (b) and (3) (b), 361 (2) (d) and (4) (e), 362 (2) (b) and 363 (1).
[5] TA 1988 s 363 (2).

of one class of ordinary shares where he disposes of shares of another class but which amount to part of the 'ordinary share capital'[6] of the company.

In practice, the Inland Revenue does not treat these provisions as applying where the partnership is incorporated into a close company or shares in the close company are exchanged for shares in another close company. This treatment applies provided that relief would have been available if the loan had been taken out to finance investment in the new company[7]. On the other hand, the Inland Revenue appears to take the view[8] that the conversion into ordinary share capital of a convertible loan stock is effected by way of an assignment of the loan stock to the company in exchange for shares, so as to result in the taxpayer being treated as recovering capital from the close company. However, in practice, a conversion into shares does not usually involve an assignment of the loan stock; instead, the issue of the shares extinguishes the company's indebtedness. Thus, the conversion of a loan into shares would not, in the author's view, normally involve the lender being treated as having recovered capital.

Where the taxpayer is treated as having repaid part of the qualifying loan, he loses the right to relief on a corresponding part of the interest even if the loan is not in fact reduced.

LOANS TO PURCHASE PARTNERSHIP MACHINERY OR PLANT

8-26 Expenditure on machinery or plant belonging to a partner, but not being partnership property, can qualify for capital allowances where the machinery or plant is used in the partnership business[9]. An individual to whom such machinery or plant belongs may claim relief for interest paid on a loan applied in the provision of that machinery or plant[10]. This relief only applies to interest falling due and payable (but irrespective of when it is paid) up to the end of the period of three years from the end of the year of assessment in which the loan was taken up. A proportion only of the interest will be relievable where the machinery or plant is only partly used for the purposes of the partnership business[11].

LOAN TO EMPLOYEE TO PURCHASE MACHINERY OR PLANT

8-27 Similarly, an individual who is charged to income tax under Sch E in respect of remuneration from an office or employment may claim relief for interest paid on a loan used to purchase machinery or plant for the purpose of the office or employment where he is entitled to capital allowances in respect of his expenditure on the machinery or plant[12]. Again, the relief is limited to interest payable before the end of three years from the year of assessment when the loan was taken, and a proportion only of the interest

---

6   TA 1988 s 832 (1).
7   Extra-statutory Concession A43.
8   Inland Revenue, 'Tax Bulletin', February 1992, p 13.
9   CAA 1990 s 65.
10   TA 1988 s 359 (1).
11   TA 1988 s 359 (2).
12   TA 1988 s 359 (3); and see CAA 1990 s 27.

is eligible for relief where there is only partial use for the purposes of the office or employment[13].

3   Interest relief for companies

BACKGROUND

8-28   Prior to the introduction of corporation tax in 1965, companies had been subject to income tax, and therefore were entitled to relief in respect of yearly interest paid under the deduction and retention procedure[14]; relief would be available in the ordinary way for any 'short' interest paid, so long as this could not be said to have been paid 'in respect of any capital employed in the trade'[15]. On the introduction of the corporation tax system, special rules were introduced with a view to placing companies in the same position as individuals in relation to the effect for taxation purposes of paying yearly interest and other charges on income paid out of profits. Because yearly interest paid by a company would not be paid out of profits or gains brought into charge to income tax, a company was, from 1965, bound to deduct income tax from yearly interest paid[16]; relief was given for such yearly interest and other charges on income paid by allowing such payments to be deducted from the 'total profits' of the company for the accounting period in which the interest was paid[17].

Also, from 1965, companies were prohibited from deducting as a trading expense payments of yearly interest, even where not payable out of trading profits, except where payable in the UK on an advance from a bank carrying on a bona fide banking business in the UK. However, even where yearly interest was paid to such a bank, relief was not regarded as being available where the interest was paid in respect of capital employed in the trade[18], until this restriction was removed in 1969[19].

It should be noted that any interest, whether yearly or 'short', which is treated as a distribution[20] for corporation tax purposes – and whether paid by a UK resident company or by a UK branch of a non-resident company – is not eligible for relief against corporation tax as either a trading expense[1] or a charge on income[2].

RELIEF AS A TRADING EXPENSE

8-29   The present position is that a company may only deduct as a trading expense yearly interest which is payable in the UK on an advance from

---

[13] TA 1988 s 359 (4); and see, as to partial use for the purpose of employment, *Hillyer v Leeke (Inspector of Taxes)* [1976] STC 490 at 492g.
[14] See Chapter 1 above.
[15] See §**8-06** above.
[16] ITA 1952 s 170.
[17] FA 1965 s 52; now, as amended, TA 1988 s 338.
[18] See §**8-06** above.
[19] FA 1969 Sch 13 para 4 (1).
[20] See TA 1988 s 209 (2) (d) and (e).
[1] TA 1988 s 337 (2) (a).
[2] TA 1988 s 338 (2) (a).

a bank carrying on a bona fide banking business in the UK[3]. There is no requirement that the lending bank be resident in the UK, but a loan from such a non-resident bank must be made from its UK branch if the interest is to qualify for relief[4]. The special rules which apply for income tax purposes where yearly interest is paid to a non-resident[5] do not apply for corporation tax purposes[6]. Yearly interest paid by a company to such a UK bank may be paid without deduction of basic rate income tax[7]. As in the case of the exemption from the obligation to deduct tax from yearly interest where it is paid to a UK bank[8], the Inland Revenue treats foreign currency interest as 'payable in the United Kingdom' even where it is payable, and paid, abroad, so long as it is brought into account as a trading receipt of a bona fide banking business of the lender carried on in the UK. As mentioned in relation to the availability of the exemption from the obligation to deduct tax from yearly interest[9], a company should seek confirmation from the bank that the circumstances are such as to satisfy the concessionary practice, in order that the interest qualifies as a trading expense.

The limitation on the deduction as a trading expense of yearly interest is subject to 'any ... provision of the Corporation Tax Acts which expressly authorises such a deduction'[10]. It is arguable that the provision in TA 1988 s 9 which requires that 'income shall for the purposes of corporation tax be computed in accordance with income tax principles' authorises a deduction for yearly interest where it would be so available for income tax purposes[11]. However, in the author's view this is not sufficiently 'express' authorisation to displace the general prohibition which is clearly expressed in s 337 (2).

8-30   'Short' interest paid by a company is not subject to any rules as to deductibility as a trade expense other than those which ordinarily apply to trade expenditure; accordingly (subject to those rules) it may be deducted as a trade expense.

8-31   The interest must, of course, satisfy the tests generally applicable to trade expenditure[12]. In particular, the interest must be wholly and exclusively incurred for the purposes of the trade[13] and when paid to a non-resident must not exceed a reasonable commercial rate[14]. Further, relief for interest as a trading expense will not be available where it is capitalised[15], although relief may be available for capitalised interest as a charge on income[16]. Where in its accounts a property development company charges interest

---

3   TA 1988 s 337 (2) (b) and (3).
4   Interest on a loan from an overseas branch of a UK resident bank would also qualify for relief – see §7-21 above.
5   See §§8-09 to 8-12 above.
6   TA 1988 s 82 (6); but see §§8-36 and 8-37 below, in relation to relief as a charge on income for interest paid to a non-resident.
7   See §7-21 above.
8   See §7-20 above.
9   See §7-20 above.
10   TA 1988 s 337 (2).
11   See Chapter 8 Part 1 above.
12   TA 1988 ss 74 and 9.
13   TA 1988 s 74 (a).
14   TA 1988 s 74 (n).
15   See §8-08 above.
16   See §8-38 below.

direct to work-in-progress then, even though it is interest which is eligible for relief as a trade expense, the interest will not be relieved until it is taken into account as a cost of sales in computing the company's profit[17].

The taxable profits of a company having two or more separate trades are first computed on a trade-by-trade basis. Where a loan is raised wholly and exclusively for the purposes of one of the trades, the interest payable in respect of that loan must be allocated as an expense of that trade and cannot be treated as an expense of the other trade or trades carried on by the company; this remains the case even though the loan in question may have been taken up for the purposes of a transaction which resulted in capital allowances in one trade being available to relieve the profits of the other trades and so improve the cash flow of both trades. This was the position in *Scorer (Inspector of Taxes) v Olin Energy Systems Ltd*[18] where relief was unsuccessfuly claimed under, in effect, the predecessor of s 393 (9) whereby relief for interest paid for the purposes of a trade, but not deductible in computing the profits of the trade, may be carried forward to later years[19]. In that particular case, the interest could not be treated as a trading expense (even after 1969) because the interest was not paid to a UK bank[20].

8-32 The rules as to deduction of interest as a trading expense for corporation tax purposes apply whether the company is resident in the UK or resident abroad; in the latter case, interest will only be deductible insofar as it is wholly and exclusively incurred for the purposes of the trade carried on through a branch or agency in the UK and in respect of which the company is within the charge to corporation tax[1].

RELIEF AS A CHARGE ON INCOME

8-33 Relief as a charge on income is available under TA 1988 s 338 in respect of certain interest which is 'paid out of the company's profits brought into charge to corporation tax'[2], and is allowed as a deduction against the 'total profits' for the accounting period. Therefore, any interest which is not taken into account in computing the trading profits of a company[3] may qualify for this treatment, subject to the conditions described below, and would typically be interest paid by a non-trading company, interest paid by a trading company otherwise than wholly and exclusively for the purposes of a trade carried on by the company (eg when it is paid on loan stock issued by the company to raise capital for the purposes of its activities generally) or yearly interest paid otherwise than to a UK bank[4].

---

[17] See Inland Revenue, 'Tax Bulletin', November 1991, p 4.
[18] [1982] STC 800; reversed in CA on a different point [1984] STC 141, [1984] 1 WLR 675.
[19] See §**8-42** below.
[20] See §**8-29** above.
[1] TA 1988 s 11.
[2] This expression is based on the original language relating to the deduction and retention procedure in Rules 19 and 21 (see §**1-10** above). The language was considered in *Allchin v Coulthard* [1943] AC 607, HL; see in particular, at 619-622.
[3] TA 1988 s 338 (2).
[4] See §**8-29** above.

8-34 In *Wilcock (Inspector of Taxes) v Frigate Investments Ltd*[5] it was held
that interest paid by a company on a loan taken from a bank in the UK
to finance the property-dealing trade of the company was 'deductible' in
computing the profits of the trade and so could not fall to be treated as
a charge on income; in that case the interest was paid on a loan to finance
dealing stock. In *Olin Energy Systems v Scorer (Inspector of Taxes)*[6], the
interest in question was paid on a twenty-year loan to finance the purchase
of a ship; the interest could not be treated as a trading expense, because
the interest, paid before 1969, was paid in respect of capital employed in
the trade[7] and was not paid to a UK bank[8], but it would seem, from the
comments of Walton J that interest on a loan to buy an asset should be
treated no differently from payments to hire an asset[9], that under the present
law such interest could in appropriate cases (ie if paid to a UK bank) be
treated as a trade expense. However, it is by no means clear that all bank
interest which is paid wholly and exclusively for the purposes of a trade
must be treated as trade expenditure and not as a charge on profits. The
proper accounting treatment in a given case may be to treat the interest
as paid out of profits, rather than as an expense in computing the profits
of the trade; although accountancy evidence will not be conclusive on the
point[10], it may be a relevant factor in resolving the issue.

The question of whether a payment of interest should be relieved as a
trading expense or as a charge on income is not necessarily of academic
interest only. This was illustrated in the *Frigate Investments* case where if
the interest in question had been relieved as a charge it could have been
set against other (rental) income of the company, leaving the trading profits
for the period to be largely relieved by losses carried forward from earlier
years. As a result of the decision in that case, the trading profits were largely
extinguished by the interest, but nearly all the rental income remained in
charge to tax because the trading loss carried forward could not be set against
that other income.

8-35 The interest to which s 338 can apply is[11]

1   Yearly interest[12]; yearly interest paid on a loan from a UK bank may
     be relieved as an expense of the trade, provided that other conditions
     are satisfied[13], and such yearly interest which is deductible as a trade
     expense will not qualify as a charge on income. Other yearly interest
     can only be relieved as a charge on income; and
2   Interest other than yearly interest, where the interest is payable in the
     UK[14] on an advance from a bank carrying on a bona fide banking business
     in the UK[15] or from a bona fide member of the London Stock Exchange

5   [1982] STC 198.
6   [1982] STC 800 – see §**8-31** above.
7   See §**8-06** above.
8   See §**8-29** above.
9   [1982] STC 800 at 814*g*.
10 See *Heather (Inspector of Taxes) v P-E Consulting Group Ltd* (1972) 48 TC293 at 322, CA.
11 TA 1988 s 338 (3).
12 See Chapter 3 Part 1.
13 See §§**8-29** to **8-32**.
14 The published Inland Revenue practice referred to in §**7-20** above is not stated to apply
    for this purpose, but in practice it is so applied.
15 See §**7-20** to **7-23** above.

or a bona fide UK discount house. 'Short' interest is not precluded from being relieved as a trading expense, and will normally be relieved in that way in the case of a trading company; when paid by an investment company, it will only be capable of being relieved as a charge on income.

Relief as a charge on income is only given in respect of interest which is *paid* and so differs from interest relieved as a trading expense which, as with trade expenditure generally, is debited on an accruals basis. Normally, interest is not treated as 'paid' when it has merely been debited by a bank or other creditor. Nor will interest be treated as paid if both debtor and creditor make up their accounts to show an amount equal to the interest as owing from the debtor to the creditor. This was decided in *Minsham Properties Ltd v Price (Inspector of Taxes)*[16], where the judge also cast doubt on the suggestion by the Inland Revenue that it might be possible for debtor and creditor to agree that an increase in the loan should be applied in effective payment of interest, 'even if cheques for the loan and accrued interest were circulated'[17]. It is doubtful whether this *obiter* comment can be correct. Although the mere entry in books of account that interest is owing or due – effectively, evidence of non-payment – cannot amount to payment, it would seem that payment by cheque, and perhaps even by book entry, from debtor to creditor would be effective where the source of the payment is a loan from a third party or from the creditor himself. Both parties would, of course, be bound by the other consequences of payment – namely, the receipt of taxable income by the creditor and, in some cases, the obligation of the debtor to deduct basic rate income tax from the interest paid. However, for the purpose of s 338 it is provided that interest payable in the UK on an advance from a bank carrying on a bona fide banking business in the UK or on an advance from a member of the London Stock Exchange or a UK discount house is treated as 'paid' when it is debited to the company's account in the books of the lender[18]. It is understood that the Inland Revenue considers that this provision only applies to interest other than yearly interest, but in the author's view this is not the correct interpretation of the legislation.

8-36 Where *yearly* interest is paid to a non-resident, certain special restrictions apply. The first general restriction is that a non-resident company may not obtain relief from corporation tax in respect of yearly interest as a charge on income where the interest is paid to a person not resident in the UK[19]. This restriction does not apply where the non-resident company paying the interest can claim the benefit of a non-discrimination Article in a double taxation agreement entered into by the UK with the state of which the non-resident payer is a resident under which a resident of the other state may be treated no less favourably than a resident of the UK. But, where a non-resident company does not have that protection, no relief is normally available for yearly interest as a charge on income paid to a non-resident. However, there is an exception to this rule in that, in practice, the Inland Revenue treats interest paid by a non-resident company as being

---

[16] [1990] STC 718.
[17] [1990] STC at 731*j* to 732*b*.
[18] Proviso to TA 1988 s 338(3).
[19] TA 1988 s 338(4).

eligible for relief as a charge on income where it is paid to a non-resident company which carries on a bona fide banking business in the UK irrespective of whether the company paying the interest has the protection of a double taxation agreement.

8-37   Where yearly interest is paid to a non-resident, one of three other conditions must also be satisfied:

1   Income tax is deducted under TA 1988 s 349 (2) and accounted for under TA 1988 Sch 16, unless the interest is paid on a quoted Eurobond[20]. Where the payer is discharged from the obligation to deduct tax from the interest by reason of the recipient being a bank carrying on a bona fide banking business in the UK[1], the company is in practice treated as satisfying this condition. Moreover, where an exemption from deduction, or a reduction in the rate of deduction, is authorised pursuant to a double taxation agreement, the company is treated as having made the required deduction[2]; or

2   The interest payment is made for the purpose of a trade and satisfies the other conditions in TA 1988 s 340. These conditions are almost exactly the same as those which apply under TA 1988 s 82 (2) in relation to interest paid abroad by individuals and relieved as an expense of a trade[3]; the conditions are relaxed, in that a trade carried on by a UK resident 75 per cent subsidiary of the borrower is treated as being carried on by the borrower[4]; this facilitates group borrowings through one company; or

3   The payment is one payable out of income brought into charge to corporation tax under Sch D Case IV or V. This enables a company to obtain relief for yearly interest paid which is not within Sch D Case III and so does not fall within the obligation to deduct tax under TA 1988 s 349 (2)[5].

These restrictions do not apply where relief for 'short' interest is claimed as a charge on income.

8-38   Until 1981, a company was unable to obtain relief as a charge on income for interest which was capitalised. As the result of an amendment contained in FA 1981 s 38, interest (but not other charges on income) charged to capital may qualify as a charge on income[6].

8-39   If the payment of interest is not ultimately borne by the company - eg the company is indemnified by a third party in respect of interest paid - no relief is available under s 338[6]. Further, if the liability to pay the interest is not incurred for valuable and sufficient consideration, no relief

---

[20] TA 1988 s 338 (4) (a) and (b); see Chapter 7 Part 1.
[1] TA 1988 s 349 (3) (a), and §§7-20 and 7-21 above.
[2] Regulation 6 of the Double Taxation Relief (Taxes on Income) (General) Regulations 1970: SI 1970 No 488.
[3] See §8-11 above.
[4] TA 1988 s 340 (3).
[5] See also §9-27 below.
[6] TA 1988 s 338 (5)(a).

is available[7]. To be 'sufficient' it is necessary that the consideration is more than legally valuable and the company must receive an adequate *quid pro quo* amounting to fair value for the interest paid[8]. Normally, where the company receives a loan in consideration for which interest is paid at a market rate, sufficient consideration would have been given; but, if, for example, a company were to assume liability for payment of interest and repayment of principal on a loan in consideration of cash or other property being transferred to the company, the consideration would be insufficient if the value of the property received were less than the value of the loan obligation assumed having regard to the principal outstanding, any accrued but unpaid interest, the terms of repayment and the rate of interest payable.

8-40 If the company is a non-resident company – liable to corporation tax by reason of carrying on a trade in the UK through a branch or agency[9] – it may only obtain relief for interest as a charge on income if the liability is incurred wholly and exclusively for the purposes of the UK trade[10].

8-41 One of the following special conditions must be satisfied where the charge on income for which relief is sought is interest, whether or not it is yearly interest:

1   The company must exist wholly or mainly for the purpose of carrying on a trade[11]; it is not clear whether a company which has been established to carry on a trade but which has not yet begun to trade can qualify for relief for interest under s 338. However, if the interest would qualify for relief as a trading expense if the trade had commenced, relief may be available as an expense of the trade once the trade has begun, so long as the interest is not incurred more than five years before trading begins[12]; that special provision does not apply to interest which is only capable of being relieved as a charge on income. Because relief under s 338 is given when the interest is *paid*, it may be possible to defer payment of interest until such time as the company can be said to exist for the purpose of carrying on a trade, provided that in the meantime the interest is not treated as paid as a result of being debited in the books of a lender bank[13]. It is doubtful whether a company which is in liquidation will satisfy this condition; or

2   The payment of interest must be wholly and exclusively applied for the purposes of a trade carried on by the company[14]. This condition is not necessarily inconsistent with the view that such interest may qualify as a deductible trading expense, because relief for yearly interest as a trading expense is only available where the interest is paid on an advance from a bank carrying on a bona fide banking business in the

---

[7] TA 1988 s 338 (5) (b).
[8] *Ball (Inspector of Taxes) v National and Grindlays Bank Ltd* [1971] 3 All ER 485, 47 TC 287, CA.
[9] TA 1988 s 11.
[10] TA 1988 s 338 (5) (b).
[11] TA 1988 s 338 (6) (a).
[12] TA 1988 s 401.
[13] See §8-35 above; but see also §§9-26 and 9-27 below.
[14] TA 1988 s 338 (6) (b).

UK; any such interest paid to any other lender may only be relieved as a charge on income; or

3   The company must be an 'investment company' or an authorised unit trust scheme[15]. An 'investment company' is a company whose business consists wholly or mainly in the making of investments and the principal part of whose income is derived from that business[16]. An authorised unit trust[17] is, in relation to its income, treated for taxation purposes as if the trustees were a UK resident company[18]. Where the company is an investment company, there is no test applied as to the purpose or use to which the loan on which the interest is paid is applied. If a new company is established with a view to carrying on a trade at a later date, interest on pre-trading borrowings which might not qualify under condition 1 or 2 above may qualify if the company carries on business as an investment company before trading commences. It is open to question whether a company in liquidation can qualify as an investment company; the Inland Revenue is understood to take the view that the business of a company in liquidation is to realise the assets and discharge the liabilities and, accordingly, it cannot satisfy the definition in TA 1988 s 130; or

4   The interest would, if the company were an individual, qualify for relief for income tax purposes under TA 1988 s 353, as being on a loan used for the purchase or improvement of land[19]. As will be seen below, relief for income tax in respect of interest on a loan to purchase or improve land is only available where, broadly, the land is occupied by the borrower as his only or main residence or is let on a commercial basis. If the land in question is occupied by the company then these conditions are treated as satisfied if the land is used as an individual's only or main residence, or if it is not used as a residence at all. Therefore, relief under s 338 will be available where the land is occupied as industrial, commercial or other premises of the company, or where the land is occupied as a residence by company personnel on behalf of the company in a representative capacity. Where the land is occupied as an individual's residence, the limit on the amount of a loan on which interest relief is available[20] applies, but without regard to other land in respect of which similar loans are made[1]; therefore, the company may obtain relief under s 338 for interest on several loans in respect of separate parcels of land occupied on its behalf by individuals, but relief will not be available if the individuals do not occupy the land in a representative capacity[2]. A trading company or an investment company will not need to rely on this condition in order to obtain relief for interest on a loan to acquire land, whether the land is occupied by or on behalf of the company, is let or is occupied by an individual as a residence; the relief may apply in the case of a non-trading members' club which pays interest

[15]   TA 1988 s 338 (6) (c).
[16]   TA 1988 s 130.
[17]   The expression 'authorised unit trust' is defined in TA 1988 s 468 (6) – see TA 1988 s 832 (1).
[18]   TA 1988 s 468 (1).
[19]   TA 1988 s 338 (6) (d); and see Part 4 of this Chaper, below.
[20]   See §§8-51 to 8-59 below.
[1]   Proviso to TA 1988 s 338 (6) (d).
[2]   See, as to representative occupation, *Tennant v Smith* [1892] AC 150, 3 TC 158, HL.

on a loan to acquire premises and where relief for the interest is sought against other income (eg bank interest received).

8–42 Interest relieved as a charge on income may be set against the total profits of the company for the accounting period in which the interest is paid. Unused relief may, subject to certain limitations[3], be surrendered by way of group relief against profits of other members of a group of UK resident companies (which satisfy the relationship tests for group relief purposes) of which the company paying the interest is a member[4], but, as with the general relief for charges on income, this is given on a current accounting period basis only; insofar as the accounting periods of the claimant and surrendering company do not coincide exactly, a proportionate part of the unused charges on income may be set against a proportionate part of the profits of the other company, the proportions being calculated by reference to the extent to which the accounting periods do correspond[5]. Where interest relieved as a charge on income is paid by a company wholly and exclusively for the purposes of a trade which it carries on and that interest exceeds the profits against which it may be relieved, then such interest may be treated as if it were an expense of the trade in question for the purpose of computing the losses of that trade which are available to be carried forward against trading income from the same trade in succeeding accounting periods under TA 1988 s 393 (1)[6]. Interest relieved as a charge on income cannot, however, be carried back against profits of a previous accounting period in the same way as can trading losses[7].

Where an 'investment company'[8] has paid interest for which relief is available as a charge on income but which exceeds the profits of the company of the accounting period in which the interest is paid, such excess interest can be carried forward to the succeeding accounting period (and so on to later accounting periods). Once carried forward, such excess interest is treated as part of the 'expenses of management' for the subsequent accounting period and can be set against the total profits (including capital gains) of the company in the subsequent accounting period[9]. However, where the 'expenses of management' of an investment company in an accounting period include an amount carried forward in that way, the amount of expenses of management which are eligible to be set off by way of group relief against the profits of another company in the same accounting period is that part of those expenses of management exclusive of that part which has been carried forward from previous accounting periods[10].

---

[3] TA 1988 s 403 (8).
[4] TA 1988 s 403 (7).
[5] TA 1988 s 408.
[6] TA 1988 s 393 (9).
[7] See TA 1988 s 393 A.
[8] As defined in TA 1988 s 130.
[9] TA 1988 s 75 (3).
[10] TA 1988 s 403 (8).

4   Interest on loans related to land etc

8-43   Relief against income tax may be claimed under TA 1988 s 353 for interest on loans taken out to acquire or improve land and buildings. This relief is subject to many conditions and constraints set out in TA 1988 ss 354 to 358, and is normally only available where the property is let commercially or is used as the main residence of the borrower. By concession[11], relief from UK income tax is also available to a resident of the Republic of Ireland for interest on a loan from an Irish building society or other lender, subject to the other conditions for relief being satisfied. The way in which relief is given for interest on most loans to acquire residences in the UK is through the Mortgage Interest Relief at Source system[12].

QUALIFYING LOANS

8-44   The relief applies where the loan is used[13]

1   to purchase an estate or interest in land or such an estate or interest absorbed into or given up to obtain the interest. This includes the outright purchase of a freehold or leasehold interest, the purchase of a freehold or leasehold reversion, or the buying out of a subsidiary leasehold interest, but not the acquisition of a rentcharge or an interest as mortgagee of land[14]. Normally, the taxpayer must own the relevant estate or interest in the land at the time when the interest is paid[15], but this requirement does not apply where a tenant pays interest to his landlord on outstanding purchase money under a conditional sale agreement to acquire the landlord's interest at a later date[16]; or

2   to improve or develop the land or buildings; this does not extend to ordinary maintenance and repair, but does include renovating a property which is in a dilapidated condition when it is acquired[17]. The application of the loan on street works (not being maintenance or repair), such as where the owner of a newly-constructed house is required to contribute to construction of the adjoining road and sewers, is treated as expenditure on the improvement or development of land[18]. The Inland Revenue has published a list of examples of work which will qualify as improvements for the purposes of interest relief[19]. Except for transitional relief, this provision does not apply to loans to improve residences made after 5 April 1988[20]; or

3   to pay off another loan which was eligible for relief (or which would have been eligible had it not been interest-free).

---

[11] Extra-statutory Concession A28.
[12] See Chapter 7 Part 2 and §8-51 below.
[13] TA 1988 s 354 (1) (a) to (c).
[14] TA 1988 s 354 (4).
[15] TA 1988 s 354 (1).
[16] TA 1988 s 354 (7).
[17] TA 1988 s 354 (2) (a).
[18] TA 1988 s 354 (2) (b).
[19] See Inland Revenue Booklet: Tax Treatment of Interest Paid – IR11 (1985), para 37 and Appendix 1 (although this booklet is no longer current).
[20] TA 1988 s 355 (2A) to (2C).

As with other circumstances when relief is specifically available for loan interest paid, the loan must be 'to defray money applied' in one of three ways summarised above[1], and must be made in connection with the application of the money in a qualifying way at the time of or within a reasonable time from that application[2].

Although credit given for unpaid purchase money is not strictly a 'loan'[3], it is treated as a loan applied in making the purchase for the purposes of interest relief[4]. In practice, interest paid by a purchaser to a vendor on the unpaid purchase price where the purchaser takes possession before completion or where the purchaser delays completion beyond the agreed date is treated as interest on a loan which can qualify for relief. Overdraft interest is not eligible for relief[5], but, where an overdraft is applied exclusively for a qualifying purpose and is replaced within twelve months by a loan, the Inland Revenue will, in practice, give relief for interest on the loan provided that the other conditions are met[6].

To qualify for interest relief, the land in question must be located in the UK or the Republic of Ireland[7] (but this does not include the Channel Islands or the Isle of Man). No relief is available for interest on a loan to purchase property outside the UK or the Republic of Ireland, even where that property is let at a rent which is taxable in the hands of the resident recipient[8]. Relief also applies where the loan is not in relation to land, but is made to finance the acquisition of a houseboat[9] or a caravan[10].

ANTI-AVOIDANCE PROVISIONS[11]

8-45 Special provisions are designed to prevent increased relief being obtained or relief being obtained for an excessive amount of loan. Relief is not available for interest on a loan to purchase an interest in land where the purchaser and seller are husband and wife, where the purchasers are trustees of a settlement and are purchasing from the settlor and it appears that the main purpose of the purchase is to obtain interest relief, or where the purchaser and seller are 'connected'[12] (including where the transaction is channelled through other parties) and the price substantially exceeds the value of the property. If the purchaser or his spouse has, since 15 April 1969, owned the property in question and disposed of it, interest relief will

---

[1] See §**8-16** above
[2] TA 1988 s 367 (2); and see §**8-16** above.
[3] *IRC v City of Buenos Ayres Tramways Co (1904) Ltd* (1926) 12 TC 1125 at 1146.
[4] TA 1988 s 367 (3).
[5] TA 1988 s 353 (3) (a).
[6] See Inland Revenue Booklet: IR11 (1985) para 33; although this booklet is no longer current, it is understood that the practice still applies – see ICAEW 'Taxline', May 1992, p 4. See also *Lawson (Inspector of Taxes) v Brooks* [1992] STC 76 as to whether this is a concession or a correct interpretation of TA 1988 s 367 (2).
[7] See Extra-statutory Concession A28 as to relief against UK income tax extended to residents of the Republic of Ireland in respect of interest paid to Irish lenders.
[8] *Ockenden (Inspector of Taxes) v Mackley* [1982] STC 513, [1982] 1 WLR 787.
[9] Defined in TA 1988 s 367 (1).
[10] Defined in the Caravan Sites and Control of Development Act 1960 s 29 (1) – see TA 1988 s 367 (1).
[11] TA 1988 s 355 (5).
[12] Within TA 1988 s 839.

not be available on a loan to repurchase the property if it appears that the main purpose of the loan is to obtain interest relief on the loan.

Further, if payment for improvement or development work substantially exceeds the value of the work done and the person making the payment is 'connected' with the person who directly or indirectly receives payment, no relief is available.

In these circumstances, it appears that none of the interest is eligible for relief and that it is not possible for relief to be obtained for interest on that part of the loan which relates to expenditure which is not excessive. This is notwithstanding the provision[13] which allows a proportion of the interest to qualify for relief where part only of the loan satisfies the condition. Such partial relief would be available where, for example, a loan of £40,000 is applied as to £20,000 in the purchase of land and as to £20,000 on other unrelated expenditure; in those circumstances, one-half of the interest would qualify for relief.

METHOD OF GIVING RELIEF

8–46 Subject to the application of the MIRAS method of giving relief[14] in the case of a residence occupied by the borrower, relief for interest on a loan to acquire or develop land is given under TA 1988 s 353 in the same way as relief for interest on a business-related loan for which specific relief is available[15]. If the interest could also qualify as a business expense (as it might, for example, where expenditure on purchase of a farm includes purchase of a farmhouse), a dual claim for relief as a business expense and under s 353 is not possible[16]. If a taxpayer elects to claim relief under s 353, relief is normally only available for the year of assessment in which the interest is paid[17], but where the interest could have been claimed as a business expense any unrelieved interest may be carried forward as a business loss[18] or carried back under terminal loss relief[19]; unrelieved interest on a loan to acquire or improve land (or a caravan or houseboat) which is let may be carried forward against subsequent rental income[20].

LAND AND BUILDINGS LET COMMERCIALLY

8–47 Relief for interest on a loan to acquire or develop property which is tenanted is available only if the property is let commercially. The conditions which must be satisfied[1] are that, in any period of 52 weeks within which interest is payable (falling wholly or partly within the year of assessment within which the interest is paid), the property must be let at a commercial rent for more than 26 weeks, and when not so let must be either available

---

13 TA 1988 s 367 (4).
14 See §8–51 below.
15 see §§8–13 to 8–15 above.
16 TA 1988 s 368 (3) to (6); see §8–13 above.
17 TA 1988 s 353 (1).
18 Under TA 1988 s 385.
19 TA 1988 s 388 – see TA 1988 s 390.
20 §8–50 below.
1 TA 1988 s 355 (1) (b).

for letting or used as a private residence in circumstances which qualify the interest for relief[2] or be prevented from being available for letting or use as a residence by works of construction or repair.

It will be noted that the period by reference to which the conditions are applied is 'any period of 52 weeks', which need not be co-terminous with a year of assessment. The interest in question need not be 'paid' within the period of 52 weeks, but must merely be 'payable' within the period. In order for relief to be obtained, the property must be let for *more than* 26 weeks in the 52-week period, and therefore interest relief may be lost where there is a significant delay before a newly-acquired (or newly-developed) property is let. Where such a delay is anticipated, careful arrangement of the interest payment dates may help to maximise relief for interest; there is no requirement that the interest when paid relates to the period of 52 weeks in which the conditions are satisfied, so the rolling-up of interest until the property is first let may result in relief being available which might otherwise have been lost[3].

Where a partnership occupies property owned by a partner rent-free but pays interest on behalf of the partner, the Inland Revenue will treat the payment as an expense in the partnership's tax computation; in the hands of the individual partner, he will be treated as receiving rent against which the interest may be set. A similar practice applies where a company occupies land owned by a controlling director[4].

8-48 Rent paid direct to a landlord whose usual place of abode is outside the UK is required to be paid under deduction of basic rate income tax[5]. Where the rent is paid to an agent in the UK, income tax on the rent can be collected from the agent[6]. This can give rise to cash flow problems for a non-resident landlord who has borrowed money to finance the acquisition or development of the property, since the agent will wish to retain sufficient of the rent to cover any tax which may be collected from him[7]. In the case of interest paid by an agent for a non-resident landlord it is sometimes possible to obtain the Inspector of Taxes' prior confirmation that interest paid by the agent on the landlord's behalf will be taken into account in determining the amount of income tax which may be assessed in the name of the agent, so that the agent is prepared to apply the rent in that way without making a retention on account of his maximum possible exposure to tax on behalf of the landlord.

8-49 Where a non-resident buys property in the UK with the aid of a loan it is normally prudent for the loan to be taken out with a UK lender. This is because in order for interest relief to be available the interest must fall within Sch D Case III or, normally, be paid in the UK on a loan from a bank carrying on a bona fide banking business in the UK[8]. Although it might be arguable that interest paid on a loan secured by a mortgage

---

[2] See §§**8-51** to **8-59** below.
[3] But see §§**9-26** and **9-27** below.
[4] Inland Revenue Statement of Practice SP4/85.
[5] TA 1988 s 43.
[6] Under TMA 1970 s 78.
[7] TMA 1970 s 83 (2).
[8] TA 1988 s 353 (1).

over land in the UK is within Sch D Case III[9], such interest would, in the absence of a double taxation agreement between the UK and the country of residence of an overseas lender, be required to be paid subject to deduction of basic rate income tax[10]. Even though a replacement loan can qualify interest for relief[11], this only applies where interest on the original loan itself qualified for relief; thus, bridging finance should also be taken out by way of a loan from a UK lender, because a replacement loan from a UK lender might not qualify the interest for relief unless the bridging loan was also from a UK lender.

8-50 Interest which is eligible for relief by reason of a property being let can be set only against the income from letting that or any other property (including a caravan or houseboat), and cannot be set against other income. Any unused relief can, however, be carried forward and set against letting income from such properties in later years, so long as the loan continues to qualify for relief[12].

LOAN TO PURCHASE A PRIVATE RESIDENCE

8-51 Subject to a number of conditions (mentioned below), relief is given for interest paid on a loan to acquire an individual's private residence. This relief is subject to two important qualifications: first, it is only given in respect of loans up to a 'qualifying maximum' amount (or on so much of a loan of a higher amount)[13]; this qualifying maximum is fixed in the annual Finance Act for each year of assessment[14] and, since 6 April 1983, has stood at £30,000. The second qualification is that relief is only given from income tax at the basic rate; this was introduced with effect from 6 April 1991, subject to certain transitional provisions which operated for twelve months where bridging loans were in place before that date[15].

In the majority of the cases of loans to acquire or improve a private residence, tax relief is given under the MIRAS system described in Chapter 7 Part 2 above rather than through the application of TA 1988 s 353[16]. The borrower obtains relief by being permitted to pay the lender the interest due net of basic rate income tax, the lender recovering the tax element direct from the Inland Revenue. Somewhat curiously, the MIRAS legislation provides[17] for the borrower to be charged to tax at the basic rate on 'an amount of income equal ... to the deduction which, in computing his total income otherwise than for the purposes of excess liability, falls to be made' in respect of the interest payments.

Quite how there would fall to be made a deduction 'in computing his total income' in the absence of TA 1988 s 353 is not clear. Prior to 1969, relief was given for all annual payments, including yearly interest, in

---

[9] See Chapter 3 Part 2 above.
[10] See §**7-16** above.
[11] TA 1988 s 354(1)(c).
[12] TA 1988 s 355(4).
[13] TA 1988 s 356A and s 357
[14] TA 1988 s 367(5).
[15] FA 1991 s 27, inserting new s 353(4) and (5) and new s 369(3A) and (3B) in TA 1988.
[16] TA 1988 s 353(2).
[17] TA 1988 s 369(3).

computing total income for surtax (now higher rate) purposes. But this treatment of interest ceased when general relief for interest was abolished[18]; interest is now expressly excluded from the annual payments to be taken into account under the third paragraph of TA 1988 s 836 for the purposes of estimating total income, although the requirement in the fifth paragraph of that section that the taxpayer shall state 'any tax which the person in question may be entitled to retain or charge against any other person' may be helpful[19], as might the statement in TA 1988 s 835 (6) (b) that deductions which are allowable in computing total income on account of sums payable under deduction of income tax at the basic rate in force for a year of assessment shall be allowed as deductions in respect of that year[20].

However, relief is in practice available at the basic rate for interest on a qualifying loan to acquire a private residence. Whether the relief is given through the MIRAS scheme or in the assessment following a claim by the taxpayer, the same conditions described below must be satisfied[1].

In the case of land used as a private residence by the borrower and not let commercially, interest relief is only available where the loan is applied in the acquisition of the property or in financing the construction of a new building (and not, in the case of a loan made after 5 April 1988, an extension or improvement to an existing building), or in replacement of such a loan[2].

RESIDENCE

8-52 The property must be used as 'the only or main residence' of the borrower at the time when the interest is paid[3]. Relief is no longer available where the loan is used to acquire or improve a property used as the only or main residence of the borrower's former or separated spouse or other dependent relative; however, relief continues to be available for interest on such loans taken out before 6 April 1988[4]. Except for the special case mentioned below, the property must be a 'residence' – that is a place where the borrower, or other person, resides. There is no definition of what amounts to residing for this purpose, but it probably amounts to more than occasional use. In *Frost (Inspector of Taxes) v Feltham*[5] a tenant of a public house in Essex successfully argued that a house in Wales belonging to him and his wife, and which they visited monthly, was his only or main residence for the purposes of relief for mortgage interest; however, it should be noted that each case must be decided objectively on its own facts, and this was the kind of case where the court is reluctant to disturb a finding of fact by the appellate Commissioners[6].

Where the interest in question is paid within twelve months after the date when the loan is made, it is sufficient if the property is used as the

---

[18] See FA 1969 Sch 13 para 21, amending ITA 1952 Sch 24; and see now TA 1988 s 836.
[19] See also TA 1988 s 835 (2).
[20] Although this is a provision concerned with the *timing* of deductions which 'are allowable'.
[1] TA 1988 s 355 (2A) to (2C).
[2] TA 1988 s 355 (2A) to (2C).
[3] TA 1988 s 355 (1) (a).
[4] FA 1988 s 44.
[5] [1981] STC 115, [1981] 1 WLR 452.
[6] See [1981] STC 115 at 119*j* to 120*a*.

residence within twelve months of the loan being made[7]. Therefore, if a property is acquired with the aid of a loan on 1 January, interest paid before 31 December of the same year may qualify for relief provided that the property is occupied as a residence before the end of that year, even if it is not so occupied at the time when the interest is paid. The twelve-month period may be extended by the Inland Revenue in any given case where the Board of Inland Revenue considers it reasonable having regard to the circumstances. This enables relief to be given when, for example, the purchaser of a new property cannot move into it because of a delay in selling his previous house. Where the taxpayer takes out a loan to purchase a new house, relief continues to be available in respect of interest on a loan to acquire the first house where the taxpayer does not sell the first house for up to one year, or longer if the Board of Inland Revenue so directs in any particular case[8], but only if the borrower does in fact use the new house as his only or main residence within twelve months of the loan being made, so as to qualify the loan for interest relief[9].

8-53   Where a taxpayer has two or more properties which qualify as 'residences' it is a question of fact which is the 'main' residence. Unlike the position for capital gains tax relief purposes[10], there is no provision for a taxpayer to elect which is his main residence. Therefore, it is possible for a taxpayer to obtain relief for interest in respect of one property which, as a matter of fact, is the main residence, whilst at the same time electing for a different property to be treated as his main residence for the purpose of obtaining relief for capital gains tax on a disposal.

Where on marriage each spouse owns a residence which qualifies for mortgage interest relief, and one spouse goes to live in the other's house, interest relief will be allowed by concession to the spouse who moves, provided that the property is sold within twelve months[11]. If both spouses move to a new residence for which a loan is taken out, relief is regarded as being available under the bridging provisions[12], on loans relating to all three properties for a period of twelve months from the date of the new loan (or longer in certain circumstances)[13].

8-54   An exception to the requirement that a property is a taxpayer's 'residence' applies where the taxpayer resides in 'job-related' accommodation but owns another property which he intends to use as his only or main residence at a later date[14]. This enables clergymen, members of the armed forces, employed publicans etc[15] to obtain relief for interest on loans to acquire or develop their own houses even though accommodation is provided for them in the course of their work.

---

[7] TA 1988 s 355 (1) (a).
[8] TA 1988 ss 354 (5) and (6) and 371.
[9] See *Hughes (Inspector of Taxes) v Viner* [1985] STC 235, [1985] 3 All ER 40.
[10] TCGA 1992 s 222 (5).
[11] Extra-statutory Concession A35.
[12] See §**8-52** above.
[13] Inland Revenue Statement of Practice SP 10/80.
[14] TA 1988 s 356.
[15] But see *Frost (Inspector of Taxes) v Feltham* [1981] STC 115, [1981] 1 WLR 452 and §**8-52** above.

Accommodation is 'job-related' if it is provided for the taxpayer or his spouse by reason of their employment and in circumstances where the provision of the accommodation falls within one of the three exceptions from that provision being treated as a taxable benefit from the employment[16]; that is, broadly, where the provision of accommodation is necessary for the proper performance of the duties of the employment, where the accommodation is provided for the better performance of the duties and accommodation is customarily provided in such cases, or where there is a special threat to the employee's security. Accommodation is not job-related where the employee is a director of the company providing the accommodation unless the director does not have a 'material interest' (ie broadly, an interest of more than 5 per cent) in the company[17] or the director is a full-time working director and the company carries on a non-trading or charitable activity and does not have the function of holding investments[18]. The provisions relating to job-related accommodation also apply to individuals who are taxed under Sch D and who are required by an arm's length contract to work from premises provided by another person and to live there or on other premises provided by that person[19].

A taxpayer may not claim relief for interest in respect of more than one property under these special provisions[20]. It is not specifically so provided, but it appears that where two or more properties may qualify in this case the taxpayer may elect between them, but if the loans are made at different times it may be necessary to take relief on the first loan first.

TEMPORARY ABSENCES

8-55   In practice[1], the Inland Revenue does not regard temporary absences of up to one year as prejudicing a person's residence in a property. Further, an absence of up to four years by reason of a taxpayer's employment elsewhere in the UK or abroad will be disregarded; after reoccupying the property for at least three months, a further period of absence of up to four years may occur without affecting the relief. Where the taxpayer works abroad in a Crown employment in circumstances where his duties are treated as performed in the UK under TA 1988 s 132 (4) (a), any property in the UK being purchased with a mortgage continues to qualify for relief.

It sometimes happens that an individual working abroad will buy a new house during a visit to the UK on leave. The Inland Revenue extends the concessionary practice described above where in such circumstances the individual uses the house as a residence for at least three months before going abroad again and satisfies the other conditions. This means that a further period of absence of up to four years would not prejudice the relief, although it is prudent to check with the Inspector of Taxes that the concessionary treatment will apply.

---

16   TA 1988 s 356 (3) (a) and see TA 1988 s 145 (4).
17   See TA 1988 s 168 (11) for the definition of 'material interest'.
18   TA 1988 s 356 (4).
19   TA 1988 s 356 (3) (b) – neither the borrower nor his spouse may have a material interest in, or carry on business in partnership with, the other person.
20   TA 1988 s 356 (2).
1   Extra-statutory Concession A27.

Except in the case of these concessions, there is no general requirement that a property must be occupied for at least three months in order that it can be treated as a 'residence'; in practice, an individual working abroad will more usually acquire a house or flat in the UK in the course of a return visit of much less than three months and occupy it for a short period before letting it. In these circumstances he will claim relief in respect of let property[2]. However, in such a case relief for interest will only be available against rental income, whereas relief against general income is available where the property is occupied as a residence; on the other hand, where the Inland Revenue's concessionary practice in relation to temporary absences is applied, relief is given for interest against general income even where the property is let[3].

LIMIT ON RELIEF

8–56   Where interest relief is available by reason of the property in question being a residence – but not where the property is let commercially – the maximum amount of borrowings which can qualify for relief is, currently, £30,000[4]; capitalised interest of up to £1,000 is disregarded in determining whether the loan exceeds the limit[5]. However, this does not generally increase the limit to £31,000 (including interest of £1,000); a loan which exceeds the £30,000 limit will not qualify for relief by reference to any capitalised interest which is added to it.

8–57   In the case of loans made before 1 August 1988[6], the limit is applied to the aggregate amount of loans interest on which would otherwise qualify for relief, and where the amount of a loan exceeds £30,000 (or takes the aggregate above £30,000) a proportion only of the interest can qualify for relief[7]. In applying the limit where a number of loans are taken out, the loans are taken in the order in which they are made, so that where the £30,000 limit is exceeded interest relief on the later loan or loans will be limited or will not be available[8]. Where more than one loan is made simultaneously, the loans are treated as one loan[9] and the limit is applied on a proportionate basis to each loan.

Only one limit of £30,000 applies to spouses who are living together[10].

Under loans taken out before August 1988 by joint borrowers who are not spouses living together, the loan is apportioned between the borrowers in the ratio in which the interest is paid[11]. Thus, where two individuals have jointly borrowed £60,000 to buy a house (held in joint names) in which

---

2 See §§**8–47** to **8–50** above.
3 Although an individual working abroad for a year or more may not have a significant amount of other income liable to UK taxation.
4 TA 1988 ss 356A, 357 and 367 (5) and FA 1992 s 10 (4).
5 TA 1988 s 357 (6).
6 TA 1988 ss 357 (1) and 356C (2).
7 TA 1988 s 357 (1).
8 TA 1988 s 357 (2) (b).
9 TA 1988 s 357 (3) (b).
10 TA 1988 s 357 (3) (a) and (5).
11 TA 1988 s 357 (2).

they live, they will each be entitled to full relief for interest paid on the loan if they each pay half of the interest.

8-58 For loans made on or after 1 August 1988, the £30,000 maximum is applied to each residence, and is shared between those who have an interest in the property[12]. The sharing of the maximum is on an equal basis between the co-owners, but where the share allocated to a person exceeds the amount of interest payable by him the excess can be re-allocated to the other co-owners[13]. Where the share of the loan on which he pays interest exceeds his share of the maximum, only a proportion of the interest qualifies for tax relief[14]. Spouses living together may elect that interest paid by one should be treated as paid by the other and that their respective shares of the maximum should be adjusted[15]. However, if spouses who are not separated each pay interest on loans in respect of separate residences, the residence first purchased shall be treated as the only or main residence of them both and the other shall be disregarded[16].

8-59 Special provisions apply in relation to the application of the MIRAS system where the £30,000 maximum limit applies. In particular, the interest does not fall within the MIRAS scheme unless the loan was made after 5 April 1987 or the lender is prepared to have MIRAS applied to limited loans[17], and, where the limit in respect of a loan is affected by an earlier loan in respect of the same residence, MIRAS does not apply unless both loans were made by the same lender[18]. Where a loan is made to two or more borrowers jointly, MIRAS only applies if each borrower is a 'qualifying borrower'[19] and if interest payable by each of them is 'relevant loan interest'[20] within the MIRAS scheme[1].

PERSONAL REPRESENTATIVES OF A DECEASED BORROWER

8-60 The personal representatives of, or the trustees of a will trust of, a deceased borrower may continue to obtain relief for interest paid on a loan[2] in respect of property which belonged to the deceased at the time of his death. This relief is available where the property was used as the deceased's only or main residence or was intended to be so used when the deceased at his death lived in 'job-related' accommodation[3]. It is not necessary that the loan in question was taken out by the deceased; the personal

---

[12] TA 1988 s 356A (1) to (3).
[13] TA 1988 s 356A (4) to (8).
[14] TA 1988 s 356D (5).
[15] TA 1988 s 356B (1) to (4); see Inland Revenue Statement of Practice SP8/89, in relation to extension of time limit for elections. See also Inland Revenue Statement of Practice A34(a), under which relief is allowed to whichever spouse pays interest irrespective of whether the property is owned wholly or partly by the other.
[16] TA 1988 s 356B (5).
[17] TA 1988 s 373 (1) and (2).
[18] TA 1988 s 373 (3).
[19] TA 1988 s 376 (1) to (3).
[20] TA 1988 s 370.
[1] TA 1988 s 373 (6).
[2] TA 1988 s 358.
[3] See §8-54 above.

representatives could, for example, take out a new loan to replace a previous loan to the deceased. It is, however, necessary that at the time when the interest is paid the property is used as the only or main residence of the deceased's widow or widower, or that at the time the deceased's widow or widower is living in job-related accommodation and either uses the property as a residence or intends to use the property in due course as his or her only or main residence[4]. The £30,000 limit applies as it would to a loan to the deceased had he survived.

Where interest paid by personal representatives qualifies for relief in these circumstances, it may qualify as 'relevant loan interest' so as to be paid net of tax under the MIRAS scheme[5].

In practice, relief is in some circumstances available where a property is inherited subject to a mortgage on which the deceased was entitled to interest relief, and the successor takes over the mortgage or takes out a new loan to redeem that mortgage[6].

LOAN TO PURCHASE LIFE ANNUITY

8-61   Relief for interest is available, against basic rate income tax only[7], where it is paid on a loan not less than nine-tenths of which is applied in the purchase of an annuity on the life of the borrower or on the life of the survivor of the borrower and another person[8]. The borrower (or each of the annuitants, where there are two) must be over the age of sixty-five years, and the loan must be secured on land in the UK or the Republic of Ireland owned by the borrower or one of the annuitants; further, the property must be used as the only or main residence of the borrower, or of each of the annuitants, at the time when the interest is paid. The amount of interest eligible for relief is limited to interest on a loan of £30,000, the limit being shared proportionately where two or more persons pay the interest[9]. Interest on such a loan may be paid net of basic rate tax under the MIRAS scheme[10].

5   Interest on loans to pay inheritance tax

8-62   Interest paid by personal representatives is eligible for relief under TA 1988 s 353 where it is paid on a loan to them which is applied in paying inheritance tax before the grant of representation[11] on the delivery of the personal representatives' account to the Inland Revenue and to the extent that it is attributable to the value of personal property[12] to which the deceased was beneficially entitled and which vests in the personal representatives as

---

4   TA 1988 s 358 (4).
5   Regulation 7A, the Income Tax (Interest Relief) Regulations 1982: SI 1982 No 1236.
6   See Inland Revenue Statement of Practice A34 (b).
7   TA 1988 s 353 (4).
8   TA 1988 s 365.
9   TA 1988 s 365 (3).
10   Regulation 4, the Income Tax (Interest Relief) Regulations 1982: SI 1982 No 1236.
11   Or, in Scotland, confirmation.
12   Inheritance tax on real property can normally be paid by interest-free instalments commencing six months after the death – IHTA 1984 s 227.

such[13]. The relief also applies where the duty is payable in respect of foreign personal property which does not vest in the personal representatives as such but which would do so if the property were UK property. Relief is not available when the property in question was held by the deceased jointly with another person and the interest passes to that other person by survivorship.

Relief is only available for interest paid in respect of a period ending within one year from the making of the loan; the date when the interest is paid or is payable is immaterial for this purpose. Relief is also available within the same period for interest on a loan replacing a previous loan where the interest qualified for this relief. The relief is given against income of the year in which it is paid, but if such income is insufficient the interest may be carried back to previous years[14] or, if relief cannot be obtained in that way, may be carried forward to later years[15].

6   Interest paid by personal representatives and trustees

8-63   Interest paid by personal representatives or trustees may qualify for relief under certain of the provisions described in the earlier Parts of this chapter. The provisions of TA 1988 s 353 apply generally to interest paid by 'a person', which includes personal representatives and trustees, but certain of the qualifying conditions cannot be fulfilled by personal representatives or trustees because they only apply to individuals. These restricted cases are those concerning loans to individual members of partnerships[16] or to an employee[17] to acquire machinery or plant, or loans to invest in a close company, a co-operative, an employee-controlled company or a partnership[18].

8-64   Yet, even where the interest does not qualify for relief against basic rate income tax, effective relief against higher rate income tax may be enjoyed by an individual beneficiary in respect of interest paid by personal representatives or trustees. This is because of the way in which beneficiaries are taxed in respect of distributions made to them. A beneficiary under a trust is treated as if the amount of income distributed to him out of trust were of a net amount which has already suffered income tax at the basic rate. This amount is grossed up to include the basic rate, and the beneficiary is charged to higher rate tax on that amount with credit being given for tax at the basic rate. (Where the trust is one which has suffered the additional rate of tax also by reason of its being an accumulation or discretionary trust, the income is grossed up to include also the additional rate of tax[19].) Because interest paid by the trustees will normally be an expense of the trust payable out of income, the interest will be paid out of the net income of the trust after suffering income tax at the basic rate (and, if appropriate, at the additional

---

13 TA 1988 s 364 (1).
14 The most recent year first.
15 TA 1988 s 364 (2).
16 §8-26 above.
17 §8-27 above.
18 §§8-17 to 8-25 above.
19 TA 1988 s 687 (2).

rate[20]). The beneficiary will then receive a payment of the net amount remaining in the trustees' hands, and it is that amount which is grossed up for higher rate purposes.

EXAMPLE

A trust receives gross income of 1,000 and pays interest of 210 which is not deductible for income tax purposes. After paying basic rate income tax (250) and the interest, the trustees distribute 540 to the beneficiary; this amount is grossed up to 720 on which he suffers income tax at, say, 40 per cent (with credit given for tax at the basic rate) – ie 108. This leaves net after-tax income of 432. Had the beneficiary received the income direct and paid the (non-deductible) interest himself, his net income after tax of 400 and interest of 210 would have been 390.

8-65   However, it is not possible for an individual who wishes to obtain effective relief at the higher rates for interest paid to do so by establishing a trust (eg to hold investments) of which he (and/or his wife) is a beneficiary. This is because of the operation of the special rules which relate to the taxation of the income of a settlement in which the settlor retains a benefit[1]. Broadly, these rules cause the undistributed income of such a settlement to be taxed as if it were the income of the settlor. The definition for this purpose of undistributed income is such as to disregard any distributions in respect of interest[2] and to exclude from the expenses disbursed by the trustees payments of interest (or a proportion of such interest, where only part of the net income of the trust is paid to the settlor or his or her spouse)[3]. Any interest which is eligible for income tax relief or which is paid to the settlor or his spouse is excluded from this special treatment[4].

A similar provision applies in relation to a settlement under which the income is paid or applied for the benefit of the unmarried minor child of the settlor[5]; in such a case, the income is treated for taxation purposes as the income of the settlor. Where interest is paid by the trustees of the settlement, a part of the interest, proportionate to the proportion which the income paid to a child of the settlor bears to the net income of the settlement, is treated as paid to or applied for the benefit of the child, and so falls to be treated as part of the income of the settlor[6]. There is excluded from this treatment any interest which qualifies for relief for income tax purposes and also any interest which is in any event paid to the settlor or his spouse[7].

8-66   Where a beneficiary of the estate of a deceased person has a limited interest in the residue of the estate he is chargeable to higher rate income tax as if distributions of income to him were of a net amount after deduction of basic rate income tax[8]. Thus, such a beneficiary is in the same position

---

[20] TA 1988 s 686 (2) (d).
[1] TA 1988 Part XV Chapter III.
[2] TA 1988 s 682 (1) (a).
[3] TA 1988 s 682 (2) to (4).
[4] TA 1988 s 682 (5).
[5] TA 1988 Part XV Chapter II.
[6] TA 1988 s 666 (1).
[7] TA 1988 s 666 (2).
[8] TA 1988 s 695.

as an income beneficiary under a settlement and will effectively enjoy relief from income tax in excess of the basic rate in respect of interest paid by the personal representatives even though such interest does not qualify for relief as interest paid by the personal representatives. Moreover, because interest on delayed payments of inheritance tax is an expense payable out of the income of the estate, relief at rates in excess of the basic rate is effectively available even though such interest is expressly not relievable for income tax purposes[9].

If the beneficiary has an absolute interest in residue, relief is available for yearly interest paid by the personal representatives as an expense of the estate[10] in computing the 'residuary income' in respect of which the beneficiary is chargeable[11]. However, because of the express prohibition against any deduction in respect of interest paid on overdue inheritance tax[12] no relief is available in this instance for such interest[13]. The difference from the case of a beneficiary with a limited interest in residue arises because such a beneficiary is taxed on the grossed up amount of the net income paid to him, whereas a beneficiary with an absolute interest is charged on the income of the estate less certain deductions (but a deduction in respect of interest on overdue inheritance tax is expressly prohibited). A similar position would apply in respect of interest on overdue income tax or capital gains tax[14].

8-67 It should be noted that interest paid on a statutory legacy in the case of an intestacy, or after one year from the death in the case of a general or pecuniary legacy, can give rise to a measure of double taxation. This is because such interest does not qualify for relief against basic rate income tax paid by the personal representatives on the income of the estate but is taxed as interest received in the hands of the beneficiary. This position can be contrasted with the treatment of income received by a beneficiary who has an interest in residue or in a specific gift; in those cases, the income from the property to which the beneficiary is entitled will be taxed once only – in the case of income from residue, income tax will be suffered by the personal representatives at the basic rate, and by the beneficiary at the higher rate, whilst income from a specific gift will be the income of the beneficiary from the date of death and will be taxed as such.

---

[9] IHTA s 233 (3), and §9-60 below; also, see paragraph 3 (d) CCAB Press Release, 3 February 1978 - [1978] STI 49.
[10] TA 1988 ss 697 (1) (a) and 701 (6).
[11] TA 1988 s 696 (2).
[12] In IHTA s 233 (3).
[13] See paragraph 3 (c), CCAB Press Release, 3 February 1978 - [1978] STI 49.
[14] See TMA 1970 s 90.

Chapter 9

SPECIAL TOPICS

9-01 The preceding chapters have described the general rules which apply for the purposes of income tax and corporation tax in relation to the payment and receipt of interest. This chapter explains special rules which apply to, or in relation to, interest in certain cases; in addition, a summary is included of the special provisions concerning discount.

1 Interest treated as a dividend distribution

9-02 The scheme of corporation tax normally permits relief for interest - either as a trading expense or as a charge on income - in computing the profits which are liable to corporation tax. When the post-tax profits of a company are distributed by way of dividend, a UK resident company is usually required to make a payment to the Inland Revenue of advance corporation tax ('ACT')[1] of a fraction, currently twenty-five seventy-fifths[2], of the amount of the dividend; the ACT may, subject to certain limitations, be set against the company's liability for corporation tax for the then current accounting period, or be either carried back for up to six years or carried forward indefinitely[3]; in some cases, ACT can be surrendered to subsidiaries[4]. Where ACT cannot be used immediately it becomes an effective tax cost to the company until the time when it can be offset. In the hands of a UK resident non-corporate recipient, the dividend is treated as being of a gross amount equal to the aggregate of the dividend and the ACT, with a tax credit being available in respect of an amount equal to the ACT which represents basic rate income tax on the gross amount[5]. Under the general law, a non-resident is not normally[6] able to recover any part of the tax credit, but certain double taxation agreements entered into by the UK do permit recovery of part of the tax credit in certain circumstances, although the amount recoverable will depend upon whether the recipient is a company or an individual and on the level of the shareholding.

9-03 It can be seen that it may often be more tax-efficient for remittances from a company in respect of the use of capital to be by way of payment of interest rather than the payment of dividends. It is for this reason that

---

[1] TA 1988 s 14.
[2] TA 1988 s 14(3) and FA 1992 s 10(1)(b).
[3] TA 1988 s 239; subject to restrictions under TA 1988 ss 245 and 245A.
[4] TA 1988 s 240.
[5] TA 1988 s 231.
[6] But see TA 1988 s 232 in relation to certain non-residents, such as Commonwealth citizens, to whom TA 1988 278(2) applies.

the definition of 'distribution' from a company includes, in TA 1988 s 209 (2), payments of interest in certain circumstances. In such cases, the interest is treated as a distribution; it cannot be relieved as a trade expense[7] or as a charge on income[8] and, where paid by a UK resident company, ACT must be paid in respect of it[9]. In this connection, it should be noted that, although s 209 (2) principally applies in relation to UK resident companies, it can also apply in relation to a non-resident company trading in the UK through a branch or agency and, accordingly, subject to corporation tax[10]; however, in such a case, the effect of the application of s 209 is merely to disallow relief as a trade expense[11] or a charge on income[12], because a non-resident company is not required to pay ACT[13].

The relevant circumstances as set out in s 209 (2) are as follows:

'(d) any interest or other distribution out of assets of the company in respect of securities[14] of the company, where they are securities under which the consideration given by the company for the use of the principal thereby secured represents more than a reasonable commercial return for the use of that principal, except so much, if any, of any such distribution as represents that principal and so much as represents a reasonable commercial return for the use of that principal;

(e) any interest or other distribution out of assets of the company in respect of securities of the company (except so much, if any, of any such distribution as represents the principal thereby secured and except so much of any distribution as falls within paragraph (d) above), where the securities are –

(i) securities issued as mentioned in paragraph (c) above, but excluding securities issued before 6 April 1965 in respect of shares and securities issued before 6 April 1972 in respect of securities; or

(ii) securities convertible directly or indirectly into shares in the company or securities issued after 5 April 1972 and carrying any right to receive shares in or securities of the company, not being (in either case) securities quoted on a recognised stock exchange nor issued on terms which are reasonably comparable with the terms of issue of securities so quoted; or

(iii) securities under which the consideration given by the company for the use of the principal secured is to any extent dependent on the results of the company's business or any part of it; or

(iv) securities issued by the company ('the issuing company') and held by a company not resident in the United Kingdom where the issuing company is a 75 per cent subsidiary of the other company or both are 75 per cent subsidiaries of a third company which is not resident in the United Kingdom; or

(v) securities issued by the company ('the issuing company') and held by a company not resident in the United Kingdom ('the non-resident company')

---

[7] TA 1988 s 337 (2) (a)
[8] TA 1988 s 338 (2) (a).
[9] TA 1988 s 14 (1) the interest is a 'qualifying distribution' (see TA 1988 s 14(2)).
[10] TA 1988 s 11 (1).
[11] TA 1988 s 337 (2) (a).
[12] TA 1988 s 338 (2) (a).
[13] TA 1988 s 14 (1); where the payment is treated as not being interest, no basic rate income tax is deductible.
[14] See TA 1988 s 254 (2) as to distributions 'in respect of' securities of other members of a group of companies.

where less than 90 per cent of the share capital of the issuing company is directly owned by a company resident in the United Kingdom and both the issuing company and the non-resident company are 75 per cent subsidiaries of a third company which is resident in the United Kingdom; or

(vi) securities which are connected with shares in the company, and for this purpose securities are so connected if, in consequence of the nature of the rights attaching to the securities or shares and in particular of any terms or conditions attaching to the right to transfer the shares or securities, it is necessary or advantageous for a person who has, or disposes of or acquires, any of the securities also to have, or to dispose of or to acquire, a proportionate holding of the shares; or

(vii) equity notes issued by the company ('the issuing company') and held by a company which is associated with the issuing company or is a funded company.'

9-04   The provisions apply in relation to 'securities of the company'. The wide definition of 'security' for these purposes[15] is such that there is no need for the indebtedness in question to be secured, whether by a fixed or floating charge, and any interest paid by a company on money 'advanced' is treated as being paid in respect of a security issued by the company. However, where a company pays interest in respect of money not borrowed but merely due from it (eg delayed payment of purchase money under a contract) there would seem to be no advance[16], so the interest would not be interest on a 'security'.

It is not only interest which can be treated as a distribution under these provisions, but any other distribution out of assets of the company in respect of securities. This would include a premium payable on redemption[17] or any element of discount paid, but not any repayment of the principal of the loan.

9-05   The securities referred to in s 209 (2) (e)(i) are bonus securities issued in respect of shares or securities of the company, or so much of any securities as are so issued by the company otherwise than wholly for 'new consideration'. 'New consideration' means, in effect, new money or other value introduced into the company[18]. An issue of bonus securities would occur where a company issues securities to shareholders according to the shareholdings and so treats itself as owing money to the shareholders when no money has in fact been lent or where the amount subscribed by the shareholders is less than the face value of the security; on the other hand, an issue of securities in satisfaction of the amounts which shareholders are entitled to be paid, for example on a reduction of capital, would not be a bonus issue because the shareholders would be providing (by way of delayed receipt) sums to which they would otherwise be entitled.

9-06   Interest on convertible securities – whether convertible into shares or other securities – is treated as a distribution under s 209 (2) (e)(ii), except

---

[15] TA 1988 s 254 (1).
[16] There is no deemed advance – cf TA 1988 s 367 (3).
[17] Which may properly be interest in any event – see §§**2-30** to **2-32** above.
[18] TA 1988 s 254 (1) and (5) to (7).

where the securities are either quoted on a recognised stock exchange or are reasonably comparable with the terms of issue of securities so quoted[19]. For this purpose, securities are only convertible where they are convertible into shares or securities of the same company[20].

9-07   Interest can be treated as a distribution under s 209 (2) (e)(vi) where the securities in respect of which it is paid are 'connected with' shares in the company; this provision does not apply to securities 'connected with' shares in another company, even if a member of the same group. Securities are 'connected with' shares if it is necessary or advantageous for a person holding, disposing of or acquiring the securities also to have, dispose of or acquire a proportionate holding of shares; but the necessity or advantage must derive from the nature of the rights attaching to the securities or shares, and in particular of any terms or conditions attaching to the right to transfer the shares or securities. It appears from these provisions that the terms in question must be imposed by the Articles of Association or the terms of issue of the securities – ie something to which the company is a party – and not merely from a private agreement between some or all of the shareholders and which does not concern the company.

9-08   Interest or other consideration which is dependent on the results of the company's business – to which TA 1988 s 209 (2) (e)(iii) applies – need not necessarily be related to the company's profits. It could be related to the level of turnover, or the profits (or losses) realised from a particular transaction (eg a property development); as in the case of the other instances of interest being treated as a distribution, there is no requirement that the interest would otherwise be capable of being distributed as a dividend under general company law.

At one time, this provision made it possible for UK resident lenders to make loan finance available to certain borrowers on very competitive terms. This resulted from the provision that distributions received by a resident company from another resident company are not subject to corporation tax[1]; advance corporation tax is payable in the ordinary way, and the distribution, together with the tax credit[2] is available to frank dividends paid by the recipient, so relieving the recipient from the obligation to account for advance corporation tax on dividends paid. Therefore, where the borrower was not concerned to obtain relief for interest paid (eg because the level of its profits or available losses prevented it paying corporation tax in any event) it could suit both borrower and lender to cause the interest to be treated as a distribution and to reduce the interest payable to a level at which the net cost to the borrower, taking into account the advance corporation tax, was less, and the net after-tax return to the lender was greater, than under a conventional loan. By reason of what is now s 209 (2) (e)(iii) this could be achieved by linking part of the interest – for commercial reasons, only a very small part – to an element in the results of the company's business.

---

[19] Securities traded on the Unlisted Securities Market of the London Stock Exchange are not treated as 'quoted on a recognised stock exchange' – see Inland Revenue Statement of Practice SP 18/80, [1980] STI 894.
[20] Cf FA 1976 s 126(2) (stamp duty) and TA 1988 Sch 18 para 1(5)(a) (group relief – anti-avoidance provisions).
[1] TA 1988 s 208.
[2] 'Franked investment income' – TA 1988 s 238(1).

However, TA 1988 s 212 provides that, normally, in the case of interest paid to a company within the charge to corporation tax, where such interest would otherwise be treated as a distribution under the provisions described above, only so much of the interest is a distribution as exceeds a reasonable commercial return for the use of the principal. This does not prevent any excessive part of the interest being treated as a distribution. This amendment does not apply where the lender is exempt from corporation tax in respect of the receipt of the interest or distribution under a provision other than the general exemption from corporation tax in respect of dividends received from resident companies[3], or where the lender is not a company or is a non-resident company which is not within the charge to corporation tax.

Loans are sometimes made on a limited recourse basis under which the borrower is only required to make payments of interest and repayments of principal to the extent of the value of income derived from a particular project. In such cases, the interest would be 'dependent on the results of the company's business'. However, normally, even though the lender may charge a higher rate of interest than under a conventional loan (to compensate for the added risk), the interest would not exceed a commercial return for the principal lent and therefore would not normally be treated as a distribution under s 209 (2) (e)(iii) where it is paid to a UK resident company or a non-resident company which is within the charge to corporation tax.

9-09 It should be noted that the circumstances described in §§**9-06** and **9-08** above in which interest can be treated as a distribution are similar to circumstances in which loans to a company can effectively be treated as equity share capital for the purposes of restrictions on the availability of group relief[4] and transfers of loan capital are not eligible for exemption from stamp duty[5]. However, there are differences between the distribution rules and the rules which apply for group relief or stamp duty.

9-10 Whether or not the interest exceeds a reasonable commercial return for the use of the principal, interest can be treated as a distribution under s 209 (2) (e)(iv) or (v) where the interest is paid to a non-resident company and either the borrower is a 75 per cent subsidiary[6] of the lender or the borrower and the lender are, broadly, under common 75 per cent ownership. The latter does not depend upon the parent company being non-resident, but, if the common parent company is a UK resident company which owns *directly* 90 per cent or more of the share capital[7] of the borrower, the interest is not treated as a distribution; this reflects the fact that if it were the parent company itself borrowing from a non-resident *subsidiary*, the interest would not be treated as a distribution by virtue of those provisions (unless the parent company were itself a 75 per cent subsidiary of a non-resident company of which the lending company is also a 75 per cent subsidiary). The operation of s 209 (2) (e)(iv) and (v) is illustrated by the following diagrams:

---

[3] TA 1988 s 208 (3).
[4] TA 1988 Sch 18 para 1(5), and see Chapter 9 Part 2 below.
[5] FA 1986 s 86 (6) and see §**11-18** below.
[6] As defined in TA 1988 s 838.
[7] Not just of the ordinary share capital.

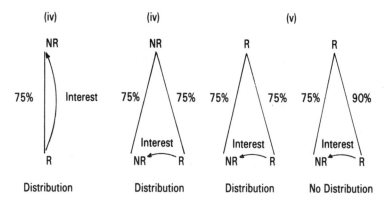

9-11   The application of s 209 (2) (e)(iv) and (v) is usually modified where there is a double taxation agreement in force between the UK and the country of residence of the recipient of the interest. Such a modification is usually in the form of a paragraph in the Article concerning interest which states that a provision of the law of the UK which causes interest paid to a non-resident to be treated as a dividend distribution shall not apply in the case of interest paid to a resident of the other party to the double taxation agreement. This will override s 209 (2) (e)(iv) and (v), but will not override the treatment of interest as a distribution under any of the other provisions in s 209 (2), because they do not depend upon the recipient of the interest being a non-resident. Interest paid to a non-resident and which is protected by a double taxation agreement can therefore be paid without the payment of advance corporation tax and also will not be prevented from qualifying for relief as an expense or as a charge on income. In some older double taxation agreements[8] which pre-dated the 1973 introduction of the imputation system, the relevant provision does not provide that the interest is not to be treated as a distribution but merely prevents the interest being left out of account in computing the taxable profits of the company[9]. In practice, the Inland Revenue does not require such interest to be treated as a distribution for the purposes of advance corporation tax. However, it is understood that the Inland Revenue might not consider that a provision based on the non-discrimination article in the OECD Model Convention relating to the taxation of income and gains is sufficient to prevent ACT being required to be paid in respect of interest paid to a resident of the other party to a double taxation agreement[10].

However, it should be noted that a provision of this kind alone does not permit the interest to be paid in full. Interest paid by a company and which is not a distribution is subject to the deduction of basic rate income tax at source unless this is reduced or removed altogether by another provision in the double taxation agreement and the payment of the interest gross has been authorised by the Inspector of Foreign Dividends[11].

[8] Eg Article 7(6) of the UK/Germany Double Taxation Agreement – 26 November 1964: SI 1967 No 25, amended in relation to Article 7(6) by SI 1971 No 874.
[9] This results from the agreement's pre-dating the introduction of the imputation system when it was sufficient for the interest to be allowed to remain deductible, since ACT was not payable and another provision of the double taxation agreement would normally reduce or eliminate the tax deductible from the interest paid.
[10] See ICAEW 'Taxline', September 1992 p 10 and Article 24.4 of the OECD Model Convention.
[11] See §§7-18 and 7-19 above.

The relief under a double taxation agreement from the treatment of interest paid as a distribution will normally be qualified by a general provision that where, by reason of a special relationship between the borrower and the lender, or between each of them and a third party, the interest paid is excessive, the interest may not be protected by the double taxation agreement. The relevant language used in the UK's double taxation agreements is not always the same. In some[12], the test as to whether the interest paid is excessive is applied by reference to the circumstances of the actual indebtedness in question; this, therefore, involves a consideration of current market interest rates as applied to the loan which was made to the particular borrower. In other more recent agreements[13], wider language is used which requires a consideration of the amount of interest or the terms of the loan which would have been agreed upon in the absence of such a relationship. For some time, the Inland Revenue regarded such language as is found in more modern agreements as preventing the application of the relieving provisions to the extent that the whole or part of the interest would not have been paid had the parties been at arm's length because the borrowings exceeded what could have been borrowed from an arm's length lender.

Following an adverse, but unpublished, decision of the Special Commissioners of Taxes, which apparently cast doubt on the Inland Revenue's position[14], new s 808A was introduced into the Taxes Act 1988[15] to provide statutory support for the Inland Revenue's view. This provides that where a double taxation agreement limits the relief available where the interest paid is excessive owing to a special relationship, account should be taken of all factors; these factors are stated to include whether the loan would have been made, and if so of what amount, in the absence of the special relationship, as well as what rate of interest and other terms would have been agreed upon in the absence of the relationship. However, this does not apply where the double taxation agreement expressly requires regard to be had to the debt in question[16]. The new provision also places the onus on 'the taxpayer' to show that there is no special relationship or what amount of interest would have been paid in the absence of that relationship; in the context of the double taxation agreement preventing the interest being treated as a distribution, it would seem that 'the taxpayer' is the company paying the interest and claiming relief from the obligation to pay ACT.

There is no published level of borrowing which is regarded as acceptable by the Inland Revenue, the appropriate level in each case depending on its own particular facts. Thus, a company undertaking a speculative venture such as offshore oil exploration might be expected to have a much lower gearing (if any) than a bank. In considering a company's gearing, regard should be had to all its borrowings and any security therefor on the one hand and its shareholders' funds (not merely the nominal amount of its issued share capital) on the other hand, although the prospect of the reserves being depleted by dividend payments should not be overlooked. Regard

---

[12] Modelled on the OECD Model Double Taxation Convention with respect to taxes on income and gains.
[13] Eg Article 11(4) of the UK/Switzerland Double Taxation Agreement SI 1978 No 1408, and Article 11(4) of the UK/Netherlands Double Taxation Agreement, SI 1980 No 1961.
[14] Inland Revenue Press Release, 15 May 1992.
[15] F(No 2)A 1992 s 52.
[16] TA 1988 s 808A(5) – thus double taxation agreements which follow the OECD Model Convention wording are not affected by the requirements of s 808A.

should also be had to the adequacy of the borrower's income to service interest payments. The basic test is what an arm's length banker would lend in the same circumstances. In practice, the Inland Revenue is normally prepared to agree an acceptable level of borrowing having regard to the consolidated assets and liabilities of a UK group, even where the borrowing is being undertaken by a subsidiary or subsidiaries (and not only by the group parent company).

In addition to this general provision, the exemption under a double taxation agreement from treatment of interest as a distribution is normally subject to a special qualification that it will not usually apply where more than 50 per cent of the recipient company is controlled, directly or indirectly, by residents of the UK.

9-12 The rules relating to interest paid to an overseas affiliate could apply to cause interest to be treated as a distribution where it is paid on a loan from an affiliated company even though the borrower is a UK bank. However, by concession, the Inland Revenue will not treat interest as a distribution under TA 1988 s 209 (2) (e)(iv) where interest is paid by a bank authorised to take deposits under the Banking Act 1987 and is paid in the ordinary course of banking business, provided that the interest is not excessive having regard to the terms and amount of the indebtedness and what the position would have been had the parties been independent persons dealing at arm's length[17]. This means that a UK banking subsidiary of an overseas group can pay interest within the same group without the interest being treated as a distribution. However, if the payer of the interest is not itself a bank, the concession does not apply, even if the recipient is a bank carrying on a bona fide banking business in the UK[18].

9-13 The final circumstance – s 209 (2) (e)(vii) – where interest can be treated as a distribution is where the interest is paid in respect of 'equity notes' held by a company associated with the issuing company or by a company which has been directly or indirectly funded by the issuing company or a company associated with it[19]. This provision was introduced in 1992[20], with a view to countering what the Inland Revenue perceived[1] as an avoidance device under which interest paid by a UK company to a company resident elsewhere (eg in the United States) would be treated as interest for UK tax purposes but would be treated as a dividend in the recipient country because the perpetual or long-term nature of the indebtedness resulted in its being characterised as equity for tax purposes in the recipient country. Therefore, the term 'equity note' is defined[2] by reference to there being no stated redemption date, the redemption date being more than (or being likely to be more than) 50 years after issue of the note or the issuer being able to secure that there is no particular redemption date or that it will fall more than 50 years after issue.

---

[17] Extra-statutory Concession C18; published on 11 June 1991, replacing the similar (but, in some respects, wider) unpublished 'Moscow Narodny' practice.
[18] TA 1988 s 212 does not disapply the distribution rules to interest paid to a company within the charge to corporation tax where the interest is treated as a distribution under TA 1988 s 209 (2) (e)(iv) or (v).
[19] TA 1988 s 209(11).
[20] F (No 2) A 1992 s 31.
[1] Inland Revenue Press Release, 15 May 1992.
[2] TA 1988 s 209 (9).

This provision is very wide and could apply to more cases than the fairly narrow circumstances at which it was originally directed; comments made by the Financial Secretary to the Treasury in the Finance Bill debate about the desirability of the provisions being 'flexible' suggest that this was intentional[3]. Companies are 'associated' for the purposes of this provision if they are, broadly, under common 75 per cent or greater control[4]. Although the wide nature of the legislation means that inter-company loans repayable on demand appear to be within the provision[5], this will not affect loans between UK companies. TA 1988 s 212 has been extended[6] so that interest on equity notes will not normally be treated as a distribution where received by a company within the charge to corporation tax, provided that the interest does not exceed a reasonable commercial return. Thus, in practice, the 'equity notes' provision will normally only apply to interest paid to non-residents; but, because that is not a term of the legislation, the relieving provision of a double taxation agreement discussed in **9-11** above will not be available to provide any relief.

2   Group relief and other group provisions: loans which are not 'normal commercial loans'

9-14   The basic requirements as to the relationship between two companies between which losses may be surrendered by way of group relief – generally, that they should be members of a group of UK resident companies under common 75 per cent control[7] – are modified so as to require that, broadly, the 75 per cent shareholding relationship must also extend to a 75 per cent true economic interest in profits available for distribution and assets on a winding-up[8]. In each case, the test is applied by reference to the entitlement of 'equity holders'.

The expression 'equity holders' is defined in TA 1988 Sch 18 para 1, and includes a loan creditor[9] in respect of a loan which is not a 'normal commercial loan'. In order to be a 'normal commercial loan', in addition to other conditions, the loan creditor must not be entitled to any amount by way of interest which depends to any extent on the results of the company's business or any part of it, or on the value of the company's assets, or which exceeds a reasonable commercial return on the new consideration lent. This condition is similar to two conditions which can cause interest paid by the company to be treated as a distribution[10], although there is no apportionment of the loan by reference only to the extent to which the interest exceeds a commercial return; similar circumstances can also cause a transfer of loan capital to fall outside the exemption from stamp duty[11]. However, the group relief provisions have been modified[12] to prevent a loan not being a normal

---

[3] Standing Committee on the Finance Bill: 30 June 1992, col 446 – Mr Stephen Dorrell MP.
[4] TA 1988 s 209(10).
[5] It is understood that, in practice, the Inland Revenue will not normally take this point.
[6] F(No 2)A 1992 s 31 (3).
[7] See TA 1988 ss 402 and 413(3) and (5).
[8] TA 1988 s 413 (7) and (10) and Sch 18.
[9] Defined in Sch 18 para 1(4).
[10] TA 1988 s 209 (2) (d) and (e)(iii), and see §**9-08** above.
[11] FA 1976 s 126 (2) (a), and see §**11-18** below.
[12] By FA 1991 s 77.

commercial loan in two particular types of case – namely, where interest on a loan to a company is to be reduced where its results improve or the value of its assets increases, and where a limited recourse loan is made to finance an investment in land[13].

9-15 Because TA 1988 s 413 (7) operates by reference to the entitlements of all the 'equity holders', the existence of a loan which is not a 'normal commercial loan' can prevent group relief being available where the loan is made by a company which is outside the group relationship. This is because the entitlement of the creditor in respect of such a loan to be repaid the principal of the loan in a winding-up will be taken into account in ascertaining the entitlements of the 'equity holders' on a notional winding-up[14]; this may result in a company holding 75 per cent or more of the ordinary share capital being treated as entitled to less than 75 per cent of the assets which would be distributed to the 'equity holders' on a winding-up[15]. Therefore, if a UK resident wholly-owned subsidiary of a resident company takes a loan from a bank or other lender on terms which relate the interest in any way to profits (including a limited recourse loan) this might have the effect of preventing group relief being available between parent and subsidiary.
A similar difficulty can arise in relation to the application of group relief to a consortium company[16].

9-16 The special provisions concerning 'equity holders' are extended to apply for the purpose of determining whether a company is entitled to surrender surplus advance corporation tax to a 51 per cent subsidiary[17], whether a 75 per cent subsidiary is a member of a group for capital gains purposes[18] and whether a company can be treated as a 51 per cent subsidiary (or a consortium company) for group income purposes[19]. Therefore, the existence of a loan bearing interest which depends on a company's business, or which exceeds a reasonable commercial return, can prejudice the required group relationship for the purpose of those reliefs.

3 Interest and transfer-pricing

9-17 TA 1988 s 770 permits the Board of Inland Revenue to direct that in computing the income, profits or losses of a person there shall be substituted for the price paid or received on a sale of property to or from certain associated persons the price at which the property would have been sold if the transaction had been between independent persons dealing at arm's length. The provisions of s 770 apply not only to sales of property but also[20] to 'the giving of business facilities of whatever kind'. Consequently, it would appear that the profits, income or losses may be adjusted where a taxpayer to whom s 770 applies

---

[13] TA 1988 Sch 18 para 1(5E) to (5I).
[14] TA 1988 Sch 18 para 3.
[15] See TA 1988 s 413 (7) (b).
[16] See TA 1988 ss 402 (3) and 413(8).
[17] TA 1988 s 240(11) (b) and (13).
[18] TCGA 1992 s 178.
[19] TA 1988 s 247(8A) and (9A).
[20] TA 1988 s 773 (4).

either pays loan interest to an associated person in excess of an arm's length rate or makes a loan to an associated person at less than an arm's length rate of interest.

Where a non-resident makes an interest-free loan to a resident of the UK, interest on that loan would normally[1] be subject to UK income tax; therefore, a s 770 adjustment could be made in those circumstances and the non-resident assessed to income tax. However, in practice the Inland Revenue would be unable to recover the tax in a foreign jurisdiction, although it is possible that the non-resident may be assessed in the name of a branch or agent in the UK[2]. It would not seem that the Inland Revenue can apply s 770 so as to assess the UK borrower in respect of the basic rate income tax which it would have been obliged to deduct under TA s 349 (2)[3] had the loan carried a commercial rate of interest and been yearly interest; this is because such an adjustment could not be made 'in computing the income, profits or losses of the [borrower]' as permitted under s 770 (2).

9-18   The circumstances to which s 770 can apply in relation to the excessive payment or the underpayment of loan interest are where the borrower or lender is a company, partnership[4] or other 'body of persons' over which the other party (whether or not a 'body of persons') has control, or both borrower and lender are 'bodies of persons' over whom the same person, or persons (whether or not 'connected persons'), has or have control[5]. 'Control' is defined in TA 1988 s 840[6] as, broadly, the power of a person to secure that the affairs of the company are conducted in accordance with that person's wishes or, in relation to a partnership, a right to a share of more than one-half of the assets or the income of the partnership. In ascertaining where control lies, there is provision for there to be attributed to any person the rights and powers of a nominee for him or of certain persons with whom he is 'connected'[7].

9-19   Section 770 cannot apply to require the interest to be adjusted in the computation of income, profits or losses of a party to a loan where the other party to the loan is resident in the UK and is carrying on a trade in the UK and the interest paid or received by him is taken into account in computing the profits or gains or losses of that trade for tax purposes[8] or, presumably, where no interest is in fact paid or received, would be so taken into account if paid or received. It should be noted that a s 770 adjustment is only avoided where the other party's UK taxable trading profit or loss would be affected by the interest. It is not sufficient that the other party is UK resident and carries on a trade in respect of which he is taxable *and also* would be taxable under Sch D Case III on interest received, or would be entitled to relief for interest paid as a charge on income (in the case of a company)[9] or under TA 1988 s 353 (in the case of an individual).

---

[1] Subject to the application of relief under a double taxation agreement.
[2] Under TMA 1970 s 78.
[3] See §§**7-16** to **7-19** above.
[4] TA 1988 s 773 (2).
[5] TA 1988 s 770 (1) (a).
[6] TA 1988 s 773 (2).
[7] TA 1988 s 773 (3).
[8] TA 1988 s 770 (2) (a) and (b).
[9] TA 1988 s 338.

4 Arrangements designed to obtain relief, or effective relief, for interest

TRANSACTIONS ASSOCIATED WITH LOANS OR CREDIT

9-20 TA 1988 s 786 is designed to prevent a taxpayer from arranging his affairs so that, although he bears the economic cost of borrowing money, he does not pay interest for which no relief would be available but either reduces his taxable income by a comparable amount or makes a payment which does not amount to interest but for which he obtains relief. The provisions of s 786 apply generally where money is lent or credit given or where the terms of a loan or credit are varied or arrangements are made to facilitate the lending of money or giving of credit. For the section to apply it is not necessary that the transaction is made between the borrower and lender, but the section may apply where persons 'connected'[10] with either or both of the borrower and lender are involved. The section applies in relation to three types of transaction described below.

9-21 Until 1977, relief could readily be obtained for both income tax and corporation tax purposes in respect of an annuity or other annual payment; indeed, until 1969, relief for annuities and annual payments was given in the same manner as for yearly interest[11]. Section 786(3) prevents relief being obtained by a transaction in which the borrower pays an annuity or annual payment – which might qualify for relief – directly or indirectly as consideration for, or to facilitate the making of, a loan (probably, on an interest-free basis) by requiring the annuity or annual payment to be treated as yearly interest. The payer of the annuity or annual payment will then only obtain relief for the payment if a payment of yearly interest in the same circumstances would qualify for relief. Since 1977 it is less likely that such a scheme could be used to obtain relief, even without the application of s 786 (3), because an annuity or other annual payment paid in consideration for something which is not itself taxable in the hands of the payer of the annuity or annual payment is not allowed as a deduction in computing total income for income tax purposes or as a charge on income for corporation tax purposes[12].

9-22 An alternative arrangement would be for the borrower to sell or otherwise transfer an income-producing asset to the lender (or to a 'connected' person) in circumstances where he subsequently repurchases the asset (normally, on repayment of the loan); in the intervening period, the lender (or the 'connected' person) would receive the income from the asset as consideration for the loan. In such a case, whether the reacquisition is of the same or any other property, and whether the reacquisition is pursuant to an agreement entered into at the outset or pursuant to a call option which is collateral to the original sale, the person making the original sale or transfer is, by virtue of s 786 (4), chargeable to tax under Sch D Case VI on an amount equal to any income which arises from the transferred property before the loan or credit comes to an end. Therefore, the borrower suffers

---

[10] As defined in TA 1988 s 839 – see s 786 (8).
[11] Subject to the special rules for companies since 1965.
[12] TA 1988 s 125.

tax on the income from the transferred property as if it had remained his income and had not been sheltered by relief for interest paid. The assessments under this sub-section can be made on an annual basis by reference to the income in each year of assessment or accounting period where an agreement to reacquire the asset is entered into at the outset; where the property is reacquired upon the exercise of an option, it would seem that the assessment would be made in one amount when the option is exercised and it is then known that the sub-section applies. It should be noted that the sub-section does not deem the income in question to be the income of the person who originally sold or transferred the asset; that remains the income of the purchaser or transferee who is taxable in respect of the income in the ordinary way. The person who sold or transferred the asset is chargeable on an equivalent amount of income. However, the sub-section was not amended on the introduction of the imputation system of corporation tax in 1973. The income which arises from shares in a company is the dividend only, and, although normally a tax credit is added to the dividend for tax purposes, this is only available to 'the person receiving the distribution'[13]; therefore, where the property transferred is shares in a UK resident company, the Case VI assessment on the person transferring the shares would appear to be on the amount of the dividend exclusive of the tax credit. Further, if a resident company were to transfer and re-acquire shares of a resident company in such circumstances, it would be chargeable under Case VI in respect of the dividend income even though it would not be subject to corporation tax on those dividends were it to receive them itself[14]. When s 786 (4) applies, the provisions of s 729 in relation to sales and repurchases of securities do not apply[15].

9–23 A similar scheme to that countered by s 786 (4) would be for the income arising from property to be assigned, surrendered, waived or otherwise foregone without any transfer of the property being made; for example, a borrower might agree to forego interest on a bank deposit account in consideration of the bank making a loan at a reduced interest rate or without any interest being paid at all. In such a case, s 786 (5) provides that the person foregoing the income shall be chargeable to tax under Sch D Case VI in respect of the income. Section 786(5) is treated as applying where for a period credit is given for the purchase price of property during which period the purchaser's rights to income from the property are suspended or restricted; the purchaser is treated as having surrendered a right to income from the property which he has effectively foregone during that period[16]. These provisions may not apply where there is a temporary transfer of non-income-producing property on terms which do not provide for any income to be paid (eg a deposit of cash) or where a transaction is entered into without making any provision for income which might otherwise have been earned. It would seem that income is only 'waived' or 'foregone' by a person where he would have received income had he not taken some action or had he not refrained from doing something which would have resulted in

---

[13] TA 1988 s 231 (1).
[14] TA 1988 s 208.
[15] See TA 1988 s 729 (b) and §**9–36** below.
[16] TA 1988 s 786 (6).

income being received, and that income is not waived or foregone merely because the terms of a transaction omit any provision for income to arise.

9-24 Where s 786(5) applies and the income foregone is paid under deduction of income tax, the income foregone is treated as being the gross amount before deduction of tax[17]. No special provision is made in respect of dividends to which a tax credit would normally attach; as suggested in §**9-22** above, it would seem that in such circumstances only a dividend – exclusive of the tax credit – is foregone and therefore is the measure of the amount on which the taxpayer may be assessed.

9-25 It is emphasised that the three provisions described above only apply where the transaction in question is made with reference to a loan or credit. If the transaction involves only the variation of the terms of a loan or credit, and nothing else, these provisions will not apply. In the author's view, it is not the case, as is sometimes suggested, that the mere waiver of interest alone will give rise to an assessment to tax under Sch D Case VI by virtue of s 786(5)[18]. However, if a waiver of loan interest is made with reference to some *other* lending or credit transaction – as in the case of the waiver of bank deposit interest in consideration of an interest-free loan – s 786(5) may apply to cause an assessment to be made on the interest waived.

SCHEMES TO OBTAIN RELIEF FOR INTEREST

9-26 TA 1988 s 787 is designed to counter schemes designed to reduce a person's tax liability by means of relief for interest paid. It provides that relief for interest as a deduction in computing profits or gains, or for a company either as a charge on income[19] or under a surrender by way of group relief of excess charges on income[20], or for an individual under TA 1988 s 353, shall not be given where a scheme has been effected or arrangements made where the sole or main benefit that might be expected to accrue to the payer of the interest is the obtaining of relief for the interest. The provisions can in theory apply to interest which is deductible as a trading expense, but such interest must, in any event, be incurred wholly and exclusively for the purposes of the trade, profession or vocation[1]. Where the relief is claimed by way of group relief, the benefit from the transaction is judged from the point of view of both the surrendering company and the claimant company taken together[2].

The 'sole or main benefit' test is an objective test which does not require a consideration of the purpose of the transaction in the mind of the party

---

[17] TA 1988 s 786(7).
[18] A view which, it is believed, is shared by the Inland Revenue – see Inland Revenue Booklet IR11 (1985) para 80 (although that booklet is no longer current).
[19] TA 1988 s 338(1).
[20] TA 1988 s 403(7).
[1] TA 1988 s 74(a).
[2] TA 1988 s 787(3).

paying the interest[3]; it should be contrasted with tests which do depend on the main object or purpose of a transaction[4].

9-27   This anti-avoidance section was introduced to counter artificial tax avoidance schemes such as the 'advance interest' scheme. This scheme – which, so far as individuals were concerned, was of limited application after interest relief was restricted in 1974 – involved the taxpayer borrowing a sum of money, paying interest for a year or more in advance and then paying an affiliate of the lender a sum of money to assume the repayment obligation; the sum paid was approximately equal to the amount of the loan less the interest paid in advance. Despite the introduction of this legislation, it has been held that this scheme was not in any event effective. In *Cairns v MacDiarmid (Inspector of Taxes)*[5] it was held that in the circumstances the interest was not yearly interest and so failed to qualify for relief under the predecessor of TA 1988 s 353.

Even though TA 1988 s 787 may not have been required to counter the scheme at which it was aimed, it remains in force and can still apply to negative relief for interest where arrangements are made which are directed only at reducing liability to tax. Although the application of the section must be considered by reference to the facts of any given case, it appears that the section will not deny relief where what is involved is a genuine borrowing which benefits the borrower. For example, it is understood that the Inland Revenue does not in practice apply the section where a company undertakes a 'Swiss roundabout'[6]. This arrangement is designed to obtain relief for interest as a charge on income where relief cannot otherwise be obtained by reason of a failure to satisfy the requirements of TA 1988 s 338 (4)[7]. If a company pays interest on a loan where income tax is not required to be deducted under TA 1988 s 349 (2) and the interest does not fall within TA 1988 s 340, the only way in which relief can be obtained is by paying the interest out of income falling within Sch D Case IV or V[8]. If a company does not have such income it may create it by placing the proceeds of the original loan on deposit with, say, a Swiss bank. The company can then borrow a like amount from the same or another Swiss bank (perhaps secured by a charge over the deposit); the interest paid on the second loan will be paid without deduction of basic rate income tax, by virtue of the UK/ Switzerland Double Taxation Agreement[9], and this will satisfy TA 1988 s 338 (4) (a) in relation to that interest[10]. Consequently, the interest on the first loan may be relieved as paid out of the Swiss deposit interest and the interest on the Swiss loan may be set against the company's profits generally. Although part of these arrangements is designed to obtain relief for interest which could not otherwise be obtained, the arrangement as a

---

[3] *Crown Bedding Co Ltd v IRC* [1946] 1 All ER 452, 34 TC 107, CA; *Star Cinemas (London) Ltd and Majestic (Derby) Ltd v IRC* [1952] TR 49, CA.

[4] Eg TCGA 1992 s 137(1) and TA 1988 s 703(1).

[5] [1983] STC 178, CA; see §3-12 above.

[6] It remains to be seen whether this attitude will be revised in the light of the House of Lords decision in *Furniss v Dawson* [1984] STC 153, [1984] 1 All ER 530.

[7] See §§8-33 to 8-42 above.

[8] TA 1988 s 338 (4) (d).

[9] Article 11(1) (SI 1978 No 1408).

[10] See §8-37(1) above.

whole is concerned with the first borrowing and obtaining finance under that borrowing is the main benefit to the taxpayer company.

5 Interest converted into capital, accrued interest and related matters

9-28 Because interest is not chargeable to tax unless and until received in that form[11], it is not surprising that attempts have been made over the years by taxpayers to arrange their affairs so that, without suffering the economic loss associated with not receiving the interest on an investment, they do not receive interest in a taxable form. Such attempts to reduce the flow of funds to the Exchequer have been met with anti-avoidance legislation. A general outline of this legislation is set out below, but it should be appreciated that much of this legislation is particularly complex and wide-ranging and can apply to circumstances which, at first sight, may not seem to be caught.

The arrangements which the legislation is designed to counter are variations of certain basic themes. From the point of view of the investor, if the value of the fruit of his investment can be converted into capital by a sale of the investment shortly before the interest is due to be received and at a price which reflects that interest, then he would not, in the absence of any special legislation, pay income tax on the element of the sale price which reflects the interest. A repurchase of the same investment a few days after the interest has been paid to the purchaser would result in the investor being approximately in the same position as he would have been had he retained the investment throughout, but without having paid income tax on the cash surplus retained[12]; normally, the price of the investment *cum div* falls on the investment becoming *ex div* by an amount approximating to the interest payable.

The legislation is also directed at the other party to the transaction. But for such legislation, a dealer in securities could buy the investment *cum div* and, after receiving the interest payment, sell the investment *ex div;* the total amount paid would approximate to the total amount received, and, subject to market fluctuations, etc, the dealer would aim to realise a modest profit overall. The distinction between the dealer and the investor is that in the dealer's computation of profits both the sale and purchase prices and the interest received fall to be dealt with on revenue account. An alternative purchaser would be a charity or other exempt investor which would be prepared to pay a price for the investment *cum div* which reflected the fact that the interest when received would be tax-free in its hands.

ACCRUED INCOME SCHEME

9-29 The rule that interest is only taxed when received is modified in relation to transfers of certain securities with or without accrued income. The securities to which these provisions apply are UK or overseas corporate,

[11] See §4-02 above.
[12] Capital gains tax may be relevant after 1965.

governmental or local authority interest-bearing securities in bearer or registered form[13], not being shares[14] (other than certain building society shares[15]), except where the interest is treated as a distribution by reason of being paid to a non-resident affiliated company of the issuer[16], and excluding securities where the only return is in the form of a discount or premium[17]; certain other securities, including certificates of deposit[18] or other securities to which TA 1988 s 56 or s 56A[19] applies, are also excluded from the accrued income scheme.

The scheme operates where securities are transferred with or without accrued income. For this purpose, 'transfer' includes conversion of securities into shares or other securities[20] and certain deemed transfers on death, transfers to trading stock, transfers to trustees, etc[1]. It should be noted that where the accrued income scheme applies on conversion of securities, a tax charge can be suffered on accrued income even though the terms of conversion are such that the income in question is never received.

9–30   Where the securities are transferred during an interest period with the benefit of interest accrued to the date of settlement of the transaction – so that, in practice, the transferor receives a price for the securities reflecting the accrued interest – the provisions apply so that the transferor is chargeable to tax under Sch D Case VI on the accrued interest[2]; the transferee, who will subsequently receive and be taxable on the whole of the interest paid for the period in which the transfer takes place, is entitled to relief by having the taxable interest reduced by the amount of the accrued interest at the time of the transaction[3]. Where the transferee accounts to the transferor for the gross accrued interest separately from the consideration for the transfer[4], the accrued interest by reference to which the accrued income scheme applies is the gross interest accounted for[5]; in other cases, it is the proportion (calculated on a daily basis to the settlement date for the transaction) of the interest payable for the current interest period[6]. If the interest payment day falls before the settlement day, the provisions apply by reference to the whole of the interest for the interest period[7]. Unless a sterling amount is to be accounted for in respect of the gross interest, the accrued amount in the case of foreign currency securities is the sterling equivalent of the relevant foreign currency amount, determined by reference to the exchange rate on the settlement day for the transaction[8].

---

[13] TA 1988 s 710 (2) (b).
[14] TA 1988 s 710 (2).
[15] TA 1988 s 710(2A).
[16] TA 1988 s 710 (3) (a); see TA 1988 s 209 (2) (e)(iv) and (v) and see §§**9–10** and **9–11** above.
[17] TA 1988 s 710 (3) (e).
[18] TA 1988 s 710 (3) (d) and (da).
[19] See §**9–47** below.
[20] TA 1988 s 710(13).
[1] TA 1988 s 711 (6).
[2] TA 1988 ss 713 (2) (a) and 714(2)
[3] TA 1988 ss 713 (2) (b) and 714(4).
[4] As in the case of a purchase of short-dated Government securities.
[5] TA 1988 s 713 (5) (a).
[6] TA 1988 s 713 (5) (b) and (6).
[7] TA 1988 s 714
[8] TA 1988 s 713 (7) to (9).

If the securities are transferred without accrued interest, the adjustments take place in the other direction; the transferor, who will receive all the interest for the period in which the transfer takes place, is given relief for the interest accruing after the transfer and the transferee is taxed on a like amount[9].

Modified rules apply[10] where the interest rate applicable to the securities is variable. The accrued amount, where such securities are transferred with accrued interest on which the transferor is taxed, is such amount as is just and reasonable, but there is no corresponding relief given to the transferee[11]. This can lead to a measure of double taxation, particularly where the transfer in question is a deemed transfer arising on conversion of the securities[12] and the same taxpayer is subsequently taxed when the actual interest is received. The rules for determining the accrued amount of interest are adjusted where the interest is in default and the value of the securities is thereby affected[13].

9-31   A number of persons are excluded from the application of the accrued income scheme[14]. These are, broadly:

1   a trader, where the sale or purchase of securities is taken into account in determining his trading profits;
2   an individual, the nominal value of whose holding of securities did not exceed £5,000 at any time in the relevant or previous year of assessment;
3   the personal representatives of a deceased person, or the trustees of a disabled person's trust, where the nominal value of the securities held did not exceed £5,000 in the relevant or previous year of assessment;
4   a charity exempt from tax in respect of interest on the securities;
5   a person neither resident nor ordinarily resident in the UK nor carrying on a trade in the UK through a branch or agency; it should be noted that this appears to mean that an individual who is not resident but who is ordinarily resident in the UK can suffer tax under the accrued income scheme in respect of non-UK securities even though no liability would arise had the interest itself been actually received by him[15];
6   a non-ordinarily resident person in respect of UK Government securities issued on terms that the interest is not taxable in the hands of non-ordinarily resident beneficial owners[16], or, where the terms of such securities allow UK tax to be charged where the non-resident is trading in the UK, a non-domiciled and non-ordinarily resident person not trading in the UK through a branch or agency;
7   an individual taxable on the remittance basis only in respect of securities situated outside the UK[17] (irrespective of whether the accrued amount, or the proceeds of sale, is remitted to the UK); and
8   an exempt approved retirement benefits scheme.

[9] TA 1988 s 713(3) and 714(2) and (4).
[10] TA 1988 s 717.
[11] TA 1988 s 717(9).
[12] See TA 1988 s 713(13).
[13] TA 1988 ss 718 and 719.
[14] TA 1988 s 715.
[15] See §5–02 above.
[16] See §6–06(1) above.
[17] See §5–06 above.

These exclusions apply by reference to the transferor or transferee who qualifies, but the other party to the transaction is not affected. Thus, if a transferor is excluded from the application of the accrued income scheme in respect of the accrued amount, the corresponding relief will still be available to a non-excluded transferee who subsequently receives the whole of the interest in respect of the period in question.

Where nominees or trustees hold securities on behalf of other persons who are absolutely entitled, it is the latter persons who are taxed under the accrued income scheme[18]. Trustees who do not hold the securities on behalf of others absolutely are subject to income tax at both the basic and additional rates where a charge arises under the scheme[19].

9-32   Special rules apply in relation to securities having accrued interest at the date of death, a tax charge normally arising by reference to the transfer of the securities to the personal representatives or to a legatee[20]. Transfers to and from trading stock are specifically brought within the scheme[1]. As in the case of relief for delayed remittance of actual income from foreign securities[2], the amount of deemed income charged to tax is reduced where the proceeds of sale of securities cannot be remitted to the UK[3]; however, the legislation does not provide for the relief to be clawed back when the proceeds become freely remittable to the UK[4]. Special provisions apply in relation to insurance companies[5] and Lloyd's underwriters[6], and where the transferee of securities is himself required to make a payment of manufactured interest to the person to whom he sells the securities[7].

Where the securities are foreign securities and the transferor is subject to foreign tax in respect of the interest, or would have been had he received the interest, credit is available in respect of the foreign tax (with a corresponding reduction in the credit available to the transferee)[8].

9-33   Where a new issue is made of securities of the same kind as securities already in issue, the terms on which interest is payable on the new securities will normally reflect the terms of the existing securities, in order to achieve fungibility. Thus, the same amount of interest will be payable on the new securities as on the existing securities, even though the new issue might occur during an interest period of the existing securities; in return for the right to an extra payment of interest on the new securities, the subscriber will make a payment in addition to the subscription price. In these circumstances, the accrued income scheme applies to the new securities as if they had been issued on the last interest payment day of the existing securities and as if they had been transferred to the subscriber with accrued interest[9]. Thus, when interest is first paid on the new securities, the subscriber is not taxed on so much

---

[18] TA 1988 s 720 (1) and (2).
[19] TA 1988 s 720 (5).
[20] TA 1988 s 721.
[1] TA 1988 s 722.
[2] See §5-04 above.
[3] TA 1988 s 723.
[4] Cf TA 1988 s 584 (2).
[5] TA 1988 s 724.
[6] TA 1988 ss 725 and 720 (3).
[7] TA 1988 s 715 (6).
[8] TA 1988 s 807.
[9] TA 1988 s 726A.

of the interest as is equal to the extra payment he made on subscription. Subsequent transactions in the new securities, including those before the first interest period has ended, are subject to the accrued income scheme as if the securities were part of the original issue.

9-34   Where securities to which the accrued income scheme applies are chargeable assets for capital gains purposes, adjustments are made to the capital gains computation to reflect the treatment of the accrued income. Broadly, this results in the amount of accrued income on securities transferred with accrued income being deducted from the consideration received by the transferor and excluded from the allowable acquisition cost of the transferee[10], with converse adjustments where the securities are transferred without accrued income[11]. Adjustments are also made where there is a disposal for capital gains purposes which is not a transfer under the accrued income scheme[12] and on a conversion or exchange of securities with accrued income the accrued amount is deducted from the consideration received (other than the new holding) or otherwise added to the base cost of the new holding (with a converse adjustment where the securities are transferred without accrued interest)[13].

OTHER SALES AND PURCHASES OF SECURITIES

9-35   In addition to the accrued income scheme, TA 1988 Chapter II Part XVII contains extensive provisions designed to counter other arrangements intended to convert income into capital by various dealings in securities. Those provisions are expressed generally to relate to 'interest', although it should be noted that this word is defined to include dividends and, in some cases, other income[14].

9-36   TA 1988 s 729 applies where an owner of securities (other than those to which the accrued income scheme applies[15] and, in certain circumstances[16], Eurobonds[17] or foreign government stock[18]) sells or otherwise transfers securities and at the same time agrees to reacquire the securities or obtains an option, which he subsequently exercises, to reacquire the securities. It will be seen that these circumstances are similar to those mentioned in TA 1988 s 786 (4)[19] in relation to the prevention of the obtaining of effective relief for loan interest; however, when s 786(4) applies, s 729 does not apply[20]. When s 729 applies, the interest on the securities is deemed to be the income of the original owner instead of the person who in fact received it, and, if the interest is paid gross, income tax may be assessed under Sch D Case

---

10 TCGA 1992 s 119(1) and (2).
11 TCGA 1992 s 119(1) and (3).
12 TCGA 1992 s 119(7).
13 TCGA 1992 s 119(10).
14 See TA 1988 ss 729(10)(a), 730(7), 731(9) and 737(6).
15 TA 1988 s 729(10)(b).
16 TA 1988 s 729(7)(b).
17 TA 1988 ss 729(9) and 732(5).
18 TA 1988 s 729(9).
19 See §**9-22** above.
20 TA 1988 s 729(6).

VI; credit is given for any tax which is shown to have been deducted from the interest[1], and relief should be available for foreign tax where the interest is not UK source interest[2].

A reacquisition of similar securities will be treated as a reacquisition of the securities originally disposed of, except that the taxpayer may not suffer any greater liability than had he reacquired the original securities[3].

Where securities (other than those to which the accrued income scheme applies[4] and, in certain circumstances[5] Eurobonds[6] foreign government securities[7]) are sold to a dealer in securities who agrees to retransfer them or later exercises a put option to retransfer them, and in consequence of the transaction any interest is receivable by him, the whole transaction is disregarded in computing his trading profit[8]. However, if he is subject to a call option under which he may be obliged to retransfer the securities, the transaction will not be disregarded from his point of view[9].

9-37 TA 1988 s 730 covers the case where the right to receive interest on any securities is transferred by the owner of the security to a third party. This may occur in particular where an investor sells coupons representing interest due on bearer securities. Where such coupons are sold in the UK, there may be an obligation on the purchaser to deduct basic rate income tax from the price paid for the coupons if the interest is due in respect of foreign government or public authority securities or in respect of interest (or other dividends) paid by a non-resident company; these deduction obligations are contained in Sch C[10] and TA 1988 s 123 (3)(c)[11].

The effect of s 730 is to deem the income in question to be the income of the original beneficial owner of the interest[12] instead of the income of the person to whom the income is transferred[13]. Where a deduction obligation arises under either Sch C or s 123(3) in relation to the sales proceeds, the amount which is deemed to be the income of the original owner is an amount equal to the proceeds of realisation of the coupons, which may be less than their face value. Where tax has not been deducted under either of those provisions or any other provision[14], the original owner may be charged to tax in respect of the income under Sch D Case VI[15]. However, except in the case of an original owner liable to corporation tax[16], tax is only charged under Case VI on the remittance basis in respect of interest within

---

[1] TA 1988 s 729 (1)(ii) and (2).
[2] Because the income is deemed to belong to the original owner of the securities 'for all the purposes of the Tax Acts': TA 1988 s 729(1)(i).
[3] TA 1988 s 729 (3).
[4] TA 1988 s 729(10) (b).
[5] TA 1988 s 729 (8) (b).
[6] TA 1988 ss 729 (9) and 732(5).
[7] TA 1988 s 729 (9).
[8] TA 1988 s 729 (4).
[9] But see §§**9-38** to **9-40** below.
[10] TA 1988 s 17 (1) Sch C para 4(b); and see §**6-15** above.
[11] See §§**7-41** and **7-42** above.
[12] Including a person whose interest in the income would have been as a beneficiary under a trust – TA 1988 s 730 (1)(a).
[13] TA 1988 s 730 (1).
[14] Eg TA 1988 s 349 (2) or 123(2).
[15] TA 1988 s 730 (4).
[16] In respect of which the remittance basis does not apply – see §**5-20** above; TA 1988 s 729 (6).

Sch D Case IV or V[17] where the remittance basis would have applied had the taxpayer received the interest himself.

9–38 Sections 731 to 735 deal with the position of a dealer in securities or other person who buys securities (other than securities to which the accrued income scheme applies)[18] and subsequently sells them or similar securities[19] in circumstances where that person receives interest on the securities. These sections do not require the resale to be part of an arrangement established with the seller of the securities originally bought, and they do not apply to transactions where the purchase and sale do not both take place within a period of six months or where the time between purchase and sale is more than one month and the transactions are at market prices and not in pursuance of an overall prior arrangement.

In the case of a dealer in securities, the adjustment under s 732 is to reduce the price paid by him for the securities by reference to the interest received by him on the securities, so reducing his loss or increasing his taxable profit. The amount of the interest by which the adjustment is made is only a proportion of the interest received by the dealer. Broadly, that proportion is the proportion which the period from when the securities last went *ex div* until the purchase by the dealer bears to the period from when they last went *ex div* until they are next quoted *ex div* following the purchase by the dealer[20]; this corresponds with the effect which the prospective receipt of interest is likely to have on the price payable by the dealer. Special provision is made for the position where the securities are not listed[1].

Section 732 does not apply where s 729 (4)[2] operates to require the purchase and sale by the dealer to be disregarded in computing his trading profit or loss[3]. Nor does it apply where the dealer in securities sells the securities while carrying on the business of a Stock Exchange market maker[4], or where the seller is a recognised clearing house or member of a recognised investment exchange[5], in each case where the securities are sold in the ordinary course of his business. If certain conditions are satisfied, the section does not apply to overseas securities bought on a stock exchange outside the UK[6] or to certain dealings by Eurobond dealers acting in the ordinary course of business[7].

9–39 Section 733 applies where the purchaser of the securities is a person who is exempt from tax on the interest received. Even if s 729 does not apply to deem the interest not to be his income, the exemption is disallowed in respect of the interest; any annual payments paid out of the interest are treated as not paid out of profits or gains brought into charge to tax, so that income tax must be deducted therefrom and paid over to the Inland

---

[17] TA 1988 s 730 (5); and see §§**5–06** and **5–07** above.
[18] TA 1988 s 731 (9).
[19] TA 1988 s 731 (5).
[20] TA 1988 s 735 (1), (3) and (4).
[1] TA 1988 s 735 (6).
[2] See §**9–36** above.
[3] TA 1988 s 732 (3).
[4] TA 1988 s 732 (2) and (6).
[5] TA 1988 s 732 (2A); and see the Income Tax (Dealers in Securites) Regulations 1992: SI 1992 No 568.
[6] TA 1988 s 732 (4).
[7] TA 1988 s 732 (5).

Revenue[8]. As in the case of s 732[9], this treatment only applies to a proportion of the interest.

9–40 Where the person who purchases and then sells the securities is not a dealer in securities but carries on another trade, the amount of income tax relief available to him in respect of a trading loss under TA 1988 s 380 or s 381 is calculated without regard to either a proportion[10] of the interest received between purchase and resale or any tax paid on that interest (ie by deduction)[11].

If the purchaser is a company which does not carry on a trade of dealing in securities, the proportion of the interest (and any tax thereon) is disregarded for corporation tax purposes, except that the company will be treated as having received a capital distribution for capital gains purposes[12]; this results in a deemed part disposal of the securities for capital gains purposes[13].

MANUFACTURED INTEREST

9–41 Where securities are sold *cum div*, the registration of the transfer of the securities may not be completed until after the dividend or interest is paid; in such circumstances the seller, as the registered holder on the relevant date, will account to the purchaser for the interest he receives; the purchaser will then be taxed on the interest in place of the seller.

A purchaser buying securities *cum div* from a person dealing on the London Stock Exchange will expect that treatment from the dealer even where the dealer may be 'selling short' and may later close his position by buying similar securities when they are *ex div*. Similarly, where a holder of securities lends those securities to another person (typically, a Stock Exchange market maker) to enable that person to satisfy a bargain to sell securities of that kind, the lender of the securities will require the borrower to make a payment equivalent to any interest paid on the securities during the term of the loan. TA 1988 s 737 and Sch 23A, together with Regulations made thereunder, provide for the treatment of payments in respect of interest (and dividends) in these circumstances. A detailed analysis of these complex provisions is outside the scope of this book, but an outline of the provisions, insofar as they apply to interest, is set out below.

9–42 Where the seller of securities passes on to the purchaser the actual interest which the seller receives as registered holder on the record date, or which he receives from the person from whom he purchases the securities, then the interest in question is treated as the income of the purchaser to whom it is passed on; the special rules concerning manufactured interest do not apply[14]. This also applies where the securities are overseas securities; in such a case, regulations may provide for what tax should be charged

---

[8] TA 1988 ss 349(1) and 733(2).
[9] See §9–38 above.
[10] Calculated as for TA 1988 s 732 – See §9–38 above.
[11] TA 1988 s 734(1).
[12] TA 1988 s 734(2).
[13] TCGA 1992 s 122.
[14] TA 1988 Sch 23A para 5.

or overseas tax credit given where the interest is passed on by a UK resident person to a non-resident[15].

9-43 More complex provisions apply[16] where the interest is 'manufactured' by the borrower – ie he pays the lender an amount equivalent to the interest but without having received the interest himself[17]. In the case of manufactured interest payments in respect of UK securities[18], the payment is treated for tax purposes as if it were a payment of interest on the securities in question but paid by the interest manufacturer. Basic rate income tax is deductible in the ordinary way[19] if the payer is a UK resident company[20]; if not, then s 737 applies to require the payment to be treated as an annual payment subject to deduction of basic rate income tax[1].

If the payment is made under an approved stock lending arrangement[2], the payer will obtain relief for the payment and otherwise treat the payment and the tax deducted from it in the same way as if the payment were an actual payment of interest or annual payment. But, if the payment is an unapproved manufactured payment[3], a paying company is not entitled to any relief for the tax deducted from the manufactured interest and may not offset[4] any tax deducted at source on interest and annual payments received against the tax for which it must account in respect of the manufactured interest paid[5].

9-44 In the case of manufactured interest payments in respect of overseas securities[6], the provisions provide[7] for tax to be deducted by reference to overseas tax which would have been deducted from the actual interest. This is done in order to prevent UK tax-exempt bodies and others obtaining tax advantages by exploiting stock lending arrangements. Although the manufactured interest is treated as an annual payment from which tax is deductible under TA 1988 s 349 (1)[8], the tax to be deducted will reflect the overseas withholding tax which would have been deducted from the actual dividend[9]; the amount of the overseas withholding tax is to be determined by reference to regulations[10].

---

[15] TA 1988 Sch 23A para 5(5).
[16] The relevant provisions were brought into force by the Finance Act 1991, s 58, (Commencement No 2) Regulations 1992: SI 1992 No 1346.
[17] In many cases, the borrower will realise a profit from the excess of the *cum div* price on sale over the *ex div* price on purchase of securities to 'repay' the borrowing, and that profit will approximate to the interest.
[18] TA 1988 Sch 23A para 3; and see para 1(1) – securities issued by the UK Government, UK local authorities and UK resident companies, but excluding quoted Eurobonds held in a recognised clearing system and shares.
[19] TA 1988 s 349 (2) (a).
[20] TA 1988 Sch 23A para 3(2).
[1] TA 1988 Sch 23A para 3 (3) and ss 737 (1) and 349(1)(a).
[2] See definition in TA 1988 Sch 23A para 1(1).
[3] See *ibid*.
[4] Under TA 1988 Sch 16 para 5.
[5] TA 1988 Sch 23A para 6(3), (6) and (7).
[6] Issued by foreign governments and public authorities and other non-UK resident bodies, together with quoted Eurobonds held in a recognised clearing system.
[7] TA 1988 Sch 23A para 4.
[8] TA 1988 Sch 23A para 4(2).
[9] TA 1988 Sch 23A para 4(5).
[10] TA 1988 Sch 23A para 4(6).

The provisions concerning manufactured payments in respect of overseas securities have not yet been brought into force but, when they are, Regulations are expected to provide for the withholding tax rates to be those which would have applied to actual interest payable to a UK resident holder of securities; in addition to this, further tax will be withheld in appropriate cases to bring the total withholding to 25 per cent (the additional withholding being equivalent to that which would have been deducted on payment of foreign interest through a UK paying agent)[11]. The notional foreign withholding tax is to be accounted for to, and retained by, the UK Exchequer, but in the hands of a UK taxable recipient of the manufactured interest it is treated as overseas tax[12]. Where the manufactured interest is paid to a non-resident, it is expected that tax will be deductible on account of notional overseas tax, but not any other UK tax; however, residents of countries[13] with which the UK has a double taxation agreement providing an exemption from tax in respect of any UK source income not otherwise dealt with in the double taxation agreement are expected to be relieved from the withholding in respect of overseas tax.

As in the case of manufactured interest in respect of UK securities, unapproved manufactured payments in respect of overseas securities attract a less favourable treatment[14]. No tax relief is available in respect of the tax deducted from the payment and the deducted tax for which the payer must account may not be offset by any overseas tax suffered in respect of overseas interest or dividends or by any UK tax deducted on account of overseas tax in respect of manufactured overseas payments received by the payer.

DISTRIBUTION MATERIALLY REDUCING VALUE OF HOLDING

9–45 If a company holds 10 per cent or more of any class of security in another company in circumstances that a profit on the sale of the holding would be taken into account in computing the company's trading profits[15] and a distribution or distributions is or are made in respect of the holding so that the value of the holding is materially reduced below its value when it was acquired, the amount of that reduction may be applied in adjusting upwards the value of the holding or the trading receipt of the company on a sale of the holding[16]. This provision, contained in TA 1988 s 736, has the effect of preventing the reduction in value of the holding which is attributable to the distribution reducing the profits of the dealing company and so cancelling out the income receipt in respect of the distribution.

This provision will most likely apply in relation to dividend distributions in respect of shares held by a dealer in securities, but it could also apply in relation to interest received on loan stocks or similar securities where this amounts to a distribution[17], particularly if the securities were purchased

---

[11] TA 1988 Sch 23A para 4(4).
[12] *Ibid.*
[13] This is expected to cover most OECD countries, other than Australia, New Zealand, Canada and Greece.
[14] TA 1988 Sch 23A para 6(4).
[15] TA 1988 s 736(1) and (6).
[16] TA 1988 s 736(2).
[17] See TA 1988 s 209(2)(d) and (e) and §§**9–02** to **9–13** above.

with an amount of past interest accrued but unpaid. If this provision applies in circumstances where a reduction can be made under TA 1988 s 732[18] in respect of the purchase price paid for securities by a dealer, the Board of Inland Revenue is directed to adjust the reduction under s 732 to avoid any double taxation as a result of a reduction in the value of the securities under s 736.

TRANSACTIONS IN SECURITIES GENERALLY – s 703

9-46 TA 1988 s 703 provides a wide power for the counteraction by the Inland Revenue of tax advantages obtained by transactions in securities. It is beyond the scope of this book to examine these provisions in detail, but they should be borne in mind in any unusual transactions concerning interests in the share or loan capital of a company. Although the provisions of s 703 which are most commonly encountered are those designed to prevent the extraction of profits of a company in such a way as to avoid the tax which would be suffered on a distribution by way of dividend, not only may interest payments be involved in such transactions but also the application of s 703 is not limited to transactions of that kind only; moreover, one of the circumstances mentioned in s 704A relates to relief for interest under TA 1988 s 353.

It should also be noted that, for the purposes of s 703, the expression 'securities' includes stock - which could include loan stock and debentures – and references to 'dividends' extend to include references to interest[19].

CERTIFICATES OF DEPOSIT

9-47 A certificate of deposit, as commonly issued by banks and some building societies, is, broadly, a document relating to money (whether in sterling or a foreign currency) which has been deposited with the issuer and which evidences the issuer's obligation to pay a stated amount (with or without interest) and where delivery of that document to a third party will transfer the right to receive the amount due under it[20]. Because the transfer of that certificate to a third party could otherwise be effected for a consideration which would not have been chargeable to tax as income, TA 1988 s 56 charges to tax under Sch D Case VI any profits or gains arising on the disposal of certificates of deposit[1]. Section 56 applies where the profits or gains on disposal of the certificate of deposit do not fall to be treated as a trading receipt, except that there are exceptions to the charge in the case of certain approved pension schemes, retirement annuity schemes and charities[2].

Normally, a Case VI loss may only be set against a Case VI profit. However, a loss on a transaction in a certificate of deposit may be set against any

---

[18] See §**9-38** above.
[19] TA 1988 s 709(2).
[20] See definition of 'certificate of deposit' in TA 1988 s 56(5).
[1] See §**9-37** above.
[2] TA 1988 s 56(3)(b) and (c).

interest derived from the certificate and which may be chargeable under Schedule C or D generally[3].

Section 56 also charges to tax under Sch D Case VI any profits or gains derived from the disposal or exercise of rights in respect of a deposit with a bank or similar institution even though no certificate of deposit or other 'security'[4] is issued, except when the profits or gains fall to be treated as receipts of a trade. Moreover, where a person has a right to receive a sum of money (with or without interest) in respect of a deposit and no certificate of deposit is issued but the taxpayer has a right to call for one then, if the taxpayer disposes of the right before the certificate of deposit is issued, the tax charge under s 56 will still apply[5].

6   Oil extraction activities: limitation of interest relief

9–48   Certain provisions contained in TA 1988 Part XII Chapter V are designed to ensure that, in charging to corporation tax profits derived from UK oil and gas production, those profits should not be reduced by expenditure or losses not derived from activities unrelated to such production; this applies whether the rights to oil and gas relate to the UK mainland or the UK Sector of the Continental Shelf ('UKCS'). There is, therefore, a one-way 'ring fence' round 'oil extraction activities' and the acquisition, enjoyment or exploitation of 'oil rights' in the UK or the UKCS; in this connection, 'oil' generally includes gas'[6]. Broadly, 'oil extraction activities' comprise the business of exploration for and production of oil and gas in the UK and the UKCS. The ring fence operates in one direction only; this means that, whereas losses and other reliefs outside the ring fence may not reduce profits within the ring fence, relief in the other direction remains unrestricted.

So far as interest is concerned, the availability of relief under TA 1988 s 338 in respect of charges on income (which under that section are set against profits of a company generally) is modified by TA 1988 s 494. Interest is only allowable as a charge on income against that part of the company's profits which are within the ring fence in the circumstances set out below:

1   To the extent that it is in respect of money borrowed by the company to finance its oil extraction activities or in acquiring UK or UKCS oil rights (except where those rights were acquired from a 'connected'[7] person). The legislation does not permit interest on a loan to qualify where it replaces an earlier qualifying loan, nor does it permit a successor company to obtain relief for interest on a loan taken over from an affiliate together with a trade which is transferred under TA 1988 s 343[8]; however, in any given case the Inland Revenue may be prepared to give sympathetic consideration to a request for continued relief, so long as the amount of interest paid does not increase.

[3] TA 1988 s 398.
[4] As defined in TCGA 1992 s 132.
[5] TA 1988 s 56A.
[6] TA 1988 s 502 (1).
[7] See TA 1988 s 839.
[8] Transfer of trade without change of ultimate control of 75 per cent of the trade.

2   Where the interest is paid to an 'associated' company[9], relief will only be available where, in addition to satisfying paragraph 1 above, the rate at which the interest is payable does not exceed a reasonable commercial rate having regard to the terms of the borrowing and the standing of the borrower. It is understood that the Inland Revenue considers that this provision restricts the availability of relief where the borrower is thinly capitalised. However, in the author's view, it is doubtful whether this approach is justified, because the legislation requires a consideration of what was borrowed rather than what might have been borrowed; this view appears to be supported by the introduction of new s 808A in relation to references to excessive interest in double taxation agreements[10].

These restrictions also apply in relation to any relief for the accrued income element of a deep discount security[11].

A company having an excess of charges on income over its total profits may surrender that excess to other members of a group of companies by way of group relief[12]; similar relief is available in relation to consortium companies. Because of the restriction on setting charges on income against ring fence profits, a situation could arise where a company's excess of charges on income over total profits is less than the amount of unused charges on income in any accounting period, because some of those charges on income may be ineligible for relief against profits within the ring fence. It is therefore provided[13] that in such circumstances the excess over non-oil profits of charges on income which may not be set against ring fence profits may be surrendered by way of group relief.

7   Beneficial loans to employees

9–49   The general rule in relation to the taxation under Sch E of benefits in kind received by reason of employment, directorship or other office[14] is that the value of such benefits is to be taken as the realisable value of the benefit to the employee[15]. Because the borrower cannot convert the benefit of an interest-free loan into money, no realisable value is received by an employee receiving an interest-free loan (or a loan at less than a market rate of interest), and therefore, under the general law, no taxation is suffered by an employee receiving such a loan from his employer or otherwise by reason of his employment.

9–50   However, the general rule is displaced in respect of directors and certain 'higher-paid' employees by TA 1988 s 160. The employees to which these[16] special provisions apply are employees earning £8,500 or more per

---

[9] Broadly, a company under common 51 per cent control with the company paying the interest – TA 1988 s 502 (3) and (4).
[10] See §**9–11** above.
[11] TA 1988 Sch 4 para 6.
[12] TA 1988 s 403 (7).
[13] TA 1988 s 494 (4).
[14] See TA 1988 s 131 (1).
[15] See, for example, *Heaton (Inspector of Taxes) v Bell* [1969] 2 All ER 70, 46 TC 211, HL.
[16] TA 1988 s 167 (1) (a).

annum. The level of earnings is ascertained by including the value of all taxable benefits on the assumption that the valuation of benefit rules apply, and without deducting any expenses of the employment[17]; special rules prevent the £8,500 threshold being avoided by fragmenting the employment[18], and also treat two or more employments with employers who are under common control as one employment[19]. Certain directorships are excluded where the director has no significant shareholding in the company and either he works full-time as a director in the company or the company is not a trading or investment company or is a charity[20]; but if the director's remuneration including the value of benefits amounts to or exceeds £8,500 per annum he will be subject to the special provisions.

9-51   TA 1988 s 160 requires the 'cash equivalent' of an interest-free, or cheap interest, loan[1] to be treated as part of the taxable earnings of the employee or director where the benefit of the loan is obtained 'by reason of his employment' and the loan is outstanding for the whole or part of the year of assessment[2]. This basic rule is qualified by an exemption when the cash equivalent does not exceed £300 for any year[3] although there is no partial exemption where the cash equivalent does exceed that amount. There are also certain other exceptions and reliefs as described below.

The loan in question must be to the employee (or director) or to a relative of the employee[4]. However, it is not necessary that the loan is made directly by the employer to the borrower. A loan is treated as obtained by reason of employment if it was 'made' by the employer[5], otherwise than by an individual employer in the normal course of his domestic, family or personal relationships[6]. However, the word 'made' has an extended meaning and will include a case where the loan in question is arranged, guaranteed or in any way facilitated by the employer[7]. This means that a loan would be within those provisions if it were made by a bank under arrangements with the employer (eg perhaps a loan at a cheap rate of interest where the employer makes the interest up to a commercial rate, or where the employer guarantees the loan), or where the employer makes an interest-free loan to a company or trust connected with the employee to whom a loan is made out of the proceeds of the first loan.

Nor is it necessary that the loan is made by the employer of the employee. If a company controlled by, or which controls, or which is under common control as, the employer makes the loan, the benefit of the loan will be treated as made by reason of the employment[8]. Further, if the employer is, has control over, or is controlled by, a close company, the loan is treated

---

17   TA 1988 s 167 (2).
18   TA 1988 s 167 (3).
19   TA 1988 s 167 (4).
20   TA 1988 s 167 (5).
1   Which includes any form of credit – TA 1988 s 160 (5) (a).
2   TA 1988 s 168(13).
3   TA 1988 s 161 (1).
4   But see *O'Leary v McKinlay (Inspector of Taxes)* [1991] STC 42, where the loan was made to trustees of a trust where the employee was entitled to the income.
5   TA 1988 Sch 7 para 1(2).
6   TA 1988 Sch 7 para 1(5).
7   TA 1988 s 160 (5) (c).
8   TA 1988 Sch 7 para 1(3); 'control' is construed by reference to TA 1988 s 840 – TA 1988 s 168(12).

as made by the employer if it is made by a person having a 'material interest' (broadly, an interest of more than 5 per cent, alone or together with certain 'associates'[9]) in the close company or the company controlling it; this means that a loan could be caught even if it were made by an individual shareholder in one of those companies. Further, in relation to these provisions, the assumption by a person of the rights and liabilities of the original lender is treated as involving the loan being 'made' by that person'[10]; consequently, these provisions cannot be avoided by the employer taking an assignment of a loan from a lender who may have lent in circumstances wholly unconnected with the employment.

If a loan to a relative of the employee is otherwise within these provisions, the employee can avoid a charge to tax under s 160 if he can show that he derives no benefit from the loan[11]. However, in relation to the employee himself, it is not a precondition of the charge to tax on the cash equivalent that there is a benefit to the employee in the sense of something advantageous to him; thus, the cash equivalent of an interest-free advance of salary was held to be taxable where the advance was made in accordance with a scheme for assisting an employee to acquire a new home where he was compulsorily moved by his employer to a more expensive locality[12].

9-52 The cash equivalent is calculated by reference to the 'official rate'. This is a rate established by Treasury Order[13]. Broadly, the cash equivalent of the benefit of the loan is equal to interest calculated at the official rate where no interest is payable, and otherwise is the amount by which interest at the official rate exceeds the interest actually paid[14]. There are two methods for calculating the amount of interest at the official rate, and the one which will be applied in practice will depend upon the profile of the repayments or further advances during the relevant year of assessment. The first method[15] involves taking the average of the amounts outstanding at the beginning and end of the year and multiplying that by the official rate; adjustments are made where the official rate changes during the year, and where the loan is made after the beginning of the year or is repaid before the end of the year. The second method[16] may be applied at the election of the Inspector of Taxes or the taxpayer and will provide a more accurate estimate of the interest where repayments or further advances fluctuate unevenly during the year; subject to adjustments where the official rate alters, this method involves adding up the amount of the loan outstanding on every day within the year, dividing that sum by 365 and multiplying the result by the official rate.

---

9 TA 1988 s 168(11).
10 TA 1988 Sch 7 para 2(a).
11 TA 1988 s 161 (4).
12 *Williams (Inspector of Taxes) v Todd* [1988] STC 676. But see Extra-Statutory Concession A5.
13 TA 1988 s 160 (5) (d) and FA 1989 s 178 (2) (m).
14 TA 1988 Sch 7 para 3.
15 TA 1988 Sch 7 para 3.
16 TA 1988 Sch 7 para 5.

EXAMPLE

Assume a loan of £10,000 is outstanding throughout the year until £5,000 of the loan is repaid on 5 March; the official rate is 12 per cent.

Method 1

$[½ (£10,000 + £5,000)] × 12\% = £900$

Method 2

$$\left[\frac{(£10,000 × 334) + (£5,000 × 31)}{365} \right] × 12\% = £1,150$$

An election for Method 2 by the Inspector must be made when the assessment (or post-appeal adjustment to the assessment) is made[17]. A taxpayer wishing to elect for Method 2 must do so when appealing against an assessment made on the Method I basis or, when no assessment has been made, within six years of the end of the year of assessment[18].

The official rate is adjusted from time to time to reflect changes in market rates of interest. However, where changes do not exactly coincide with changes to market rates, this can result in employees of banks, building societies and other financial institutions having loans from their employers suffering a liability to income tax by reference to the official rate where the official rate is higher than the market rate of interest which would be charged by the lender even if the borrower were not an employee. But, where a loan is obtained at a fixed rate and for a fixed period at a time when the interest payable on the loan in the first year of assessment is at a rate no lower than the official rate, the loan will not be brought within these provisions by reason only of a subsequent increase in the official rate[19].

9–53 Section 160 is qualified if any interest paid on the loan qualifies for tax relief, or interest if paid would have qualified for tax relief[20]. 'Tax relief' means relief under TA 1988 s 353; the fact that the loan falls under the MIRAS scheme, so that the interest is not relievable under s 353, does not affect this[1]. For example, where an employee receives an interest-free loan from his employer to finance the purchase of his main residence, and the loan does not exceed £30,000 and the other conditions are fulfilled[2], the employee's earnings will not be treated as increased by reference to the loan, except (as explained below) where the employee pays income tax at the higher rate. Where only part of the loan qualifies the interest for relief – eg where the employee receives a loan of more than £30,000 to purchase his house – adjustments are made to the methods described in §9–52 above to ensure that the cash equivalent of the loan is calculated by reference to the extent that the official rate on that part of the loan which does not qualify for relief exceeds any interest actually paid on that part of the loan.

To prevent an employee effectively obtaining excessive relief for loans to acquire his residence, it is provided[3] that, in determining whether interest,

---

[17] TA 1988 Sch 7 para 5(1)(a).
[18] TA 1988 Sch 7 para 5(1)(b) and (2).
[19] TA 1988 s 161 (2).
[20] TA 1988 Sch 7 para 7; and see Chapter 8 above.
[1] TA 1988 Sch 7 para 19(1) and (2).
[2] See Chapter 8 Part 4 above.
[3] TA 1988 Sch 7 para 10.

had it been paid, on a loan by reason of employment would have qualified for relief, that loan shall be treated as made after any other loan made to the taxpayer or his spouse interest on which is eligible for relief. Consequently, in applying to the employer's loan the limit of eligibility of relief, any simultaneous or later loan which qualifies for relief for interest actually paid would be taken into account first.

EXAMPLE

An employee obtains from his employer an interest-free loan of £25,000 to purchase his main residence; this loan is taken up on 1 January. If interest had been paid it would have qualified for relief, and therefore no 'cash equivalent' is added to his taxable earnings.

On 2 January the taxpayer obtains a bank loan of £10,000 to finance the balance of the purchase price of the house. Interest on this loan qualifies for relief. As a result, only £20,000 of the employer's loan is protected by reference to TA 1988 s 353, and £5,000 of the loan will be taken into account under TA 1988 s 160.

Where two or more interest-free loans are taken by an employee or his spouse in relation to the acquisition of the residence, the limit of £30,000 is applied as if those loans were a single loan but is attributed to the loans in the order in which they are made[4].

9-54 Because interest relief on a loan to purchase a residence is only available against tax chargeable at the basic rate[5], an employee who is a higher rate taxpayer cannot avoid an income tax charge in respect of a beneficial loan on the grounds that it is used to purchase his residence[6]. However, so much of the cash equivalent of the beneficial loan as would otherwise have been exempt from a tax charge is treated as interest eligible for relief under TA 1988 s 353[7]; the effect of this is that only tax at the higher rate is payable on the benefit of the loan to the extent that basic rate tax relief would be available on interest on the loan if paid (or if paid at the official rate).

9-55 It should be noted that an employee having the benefit of a loan (whether or not at a beneficial rate of interest) from his employer may suffer income tax in respect of the principal amount of the loan if this is ever released or written off[8], even if the loan is released or written off after the employment has ceased[9].

ACQUISITION OF SHARES PARTLY PAID

9-56 If an employee (or director) is given the opportunity to acquire (whether by subscription, purchase or otherwise[10]) shares in a company by

---

[4] TA 1988 Sch 7 para 11.
[5] See §8-51 above.
[6] TA 1988 Sch 7 para 15.
[7] TA 1988 Sch 7 para 16.
[8] TA 1988 s 160(2); see *Collins v Addies (Inspector of Taxes)* [1992] STC 746, CA, as to the circumstances amounting to a 'release'.
[9] TA 1988 s 160(3).
[10] TA 1988 s 162(10)(c).

reason of his employment and acquires those shares on a partly-paid basis, he will be treated by TA 1988 s 162 as having the benefit of an interest-free loan for the purposes of s 160. Section 162 applies generally where shares are acquired in such circumstances but are not then paid for in full unless the under-value is otherwise taxable[11]. If shares are acquired at an under-value with no obligation to pay any further sum at a later date, the employee will normally suffer an immediate income tax charge on the whole of the under-value[12]. Section 162 therefore normally applies to shares acquired on a partly-paid basis. Were it not for s 162, the unpaid amount on shares issued partly paid would not be caught by s 160 because until a call is made by the company there is no indebtedness on the part of the shareholder and no credit[13] given by the company.

In practice, the Inland Revenue may be prepared to regard the benefit of the notional loan as not being taxable where the shares acquired are ordinary shares in a close company if the employee would have qualified for tax relief had interest been paid on an actual loan to acquire the shares[14]. However, strictly, the legislation does not appear to require this treatment, because, although s 162 provides for s 160 to apply 'as if' there were an interest-free loan, the loan is not deemed to have been applied in acquiring the shares[15].

Any further payments made for the shares by the employee – eg on calls being made – will reduce the amount to which s 162 applies[16]. The notional loan is treated as remaining outstanding until[17] the whole of the amount of the under-value is made good or released, the shares are disposed of or the employee dies. On the release of the balance outstanding, or on disposal of the shares without the balance being made good, the employee is treated as if the notional loan had been written off and may suffer an income tax charge accordingly[18].

For the purposes of s 162, 'shares' is widely defined to include stock and other securities irrespective of whether there is any charge given by way of security[19]. Consequently, the provisions of the section cannot be avoided by the employee subscribing for partly-paid convertible loan stock which is later converted into share capital.

8   Interest and repayment supplement on underpaid and overpaid tax

9-57 The tax legislation normally makes provision for the payment of interest on tax which is paid later than the due date and provides for the taxpayer to receive interest in respect of certain delayed repayments of tax. Such interest when received by the taxpayer would, in the absence of any special provision, be subject to tax in his hands when received. When paid by a taxpayer it would not qualify for relief as a business expense – since

---

[11] TA 1988 s 162(3) and (11).
[12] See *Salmon v Weight* (1935) 153 LT 55, 19 TC 174, HL, or TA 1988 s 136.
[13] TA 1988 s 160(5)(a).
[14] See §§**9-53** and **8-17** to **8-19** above.
[15] See TA 1988 s 360(1)(a).
[16] TA 1988 s 162(3)(b).
[17] TA 1988 s 162(4).
[18] TA 1988 s 162(5).
[19] TA 1988 s 162(10)(a).

it would not be wholly and exclusively incurred for the purposes of the trade, profession or vocation – nor does it qualify for relief for income tax purposes under TA 1988 s 353[20]. Interest paid to the Inland Revenue would not normally be yearly interest[1]; if such interest is not yearly interest, a company could not obtain relief for such interest as a charge on income[2].

There is set out below a summary of the provisions relating to the treatment of the compensation payable in respect of the delayed payment or repayment of taxes. It is beyond the scope of this book to examine the circumstances in which such compensation is due.

INCOME TAX AND CAPITAL GAINS TAX

9-58   Interest on any overdue tax[3] and any default interest paid in respect of tax assessed to make good loss of tax by reason of the taxpayer's fraud, wilful default or neglect[4] is paid without deduction of tax and is not allowed as a deduction for taxation purposes[5].

Where a repayment of income tax[6] or capital gains tax[7] is made to an individual, a partnership, the trustees of a settlement or personal representatives[8], there may be added a 'repayment supplement'. This supplement is not treated as the income of any person for taxation purposes, and is therefore tax-free[9].

COMPANIES

9-59   Interest on overdue corporation tax[10], advance corporation tax or income tax on yearly interest and other annual payments paid by a company[11], and any default interest[12] payable by a company, is paid without deduction of tax and is not allowed as a deduction for taxation purposes[13].

A UK resident company[14] may be entitled to a repayment supplement in respect of tax repaid to it[15], which supplement is not liable to taxation in the company's hands[16].

---

[20] See Chapter 8 above.
[1] See Chapter 3 Part 1 above.
[2] See Chapter 8 Part 3 above.
[3] TMA 1970 s 86.
[4] TMA 1970 s 88.
[5] TMA 1970 s 90.
[6] TA 1988 s 842.
[7] TCGA 1992 s 283.
[8] TA 1988 s 842 (9) and TCGA 1992 s 283 (4).
[9] TA 1988 s 842 (8).
[10] TMA 1970 s 86.
[11] TMA 1970 s 87.
[12] TMA 1970 s 88.
[13] TMA 1970 s 90.
[14] See *R v IRC, ex p Commerzbank AG* [1991] STC 271, [1991] 3 CMLR 633.
[15] TA 1988 s 843.
[16] TA 1988 s 843 (7).

INHERITANCE TAX

9-60   Inheritance tax which remains unpaid after the due date for payment bears interest[17]. Any repayment of overpaid inheritance tax or of interest on inheritance tax also carries interest at the same rates as overdue tax[18].

Neither interest on overdue tax nor interest on repaid tax is taken into account in computing income, profits or losses for taxation purposes[19]. This is not stated in relation to interest paid on inheritance tax payable by instalments[20], although it would not qualify for relief under TA 1988 s 353 in any event[1].

PETROLEUM REVENUE TAX

9-61   Interest on overdue petroleum revenue tax bears interest from two months after the end of the chargeable period to which it relates until payment[2], but is not allowed as a deduction in computing income, profits or losses for any tax purposes[3]. Interest on repaid petroleum revenue tax also carries interest[4] but is disregarded in computing income for corporation tax purposes[5]; such interest on repaid petroleum revenue tax is not treated as part of the participator's gross profit for petroleum revenue tax purposes.

Interest is also charged on delayed payments of advance petroleum revenue tax ('APRT')[6] and on delayed instalments on account of APRT[7]. Such interest does not qualify for relief for any tax purposes[8]. Interest paid on repayments of APRT[9] is expressed to be disregarded in computing income for income tax[10] or corporation tax purposes[11].

VALUE ADDED TAX

9-62   Any unpaid value added tax is recoverable as a debt due to the Crown[12]; whether any interest is awarded on the recovery of such a debt from a taxable person depends upon the court making such an order.

Where value added tax is found to be payable on determination of an appeal, the Tribunal may order interest to be paid on the unpaid tax at such rate as it determines; similarly, any tax repaid to the appellant in

---

[17]   IHTA 1984 ss 233, 234 and 236(1) and (2).
[18]   IHTA 1984 s 235.
[19]   IHTA 1984 ss 233(3) and 235(2).
[20]   IHTA 1984 s 234.
[1]   See Chapter 8 above.
[2]   OTA 1975 Sch 2 para 15(1).
[3]   TMA 1970 s 90, applied by OTA 1975 Sch 2 para 1(1).
[4]   OTA 1975 Sch 2 para 16.
[5]   TA 1988 s 501.
[6]   FA 1982 Sch 19 para 10(1).
[7]   FA 1982 Sch 19 para 10(2).
[8]   TMA 1970 s 90, applied by OTA 1975 Sch 2 para 1(1) – see FA 1982 s 157(5).
[9]   FA 1982 Sch 19 para 10(4) – but no interest is payable on any excess APRT credit repaid after 1987 under FA 1982 Sch 19 para 14(1) and (5).
[10]   TA 1988 s 501, which does not mention 'income tax'.
[11]   FA 1982 Sch 19 para 10(7).
[12]   VATA 1983 Sch 7 para 6(1).

consequence of an appeal being decided in his favour carries interest at such rate as the Tribunal decides[13]. Such interest is not prevented from being subject to income tax or corporation tax in the hands of the recipient; nor is any interest payable expressly prevented from being relieved. It is doubtful whether interest paid by a taxable individual or partnership in respect of unpaid value added tax could be treated as a deductible expense of earning the profits of that trade, and it would not qualify for relief under TA 1988 s 353[14]; such interest paid by a company, probably not being yearly interest, would not be eligible for relief as a charge on income[15].

A VAT assessment can charge interest in certain cases[16]. Any interest so charged is expressed to be payable without deduction of tax[17], and no tax relief is allowed in respect of such interest[18].

Repayment supplement can be paid together with certain repayments of VAT[19], except where interest is paid in respect of an official error[20]. Repayment supplement is disregarded for income tax and corporation tax purposes[1]. Interest paid in respect of official error is taxable under general principles[2].

STAMP DUTY AND STAMP DUTY RESERVE TAX

9-63 Interest on delayed payment of stamp duty runs at the rate of 5 per cent per annum[3]. Where a person successfully appeals against an assessment to stamp duty, any stamp duty already paid is repaid to him[4]; the court may order interest, at such rate as it determines, to be paid in respect of such repaid duty. No provision is made for such interest to be disregarded for taxation purposes, although, as in the case of interest paid on underpaid value added tax[5] it is doubtful whether relief could be obtained for interest paid on delayed payment of stamp duty.

9-64 Overdue stamp duty reserve tax carries interest[6], which is expressed[7] to be payable without any deduction of income tax and not to be deductible in computing income, profits or losses for any tax purposes. Repaid stamp duty reserve tax can carry interest[8], which is not income for any tax purposes[9].

---

[13] VATA 1983 s 40(4).
[14] See Chapter 8 above; although partners could effectively obtain relief by borrowing to provide further contributions to the partnership – see §8-23 above.
[15] See TA 1988 s 338(3) and §8-35(2) above.
[16] FA 1985 s 18.
[17] FA 1985 s 18(9).
[18] TA 1988 s 827(1)(b).
[19] FA 1985 s 20.
[20] VATA 1983 s 38A(1) and (2)(a).
[1] TA 1988 s 827(2).
[2] See §§2-11 and 2-12 above.
[3] Stamp Act 1891 s 15(1).
[4] Stamp Act 1891 s 13(4).
[5] See §9-62 above.
[6] Regulation 86, the Stamp Duty Reserve Tax Regulations 1986: SI 1986 No 1711
[7] Regulation 90, the Stamp Duty Reserve Tax Regulations 1986: SI 1986 No 1711.
[8] FA 1986 s 92(2).
[9] FA 1986 s 92(4A).

9   Interest and statutory settlements

9-65   The income tax legislation contains wide-ranging provisions which can result in the income of certain settlements being treated as the income of the settlor in relation to the settlement. It is beyond the scope of this book to examine these provisions in detail, but the circumstances where the income of settlements can be treated as the income of the settlor and related provisions include the following (all section numbers referring to TA 1988):

(a)   Section 663: settlements made for the benefit of unmarried minor children of the settlor;

(b)   Section 672: irrevocable settlements under which the settlor could become entitled to the trust property;

(c)   Section 673: settlements where the settlor retains an interest in the income of the settlement;

(d)   Section 674: settlements under which there is a power to benefit the settlor;

(e)   Section 676: disallowance as a deduction of payments made by the settlor by virtue of or in consequence of the settlement;

(f)   Section 677: settlements under which the trustees make payments – including by way of loan or repayment of loan – to the settlor;

(g)   Section 683(1)(d): settlements where the settlor has not absolutely divested himself of income-producing property.

It should be noted that benefits enjoyed, or which could be enjoyed, by the spouse of the settlor can also trigger the operation of the above provisions. The definition of 'settlement' for these purposes is very wide indeed; the expression 'includes any disposition, trust, covenant, agreement or arrangement', and the settlor is the person who has made the 'settlement' or, broadly, has directly or indirectly provided the funds comprised within it[10]. It should not, therefore, be assumed that, because the arrangements in question do not involve a formal settlement or trust, those arrangements do not attract the operation of the 'settlement' provisions.

9-66   The extension of the concept of a statutory 'settlement' beyond an ordinary trust is illustrated by *IRC v Pay*[11]. There, the taxpayer had settled a sum which was immediately applied by way of loan to the settlor secured by a charge on certain property. It was held that the interest paid by the settlor under the charge was paid because of the charge on the property which was part of the overall 'settlement'. In those circumstances, the interest was paid 'by virtue or in consequence of any settlement' to which what is now TA 1988 s 676[12] applied, and therefore a deduction for the interest was disallowed. A similar overall view of related transactions was taken in *IRC v Leiner*[13] which involved the rearrangement of a loan to a company made by the mother of the alleged 'settlor'. Essentially, an outstanding loan by the mother to the company was repaid and the mother then settled that

---

[10]   TA 1988 ss 670, 681 (4) and 685(4) to (4C).

[11]   (1955) 36 TC 109.

[12]   Formerly, ITA 1952 s 407.

[13]   (1964) 41 TC 589.

sum for the benefit of, among others, her son and his child; the trustees then lent the money at interest to the son, who then lent the money interest-free to the original debtor company. The whole arrangement was treated as a settlement for the purposes of the special statutory provisions, and the son was held to be a settlor (together with his mother). Moreover, it was held that the arrangement could not be excluded from the special statutory provisions on the basis that it was a commercial transaction devoid of any bounty; comparing the positions of the company and the son before and after the transactions, it could be seen that the company was in the same position, owing the same amount of money and not paying interest on it, whereas the son had become liable to pay interest on the loan to him but without any compensating benefit, because his loan to the company was interest-free.

9-67 In *IRC v Levy*[14], the Inland Revenue sought to have an interest-free loan from a sole proprietor to his investment company treated as a settlement for the purposes of these provisions. The taxpayer owned beneficially the whole of the issued share capital[15] of a company engaged in share dealing. In addition to money owed to outside creditors, the company was indebted to the taxpayer in the sum of about £108,000; he was treated as a deferred creditor in respect of this indebtedness, since otherwise the auditors would have qualified the audit report because the company would have been regarded as insolvent. In relation to various prospective share acquisitions, which in the main did not proceed, the taxpayer made an interest-free loan to the company of £3.33 million. This was invested on deposit, and the Inland Revenue claimed that the income arising to the company was to be treated as the income of the taxpayer as settlor of a statutory settlement; it was argued that, if the arrangement constituted a settlement, the income was assessable on the taxpayer under what are now TA 1988 ss 672, 674 and 683(1)(d).

Although the case raised several questions about the application of the settlement provisions to interest-free loans, the Crown's case was disposed of by both the Special Commissioners and the High Court on the basis that the interest-free loan, lacking any element of bounty, could not amount to a settlement for these purposes. Although the absence of any obligation on the company to pay interest was a material factor in considering this question, it was not regarded as conclusive[16]. Applying an objective test[17], the appellate Commissioners had found that no element of bounty was involved in the arrangements. This view was based on the fact that the loan monies were invested in a way which produced a greater net after-tax amount than would have been the case had the taxpayer invested the money himself[18], and this benefitted the taxpayer in his capacity as loan creditor in respect of an amount which the company might not otherwise

---

[14] [1982] STC 442.
[15] Although the headnote refers to a holding of 99 per cent of the share capital, it appears that this was the legal ownership and that the whole of the share capital was beneficially owned by the taxpayer – [1982] STC 442 at 444*j* and 455*j*.
[16] [1982] STC 442 at 457*c*.
[17] Nourse J thought that the test should be objective rather than subjective – [1982] STC 442 at 457*f*.
[18] Because of the difference between the rates of tax borne by companies and individuals.

have been able to repay in full[19] and as shareholder; therefore, the taxpayer was not worse off but better off as a result of the arrangements and, applying the decision in *Leiner,* there could be no settlement.

9-68   *Levy*[20] concerned a case where the taxpayer alone (disregarding the company for this purpose) benefitted from the interest-free loan. But what of interest-free loans to third parties or to companies in which third parties have shareholding interests? This question can really only be considered in the light of the particular circumstances which are alleged to constitute a statutory settlement. However, it would seem that, as in *Leiner*[1], an interest-free loan can be an element in a settlement; in that case the consequence was to treat the income of the settlement (namely, the interest paid to the trustees on the interest-bearing loan) as the income of the settlor taxpayer. If, unlike the position in *Levy,* the taxpayer makes an interest-free loan from which he derives no benefit, it will not always be clear what is the income arising under the settlement which can be treated as the income of the settlor and, in some cases[2], whether the income arises 'from ... property comprised in the settlement'. These difficult questions were canvassed in *IRC v Levy,* but were not considered by the court because there was held to be no settlement. It does seem, however, that income derived from a loan made by a father to a child where the proceeds of the loan are to be invested in a particular way might be identified as income arising under a settlement from property comprised in the settlement, whereas there would seem to be no income susceptible to assessment where an interest-free loan is made to enable a person to acquire a non-income-producing property (eg a house) even though this would reduce the amount of interest which would otherwise be payable by the borrower had he raised the money by a commercial loan. Where the recipient of an interest-free loan is a company it may be difficult, or even impossible, to ascertain what is the income arising under the statutory settlement where the proceeds of the loan are used generally in the company's business[3].

10   Discounts

GENERAL INCOME TREATMENT

9-69   It has already been seen[4] that, although in economic terms it closely resembles interest, discount is not treated in the same way as interest for taxation purposes. There is no requirement to deduct basic rate income tax from discount, as there is from yearly interest, and, until 1984, there was no specific provision for discount to be allowed as a deduction in computing taxable income in the same way as interest. Because of the similarity between discount and interest, this Part of this Chapter summarises the

[19] The original loan of £108,000.
[20] See §**9-67** above.
[1] See §**9-66** above.
[2] Eg TA 1988 s 672(1).
[3] See [1982] STC 442 at 457*h–j*.
[4] Chapter 2 Part 2 above.

legislation which provides specific relief for certain discounts and sets out the way in which discount is taxable in certain cases.

Part 2 of Chapter 2 addresses the treatment of discounts as a matter of general tax law, from which it can be seen that a discount in return for the use of money is taxable under Sch D Case III and there is limited scope for relief in the hands of the payer. In the case of bills of exchange drawn by a company, accepted by a UK bank and discounted by a UK bank or discount house, the discount when paid is by statute treated as a charge on income for corporation tax purposes[5]. The company must ultimately bear the discount and must exist for the purpose of carrying on a trade, raise the funds on the bill of exchange for the purposes of a trade or be an investment company. Moreover, the bank or discount house must be bona fide carrying on business in the UK. Apart from other cases where relief for discounts is specifically given[6], relief for discounts would only be available as a trade expense where the trader is carrying on a financial trade or, arguably[7], otherwise where the discount is a proper trade expense of a revenue nature in connection with borrowings for the purposes of a trade.

In the case of the taxation of discounts, it is specifically provided[8] that discounts on Treasury bills are not taxable under Sch D Case III and that this shall not cause them to be taxable under Sch D Case VI. Discounts on Treasury bills will, however, be taken into account in computing trading profits of financial institutions dealing in Treasury bills.

DEEP DISCOUNT SECURITIES

9-70   TA 1988 Sch 4 provides for the taxation treatment of discount in respect of 'deep discount securities'. Subject to special rules described below, the regime for deep discount securities taxes the holder of the securities on disposal (in most cases) in respect of the element of the discount which accrues over his period of ownership, but allows the issuing company relief for the discount (in most cases) as it accrues throughout its life.

A deep discount security is a redeemable security, other than a share, issued by a company at a deep discount after 13 March 1984, but excluding a security where the redemption price is index-linked or where the security was issued in respect of shares or securities of a company otherwise than wholly for new consideration[9]. A redeemable security issued by a public body at a deep discount will also be a deep discount security, unless the redemption price is index-linked or it is a gilt-edged security issued before 14 March 1989 where, broadly, other securities issued under the same prospectus are not deep discount securities[10]. Generally, special rules apply in relation to securities issued under the same prospectus as securities issued at other times[11]. A security issued on or after 1 August 1990 will not be a deep discount security if it is convertible into any share capital or if it

---

[5] TA 1988 s 78.
[6] See §9-71(2) below.
[7] See §8-06 above, as to expenditure 'in respect of capital'.
[8] TA 1988 s 126.
[9] TA 1988 Sch 4 para 1(1)(d).
[10] TA 1988 Sch 4 para 1(1)(dd).
[11] TA 1988 Sch 4 paras 19 and 20.

can be redeemed on more than one occasion at the option of the holder[12]. A qualifying convertible security is not a deep discount security[13].

The 'discount' is the amount by which the amount payable on redemption exceeds the issue price[14]. The amount payable on redemption does not include 'any amount payable by way of interest'[15]. Thus, since a premium payable on redemption will generally be interest[16] – at least, if it is taxable as income – a security redeemable at a premium will not normally be a deep discount security; the premium might nevertheless be taxable as income in the hands of the holder when received[17] and relievable in the hands of the issuer when paid[18]. It should be noted that there is no definition of 'issue price'. Normally, the issue price will be clearly known, since the issue will be priced at a fixed amount. But, where the security is issued in exchange for consideration other than cash, it would appear to be necessary to value the consideration at the time of the issue. Where the issue price and the amount payable on redemption are denominated in foreign currency, the question of whether the security is a deep discount security should be determined by reference to the foreign currency amounts, the resulting difference being translated into sterling at the time of the issue in order to ascertain the discount in sterling which will accrue over the life of the security.

A discount is a deep discount if it represents more than 15 per cent of the amount payable on redemption, or not more than 15 per cent but more than half Y per cent where Y is the number of complete years between the date of issue and redemption[19]. Thus, a discount on a security having less than one complete year to run from issue to redemption will always be a deep discount. The redemption date is the earliest date on which the security may be redeemed but, as already noted, if the security was issued on or after 1 August 1990 and can be redeemed at the option of the holder on more than one occasion it will not be a deep discount security.

9–71 The principal taxation treatment of a deep discount security is as follows:

1   On disposal, the holder is charged to tax as income on the income element in respect of the discount accrued over his period of ownership of the security[20]. Tax is charged under Sch D Case III or IV[1]; in the case of tax chargeable under Case IV, the remittance basis can apply to non-domiciled and certain other individuals as in relation to tax on interest[2]. It is expressly provided that so much of the proceeds of redemption as are taxable in this way are not subject to deduction of basic rate income tax in respect of UK source yearly interest or foreign

---

[12] TA 1988 Sch 4 para 1(1A) and 1(1B).
[13] TA 1988 Sch 4 para 21.
[14] TA 1988 Sch 4 para 1(1)(e).
[15] TA 1988 Sch 4 para 1(1)(b).
[16] See §§2–30 and 2–31 above.
[17] See §4–02 above.
[18] See Chapter 8 above.
[19] TA 1988 Sch 4 para 1(1)(c).
[20] TA 1988 Sch 4 para 4.
[1] Even if the security is not secured, the draftsman seems to have thought (wrongly) that income from securities was chargeable under Case IV (see §3–21 above).
[2] TA 1988 Sch 4 para 4(5) and (6); and see §§5–06 and 5–07 above.

dividends³; this is a somewhat curious provision, since no withholding applies in any event to discount. For the purpose of the tax charge, 'disposal' is determined as for capital gains purposes, except that there is a deemed disposal on death, and the exchange or conversion of deep discount securities for shares or securities (other than, in certain cases, new deep discount securities) results in a disposal⁴. Any actual interest payable on the securities is subject to the usual tax regime for interest on securities, including the accrued income scheme⁵.

2   In each accounting period during the life of the security, the company is entitled to relief, against profits as reduced by other reliefs except for group relief, for the element of discount accrued in any income period⁶ in respect of the security ending in that period⁷. Relief is given as for a charge on income, although the amount is not treated as a charge on income for the purposes of TA 1988 s 338. Relief is only given if the company ultimately bears the cost of the discount and if either the company exists for the purpose of carrying on a trade, the security was issued to raise money for the purposes of a trade carried on by the company or the company is an investment company⁸. Relief is not given if any part of the amount payable on redemption would be a distribution within TA 1988 s 209 (2)(d) or (e)⁹ or if a scheme has been effected such that the sole or main benefit from the arrangements might be expected to be the obtaining of tax relief¹⁰.

A company or public body which issues a deep discount security is required to show the income element for the security on each certificate of the security¹¹. However, the taxation treatment of holder and issuer is not affected by the failure to show this; there is no sanction for failure to show the income element on the certificate, which is an obligation which purports to apply to both UK and foreign companies and public bodies.

9–72   Relief is not available for the accrued income element, but only for the discount when actually paid on redemption, where the holder of the security and the issuing company are under common 51 per cent or greater control or are otherwise associated¹², or where the issuing company is a close company and the holder is a participator in the company, an associate of a participator or a company controlled by a participator¹³.

To prevent income being accumulated in a company which acquires income-producing securities with the proceeds of a deep discount security issue, the above rules are modified from the point of view of the holder of the security in certain cases. Where a deep discount security is issued by a company and the company's assets largely comprise certain other securities, the holder of the security can be taxed by reference to the element

---

³ TA 1988 Sch 4 para 4(7).
⁴ TA 1988 Sch 4 para 7.
⁵ See §§9–29 to 9–34 above.
⁶ Defined in TA 1988 Sch 4 para 1(1)(f).
⁷ TA 1988 Sch 4 para 5.
⁸ TA 1988 Sch 4 para 5(3) and (4).
⁹ TA 1988 Sch 4 para 5(5); see Chapter 9 Part 1 above.
¹⁰ TA 1988 Sch 4 para 5(6); see §§9–26 and 9–27 above.
¹¹ TA 1988 Sch 4 para 13.
¹² TA 1988 Sch 4 para 9.
¹³ TA 1988 Sch 4 para 10.

of the discount which accrues in each income period, rather than on disposal of the security[14].

9-73   To ensure that the full amount of the discount is taxed, special rules apply on early redemption so that the holder of the security at the time of the redemption is taxed on the discount less so much as accrued before his acquisition[15]. A similar adjustment provides the company with full relief for the discount. If a further issue is made of a tranche of securities of the same kind as that already in issue, but with an additional payment being made by the subscribers to reflect the interest accrued on the securities to the date of subscription, the issue price is reduced by the amount of the extra payment[16]; although this adjusts the discount so far as the issue of the new securities is concerned, it does not have the effect of making them fungible with the existing tranche in relation to the discount itself.

Special rules apply to certain types of taxpayer. Charities[17] and the trustees of an exempt approved retirement benefit scheme[18] are not taxed in respect of the accrued income element on a disposal; the transfer of securities under approved stock lending arrangements does not trigger a tax charge in respect of the accrued income element[19], and trustees (other than trustees of certain unauthorised unit trusts) are taxable at both the basic rate and the additional rate in respect of the accrued income on a disposal of deep discount securities[20]. Special provisions apply to Lloyd's underwriters[1]. Where the disposal of a deep discount security is relevant also for capital gains purposes, the chargeable gain or allowable loss is computed after reducing the disposal proceeds by the accrued income element which is taxable as income on disposal[2].

DEEP GAIN SECURITIES

9-74   The regime applying to deep gain securities is less favourable than that which applies to deep discount securities. Although the holder is taxed on the gain arising on disposal of the securities as income, there is no corresponding relief provided for the issuer. Thus, where a discount is paid in respect of deep gain securities, relief is only available under general principles – namely, as an expense incurred wholly and exclusively for the purposes of a trade, so long as this is not prevented as being an expense 'in respect of... any sum employed or intended to be employed as capital in the trade'[3]. This would appear to limit relief to discounts incurred in providing short-term finance and, probably, discounts incurred by banks and financial traders; an investment company would not be entitled to relief in respect of discount paid on a deep gain security.

[14] TA 1988 Sch 4 paras 2 and 3.
[15] TA 1988 Sch 4 para 11.
[16] TA 1988 Sch 4 para 11B.
[17] TA 1988 Sch 4 para 14.
[18] TA 1988 Sch 4 para 15.
[19] TA 1988 Sch 4 para 16.
[20] TA 1988 Sch 4 para 17.
[1] TA 1988 Sch 4 para 18.
[2] TCGA 1992 s 118.
[3] TA 1988 s 74 (a) and (f); and see §§**8-02** to **8-06** above.

9-75 The provisions relating to deep gain securities are contained in FA 1989 Sch 11. A deep gain security is a redeemable security which, assuming redemption at any of the times when it is redeemable, *might* provide a deep gain on redemption[4]. A deep gain arises if the redemption amount exceeds the issue price by an amount which would be a deep discount under the deep discount securities rules[5]. Moreover, to be a deep gain security, the security must be neither a deep discount security, a share, a 'qualifying indexed security'[6] nor a 'convertible security'[7], and must not be a gilt-edged security issued before 14 March 1989 or fall within certain categories of security relating to different issues made under the same prospectus[8]. Generally, special rules apply in relation to securities issued under the same prospectus as securities issued at other times[9].

Because a security issued at a very small discount could be a deep gain security if regard were had to potential early redemption, early redemption is disregarded in certain instances which are not under the control of the holder of the security – namely, where redemption is only at the option of the issuer[10] and where early redemption might occur as a result of the operation of certain default provisions[11]. Special provisions can apply to cause the security nevertheless to be treated as a deep gain security if immediately before the redemption it is held by a person connected with the issuer or if it is transferred by such a person within one year before redemption[12].

9-76 The tax charge imposed in relation to deep gain securities arises on transfer or redemption[13] of the securities; 'transfer' means transfer by sale, exchange, gift or otherwise, but does not include a conversion into share capital in a company[14]. The tax charge is imposed on the excess of the proceeds of sale or redemption over the acquisition cost (including incidental acquisition costs)[15]. A deemed transfer at market value occurs on death[16], and market value is also taken into account (instead of the actual proceeds) on a transfer to a connected person[17] and on transfer otherwise than for money or money's worth or otherwise than on arm's length terms[18].

The taxable amount is treated as income within Sch D Case III or IV[19], and, in the case of foreign securities, the remittance basis applies in relation to non-domiciled individuals and certain other taxpayers[20]. Trustees, other than trustees of certain unauthorised unit trusts, are charged to tax at the basic rate and the additional rate[1].

---

[4] FA 1989 Sch 11 para 1(1) and (2).
[5] FA 1989 Sch 11 para 1(9); see §9-77 above.
[6] Defined in FA 1989 Sch 11 para 2.
[7] Defined in FA 1989 Sch 11 para 3.
[8] FA 1989 Sch 11 para 1(4), (5), (6) and (7).
[9] FA 1989 Sch 11 paras 20, 21 and 21A.
[10] FA 1989 Sch 11 para 1(3).
[11] FA 1989 Sch 11 para 1(3A) to (3G).
[12] FA 1989 Sch 11 para 19A.
[13] FA 1989 Sch 11 para 6.
[14] FA 1989 Sch 11 para 4(2) and (2A).
[15] FA 1989 Sch 11 para 5.
[16] FA 1989 Sch 11 para 7.
[17] FA 1989 Sch 11 para 8.
[18] FA 1989 Sch 11 para 9.
[19] FA 1989 Sch 11 para 5(2)(b).
[20] FA 1989 Sch 11 para 13; see §§5-06 and 5-07 above.
[1] FA 1989 Sch 11 para 11.

As in the case of deep discount securities, special provisions apply in relation to further issues of securities where the subscribers make a payment in respect of accrued interest[2], Lloyd's underwriters[3] and stock lending[4]. No tax is deductible on payment of any discount or redemption of securities to which these provisions apply[5]. The accrued income scheme does not apply to a transfer of deep gain securities[6]. A number of special rules also apply in relation to securities issued under the same prospectus as securities issued at other times[7], indexed securities[8] and qualifying convertible securities[9].

A deep gain security is a qualifying corporate bond[10]. Therefore, no chargeable gain or allowable loss can arise on disposal of a deep gain security[11].

QUALIFYING CONVERTIBLE SECURITIES

9-77 Provisions similar to those which apply to deep gain securities can apply in relation to qualifying convertible securities within FA 1990 Sch 10. This is a hybrid type of security which has a listing on a recognised stock exchange and which carries an option for conversion into shares or for redemption on terms that provide an excess of redemption proceeds over issue price which would constitute a deep gain[12]. On transfer when the security remains redeemable or on redemption, a 'chargeable amount' is taxed under Sch D Case III or IV[13]. The chargeable amount is, broadly, whichever is the lower of the amount received on transfer or redemption and the income element which has accrued at that time[14]. Non-UK domiciled individuals and certain others may be taxed on the remittance basis in relation to foreign securities[15]. A deemed transfer occurs on death, when market value is deemed to be received[16]; market value is also substituted for the actual consideration received on transfers to connected persons or otherwise on non-arm's length terms or for non-monetary consideration[17]. Where the charge arises on redemption, the issuing company obtains a deduction for the excess of the amount paid on redemption over the issue price[18].

The legislation includes provisions similar to those under the deep discount and deep gains securities legislation in relation to trustees[19], charities[20], exempt

---

2 FA 1989 Sch 11 para 3A.
3 FA 1989 Sch 11 para 10.
4 FA 1989 Sch 11 para 16.
5 FA 1989 Sch 11 para 18.
6 FA 1989 Sch 11 para 17.
7 FA 1989 Sch 11 paras 20 to 21A.
8 FA 1989 Sch 11 para 22.
9 FA 1989 Sch 11 paras 22A and 22B.
10 TCGA 1992 s 117 (3)(a).
11 TCGA 1992 s 115 (1).
12 FA 1990 Sch 10 para 2(4) to (8).
13 FA 1990 Sch 10 para 12.
14 FA 1990 Sch 10 para 13.
15 FA 1990 Sch 10 para 20.
16 FA 1990 Sch 10 para 16.
17 FA 1990 Sch 10 para 17.
18 FA 1990 Sch 10 para 25.
19 FA 1990 Sch 10 para 19.
20 FA 1990 Sch 10 para 21.

approved retirement benefit schemes[1], Lloyd's underwriters[2] and stock lending[3].

Where the disposal of a qualifying convertible security is also relevant for capital gains purposes, the amount taxed as income under Sch D Case III or IV is excluded from the consideration in computing the capital gain[4].

NON RESIDENT INVESTORS

9-78 Although the provisions relating to taxation of deep discount securities and deep gain securities operate so that the tax charge arises under Sch D Case III in relation to UK securities, non-UK resident investors will not, in practice, normally suffer a tax charge. As has been seen, the discount payable on redemption is not subject to deduction of UK tax. In such circumstances, the Inland Revenue will, by concession, not seek to recover the income tax liability of a person who is non-resident for the whole of a year of assessment, except where it can be recovered by set-off in a claim to relief in respect of taxed income from UK sources or where the tax can be assessed under TMA 1970 s 78 in the name of a UK branch or agent or other person[5]; a non-UK resident company or other person trading in the UK through a branch or agency is taxable in the ordinary way where the securities are held in connection with that UK trade. Although this concessionary practice is not expressed to apply to a chargeable amount realised by a non-resident in respect of qualifying convertible securities, it is understood that, in practice, the same concession would be applied.

11 Miscellaneous exemptions and related matters

SAVINGS BANKS

9-79 A savings bank[6] is entitled to exemption from income tax and corporation tax in respect of the income from its funds to the extent that such income is applied in payment of interest to a depositor with the savings bank; the interest paid to the depositor remains liable to tax under Sch D Case III, except to the extent of the first £70 of interest derived from an ordinary (but not an investment) deposit with the National Savings Bank[7].

INDUSTRIAL AND PROVIDENT SOCIETIES AND CREDIT UNIONS

9-80 Interest paid by an industrial and provident society is normally subject to tax under Sch D Case III in the ordinary way[8] although it is paid without

---

[1] FA 1990 Sch 10 para 22.
[2] FA 1990 Sch 10 para 18.
[3] FA 1990 Sch 10 para 23.
[4] TCGA 1992 s 37(1).
[5] Extra-statutory Concession B13.
[6] Other than certain companies within the TSB Group.
[7] TA 1988 ss 484(1) and 325.
[8] TA 1988 s 486(4).

deduction of income tax under TA 1988 s 349 (2) unless the usual place of abode of the recipient is outside the UK[9].

Interest paid by an industrial and provident society is eligible for relief in computing the taxable profits of the society[10]. However, a credit union is not regarded as carrying on a trade in relation to making loans to its members or depositing surplus funds, nor is it regarded as an investment company[11]; further, interest received by a credit union on loans to its members is not taxable in its hands[12].

CO-OPERATIVE HOUSING ASSSOCIATIONS

9–81   Where an approved co-operative housing association pays yearly interest on a loan to finance the acquisition and improvement of dwellinghouses, the interest payable by the association is treated as if it were payable by the members of the association who are tenants of property belonging to the association; the interest paid is apportioned among those tenants in proportion to the rents payable by the members of the association for the year in respect of which the interest is paid. Rent which is paid by members of the association to the association is disregarded for tax purposes. Each member of the association who is a tenant of property belonging to the association is treated as being the owner of the estate or interest in the property which belongs to the association, so that the member is then eligible for relief under TA 1988 s 353 in respect of the interest paid by the association which is apportioned to the member[13]. Loans to housing associations can be brought within the MIRAS scheme[14].

CONTRACTUAL SAVINGS SCHEMES – 'SAVE AS YOU EARN'

9–82   Any interest or other sum and any terminal bonus payable under a certified contractual savings scheme[15] whether in respect of a deposit with the Department of National Savings, shares in a building society or a deposit with a bank, is disregarded for all income tax purposes (and for capital gains tax purposes)[16].

---

[9] TA 1988 s 486 (2) and (3).
[10] TA 1988 s 486 (1).
[11] TA 1988 s 486 (1) (a) and (4).
[12] TA 1988 s 486 (1) (b).
[13] TA 1988 s 488.
[14] TA 1988 s 378 and the Income Tax (Interest Relief) (Housing Associations) Regulations 1988: SI 1988 No 1347.
[15] TA 1988 s 326 (2) and TCGA 1992 s 271 (4).
[16] TA 1988 s 326 (1).

Chapter 10

RETURNS AND STATEMENTS

10-01 This chapter summarises the principal returns and statements which may be required in connection with the income tax and corporation tax treatment of interest.

CERTIFICATE OF DEDUCTION OF INCOME TAX

10-02 Any person making a deduction of income tax from yearly interest pursuant to TA 1988 s 349 (2)[1] may be required by the recipient to state in writing the gross amount of the interest, the amount of tax deducted and the net amount of interest paid over[2]. A certificate as to this is normally provided on Form R 185. The obligation to produce the certificate if so requested may be enforced by the recipient of the interest.

10-03 Irrespective of whether it is so requested by the recipient, a company must, when sending to the recipient a warrant, cheque or other order for the payment of interest which is not a qualifying distribution, also send him a written statement showing the gross amount of interest paid, the rate of and amount of income tax deducted, the net amount paid over and the date of the payment[3].

If a payment of interest amounts to a qualifying distribution for taxation purposes[4] the company must similarly deliver to the recipient a statement as to the amount of interest paid, the amount of the tax credit which attaches to the distribution and the date of the payment[5]. Where the company makes payment direct to a bank or building society account of the recipient, a statement must be sent to the bank or building society or direct to the recipient[6]. And, where a nominee receives such a payment from a company and pays it over to the beneficial owner (or to his account with a bank or building society), the nominee must send a similar statement to the beneficial owner (or to his bank or building society)[7].

Failure to comply with these obligations incurs a penalty of £60 for each offence, but the total of the penalties imposed on the company in relation to any one distribution of interest may not exceed £600[8].

---

[1] See Chapter 7 Part 1 above.
[2] TA 1988 s 352.
[3] TA 1988 s 234A (2) and (6).
[4] See TA 1988 s 14 (2), and see Chapter 9 Part 1 above.
[5] TA 1988 s 234A (2) and (7).
[6] TA 1988 s 234A (3).
[7] TA 1988 s 234A (4) and (5).
[8] TA 1988 s 234A (9).

RETURNS OF YEARLY INTEREST PAID BY A COMPANY

10-04 A company must make returns to the Collector of Taxes, normally quarterly to 31 March, 30 June, 30 September, 31 December, but also to the end of any accounting period which ends on a date other than one of those dates, in respect of yearly interest and other payments which are paid subject to deduction of income tax[9]. The return must be made within fourteen days of the date to which the return is to be made up[10], and must show, *inter alia,* the amount of interest paid by the company during the period and the income tax for which the company is accountable[11]. The return should also include details of yearly interest and other annual payments received by the company under deduction of income tax during the return period where the company claims to have the income tax suffered by deduction set against any income tax for which it must account[12].

The return is made to the Collector of Taxes on Form CT 61(Z).

RETURNS OF QUALIFYING DISTRIBUTIONS

10-05 Where a company pays interest which is treated as a qualifying distribution[13] the interest must be included in the company's returns of franked investment income received and franked payments made. These returns are normally made by reference to quarters ending on 31 March, 30 June, 30 September and 31 December, and to the end of any accounting period ending on any other date[14]. The returns are to be made within fourteen days of the date to which the returns are made up[15], and are made to the Collector of Taxes[16] on Form CT 61 (Z).

PAYING AGENTS AND OTHERS DEDUCTING TAX ON COUPONS ETC

10-06 TA 1988 Sch 3 sets out the machinery relating to the collection of basic rate income tax charged under Sch C[17] and under TA 1988 s 123 in respect of certain foreign source interest and other dividends[18]. That machinery requires the Bank of England, the Bank of Ireland and the National Debt Commissioners to deliver to the Inland Revenue 'true accounts' of the interest and other dividends which they distribute[19]. Other chargeable persons entrusted with the payment of or obtaining payment of interest and other foreign dividends, and selling and accounting for the proceeds of coupons, or purchasing coupons which are chargeable to tax under Sch

---

[9] TA 1988 Sch 16 para 2; and see §7-11 above.
[10] TA 1988 Sch 16 para 2 (3).
[11] TA 1988 Sch 16 para 3.
[12] TA 1988 Sch 16 para 5; and see §7-11 above.
[13] TA 1988 s 14 (2); and see Chapter 9 Part 1 above.
[14] TA 1988 Sch 13 para 1 (2).
[15] TA 1988 Sch 13 para 1 (3).
[16] TA 1988 Sch 13 para 1 (1).
[17] See Chapter 6 above.
[18] See Chapter 7 Part 3 above.
[19] TA 1988 Sch 3 para 1.

C or Sch D, must make quarterly returns to the Inland Revenue of the sums handled by them and of the income tax deducted[20]. The tax for which the chargeable person is accountable must be paid to the Inland Revenue within 14 days of the end of the month in which the transaction took place[1], and, if not paid by the due date, carries interest[2].

The Inland Revenue may serve notice on a person requiring him to make his books available for inspection at his premises in order to check that the returns made are correct and complete. But the Inland Revenue may exempt a person from this obligation by issuing a certificate to that effect, and thereafter shall not exercise this inspection power until the certificate has been revoked[3]. A banker is not required to disclose particulars relating to the affairs of any person on whose behalf he may be acting, notwithstanding the obligation to account for income tax and make returns[4].

10-07 Information relating to interest paid or received in respect of securities issued by the UK government or by any company incorporated (irrespective of its place of residence) in the UK may be obtained by the Inland Revenue issuing a notice in certain cases[5]. These cases are where the holder of the securities receives the interest on behalf of a third party, or where the securities in question are bearer securities; but such a notice cannot require a bank to disclose details of interest beneficially owned by a non-resident.

INTEREST PAID BY BANKS ETC

10-08 A bank, or other person which in the course of trade or business takes deposits, may be required by an Inspector of Taxes to make a return of interest paid or credited, showing the names and addresses of the persons to whom interest is paid or credited, the amount of interest involved and the amount of any tax deducted[6]. The requirement cannot relate to a year ending more than three years before the date of the notice; the expression 'year' is not defined. The Director of Savings may also be required to make a similar return of interest paid gross[7]. Because banking businesses are often carried on at separate branches, the legislation provides that separate returns may be required in relation to separate branches by serving notices on the managers of the branches[8]. This provision does not apply to interest on deposits taken outside the UK (eg at overseas branches of UK banks)[9].

Information can be provided to the Inland Revenue electronically or in writing. There is no longer a statutory *de minimis* level of interest (£15) below which details were not required to be provided to the Inland Revenue, and the *de minimis* level of interest (£500) which was previously applied in practice by the Inland Revenue no longer applies either. However, in

[20] TA 1988 Sch 3 para 6C.
[1] TA 1988 Sch 3 para 6A.
[2] TA 1988 Sch 3 para 6C.
[3] TA 1988 Sch 3 para 13.
[4] TA 1988 Sch 3 para 11.
[5] TMA 1970 s 24.
[6] TMA 1970 s 17(1).
[7] TMA 1970 s 17(3).
[8] TMA 1970 s 17(2).
[9] TMA 1970 s 17(4).

practice the Inland Revenue does not require details of certain interest paid to be provided; this relates to interbank interest, interest paid to exempt approved retirement benefit schemes, interest on SAYE accounts, interest on transferable certificates of deposit and interest on TESSAs[10]. Previously, where the *de minimis* level applied, the fact that an Inspector of Taxes had received details of bank interest paid to a taxpayer did not prevent him making an estimated assessment in a higher amount than that notified to him by the bank, because the taxpayer might have received bank interest from other banks of an amount lower than the level of the Inland Revenue's enquiry to those banks[11].

An account holder who, by notice in writing to the bank or other person holding the deposit, declares that the person beneficially entitled to the interest is a company not resident in the UK may require details of the interest credited not to be included in a return to the Inland Revenue[12]. Further, where any other person has qualified to receive interest without deduction of basic rate income tax, because the person or persons beneficially entitled to the interest are not ordinarily resident in the UK (or, in the case of depositors who are personal representatives, the deceased was not ordinarily resident in the UK immediately before his death), he may require details of interest credited not to be given to the Inland Revenue[13].

The fact that details of interest paid or credited to a non-resident are omitted from a return made by a bank does not mean that the interest is not liable to tax in the UK. Although tax in respect of bank interest paid gross is not normally assessed on non-residents, it can be assessed where there is a UK agent or branch business from which the tax may be collected[14].

The power of the Inland Revenue to obtain details of bank deposit interest under TMA 1970 s 17 does not prevent the Commissioners of Taxes issuing a precept under s 51 of that Act requiring a taxpayer appealing against an assessment to provide information relating to the appeal[15].

10-09   Any person other than a bank paying interest in the ordinary course of carrying on a bona fide banking business in the UK may also be required by notice to provide an Inspector of Taxes with details concerning interest (whether or not yearly interest) paid and the amount of any tax deducted[16]. These details are the names and addresses of persons to whom the interest was paid or the persons on whose behalf the interest was received and the amount of the interest. This obligation is not subject to the qualifications described in §**10-08** above in relation to interest paid by banks and similar institutions to non-resident persons; however, a notice under this provision may not be given in relation to interest paid by a UK bank in respect of interest paid in the ordinary course of banking business. Similar information can be required from any person who receives interest gross on behalf of another person.

---

[10] See §**4-14** above; separate information is required in respect of TESSAs – see the Tax-exempt Special Savings Account Regulations 1990: SI 1990 No 2361.
[11] *Blackpool Marton Rotary Club v Martin (Inspector of Taxes)* [1990] STC 1, CA.
[12] TMA 1970 s 17 (4A).
[13] TMA 1970 s 17 (4B).
[14] See §§**4-27** and **4-28** above.
[15] *Eke v Knight (Inspector of Taxes)* [1977] STC 198, CA.
[16] TMA 1970 s 18.

10-10   Regulations have been made providing for additional information to be given by banks and others in connection with details of interest paid[17].

BUILDING SOCIETIES

10-11   Provisions similar to those concerning details of interest paid by banks also apply in relation to interest paid by building societies[18].

INTEREST QUALIFYING FOR TAX RELIEF

10-12   A person claiming income tax relief under TA 1988 s 353 for interest paid is required to provide the Inspector of Taxes with a statement showing the date when the debt was incurred, the amount of the debt, the name and address of the debtor and the year of assessment for which interest relief is claimed[19]. The debtor is entitled to require the person to whom the interest is paid to provide such a statement[20]; such statements are made on Form 38E-1 (1974) or, in the case of interest paid to banks, Form 38E-2 (1975). Building societies and certain other lenders provide details direct to the Inland Revenue.

---

[17] The Income Tax (Interest Payments) (Information Powers) Regulations 1992: SI 1992 No 15.
[18] Regulations 12 to 14 of the Income Tax (Building Societies) (Dividend and Interest) Regulations 1990: SI 1990 No 2231. See also, Inland Revenue Press Release, 24 November 1992.
[19] TA 1988 s 366 (1).
[20] TA 1988 s 366 (2).

Chapter 11

INTEREST AND OTHER TAXES

11-01 The previous chapters have been concerned with the treatment of interest in relation to income tax and corporation tax. This chapter summarises the treatment of interest in relation to other taxes. A basic knowledge on the part of the reader of the principles of those taxes is assumed.

1 Capital gains

11-02 Generally, interest is not taken into account in the computation of capital gains, either as an element in the allowable acquisition cost of an asset or as an element in the consideration for a disposal of an asset. Where interest is paid on delayed payment of the purchase price receivable on disposal of an asset, such interest will be charged to income tax in the ordinary way and is therefore excluded from the consideration on the disposal as being charged to income tax or taken into account in computing the income, profits or losses of the person making the disposal[1]. However, where an 'interest' adjustment is made to the consideration payable for an asset in circumstances that the 'interest' is not interest proper[2] this would be treated as part of the consideration for the disposal and acquisition of the asset.

11-03 With one exception, interest paid is expressly prevented from being treated as a deductible amount in the computation of the gain[3]. This means that, normally, whether the interest was paid on a loan to acquire the asset or on delayed payment of the purchase price, no relief can be obtained for interest even if it is not allowable for income tax purposes.

The one exception applies to interest paid by a company (but not by an individual) for a period prior to disposal of property on a loan to finance expenditure on the construction of any building, structure or works where such expenditure itself qualifies as a deduction in computing the chargeable gain on a disposal[4]. This relief only applies to interest which is not a charge on income[5]. This means that the relief will normally only apply in respect of interest paid before 1 April 1981 and which was capitalised[6]; relief would also be available if the company is not a trading company and the property is sold before it is let in circumstances that the company never becomes

---

[1] TCGA 1992 s 37 (1).
[2] See §2-17 above.
[3] TCGA 1992 s 38 (3).
[4] TCGA 1992 s 40.
[5] TCGA 1992 s 40 (2).
[6] See §8-38 above.

an investment company[7]. Interest which is relievable as a trading expense, or which would be so treated if the asset disposed of were a fixed asset of a trade whose profits were chargeable to income tax, cannot be treated as part of the allowable acquisition or enhancement expenditure in the computation of a chargeable gain[8].

11-04 Although non-UK resident trustees are not normally subject to UK capital gains tax, in certain circumstances UK resident beneficiaries of non-resident trusts can suffer capital gains tax in respect of gains realised by the trustees and attributed to the beneficiaries[9]. Gains are attributed to beneficiaries according to their receipt of 'capital payments'[10]. The expression 'capital payment' is widely defined, and it should be noted that it can include the value of a loan which is not at a commercial rate of interest[11].

2 Petroleum revenue tax

11-05 The computation of the amount of profits from oil and gas production which is charged to petroleum revenue tax is subject to rules which are quite different from the computation of income and gains for income tax, corporation tax and capital gains tax purposes. No distinction is made between expenditure of a revenue nature and expenditure of a capital nature. Further, there is an express prohibition against the deduction of 'expenditure in respect of interest or any other pecuniary obligation incurred in obtaining a loan or any other form of credit'[12].

11-06 In order to compensate oil companies for the absence of any relief for interest, the legislation provides a special 'supplement' (commonly called 'uplift') in respect of items of expenditure which might be classed as being of a broadly capital nature. By this provision, expenditure on searching for the oil, appraising the discovery, installing production equipment and transportation equipment (eg pipelines), and drilling production wells, and certain other expenditure incurred prior to the commencement of production, qualifies to be increased by a flat rate of 35 per cent[13].

11-07 The prohibition on relief for interest and credit charges led oil companies to seek ways of contracting for the supply of production equipment in a way which would provide effective relief (including uplift) for the interest element in the overall cost of equipment. The nature of the offshore oil production industry is such that the fabrication of production equipment extends over long periods, normally with instalment payments due from the oil company to the manufacturer. In some instances, oil companies negotiated contracts with payment of the full contract price being due upon delivery, the manufacturer bearing the interest cost of payment being delayed until later than would normally occur; that interest cost would be taken

---

[7] See TA 1988 ss 338 (6) and 130.
[8] TCGA 1992 s 39.
[9] TCGA 1992 s 87 (4).
[10] TCGA 1992 s 87 (5).
[11] TCGA 1992 s 97 (4).
[12] OTA 1975 s 3 (4) (a).
[13] OTA 1975 ss 2 (9) (b) (ii) and (c) (ii) and 3 (5).

into account in agreeing the contract price, and so would qualify for relief (and, where appropriate, uplift) provided that it was properly part of the price for the equipment and not truly interest for delayed payment.

However, FA 1981 s 115 prevents expenditure under a contract qualifying for uplift unless it is less than £10 million or it can be reasonably expected that either not less than 90 per cent of the expenditure would be paid (not 'incurred') within nine months of commencement of work under the contract or the amounts to be paid under the contract at any time would be not less than 75 per cent of what would be paid if instalments were paid at regular half-yearly intervals and were proportionate to the work performed under the contract. The effect of this provision is to lay down what the Inland Revenue regards as an acceptable basis for making payments under contracts lasting for more than nine months and to penalise oil companies which negotiate more favourable payment terms.

3   Inheritance tax

INTEREST AS AN ASSET OF THE ESTATE

11-08   Interest received by a deceased person in his lifetime clearly becomes an asset in his estate, although the net increase in the value of his estate will be offset by any income tax liability which relates to the interest received[14]. Where at the death the deceased held a loan stock or other interest-bearing security, no apportionment is made of the accruing interest for the period in which the death occurred for the purpose of ascertaining the assets comprised in the deceased's estate. The market value of the security will be taken as at the date of death; if at that date the security is quoted *ex div*, the value will not include the interest about to be paid and this will separately form an asset of the estate as being an amount to which the deceased was entitled at his death – otherwise the quotation will be *cum div* and the price will take into account a purchaser's entitlement to the next interest payment. In the case of certain short-dated UK government and public authority stocks, the price paid on a stock exchange dealing is the quoted price with an adjustment[15] for a proportion of the interest due on the next interest payment date, so that the buyer effectively receives the value of the interest accruing after purchase and the seller receives the value of the interest which accrued prior to the sale. Therefore, the value of such securities for inheritance tax purposes is taken as the quoted price as adjusted.

Interest on bank deposit accounts accrues on a daily basis but is normally credited half-yearly or on withdrawal. On death, the interest accrued down to the date of death is treated as an asset of the deceased's estate. If a deposit account is in the joint names of the deceased and another person, a proportion of the interest accrued to the date of death (calculated by reference to the proportion of the interest which was normally treated as the deceased's during his lifetime) would normally form part of the deceased's estate. Such interest, when received, will be chargeable to income tax in the administration

---

[14]   See, as to liabilities, IHTA 1984 s 5 (3) to (5).
[15]   Plus or minus, according to whether the bargain is effected before or after the stock goes *ex div*.

of the deceased's estate; however, in ascertaining the income of a beneficiary having an absolute interest in residue, a reduction is made in respect of the gross equivalent of an amount net of basic rate income tax which is equal to the amount of inheritance tax attributable to the accrued income[16]; this is designed to give relief for double taxation where the same income is taken into account for both income tax and inheritance tax purposes.

11-09 The same principles as are described above apply in relation to the value of assets comprised in a person's estate for the purpose of lifetime transfers of value, except that the problems of charges to both income tax and inheritance tax, and the relieving provision just described, do not arise. If a person transfers the balance of a deposit account, this would normally involve the accrued interest being credited to the account and then transferred together with the principal deposited; the value transferred would therefore be comprised of the principal and the accrued interest, although the transferor might be able to claim that the transfer of the interest element (if not any of the capital) came within the exception in respect of normal expenditure out of income[17]. The fact that the transferor would be liable to income tax in respect of the interest credited to the account[18] would not reduce the value transferred unless, which would be unusual, the donee assumed responsibility for paying the transferor's income tax in respect of the interest element in the transferred balance.

Even though a person entitled to interest may not be liable to income tax in respect of interest due to him but which he omits to claim or recover[19], such an omission may result in a transfer of value by reason of a deemed disposition under IHTA s 3(3). Such a transfer of value might be exempt from inheritance tax if the transfer forms part of the transferor's normal expenditure out of income[20].

INTEREST-FREE LOANS

11-10 No inheritance tax charge will arise where a loan repayable on demand is made at less than a market rate of interest or on an interest-free basis. However, a transfer of value may still occur where a loan is made for a fixed term at less than a market rate of interest; in such circumstances it will be possible to measure the fall in the value of the lender's estate by reference to the difference between the amount of the loan and the value of the loan to the lender, taking into account any interest which may be payable and the commercial rate which would be expected to be paid in the circumstances having regard to the currency, the term of the loan and the credit rating of the borrower. Where a transfer of value occurs in such a case, it will be made at the time when the loan is made, because that is when the transferor's estate falls in value, and not on an annual basis by reference to the amount of the interest treated as foregone.

[16] TA 1988 s 699.
[17] IHTA 1984 s 21.
[18] See §4-02 above.
[19] See §4-02 above.
[20] IHTA 1984 s 21.

An inheritance tax liability could also arise where the trustees of a settlement make a fixed term interest-free loan. This is because the making of the loan would involve a disposition as a result of which the value of property comprised in the settlement is less than it would be but for the loan being made[1].

11-11   Where an interest-free loan gives rise to a transfer of value, the rule which exempts normal expenditure from being a chargeable transfer[2] is modified[3]. It is not necessary to satisfy the conditions as to the transfer being part of the transferor's normal expenditure and made out of income. It is merely necessary to show that the transfer of value was a normal one on the part of the transferor and that, after allowing for all transfers forming part of his normal expenditure, the transferor is left with sufficient income to maintain his usual standard of living[4]. It is therefore possible for a transfer of value arising by reason of making an interest-free loan for a fixed period to be an exempt transfer, but only 'to the extent that it is a disposition whereby the use of money ... is allowed by one person ... to another'. It is arguable that the exemption is only available in respect of so much of the transfer of value as represents the loss of interest over the period of the loan. If the loan is made in circumstances that the loan is unlikely to be repaid in full (perhaps, because of the financial circumstances of the borrower), the fall in value of the transferor's estate which is attributable to this factor may not qualify for exemption, although against this it might be argued that such circumstances would merely justify an increased rate of interest[5].

4   Value added tax

11-12   Although it is the consideration for the making of a loan or the granting of credit, and anything which is done for a consideration and which is not a supply of goods is a supply of services[6], the payment of interest by the person in receipt of the loan or credit is not treated as involving a supply being made *by* him[7].

11-13   On the other hand, provision of a loan or credit in respect of which interest is received is a supply of services by the person making the loan or credit available. The supply of such service is normally an exempt supply[8] (of which the value is the interest received) except in the case of certain loans to persons outside the UK[9]. Although such a transaction does not

---

[1] See, for example, IHTA 1984 ss 52 (3), 65 (1) (b), 70 (2) (b), 71 (3) (b), 72 (2) (c) and 74 (2) (b).
[2] IHTA 1984 s 21.
[3] IHTA 1984 s 29 (4).
[4] IHTA 1984 ss 21(1)(c) and 29(4).
[5] See §§2–03 (2) and 2–31 above.
[6] VATA 1983 s 3 (2) (b).
[7] Customs and Excise VAT leaflet No 701/29/92, Finance, does not include the statement to this effect which appeared in VAT leaflet No 701/29/85, Finance, amended 1 October 1990 (see para 5). However, it is understood that this does not result from any change in the view of Customs and Excise on this point.
[8] VATA 1983 Sch 6 Group 5 Item 2.
[9] See §11–15 below.

involve the payment of interest proper[10], the interest or credit charge element in a hire purchase transaction (ie the difference between the hire purchase price and the cash price) is the consideration for an exempt supply. However, an exempt supply is only treated as made in a hire purchase, credit sale or conditional sale transaction where a separate charge is made for the credit and is disclosed to the purchaser or hire purchaser. In these circumstances, where the supply is an exempt supply, no value added tax is chargeable in addition to the interest or other credit charge paid[11].

11-14 Where the making of a loan or other credit by a bank or other financial institution is an exempt supply, there will be a consequential restriction on the input tax which may be credited against output tax[12]. However, most taxable persons will receive bank interest in respect of surplus funds deposited, and this could affect the calculation of the deductible proportion of input tax relating to both taxable and exempt supplies. For this reason it is provided[13] that, in calculating the proportion of input tax which may be attributed to taxable supplies, there shall be excluded any sums (which includes interest) received for making loans or supplying certain other financial services, so long as the supply is incidental to one or more of the trader's business activities. Moreover, input tax incurred by a taxable person in relation to his making a deposit is to be treated as attributable to a taxable supply made by him unless the deposit is made by him in the course of carrying on the business of a bank or certain other financial trades[14]. Therefore, interest received by a non-financial trader in respect of bank deposits will not adversely affect the question of the deduction of input tax.

11-15 A loan or credit made available to a person who belongs in a country, other than the Isle of Man, outside the European Community is not an exempt supply but a zero-rated supply[15]. Further, the making of a loan or provision of credit facilities is a zero-rated supply wherever the recipient belongs where it is in connection with either the export of specific goods from the UK or the transhipment of goods (whether within or outside the UK) so long as, in either case, the ultimate destination of the goods is a place, other than the Isle of Man, outside the European Community[16].

The treatment of interest as consideration for a zero-rated supply is not available where the supply is made to a person who belongs in a member state of the European Community[17] unless the loan or credit relates to the

[10] See §2-19 above.
[11] VATA 1983 Sch 6 Group 5 Item 3.
[12] VATA 1983 s 15 and Part V of the Value Added Tax (General) Regulations 1985: SI 1985 No 886, as amended. The summary in this Part of this Chapter is based on Part V of the General Regulations as it applies to tax years commencing on or after 1 April 1992 – see Regulations 1 to 3 of the Value Added Tax (General) (Amendment) Regulations 1992: SI 1992 No 645.
[13] Regulation 30 (3)(b)(ii) and (vi) of the Value Added Tax (General) Regulations 1985: SI 1985 No 886, as amended.
[14] Regulation 33 of the Value Added Tax (General) Regulations 1985: SI 1985 No 886, as amended.
[15] VATA 1983 Sch 5 Group 9 Item 6.
[16] VATA 1983 Sch 5 Group 9 Item 9.
[17] VATA 1983 Sch 5 Group 9 Item 5, as applied by note (3).

export or transhipment of goods to an ultimate destination, other than the Isle of Man, outside the European Community[18].

Where such a loan or credit gives rise to a zero-rated supply, no value added tax is chargeable in respect of the interest or other charge made for the provisions of the loan or credit. However, the difference from the exempt treatment lies in the fact that any input tax attributable to the transaction will be deductible against output tax. Moreover, in the case of a loan or credit which is not related to the export or transhipment of goods, the interest or other credit charge will be excluded from the calculation of the deductible proportion of non-specifically attributable input tax[19], where the supply is incidental to the trader's business activities.

11-16   The making of a loan on an interest-free basis may be relevant for value added tax purposes where the omission to charge interest is consideration for a taxable supply. In *Exeter Golf and Country Club Ltd v Customs and Excise Comrs*[20] the Court of Appeal upheld a decision in the High Court to the effect that, when members of a club made interest-free loans to the club, both on joining a club and on an annual basis, the benefit of such interest-free loans was part of the consideration given for taxable supplies made by the club to its members. Because part of the consideration – namely, the use of the interest-free money – was not itself 'money', what is now VATA 1983 s 10 (3) prescribed that the supply by the club should be treated as being made for a consideration equal to the open market value of the supply. That value was to be ascertained by looking at what the members were prepared to pay, which, in that case, was the cash subscription plus the value to the members of the money lent interest-free; since, had they not lent the money to the club, they could have invested it on deposit, it was convenient to take as that value a reasonable rate of interest. The rate of interest adopted for this purpose by the Commissioners of Customs and Excise and the club was minimum lending rate[1]; since minimum lending rate no longer operates, the Customs and Excise in practice adopt the base rate of the clearing banks as at the date when subscriptions are due for the relevant year[2].

VATA 1983 s 10 (3) is to be amended[3] so that, where there is no monetary consideration for the supply, or the consideration is not wholly in money, the value of the supply is the monetary equivalent of the consideration rather than the open market value of the supply. Where an interest-free loan is made as, or as part of, the consideration for a supply, the VAT treatment should be much the same as in the *Exeter Golf and Country Club* case. The

---

[18]   VATA 1983 Sch 5 Group 9 Item 9.

[19]   Regulation 30 (3) (b) (ii) of the Value Added Tax (General) Regulations 1985: SI 1985 No 886, as amended.

[20]   [1981] STC 211.

[1]   Which Cumming-Bruce LJ thought was on the low side – [1981] STC 211 at 217*d*.

[2]   Cf also *Dyrham Park Country Club v Customs and Excise Comrs* [1978] VATTR 244, where a subscription paid by a club member for a bond (entitling him to repayment of the sum in certain circumstances and also to membership of the club) was held to involve two separate supplies by the club – one, an exempt supply of the bond, and the other, a taxable supply of services.

[3]   With effect from a date to be appointed: F(No 2)A 1992 s 14 (3) and Sch 3 paras 1 and 12; see also *Naturally Yours Cosmetics Ltd v Customs and Excise Comrs*: 230/87 [1988] STC 879, [1989] 1 CMLR 797, ECJ.

interest foregone by the lender, computed at a market rate, would be the value of the consideration.

5 Stamp duty

11-17 Stamp duty is paid in respect of documents effecting transactions. No stamp duty is payable by reference to interest itself; stamp duty is not payable on a document evidencing or securing a loan whether or not at interest[4].

11-18 A document assigning a debt may be exempt from stamp duty[5]. The transfer of loan capital[6] of the OECD and certain other international organisations is exempt from stamp duty[7]. Other transfers of loan capital are exempt from stamp duty[8] unless the interest on the loan exceeds a reasonable commercial return on the nominal amount of the capital or is determined to any extent by reference to the results of a business or the value of any property or the loan is convertible into shares or securities or carries a right to an amount on repayment which exceeds the nominal amount of the capital and is not reasonably comparable with loan capital listed on the London Stock Exchange[9]. These conditions are similar to those which can cause interest paid by a company to be treated as a dividend distribution[10], or cause the loan in question to be treated as equity capital for the purpose of restrictions on the availability of group relief[11]. Interest would depend on the results of business where it is related to the company's profits or turnover[12]. However, where the amount of the payment is calculated by reference to a company's profits it is not clear that it is interest properly so called rather than a share of profits[13].

It is specifically provided that interest shall not be treated as exceeding a reasonable commercial return where the interest is determined to any extent by reference to an index showing changes in the general[14] level of prices payable in the UK over a period substantially corresponding to the period of the loan[15]. This permits the rate of interest to be index-linked without prejudicing the exemption from stamp duty on transfers of loan capital.

[4] FA 1971 s 64(1).
[5] FA 1971 s 64(2).
[6] FA 1986 s 73(7); see FA 1986 s 79(12).
[7] FA 1986 s 79(3).
[8] FA 1986 s 79(4).
[9] FA 1986 s 79(5) and (6).
[10] TA 1988 s 209(2)(d) and see Chapter 9 Part 1 above.
[11] TA 1988 Sch 18 para 1(5)(d); and see Chapter 9 Part 2 above.
[12] See *IRC v Pullman Car Co Ltd* [1954] 2 All ER 491, 35 TC 221; and see §2-07 above.
[13] See *A W Walker Co v IRC* [1920] 3 KB 648, 12 TC 297; and see §2-08 above.
[14] Ie not related to any specific industry.
[15] FA 1986 s 79(7).

INDEX

243